15 BIG STORIES

IN ONE BOOK!

DeCONNICK and De LANDRO present

★RATED Ⓜ MATURE

TRIPLE FEATURE!

ISSUE 1

ANDREW AYDIN   JOANNA ESTEP

WITHOUT *and* WITHIN

CHERYL LYNN EATON   MARIA FRÖHLICH

WINDOWS

CONLEY LYONS   CRAIG YEUNG

THE INVISIBLE WOMAN

# TRIPLE B

ISSUE 3

ALISSA SALLAH   ALEC VALERIUS

THOSE PEOPLE

DYLAN MECONIS

BIG GAME

KIT COX   VANESA R. DEL REY

*Love,* HONOR & OBEY

COLORS ON
"THE INVISIBLE WOMAN"
MARCO D'ALFONSO

LETTERING ON "THOSE PEOPLE"
ALEC VALERIUS

COLORS ON
"LIFE OF A SPORTSMAN"
LEONARDO OLEA

COLORS ON
"EVERYBODY'S GRANDMA
IS A LITTLE BIT FEMINIST"
NICK FILARDI

LETTERS
(EXCEPT "THOSE PEOPLE")
CLAYTON COWLES

COVERS
VALENTINE DE LANDRO

LOGO, ORIGINAL COVERS DESIGN,
BOOK DESIGN
RIAN HUGHES

BACKMATTER DESIGN
LAURENN MCCUBBIN

PRODUCTION
TRICIA RAMOS

EDITOR
LAUREN SANKOVITCH

# BITS AND PIECES

CHE GRAYSON

SHARON LEE DE LA CRUZ

## THIS IS GOOD FOR YOU

DANIELLE HENDERSON

RO STEIN

TED BRANDT

**ISSUE 2**

## WHAT'S LOVE GOT TO DO WITH IT?

JORDAN CLARK

NAOMI FRANQUIZ

# FEATURE!

MARC DESCHAMPS

MINDY LEE

## LIFE of a SPORTSMAN

**ISSUE 5**

VITA AYALA

ROSSI GIFFORD

## TO BE FREE

**ISSUE 4**

SARA WOOLLEY

## BODYMODS

## EVERYONE'S GRANDMA IS A LITTLE BIT FEMINIST

MATT FRACTION

ELSA CHARRETIER

## MIRROR, MIRROR

JON TSUEI

SASKIA GUTEKUNST

## BASIC BITCH

ALOBI, BASSEY & NYAMBI NYAMBI

CHRIS VISIONS

DeCONNICK and De LANDRO

present

A

BITCH PLANET

$3.99
★★★

Nº 1

THE FUTURE OF COMICS
25
EST. 1992

TRIPLE FEATURE!

CHERYL LYNN
EATON
MARIA
FRÖHLICH

WINDOWS

ANDREW
AYDIN
JOANNA
ESTEP

Featuring
CLAYTON
COWLES

WITHOUT and
WITHIN

CONLEY
LYONS
CRAIG
YEUNG

THE
INVISIBLE
WOMAN

BIG STORIES
3
IN ONE BOOK!

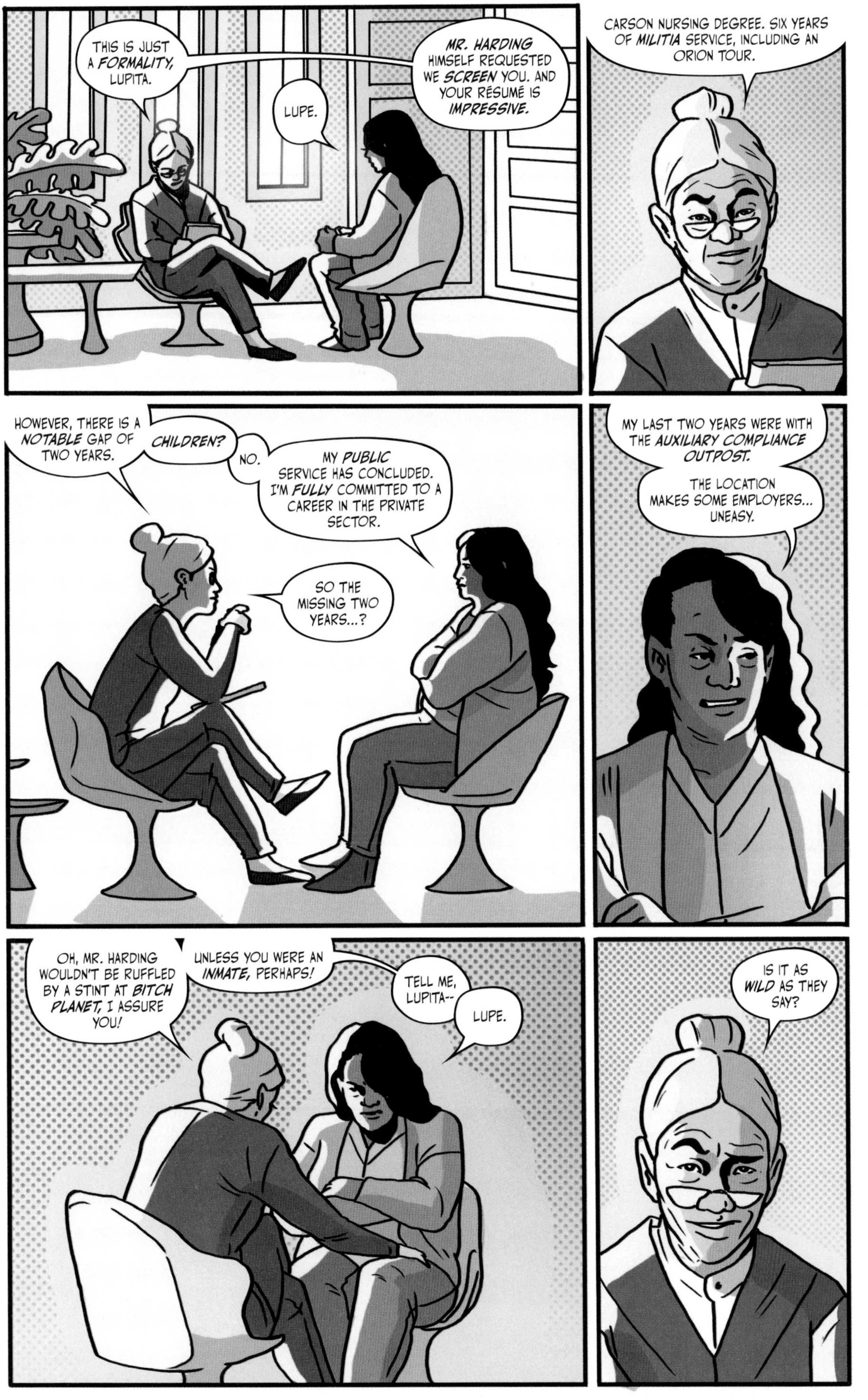
THIS IS JUST A *FORMALITY,* LUPITA.
LUPE.
*MR. HARDING* HIMSELF REQUESTED WE *SCREEN* YOU. AND YOUR RÉSUMÉ IS *IMPRESSIVE.*
CARSON NURSING DEGREE. SIX YEARS OF *MILITIA* SERVICE, INCLUDING AN ORION TOUR.
HOWEVER, THERE IS A *NOTABLE* GAP OF TWO YEARS.
*CHILDREN?*
NO.
MY *PUBLIC* SERVICE HAS CONCLUDED. I'M *FULLY* COMMITTED TO A CAREER IN THE PRIVATE SECTOR.
SO THE MISSING TWO YEARS...?
MY LAST TWO YEARS WERE WITH THE *AUXILIARY COMPLIANCE OUTPOST.*
THE LOCATION MAKES SOME EMPLOYERS... UNEASY.
OH, MR. HARDING WOULDN'T BE RUFFLED BY A STINT AT *BITCH PLANET,* I ASSURE YOU!
UNLESS YOU WERE AN *INMATE,* PERHAPS!
TELL ME, LUPITA--
LUPE.
IS IT AS *WILD* AS THEY SAY?

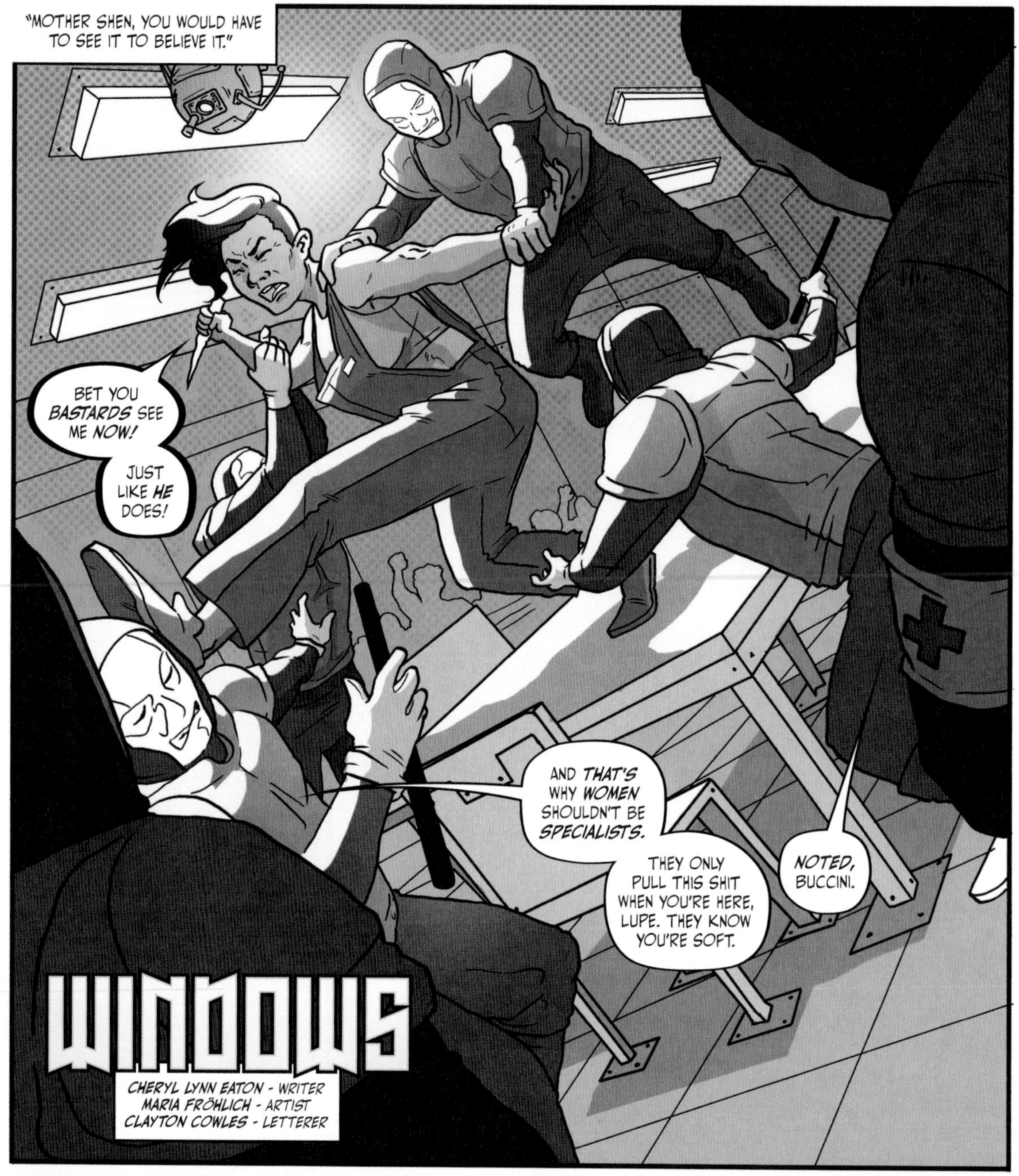
"MOTHER SHEN, YOU WOULD HAVE TO SEE IT TO BELIEVE IT."
BET YOU *BASTARDS* SEE ME *NOW!*
JUST LIKE *HE* DOES!
AND *THAT'S* WHY *WOMEN* SHOULDN'T BE *SPECIALISTS.*
THEY ONLY PULL THIS SHIT WHEN YOU'RE HERE, LUPE. THEY KNOW YOU'RE SOFT.
*NOTED,* BUCCINI.
WINDOWS
CHERYL LYNN EATON - WRITER
MARIA FRÖHLICH - ARTIST
CLAYTON COWLES - LETTERER

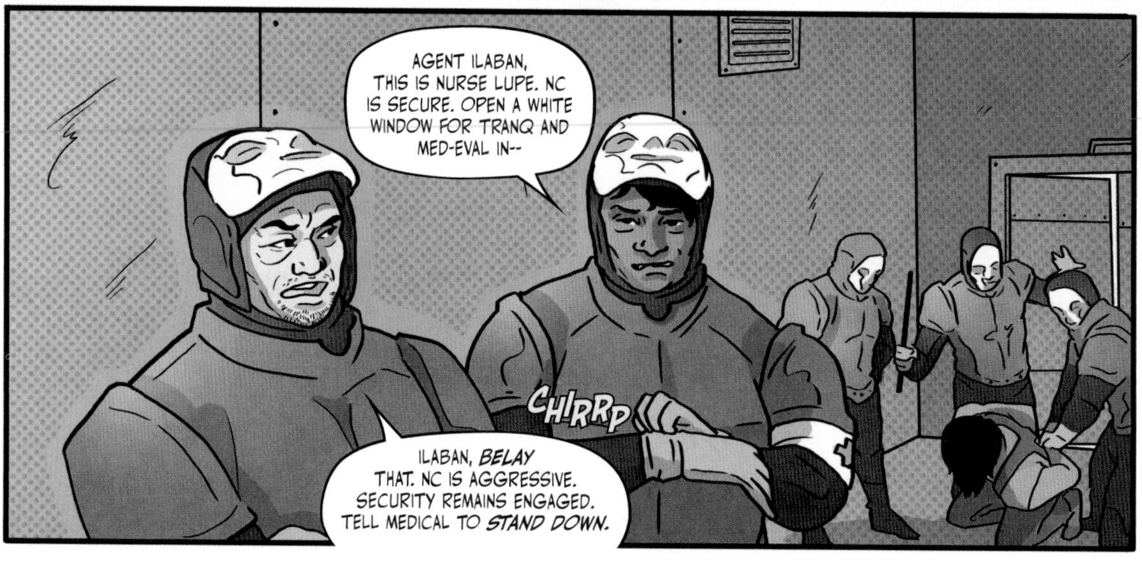
AGENT ILABAN, THIS IS NURSE LUPE. NC IS SECURE. OPEN A WHITE WINDOW FOR TRANQ AND MED-EVAL IN--
CHIRRP
ILABAN, *BELAY* THAT. NC IS AGGRESSIVE. SECURITY REMAINS ENGAGED. TELL MEDICAL TO *STAND DOWN.*

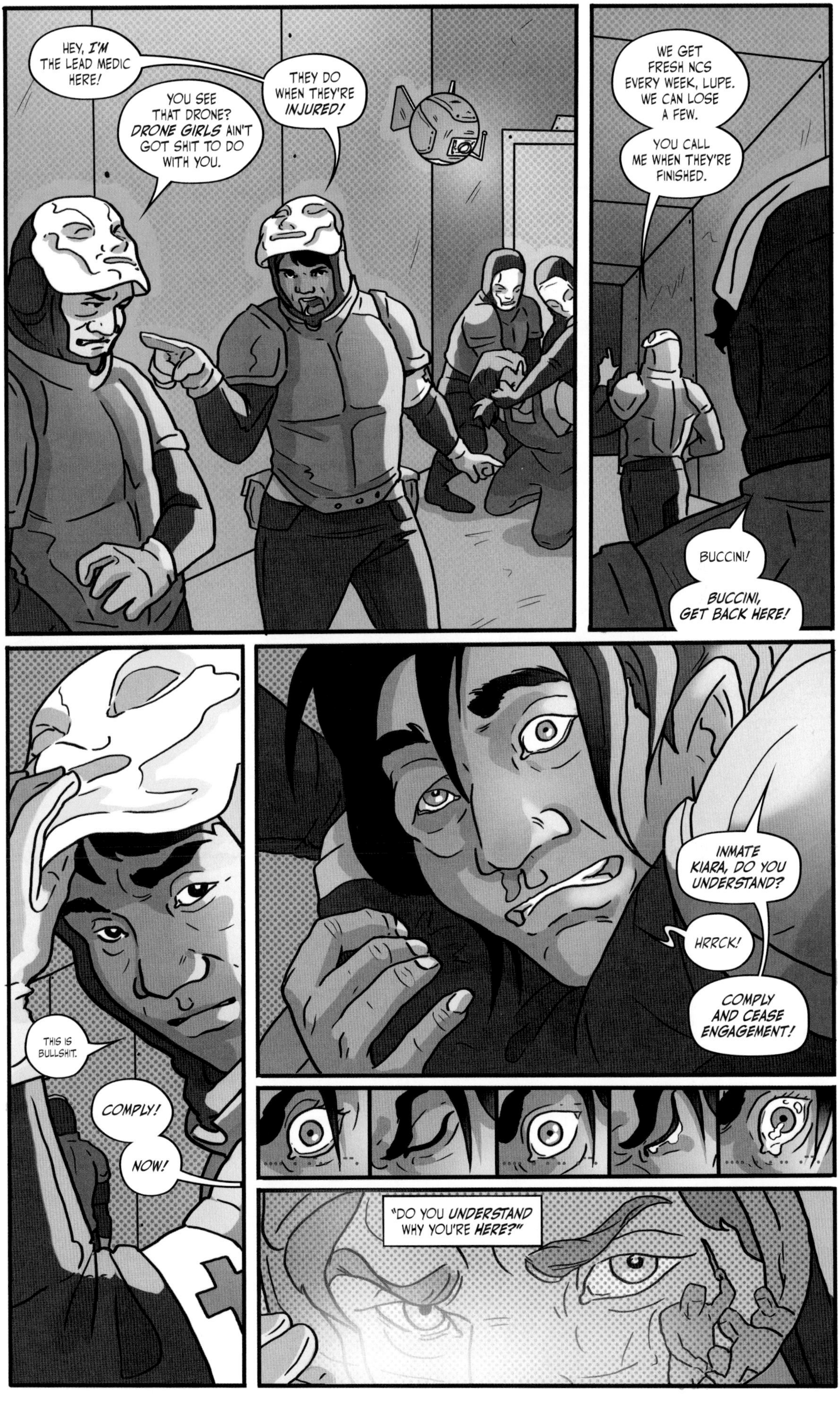
HEY, I'M THE LEAD MEDIC HERE!
YOU SEE THAT DRONE? DRONE GIRLS AIN'T GOT SHIT TO DO WITH YOU.
THEY DO WHEN THEY'RE INJURED!
WE GET FRESH NCS EVERY WEEK, LUPE. WE CAN LOSE A FEW.
YOU CALL ME WHEN THEY'RE FINISHED.
BUCCINI!
BUCCINI, GET BACK HERE!
THIS IS BULLSHIT.
COMPLY!
NOW!
INMATE KIARA, DO YOU UNDERSTAND?
HRRCK!
COMPLY AND CEASE ENGAGEMENT!
"DO YOU UNDERSTAND WHY YOU'RE HERE?"

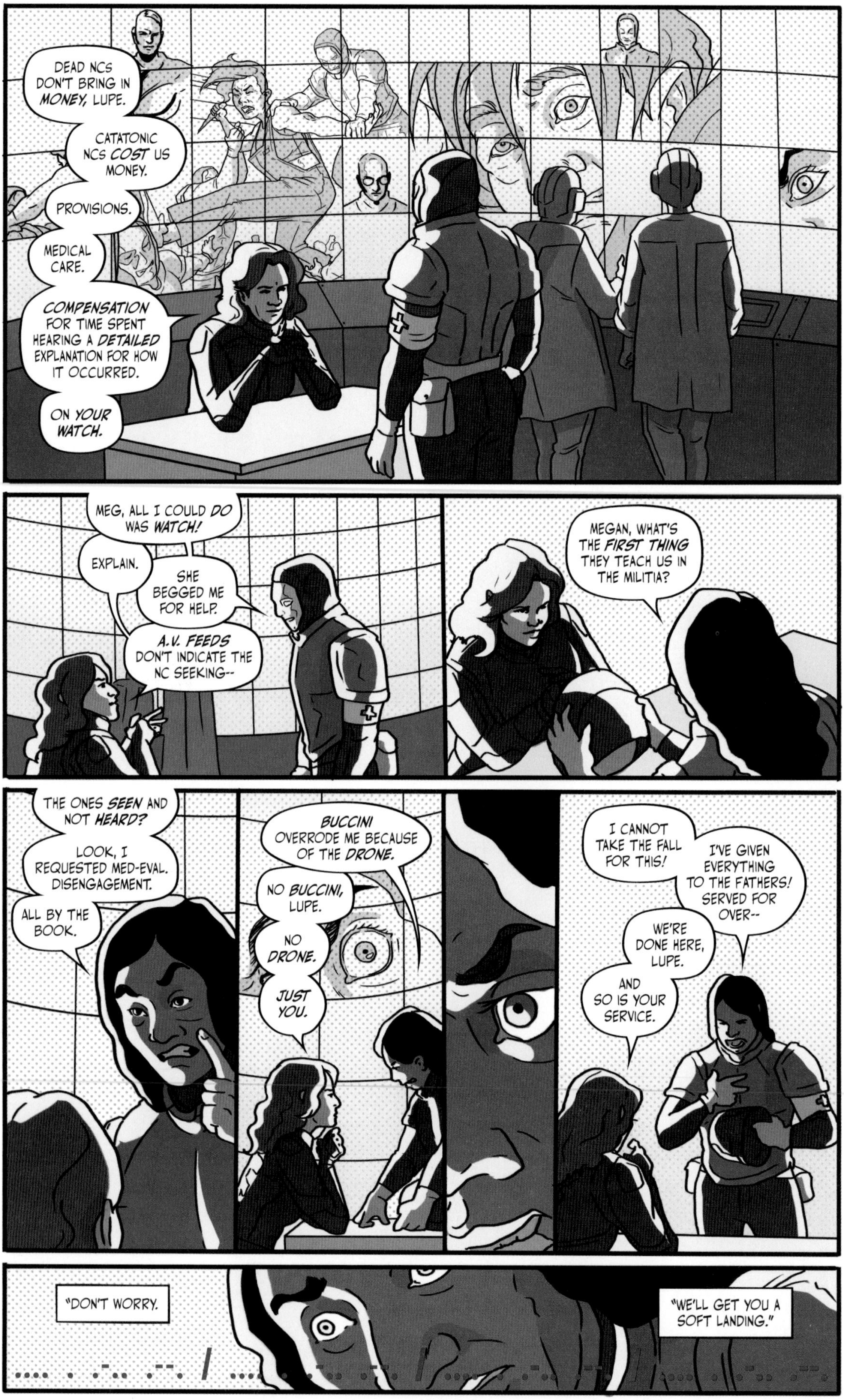
DEAD NCs DON'T BRING IN MONEY, LUPE.
CATATONIC NCs COST US MONEY.
PROVISIONS.
MEDICAL CARE.
COMPENSATION FOR TIME SPENT HEARING A DETAILED EXPLANATION FOR HOW IT OCCURRED.
ON YOUR WATCH.
MEG, ALL I COULD DO WAS WATCH!
EXPLAIN.
SHE BEGGED ME FOR HELP.
A.V. FEEDS DON'T INDICATE THE NC SEEKING--
MEGAN, WHAT'S THE FIRST THING THEY TEACH US IN THE MILITIA?
THE ONES SEEN AND NOT HEARD?
LOOK, I REQUESTED MED-EVAL. DISENGAGEMENT.
ALL BY THE BOOK.
BUCCINI OVERRODE ME BECAUSE OF THE DRONE.
NO BUCCINI, LUPE.
NO DRONE.
JUST YOU.
I CANNOT TAKE THE FALL FOR THIS!
I'VE GIVEN EVERYTHING TO THE FATHERS! SERVED FOR OVER--
WE'RE DONE HERE, LUPE.
AND SO IS YOUR SERVICE.
"DON'T WORRY.
"WE'LL GET YOU A SOFT LANDING."

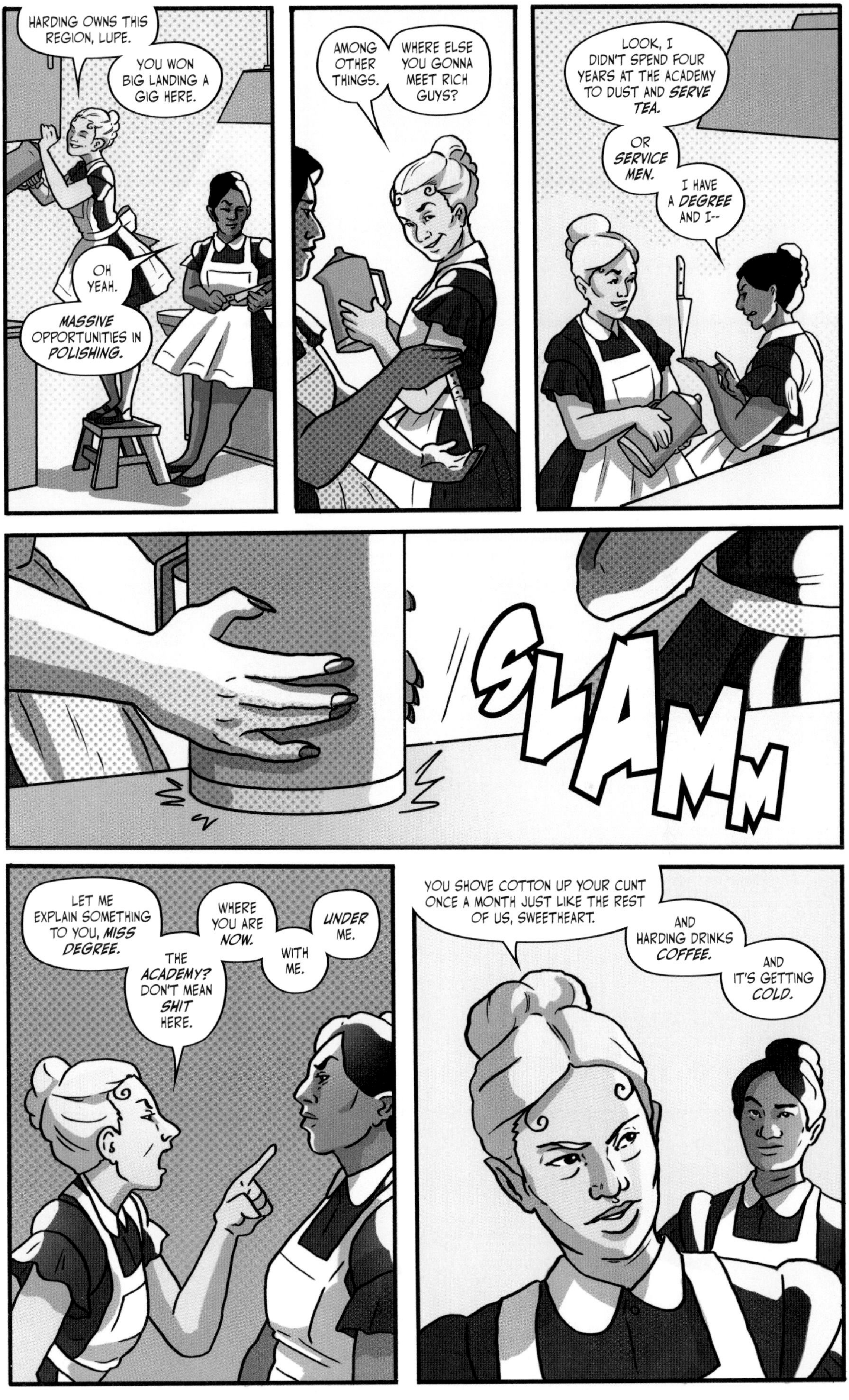
HARDING OWNS THIS REGION, LUPE.
YOU WON BIG LANDING A GIG HERE.
OH YEAH.
MASSIVE OPPORTUNITIES IN POLISHING.
AMONG OTHER THINGS.
WHERE ELSE YOU GONNA MEET RICH GUYS?
LOOK, I DIDN'T SPEND FOUR YEARS AT THE ACADEMY TO DUST AND SERVE TEA.
OR SERVICE MEN.
I HAVE A DEGREE AND I--
SLAMM
LET ME EXPLAIN SOMETHING TO YOU, MISS DEGREE.
THE ACADEMY? DON'T MEAN SHIT HERE.
WHERE YOU ARE NOW.
WITH ME.
UNDER ME.
YOU SHOVE COTTON UP YOUR CUNT ONCE A MONTH JUST LIKE THE REST OF US, SWEETHEART.
AND HARDING DRINKS COFFEE.
AND IT'S GETTING COLD.

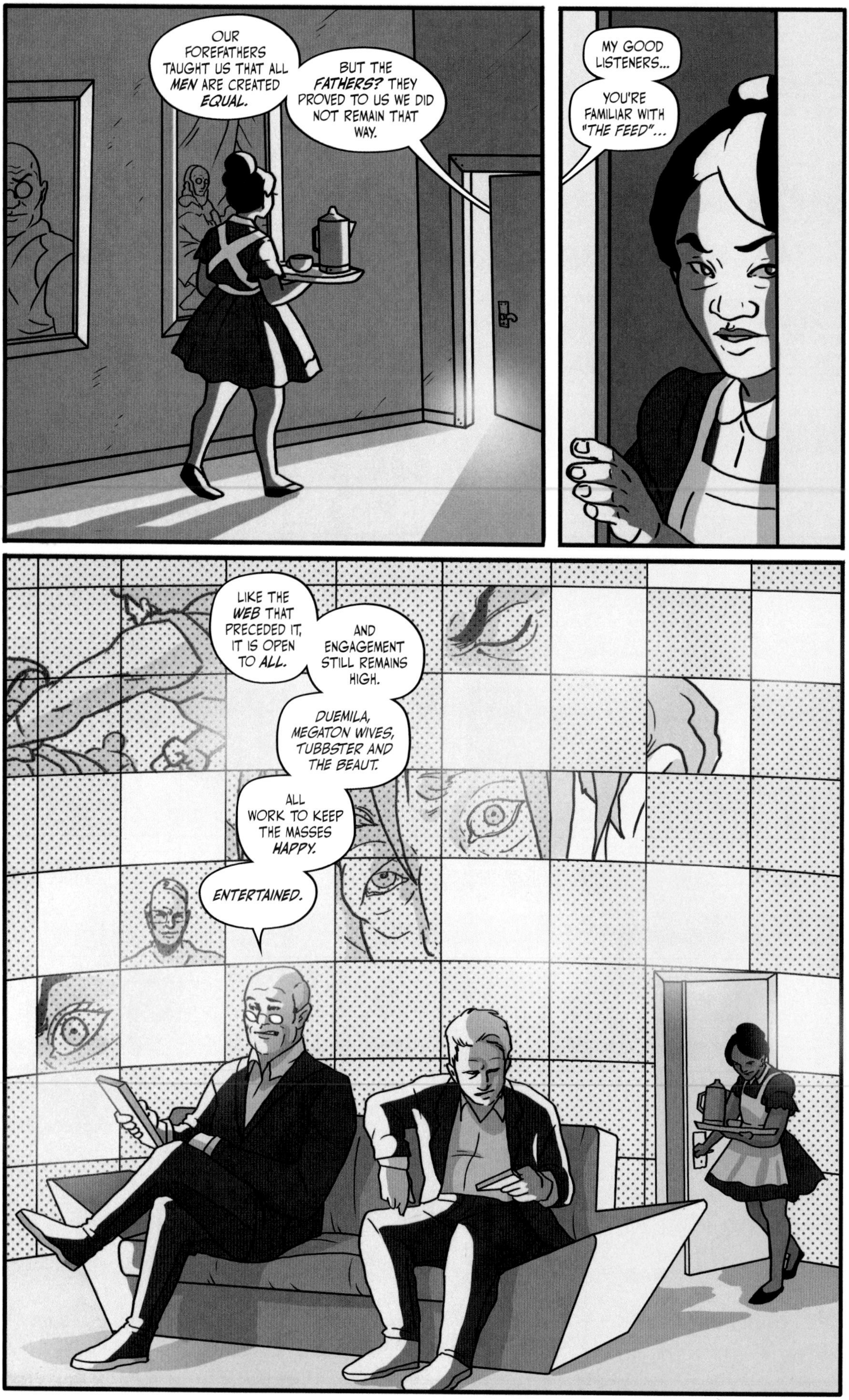
OUR FOREFATHERS TAUGHT US THAT ALL *MEN* ARE CREATED *EQUAL.*
BUT THE *FATHERS?* THEY PROVED TO US WE DID NOT REMAIN THAT WAY.
MY GOOD LISTENERS...
YOU'RE FAMILIAR WITH *"THE FEED"*...
LIKE THE *WEB* THAT PRECEDED IT, IT IS OPEN TO *ALL.*
AND ENGAGEMENT STILL REMAINS HIGH.
*DUEMILA, MEGATON WIVES, TUBBSTER AND THE BEAUT.*
ALL WORK TO KEEP THE MASSES *HAPPY.*
*ENTERTAINED.*

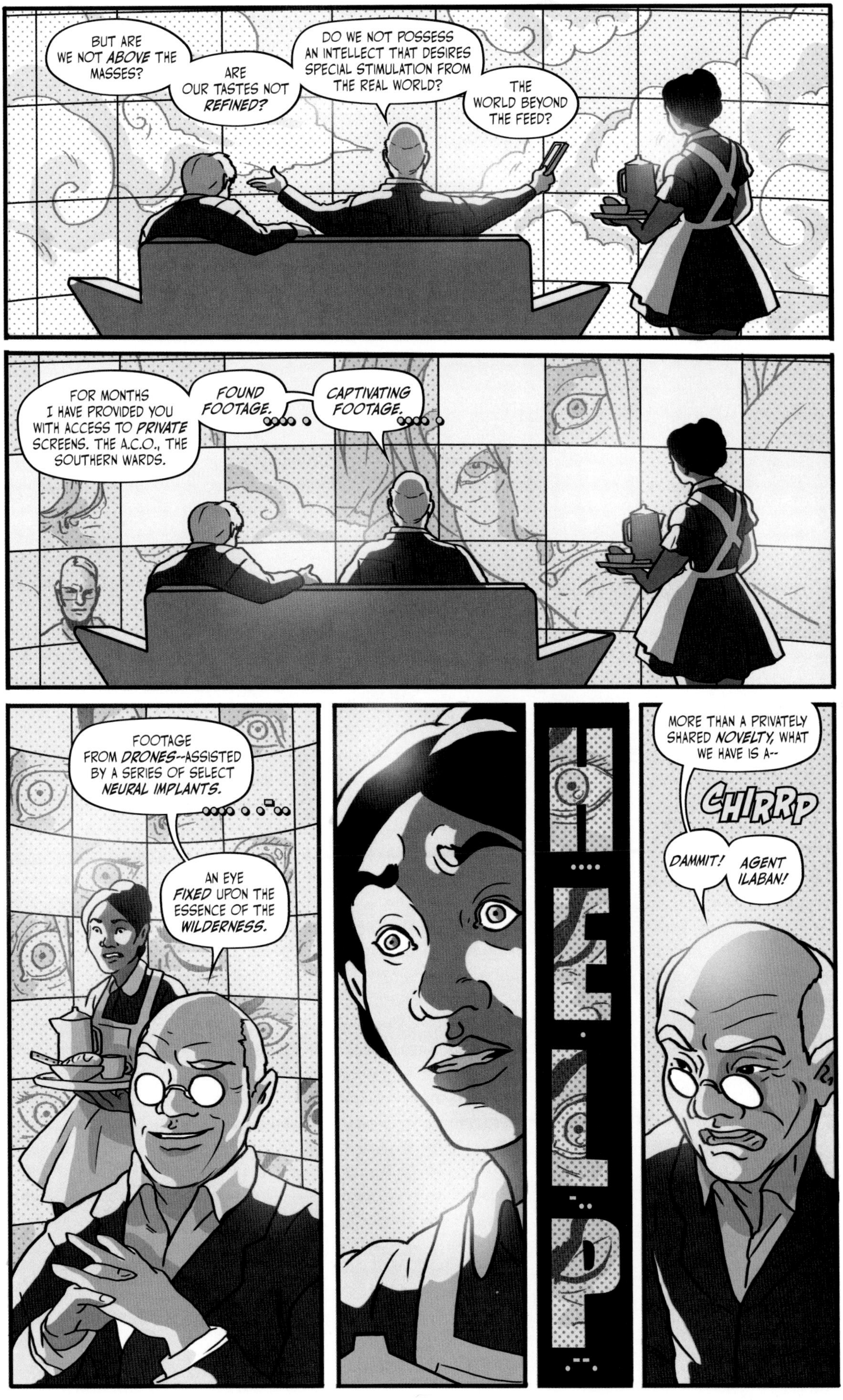

BUT ARE WE NOT ABOVE THE MASSES?
ARE OUR TASTES NOT REFINED?
DO WE NOT POSSESS AN INTELLECT THAT DESIRES SPECIAL STIMULATION FROM THE REAL WORLD?
THE WORLD BEYOND THE FEED?
FOR MONTHS I HAVE PROVIDED YOU WITH ACCESS TO PRIVATE SCREENS. THE A.C.O., THE SOUTHERN WARDS.
FOUND FOOTAGE.
CAPTIVATING FOOTAGE.
FOOTAGE FROM DRONES--ASSISTED BY A SERIES OF SELECT NEURAL IMPLANTS.
AN EYE FIXED UPON THE ESSENCE OF THE WILDERNESS.
HELP
MORE THAN A PRIVATELY SHARED NOVELTY, WHAT WE HAVE IS A--
CHIRRP
DAMMIT!
AGENT ILABAN!

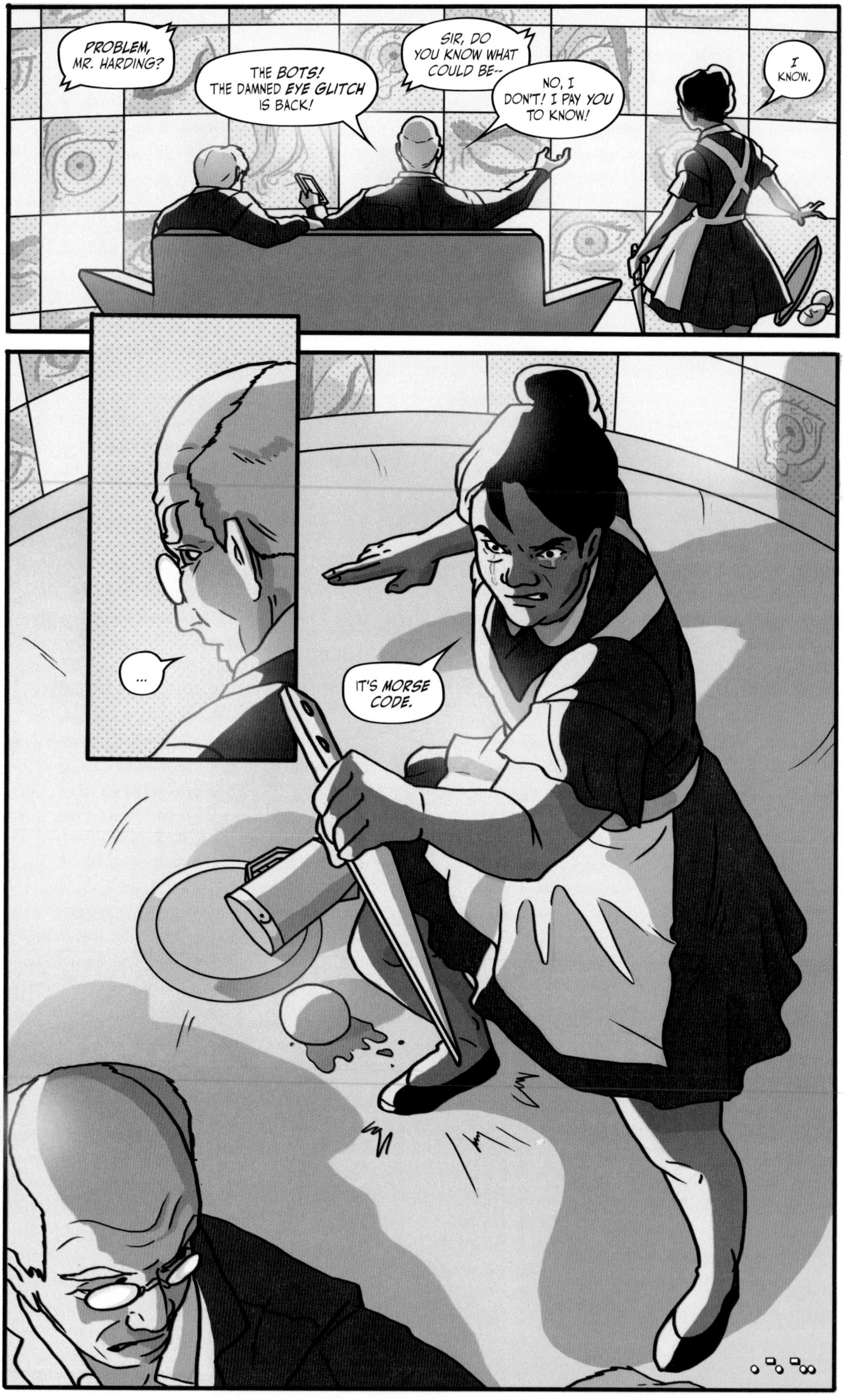
PROBLEM, MR. HARDING?
THE BOTS! THE DAMNED EYE GLITCH IS BACK!
SIR, DO YOU KNOW WHAT COULD BE--
NO, I DON'T! I PAY YOU TO KNOW!
I KNOW.
...
IT'S MORSE CODE.

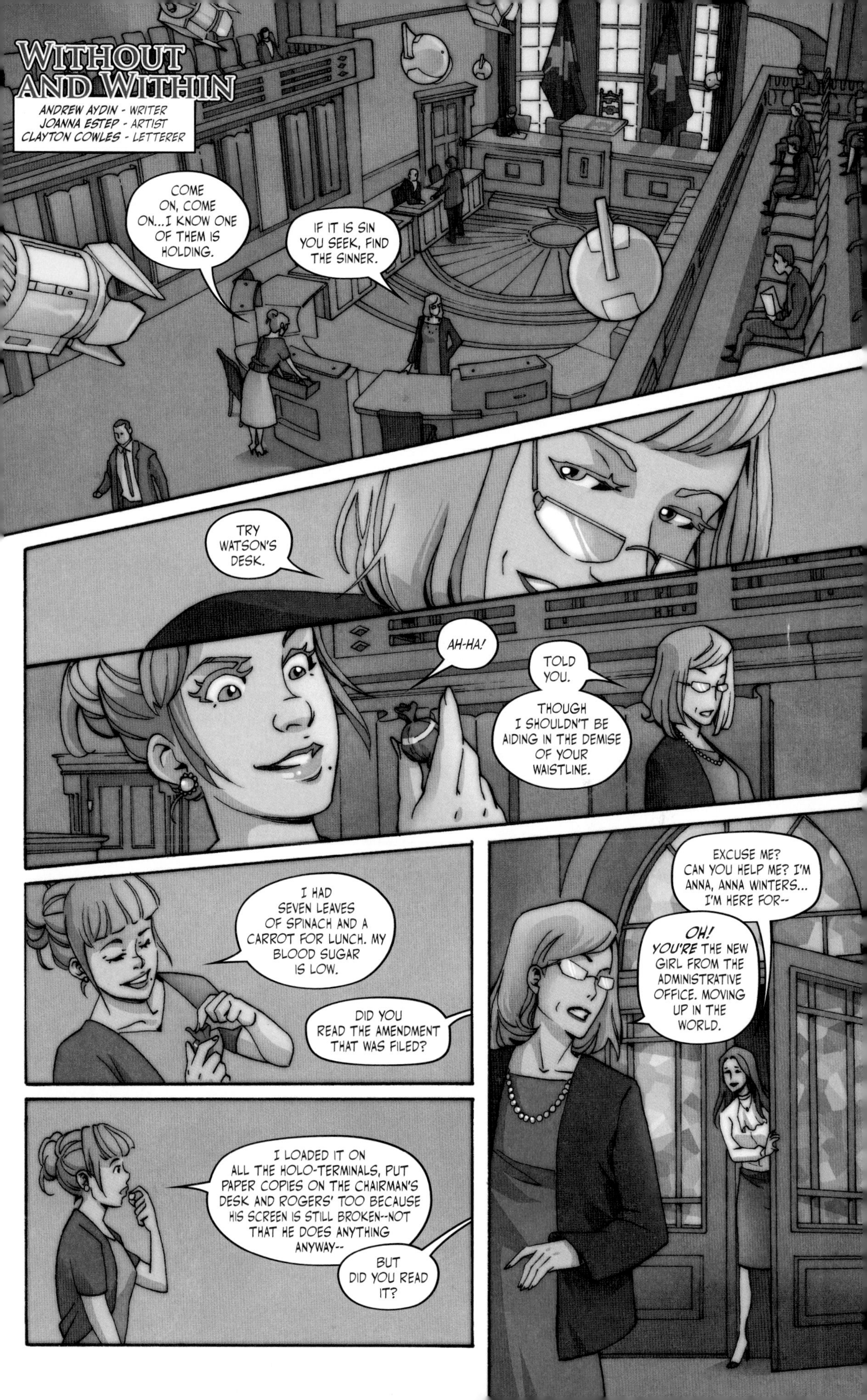
WITHOUT AND WITHIN
ANDREW AYDIN - WRITER
JOANNA ESTEP - ARTIST
CLAYTON COWLES - LETTERER
COME ON, COME ON...I KNOW ONE OF THEM IS HOLDING.
IF IT IS SIN YOU SEEK, FIND THE SINNER.
TRY WATSON'S DESK.
AH-HA!
TOLD YOU.
THOUGH I SHOULDN'T BE AIDING IN THE DEMISE OF YOUR WAISTLINE.
I HAD SEVEN LEAVES OF SPINACH AND A CARROT FOR LUNCH. MY BLOOD SUGAR IS LOW.
DID YOU READ THE AMENDMENT THAT WAS FILED?
I LOADED IT ON ALL THE HOLO-TERMINALS, PUT PAPER COPIES ON THE CHAIRMAN'S DESK AND ROGERS' TOO BECAUSE HIS SCREEN IS STILL BROKEN--NOT THAT HE DOES ANYTHING ANYWAY--
BUT DID YOU READ IT?
EXCUSE ME? CAN YOU HELP ME? I'M ANNA, ANNA WINTERS... I'M HERE FOR--
OH! YOU'RE THE NEW GIRL FROM THE ADMINISTRATIVE OFFICE. MOVING UP IN THE WORLD.

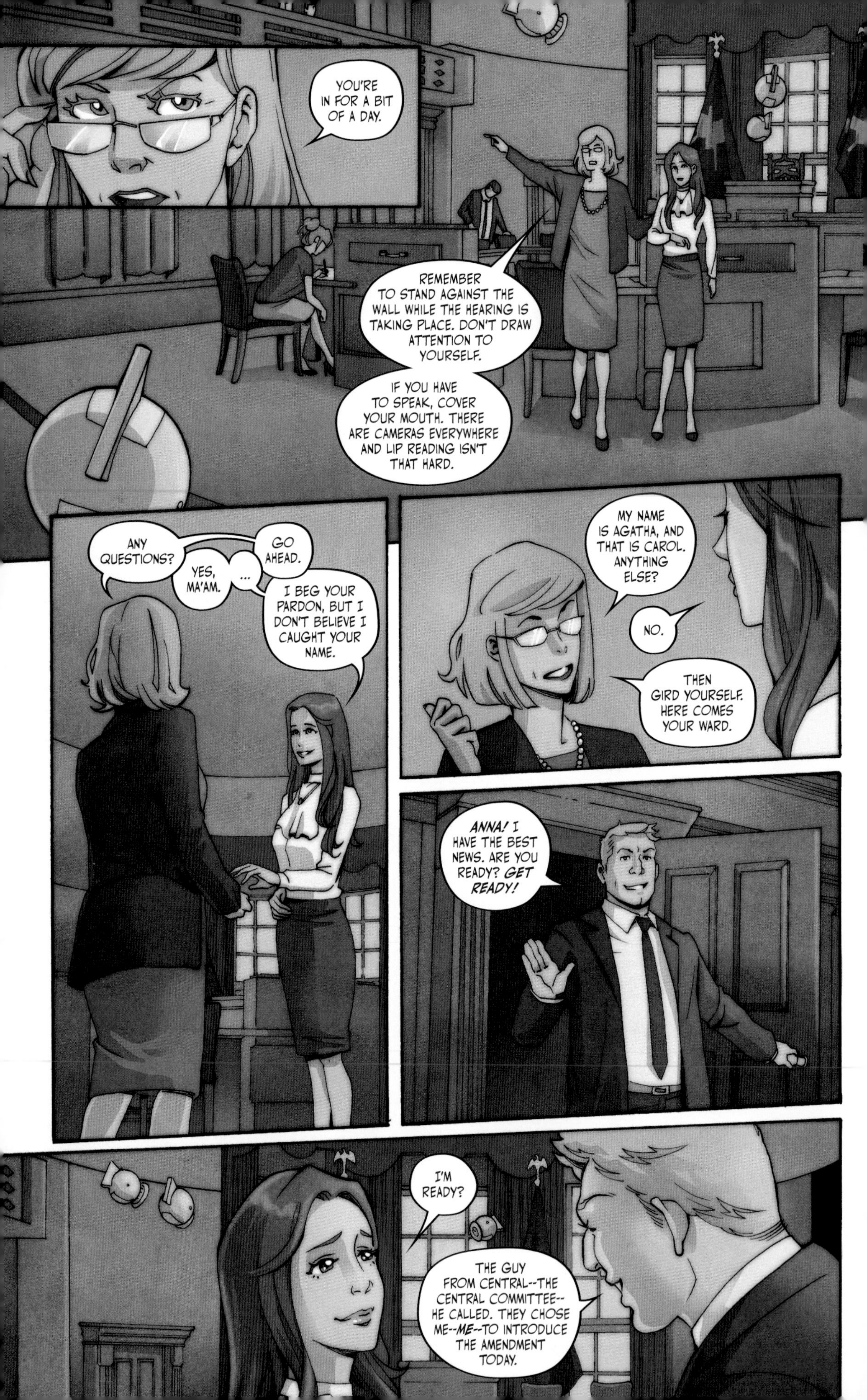

YOU'RE IN FOR A BIT OF A DAY.
REMEMBER TO STAND AGAINST THE WALL WHILE THE HEARING IS TAKING PLACE. DON'T DRAW ATTENTION TO YOURSELF.
IF YOU HAVE TO SPEAK, COVER YOUR MOUTH. THERE ARE CAMERAS EVERYWHERE AND LIP READING ISN'T THAT HARD.
ANY QUESTIONS?
YES, MA'AM.
...
GO AHEAD.
I BEG YOUR PARDON, BUT I DON'T BELIEVE I CAUGHT YOUR NAME.
MY NAME IS AGATHA, AND THAT IS CAROL. ANYTHING ELSE?
NO.
THEN GIRD YOURSELF. HERE COMES YOUR WARD.
ANNA! I HAVE THE BEST NEWS. ARE YOU READY? GET READY!
I'M READY?
THE GUY FROM CENTRAL--THE CENTRAL COMMITTEE--HE CALLED. THEY CHOSE ME--ME--TO INTRODUCE THE AMENDMENT TODAY.

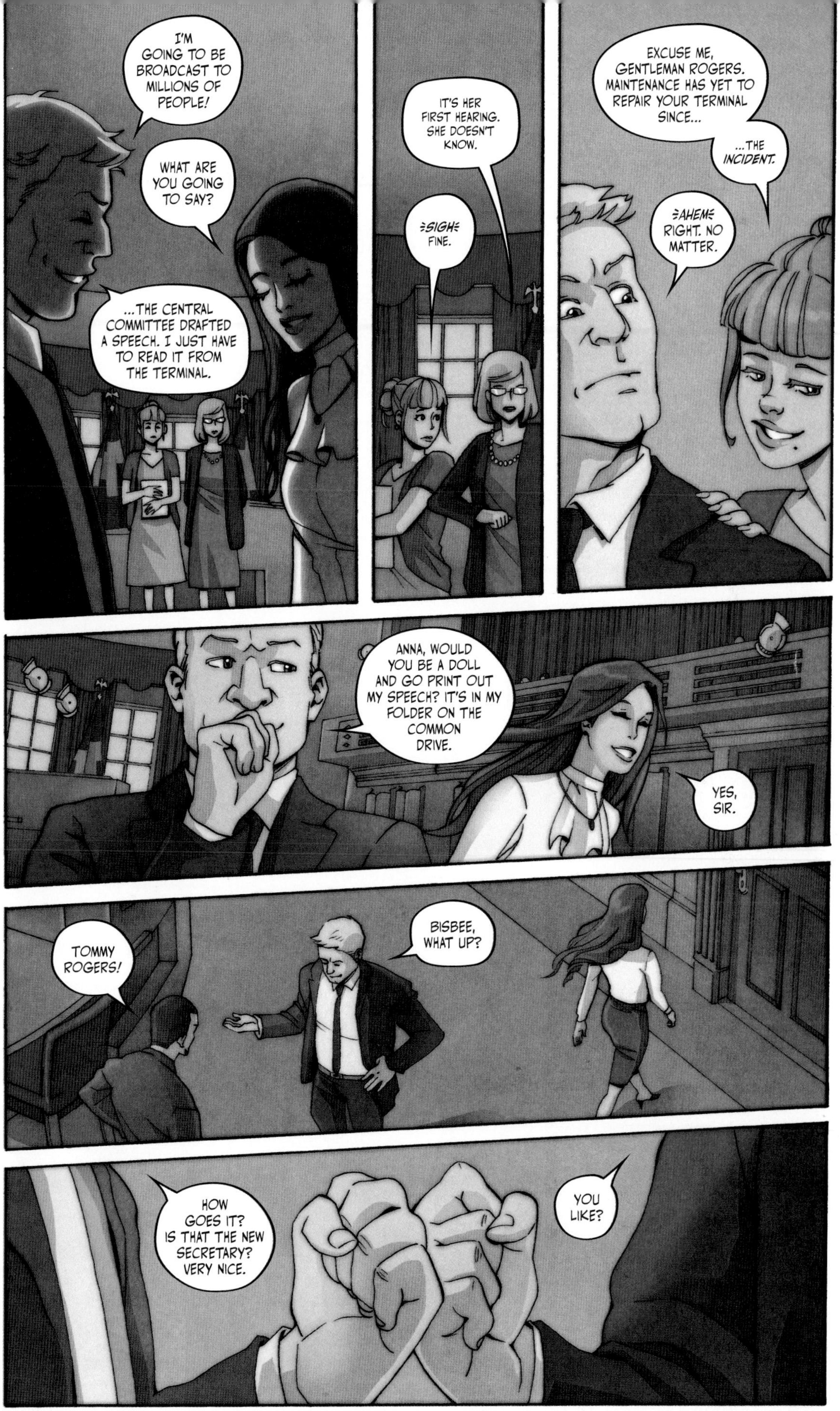
I'M GOING TO BE BROADCAST TO MILLIONS OF PEOPLE!
WHAT ARE YOU GOING TO SAY?
...THE CENTRAL COMMITTEE DRAFTED A SPEECH. I JUST HAVE TO READ IT FROM THE TERMINAL.
IT'S HER FIRST HEARING. SHE DOESN'T KNOW.
SIGH FINE.
EXCUSE ME, GENTLEMAN ROGERS. MAINTENANCE HAS YET TO REPAIR YOUR TERMINAL SINCE...
...THE *INCIDENT.*
AHEM RIGHT. NO MATTER.
ANNA, WOULD YOU BE A DOLL AND GO PRINT OUT MY SPEECH? IT'S IN MY FOLDER ON THE COMMON DRIVE.
YES, SIR.
TOMMY ROGERS!
BISBEE, WHAT UP?
HOW GOES IT? IS THAT THE NEW SECRETARY? VERY NICE.
YOU LIKE?

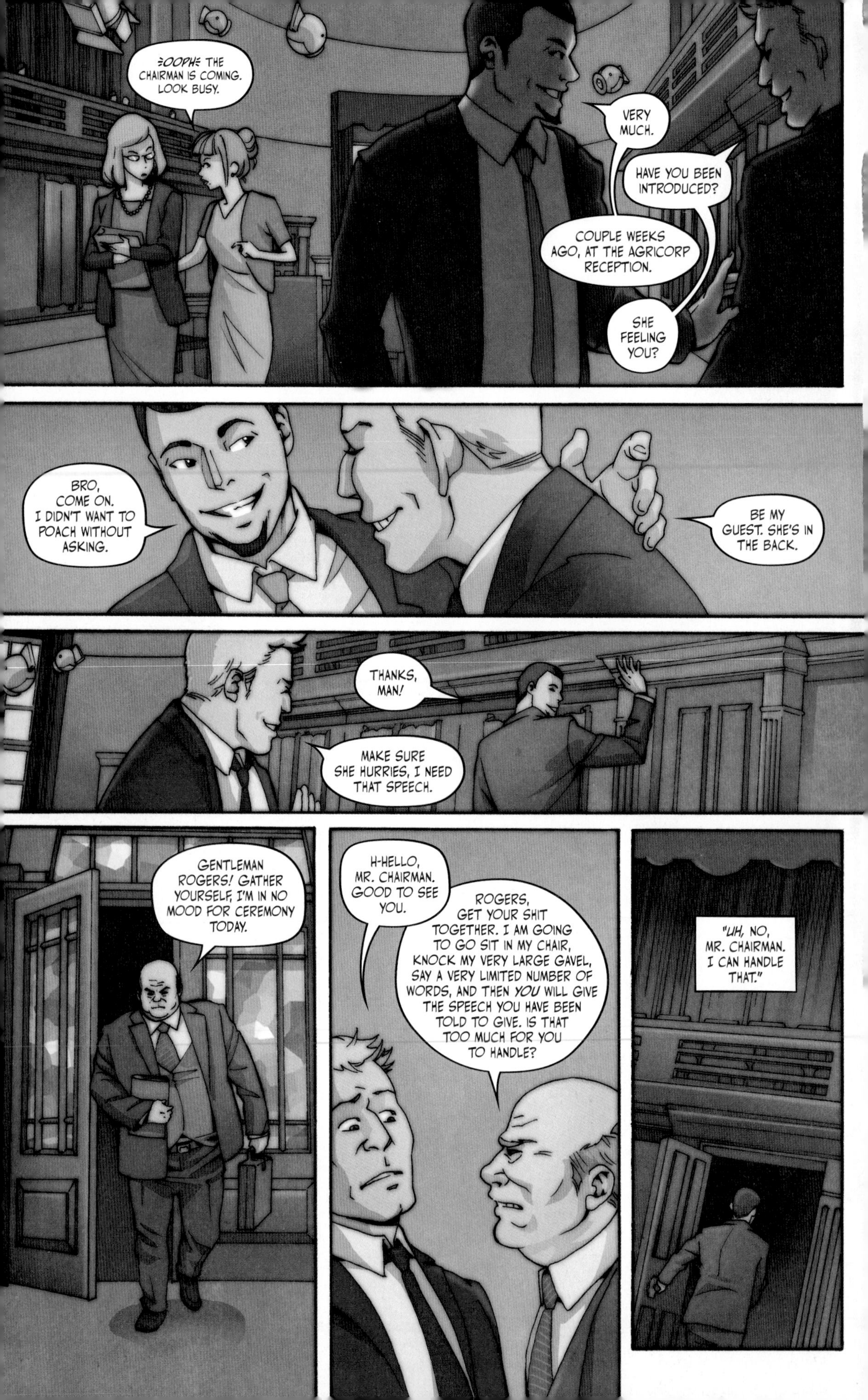

OOPH! THE CHAIRMAN IS COMING. LOOK BUSY.
VERY MUCH.
HAVE YOU BEEN INTRODUCED?
COUPLE WEEKS AGO, AT THE AGRICORP RECEPTION.
SHE FEELING YOU?
BRO, COME ON. I DIDN'T WANT TO POACH WITHOUT ASKING.
BE MY GUEST. SHE'S IN THE BACK.
THANKS, MAN!
MAKE SURE SHE HURRIES, I NEED THAT SPEECH.
GENTLEMAN ROGERS! GATHER YOURSELF, I'M IN NO MOOD FOR CEREMONY TODAY.
H-HELLO, MR. CHAIRMAN. GOOD TO SEE YOU.
ROGERS, GET YOUR SHIT TOGETHER. I AM GOING TO GO SIT IN MY CHAIR, KNOCK MY VERY LARGE GAVEL, SAY A VERY LIMITED NUMBER OF WORDS, AND THEN YOU WILL GIVE THE SPEECH YOU HAVE BEEN TOLD TO GIVE. IS THAT TOO MUCH FOR YOU TO HANDLE?
"UH, NO, MR. CHAIRMAN. I CAN HANDLE THAT."

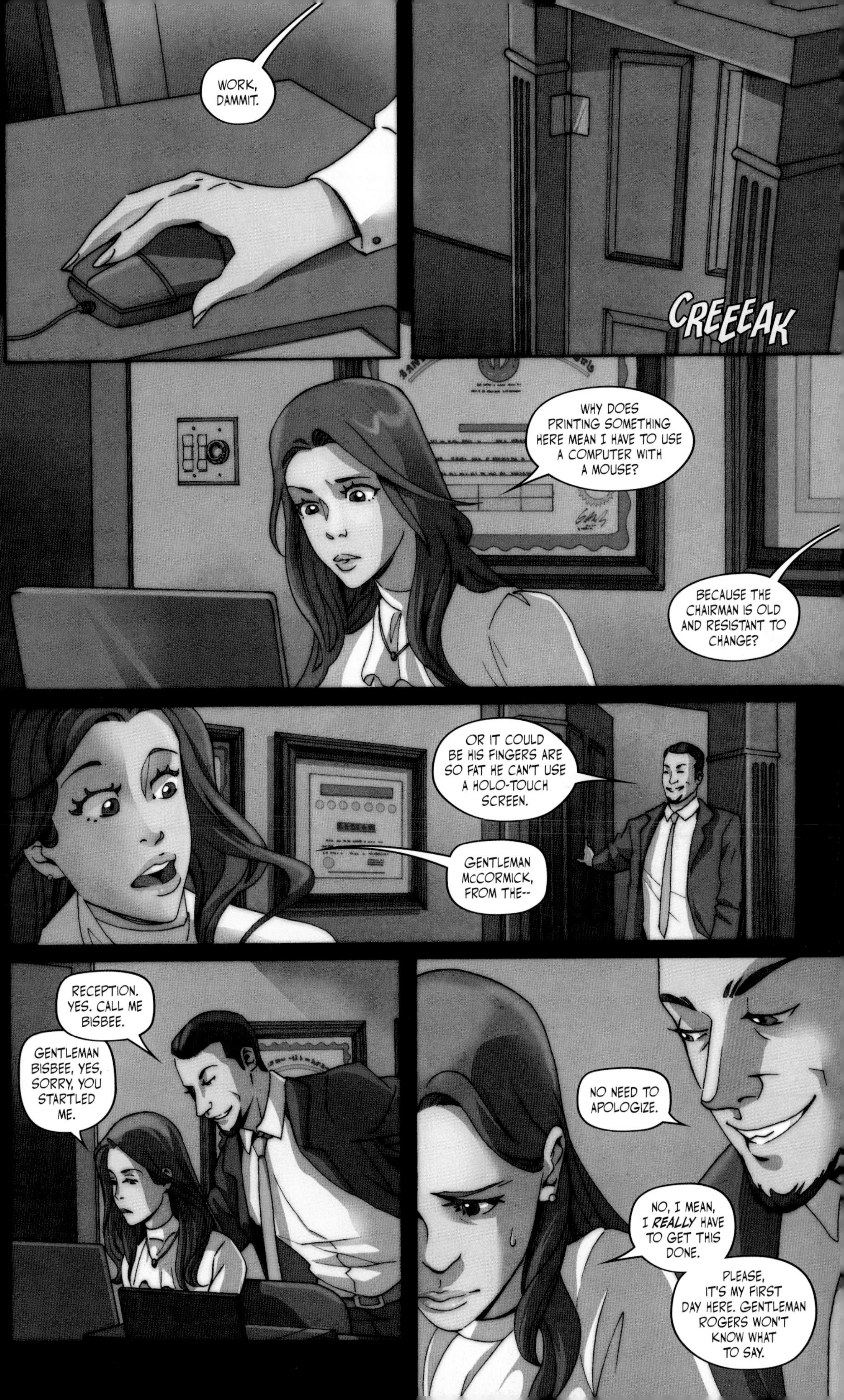
WORK, DAMMIT.
CREEEAK
WHY DOES PRINTING SOMETHING HERE MEAN I HAVE TO USE A COMPUTER WITH A MOUSE?
BECAUSE THE CHAIRMAN IS OLD AND RESISTANT TO CHANGE?
OR IT COULD BE HIS FINGERS ARE SO FAT HE CAN'T USE A HOLO-TOUCH SCREEN.
GENTLEMAN McCORMICK, FROM THE--
RECEPTION. YES. CALL ME BISBEE.
GENTLEMAN BISBEE, YES, SORRY, YOU STARTLED ME.
NO NEED TO APOLOGIZE.
NO, I MEAN, I *REALLY* HAVE TO GET THIS DONE.
PLEASE, IT'S MY FIRST DAY HERE. GENTLEMAN ROGERS WON'T KNOW WHAT TO SAY.

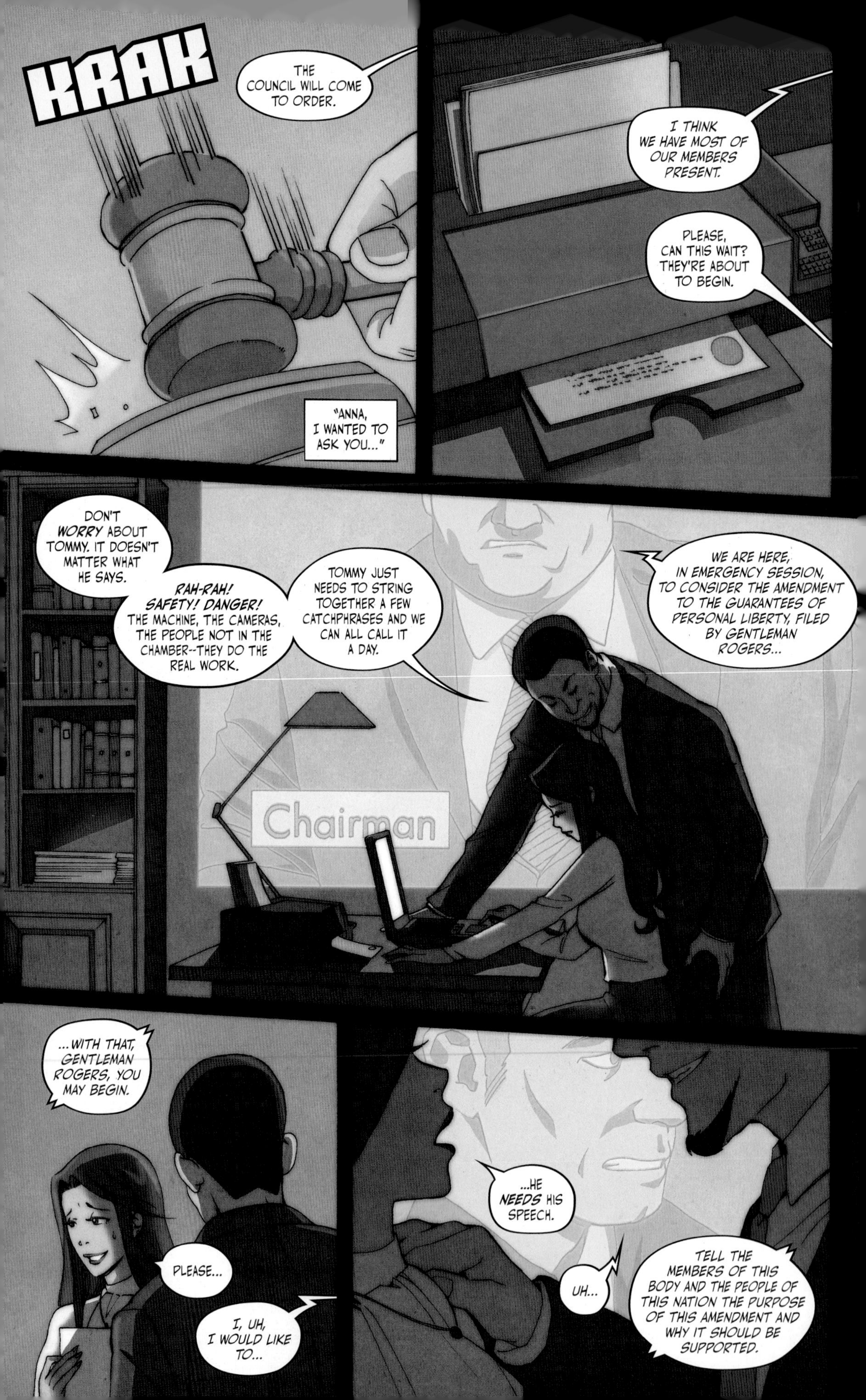

KRAK
THE COUNCIL WILL COME TO ORDER.
"ANNA, I WANTED TO ASK YOU..."
I THINK WE HAVE MOST OF OUR MEMBERS PRESENT.
PLEASE, CAN THIS WAIT? THEY'RE ABOUT TO BEGIN.
DON'T WORRY ABOUT TOMMY. IT DOESN'T MATTER WHAT HE SAYS.
RAH-RAH! SAFETY! DANGER! THE MACHINE, THE CAMERAS, THE PEOPLE NOT IN THE CHAMBER--THEY DO THE REAL WORK.
TOMMY JUST NEEDS TO STRING TOGETHER A FEW CATCHPHRASES AND WE CAN ALL CALL IT A DAY.
WE ARE HERE, IN EMERGENCY SESSION, TO CONSIDER THE AMENDMENT TO THE GUARANTEES OF PERSONAL LIBERTY, FILED BY GENTLEMAN ROGERS...
Chairman
...WITH THAT, GENTLEMAN ROGERS, YOU MAY BEGIN.
PLEASE...
I, UH, I WOULD LIKE TO...
...HE NEEDS HIS SPEECH.
UH...
TELL THE MEMBERS OF THIS BODY AND THE PEOPLE OF THIS NATION THE PURPOSE OF THIS AMENDMENT AND WHY IT SHOULD BE SUPPORTED.

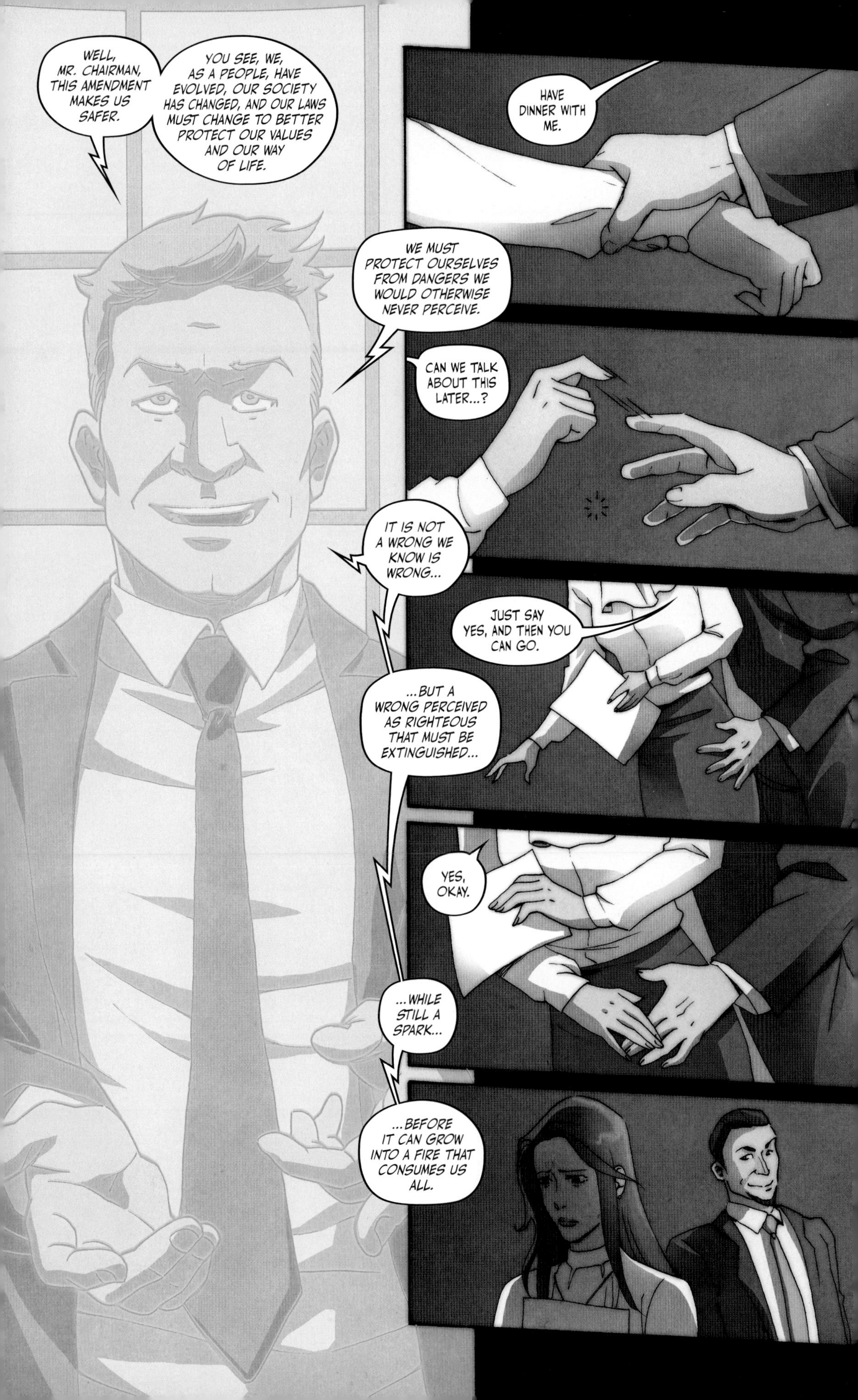
WELL, MR. CHAIRMAN, THIS AMENDMENT MAKES US SAFER.
YOU SEE, WE, AS A PEOPLE, HAVE EVOLVED, OUR SOCIETY HAS CHANGED, AND OUR LAWS MUST CHANGE TO BETTER PROTECT OUR VALUES AND OUR WAY OF LIFE.
HAVE DINNER WITH ME.
WE MUST PROTECT OURSELVES FROM DANGERS WE WOULD OTHERWISE NEVER PERCEIVE.
CAN WE TALK ABOUT THIS LATER...?
IT IS NOT A WRONG WE KNOW IS WRONG...
JUST SAY YES, AND THEN YOU CAN GO.
...BUT A WRONG PERCEIVED AS RIGHTEOUS THAT MUST BE EXTINGUISHED...
YES, OKAY.
...WHILE STILL A SPARK...
...BEFORE IT CAN GROW INTO A FIRE THAT CONSUMES US ALL.

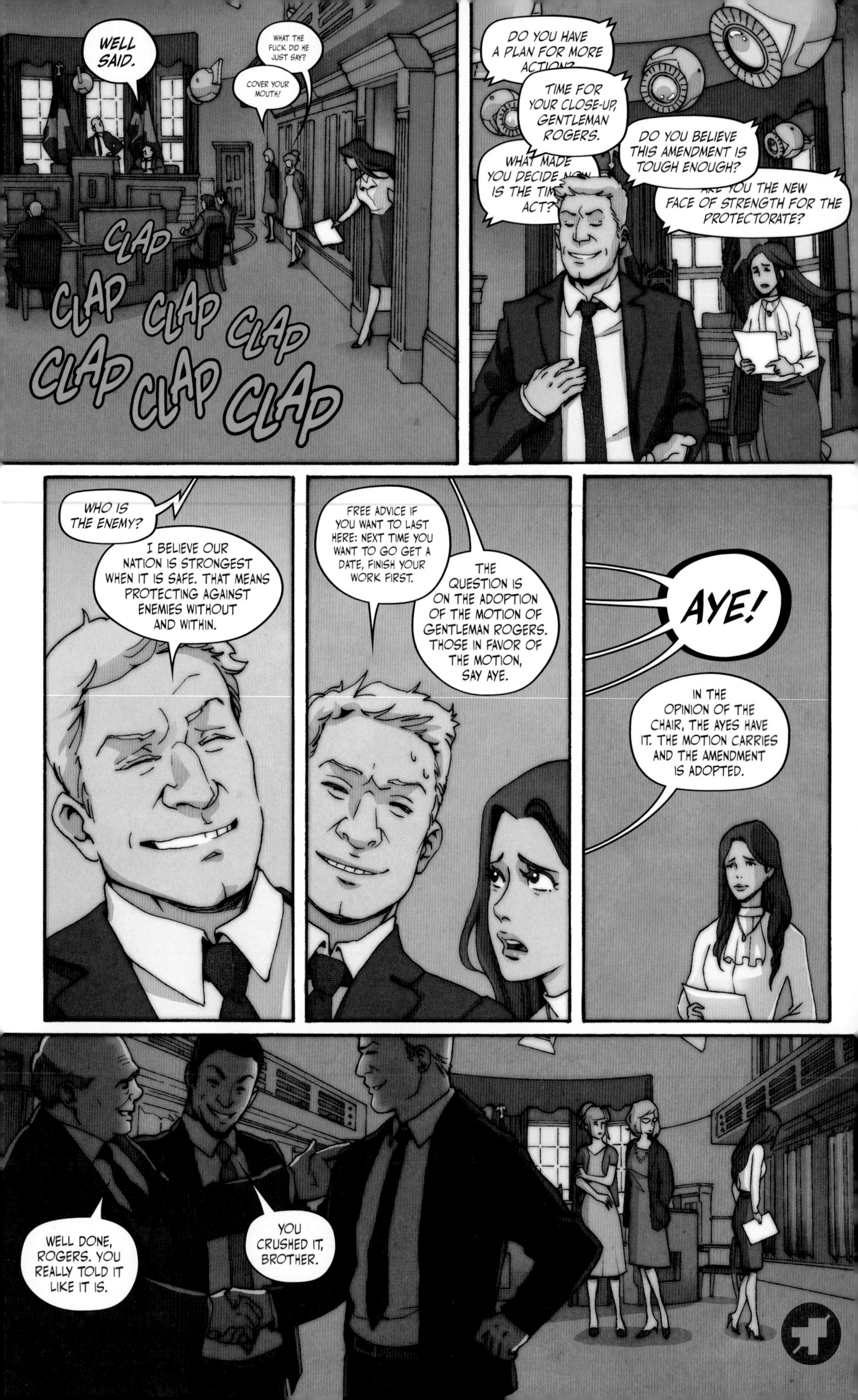
WELL SAID.
WHAT THE FUCK DID HE JUST SAY?
COVER YOUR MOUTH!
CLAP CLAP CLAP CLAP CLAP CLAP CLAP CLAP
DO YOU HAVE A PLAN FOR MORE ACTION?
TIME FOR YOUR CLOSE-UP, GENTLEMAN ROGERS.
WHAT MADE YOU DECIDE NOW IS THE TIME TO ACT?
DO YOU BELIEVE THIS AMENDMENT IS TOUGH ENOUGH?
ARE YOU THE NEW FACE OF STRENGTH FOR THE PROTECTORATE?
WHO IS THE ENEMY?
I BELIEVE OUR NATION IS STRONGEST WHEN IT IS SAFE. THAT MEANS PROTECTING AGAINST ENEMIES WITHOUT AND WITHIN.
FREE ADVICE IF YOU WANT TO LAST HERE: NEXT TIME YOU WANT TO GO GET A DATE, FINISH YOUR WORK FIRST.
THE QUESTION IS ON THE ADOPTION OF THE MOTION OF GENTLEMAN ROGERS. THOSE IN FAVOR OF THE MOTION, SAY AYE.
AYE!
IN THE OPINION OF THE CHAIR, THE AYES HAVE IT. THE MOTION CARRIES AND THE AMENDMENT IS ADOPTED.
WELL DONE, ROGERS. YOU REALLY TOLD IT LIKE IT IS.
YOU CRUSHED IT, BROTHER.

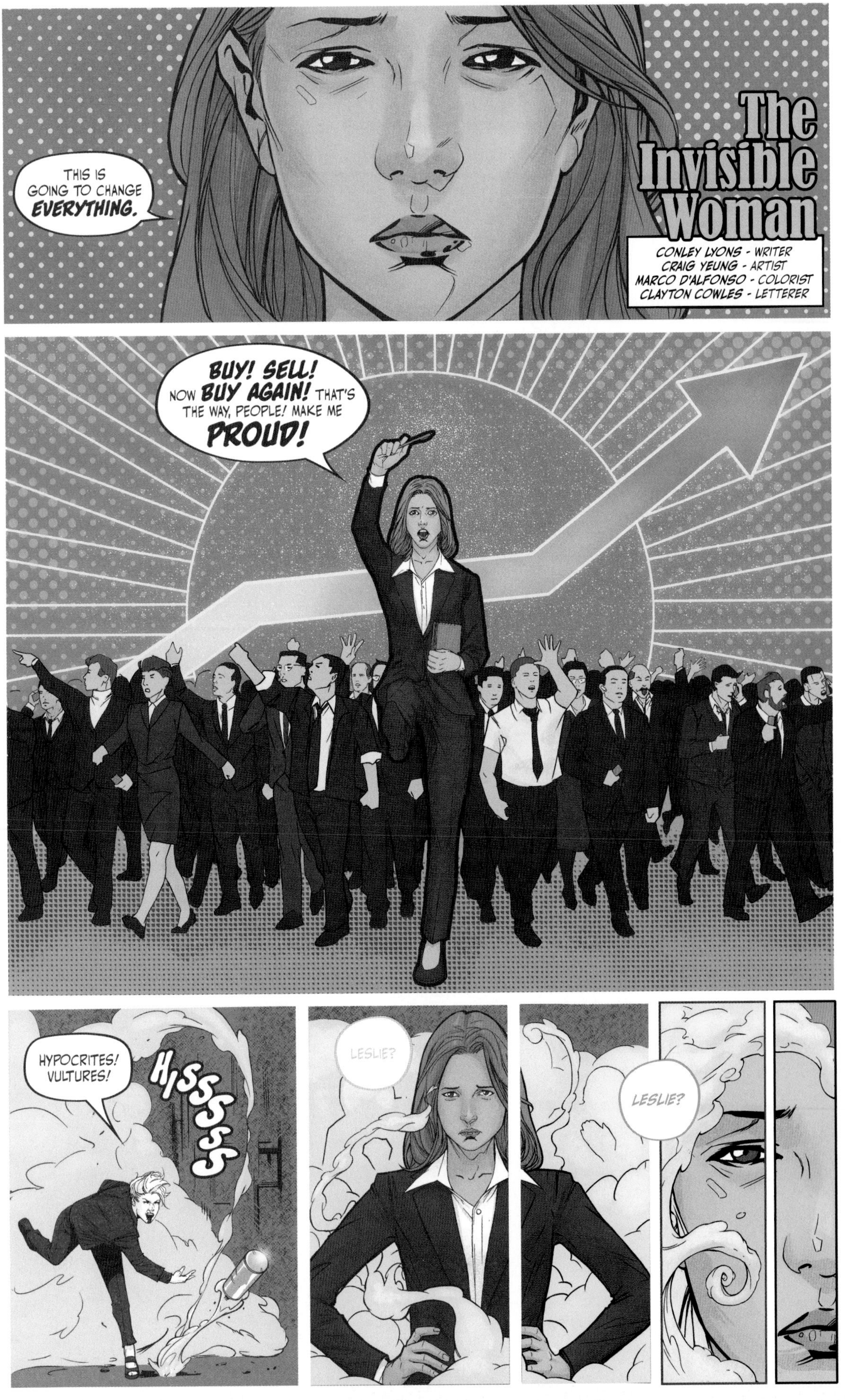
THIS IS GOING TO CHANGE EVERYTHING.
The Invisible Woman
CONLEY LYONS - WRITER
CRAIG YEUNG - ARTIST
MARCO D'ALFONSO - COLORIST
CLAYTON COWLES - LETTERER
BUY! SELL! NOW BUY AGAIN! THAT'S THE WAY, PEOPLE! MAKE ME PROUD!
HYPOCRITES! VULTURES!
HISSSS
LESLIE?
LESLIE?

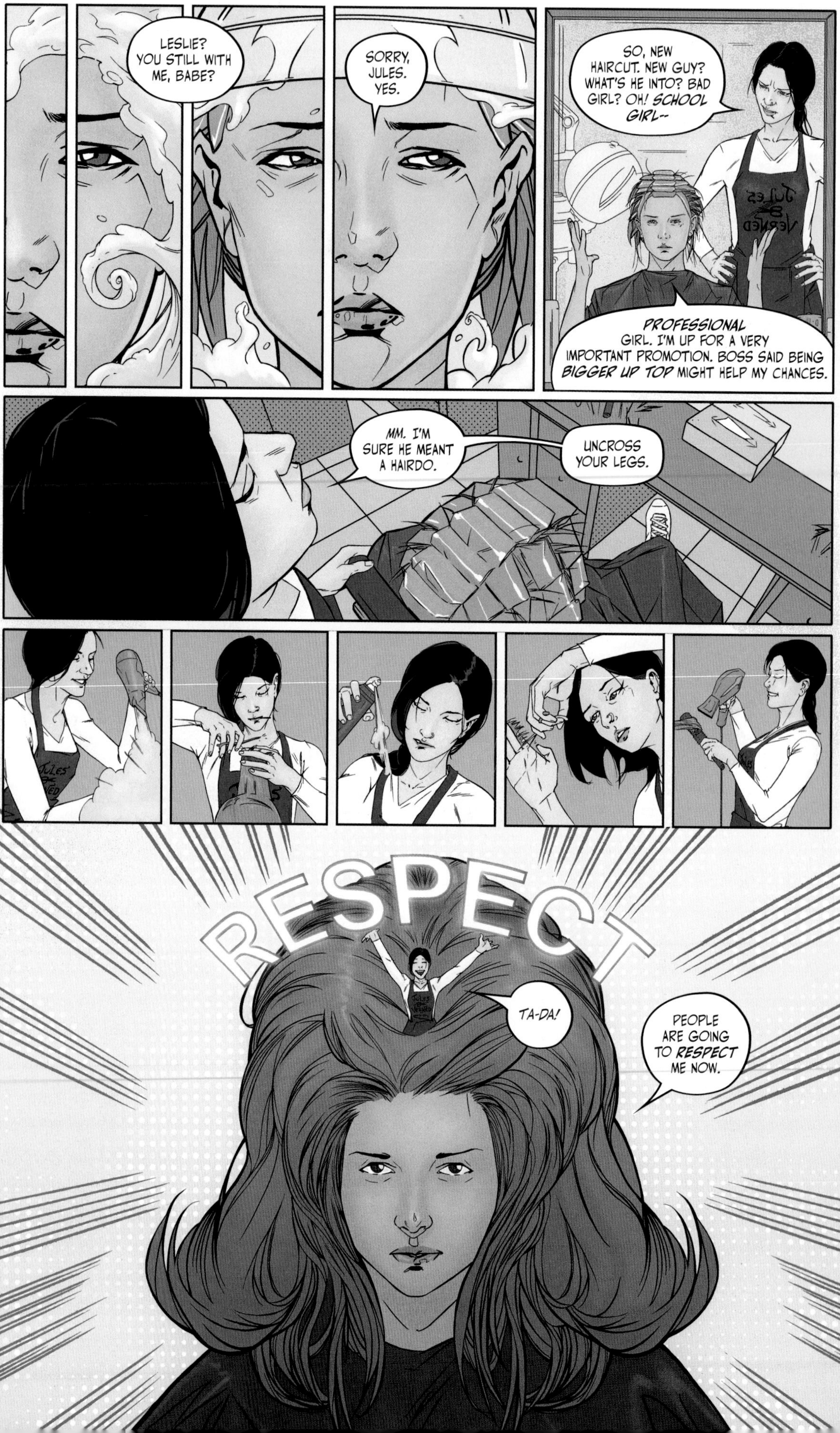
LESLIE? YOU STILL WITH ME, BABE?
SORRY, JULES. YES.
SO, NEW HAIRCUT. NEW GUY? WHAT'S HE INTO? BAD GIRL? OH! SCHOOL GIRL--
PROFESSIONAL GIRL. I'M UP FOR A VERY IMPORTANT PROMOTION. BOSS SAID BEING BIGGER UP TOP MIGHT HELP MY CHANCES.
MM. I'M SURE HE MEANT A HAIRDO.
UNCROSS YOUR LEGS.
RESPECT
TA-DA!
PEOPLE ARE GOING TO RESPECT ME NOW.

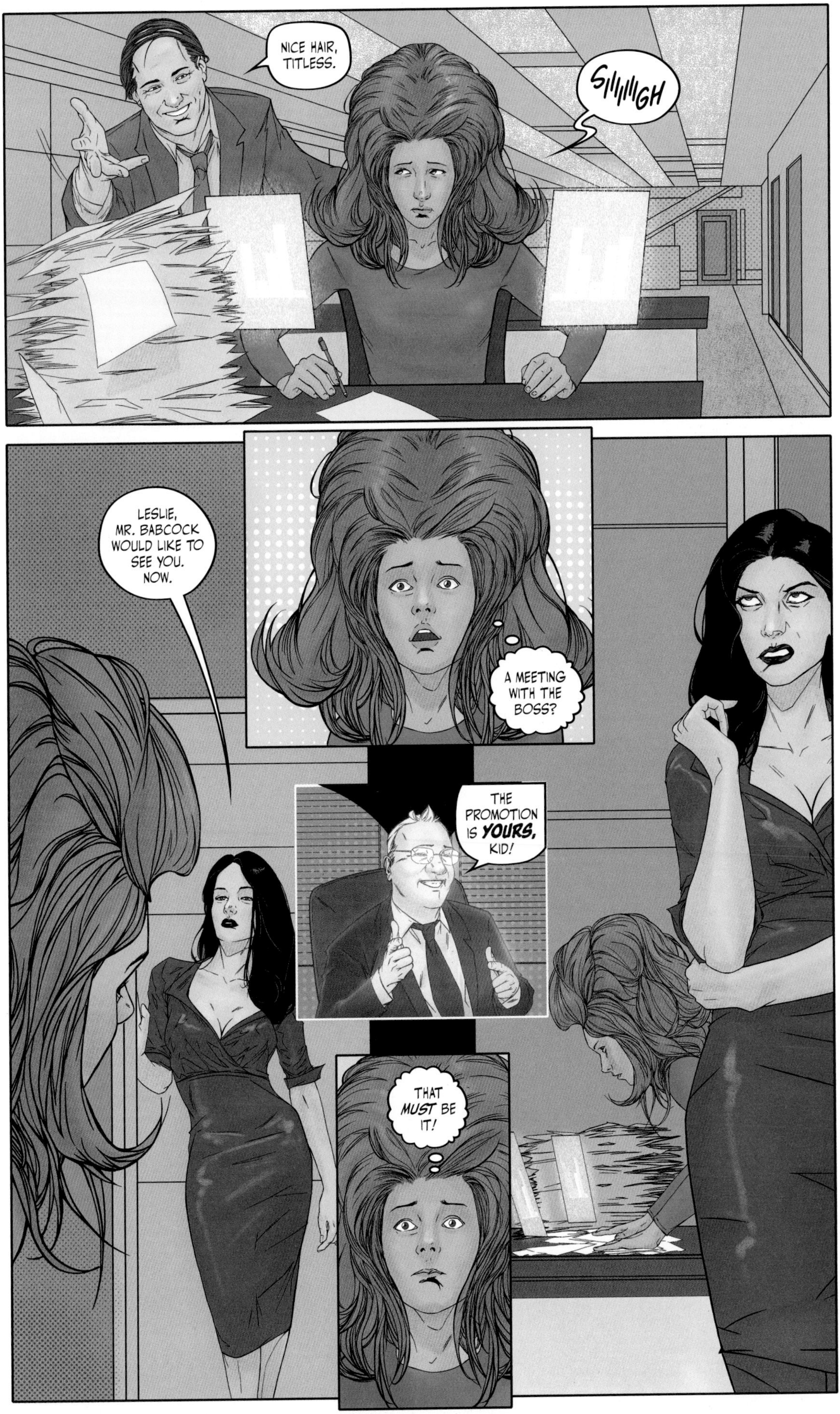

NICE HAIR, TITLESS.
SIIIIIGH
LESLIE, MR. BABCOCK WOULD LIKE TO SEE YOU. NOW.
A MEETING WITH THE BOSS?
THE PROMOTION IS *YOURS,* KID!
THAT *MUST* BE IT!

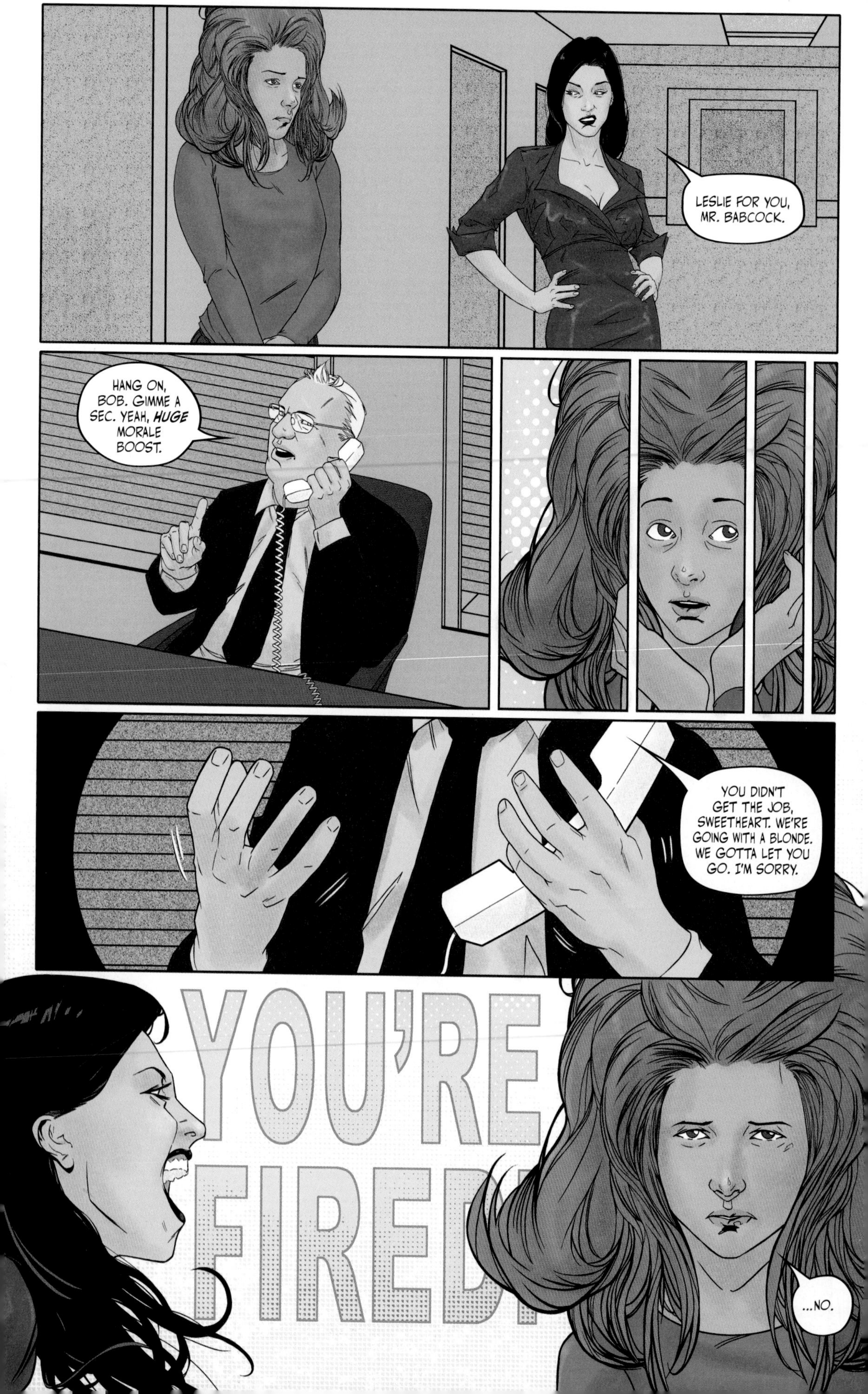
LESLIE FOR YOU, MR. BABCOCK.
HANG ON, BOB. GIMME A SEC. YEAH, ***HUGE*** MORALE BOOST.
YOU DIDN'T GET THE JOB, SWEETHEART. WE'RE GOING WITH A BLONDE. WE GOTTA LET YOU GO. I'M SORRY.
YOU'RE FIRED!
...NO.

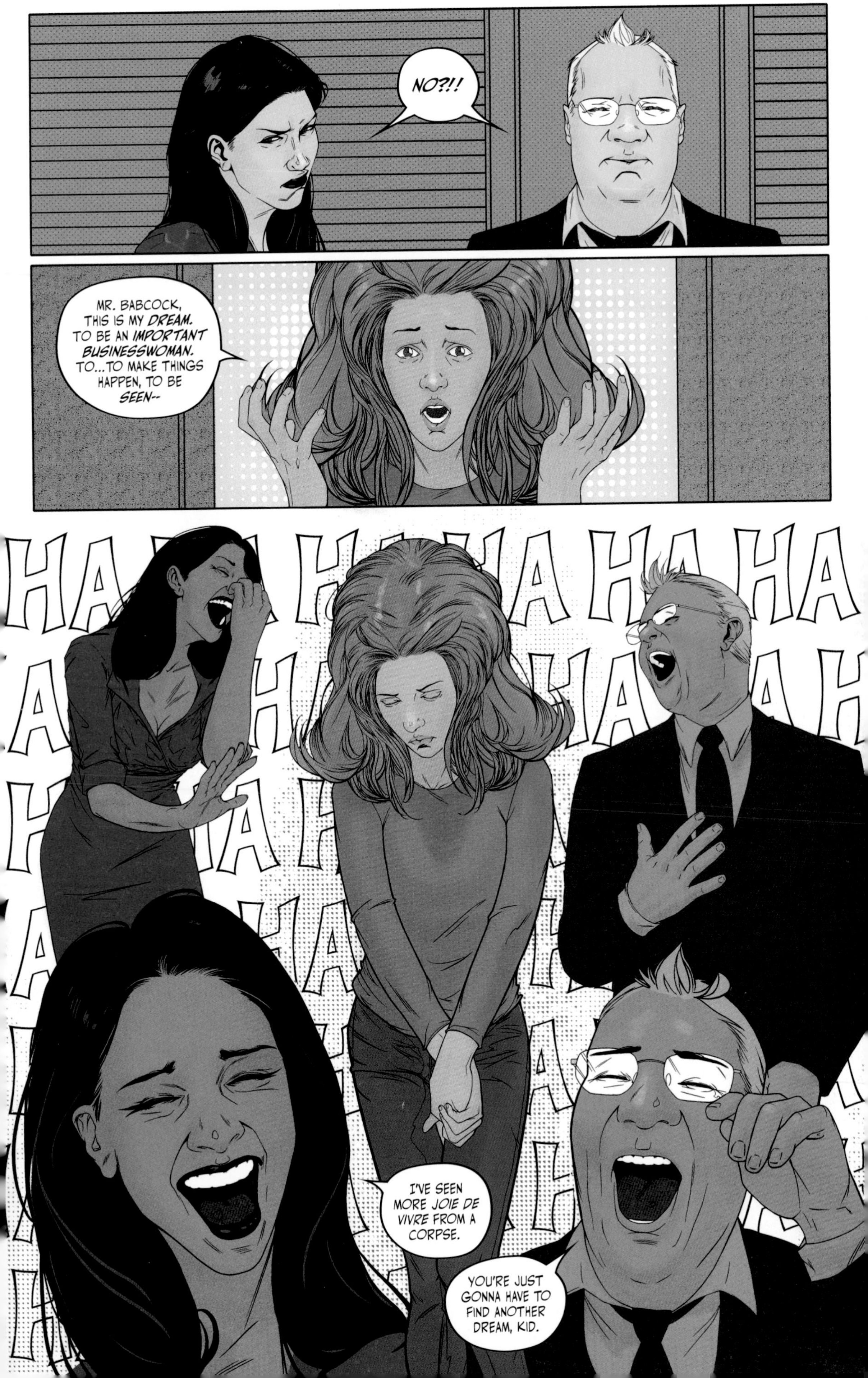
NO?!!
MR. BABCOCK, THIS IS MY *DREAM.* TO BE AN *IMPORTANT BUSINESSWOMAN.* TO...TO MAKE THINGS HAPPEN, TO BE *SEEN*--
HA HA HA HA HA HA
I'VE SEEN MORE *JOIE DE VIVRE* FROM A CORPSE.
YOU'RE JUST GONNA HAVE TO FIND ANOTHER DREAM, KID.

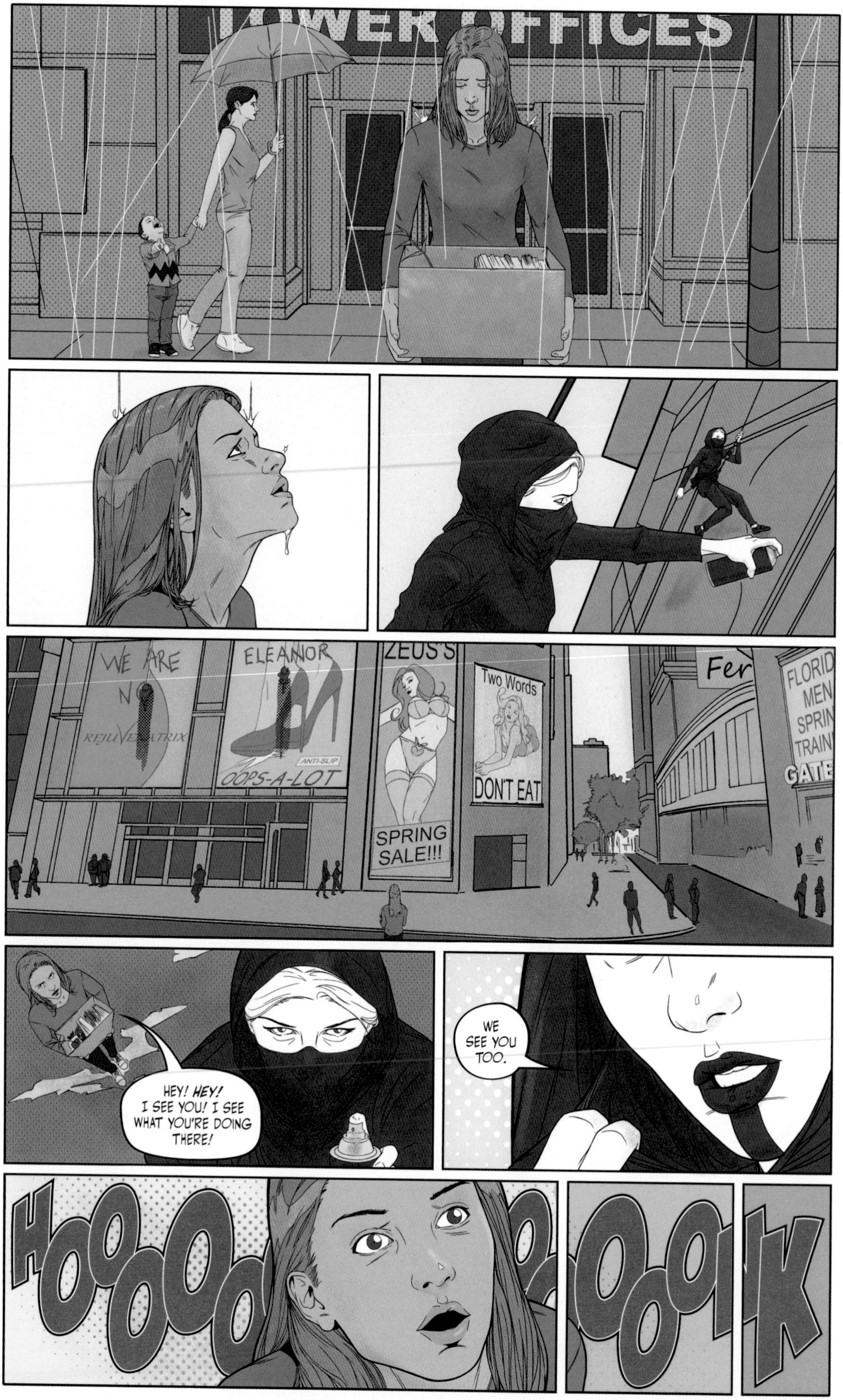
TOWER OFFICES
WE ARE
N
REJUVENATRIX
ELEANOR
ANTI-SLIP
OOPS-A-LOT
ZEUS'S
SPRING SALE!!!
Two Words
DON'T EAT
Fer
FLORID
MEN
SPRIN
TRAIN
GATE
HEY! HEY! I SEE YOU! I SEE WHAT YOU'RE DOING THERE!
WE SEE YOU TOO.
HOOOOOOOOOOOOK

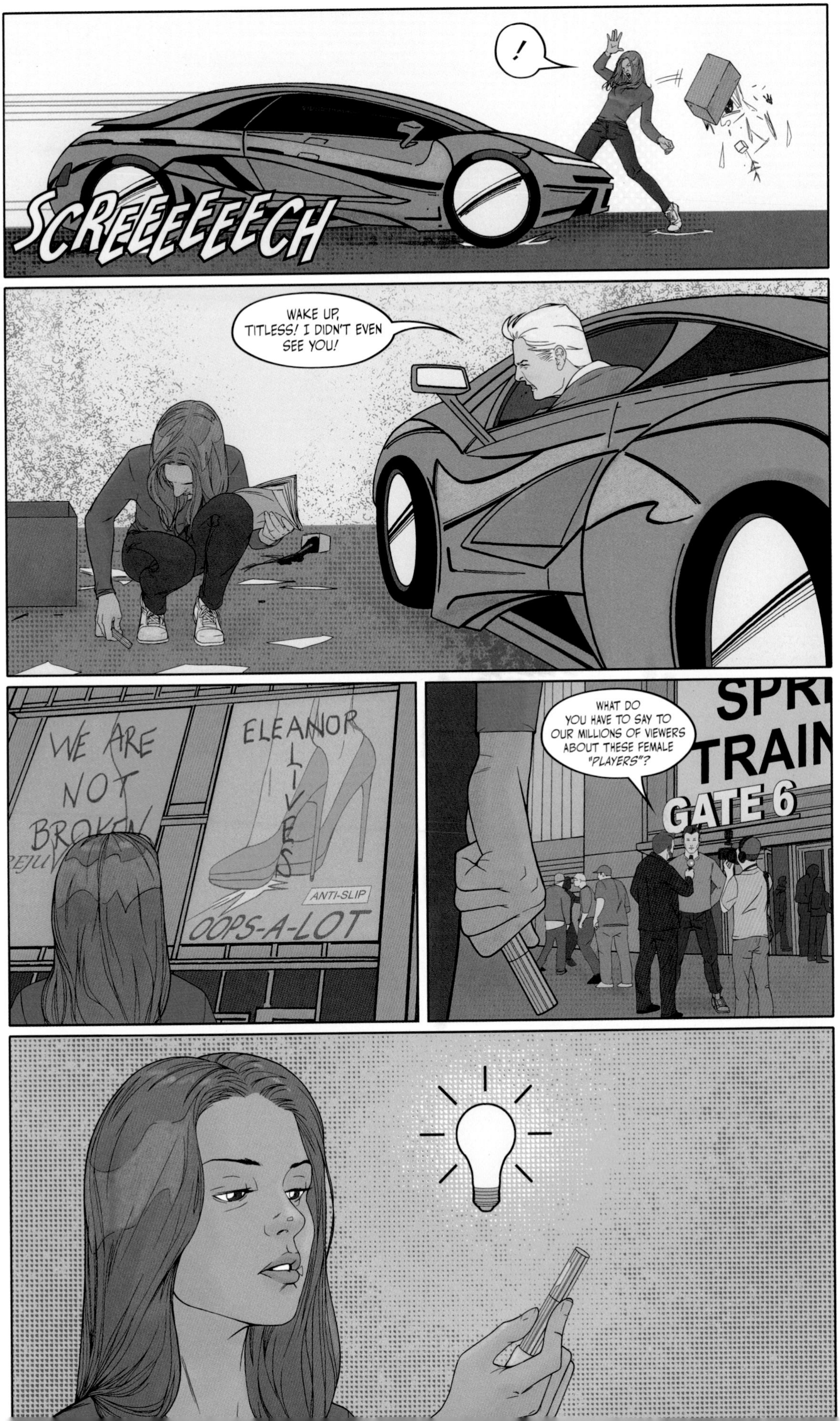

!
SCREEEEEEECH
WAKE UP, TITLESS! I DIDN'T EVEN SEE YOU!
WE ARE NOT BROKEN
ELEANOR LIVES
ANTI-SLIP
OOPS-A-LOT
WHAT DO YOU HAVE TO SAY TO OUR MILLIONS OF VIEWERS ABOUT THESE FEMALE "PLAYERS"?
GATE 6

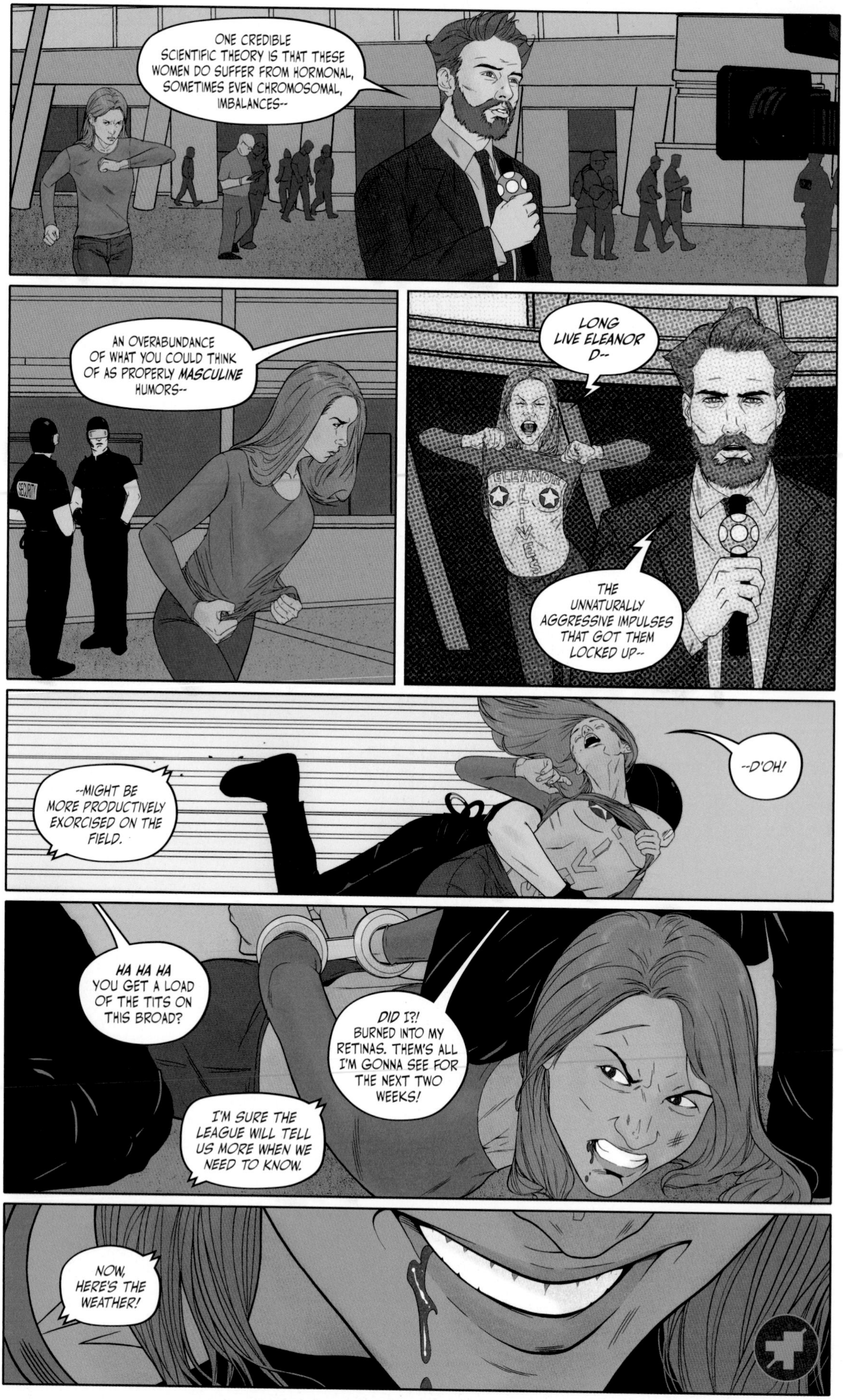
ONE CREDIBLE SCIENTIFIC THEORY IS THAT THESE WOMEN DO SUFFER FROM HORMONAL, SOMETIMES EVEN CHROMOSOMAL, IMBALANCES--
AN OVERABUNDANCE OF WHAT YOU COULD THINK OF AS PROPERLY *MASCULINE* HUMORS--
*LONG LIVE ELEANOR D--*
ELEANOR LIVES
THE UNNATURALLY AGGRESSIVE IMPULSES THAT GOT THEM LOCKED UP--
*--MIGHT BE MORE PRODUCTIVELY EXORCISED ON THE FIELD.*
*--D'OH!*
***HA HA HA*** YOU GET A LOAD OF THE TITS ON THIS BROAD?
*DID I?!* BURNED INTO MY RETINAS. THEM'S ALL I'M GONNA SEE FOR THE NEXT TWO WEEKS!
*I'M SURE THE LEAGUE WILL TELL US MORE WHEN WE NEED TO KNOW.*
*NOW, HERE'S THE WEATHER!*

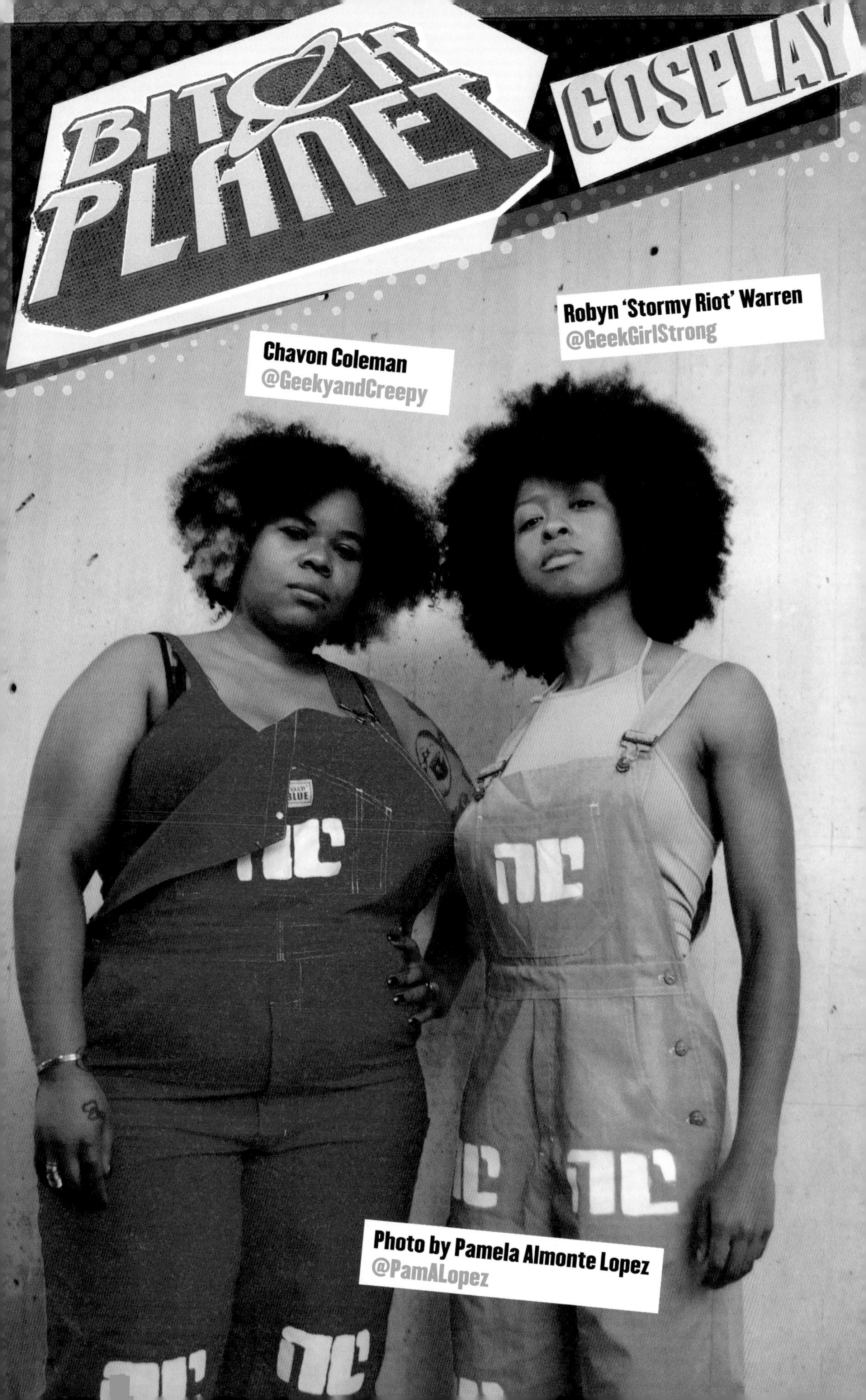
BITCH PLANET
COSPLAY
Robyn 'Stormy Riot' Warren
@GeekGirlStrong
Chavon Coleman
@GeekyandCreepy
Photo by Pamela Almonte Lopez
@PamALopez

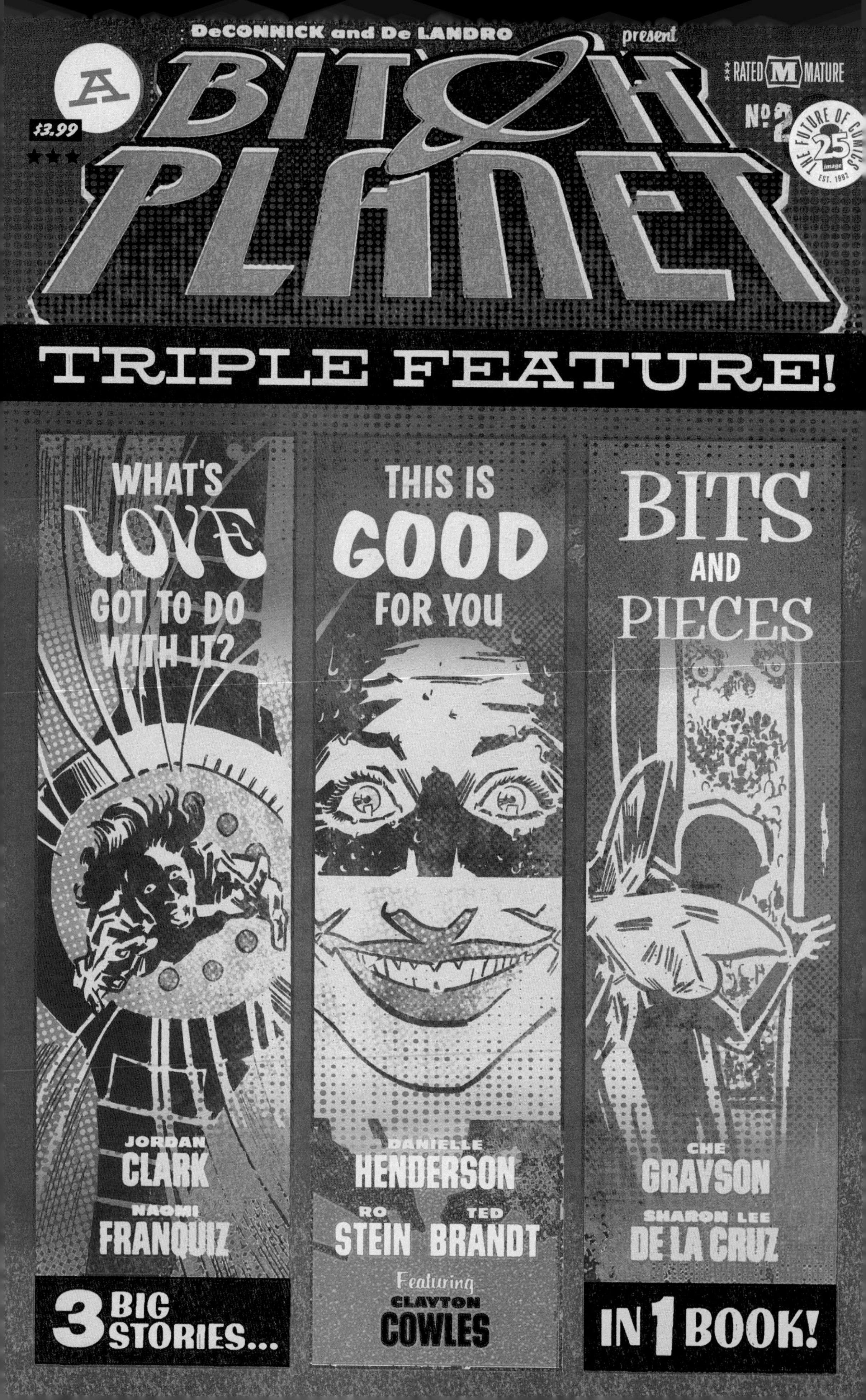

DeCONNICK and De LANDRO present
A
$3.99
BITCH PLANET
RATED M MATURE
Nº 2
THE FUTURE OF COMICS 25 image EST. 1992
TRIPLE FEATURE!
WHAT'S LOVE GOT TO DO WITH IT?
JORDAN CLARK
NAOMI FRANQUIZ
THIS IS GOOD FOR YOU
DANIELLE HENDERSON
RO STEIN
TED BRANDT
Featuring
CLAYTON COWLES
BITS AND PIECES
CHE GRAYSON
SHARON LEE DE LA CRUZ
3 BIG STORIES...
IN 1 BOOK!

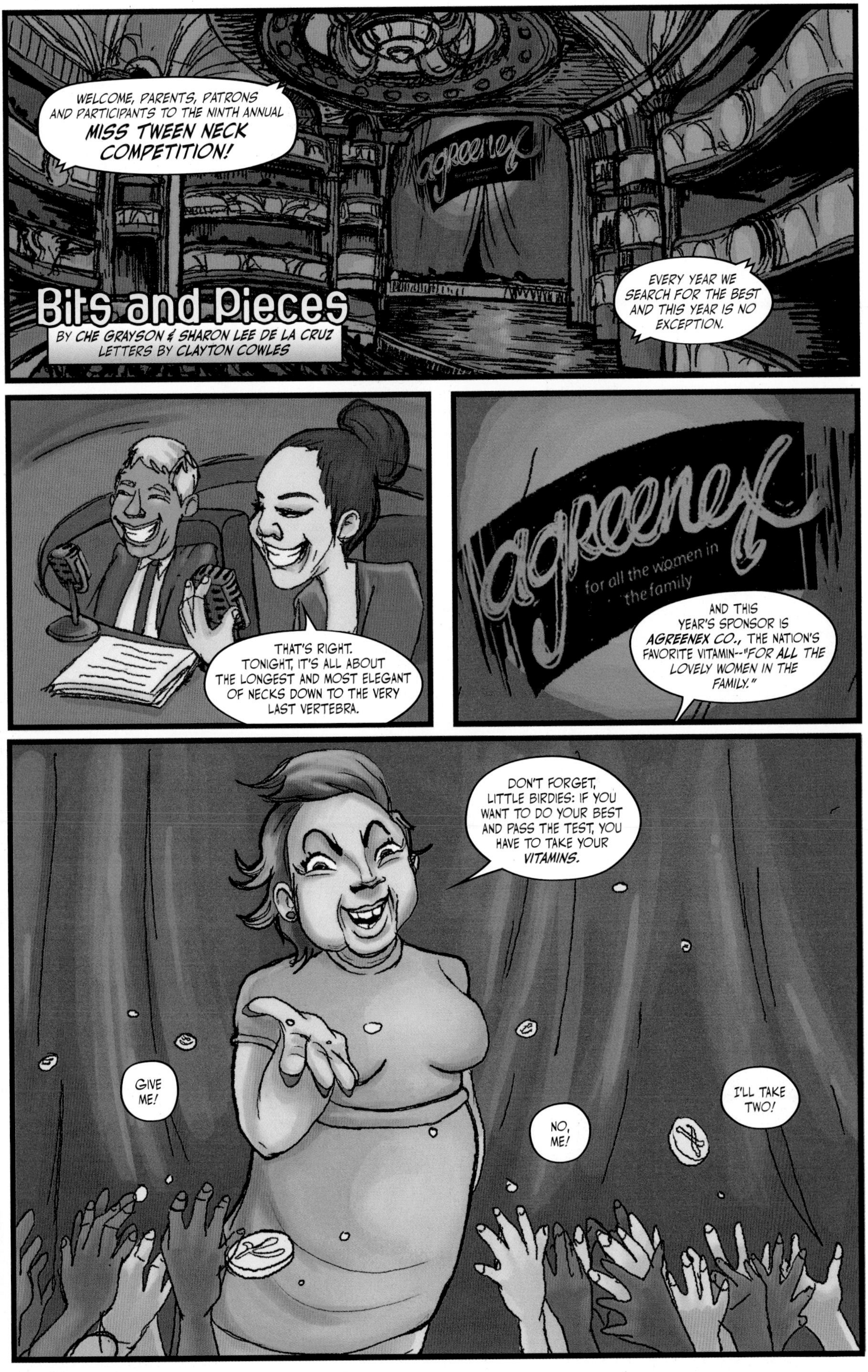
WELCOME, PARENTS, PATRONS AND PARTICIPANTS TO THE NINTH ANNUAL MISS TWEEN NECK COMPETITION!
agreenex
Bits and Pieces
BY CHE GRAYSON & SHARON LEE DE LA CRUZ
LETTERS BY CLAYTON COWLES
EVERY YEAR WE SEARCH FOR THE BEST AND THIS YEAR IS NO EXCEPTION.
THAT'S RIGHT. TONIGHT, IT'S ALL ABOUT THE LONGEST AND MOST ELEGANT OF NECKS DOWN TO THE VERY LAST VERTEBRA.
agreenex
for all the women in the family
AND THIS YEAR'S SPONSOR IS AGREENEX CO., THE NATION'S FAVORITE VITAMIN--"FOR ALL THE LOVELY WOMEN IN THE FAMILY."
DON'T FORGET, LITTLE BIRDIES: IF YOU WANT TO DO YOUR BEST AND PASS THE TEST, YOU HAVE TO TAKE YOUR VITAMINS.
GIVE ME!
NO, ME!
I'LL TAKE TWO!

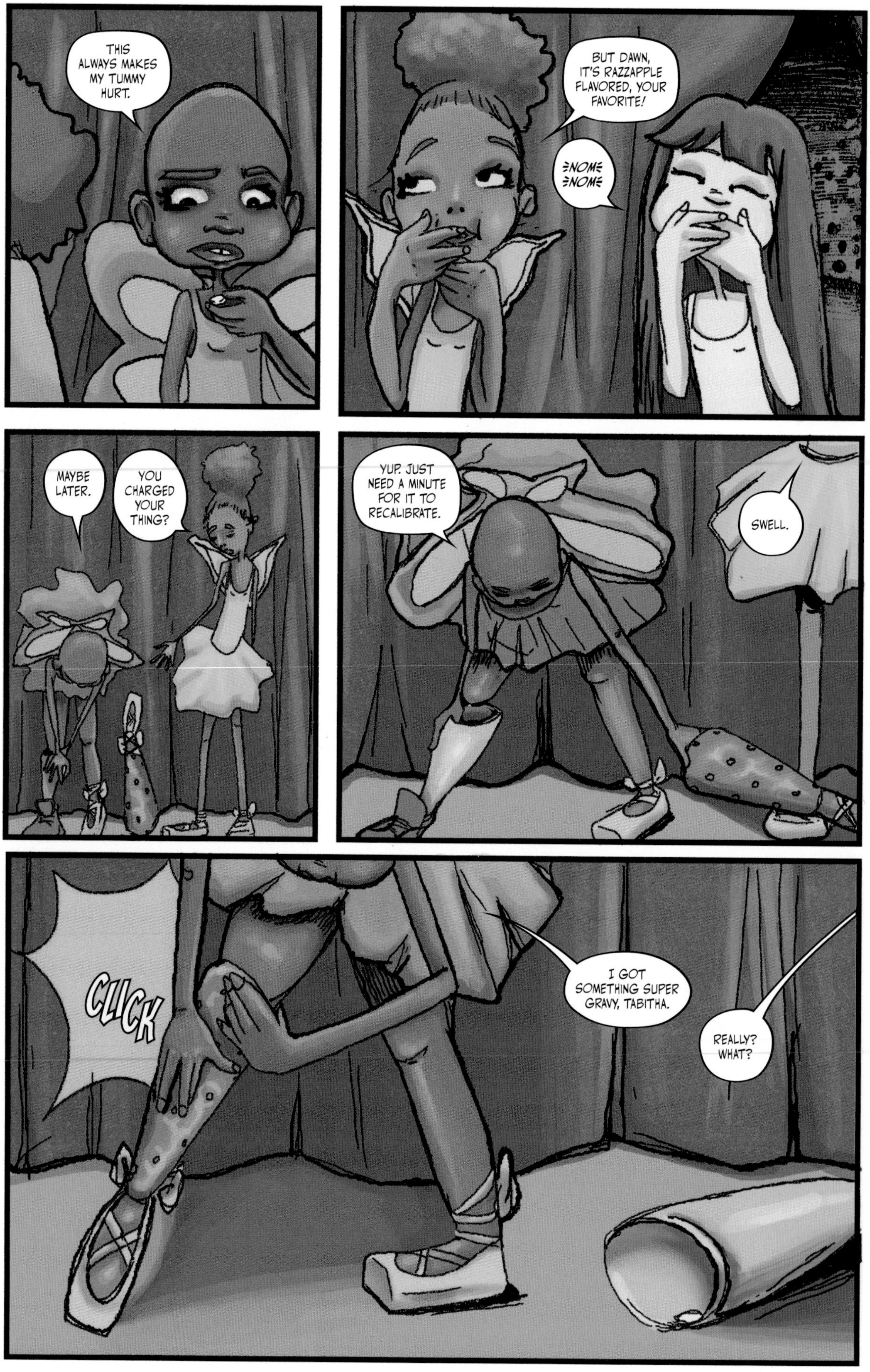
THIS ALWAYS MAKES MY TUMMY HURT.
BUT DAWN, IT'S RAZZAPPLE FLAVORED, YOUR FAVORITE!
NOM NOM
MAYBE LATER.
YOU CHARGED YOUR THING?
YUP. JUST NEED A MINUTE FOR IT TO RECALIBRATE.
SWELL.
CLICK
I GOT SOMETHING SUPER GRAVY, TABITHA.
REALLY? WHAT?

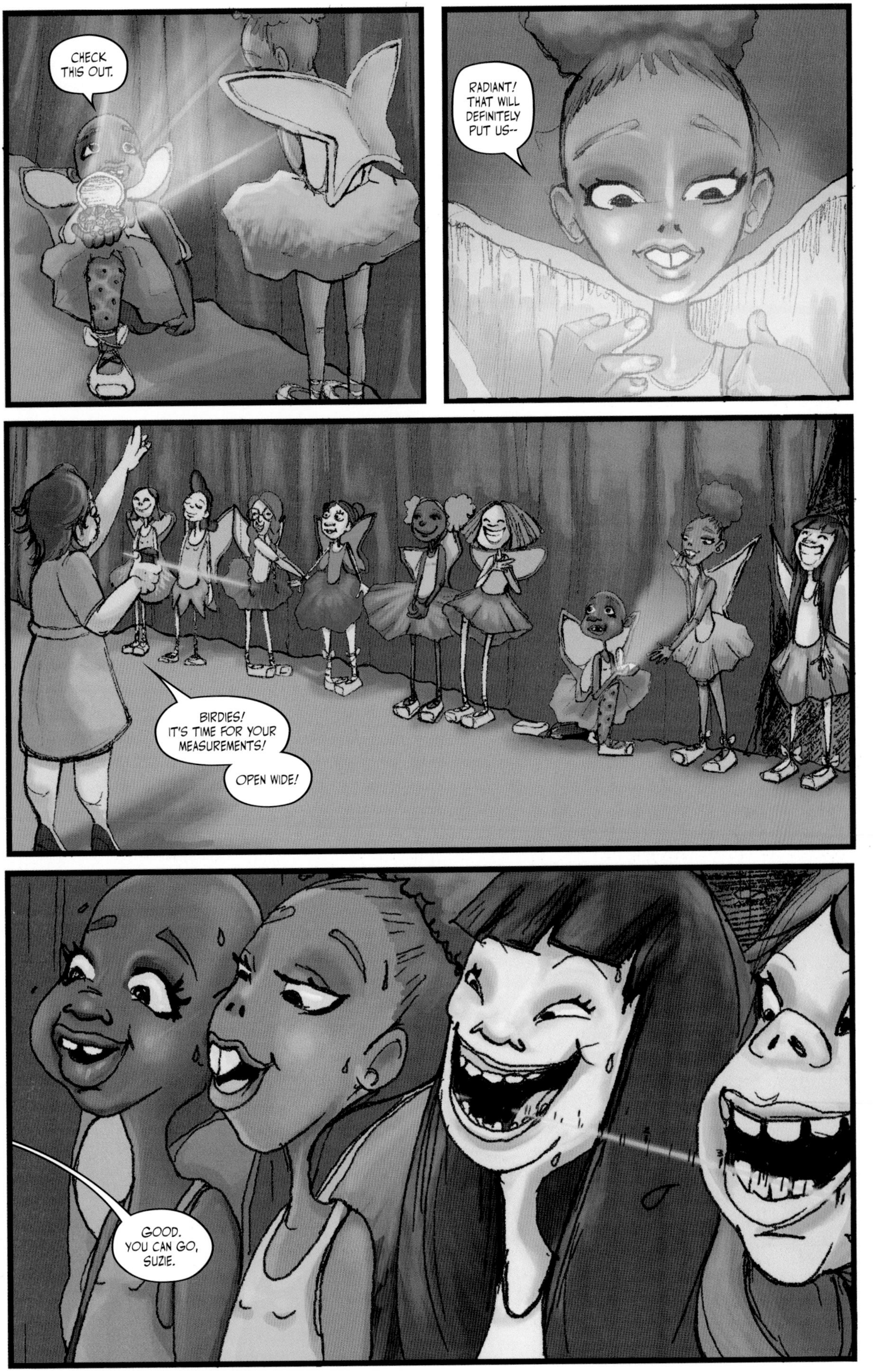
CHECK THIS OUT.
RADIANT! THAT WILL DEFINITELY PUT US--
BIRDIES! IT'S TIME FOR YOUR MEASUREMENTS!
OPEN WIDE!
GOOD. YOU CAN GO, SUZIE.

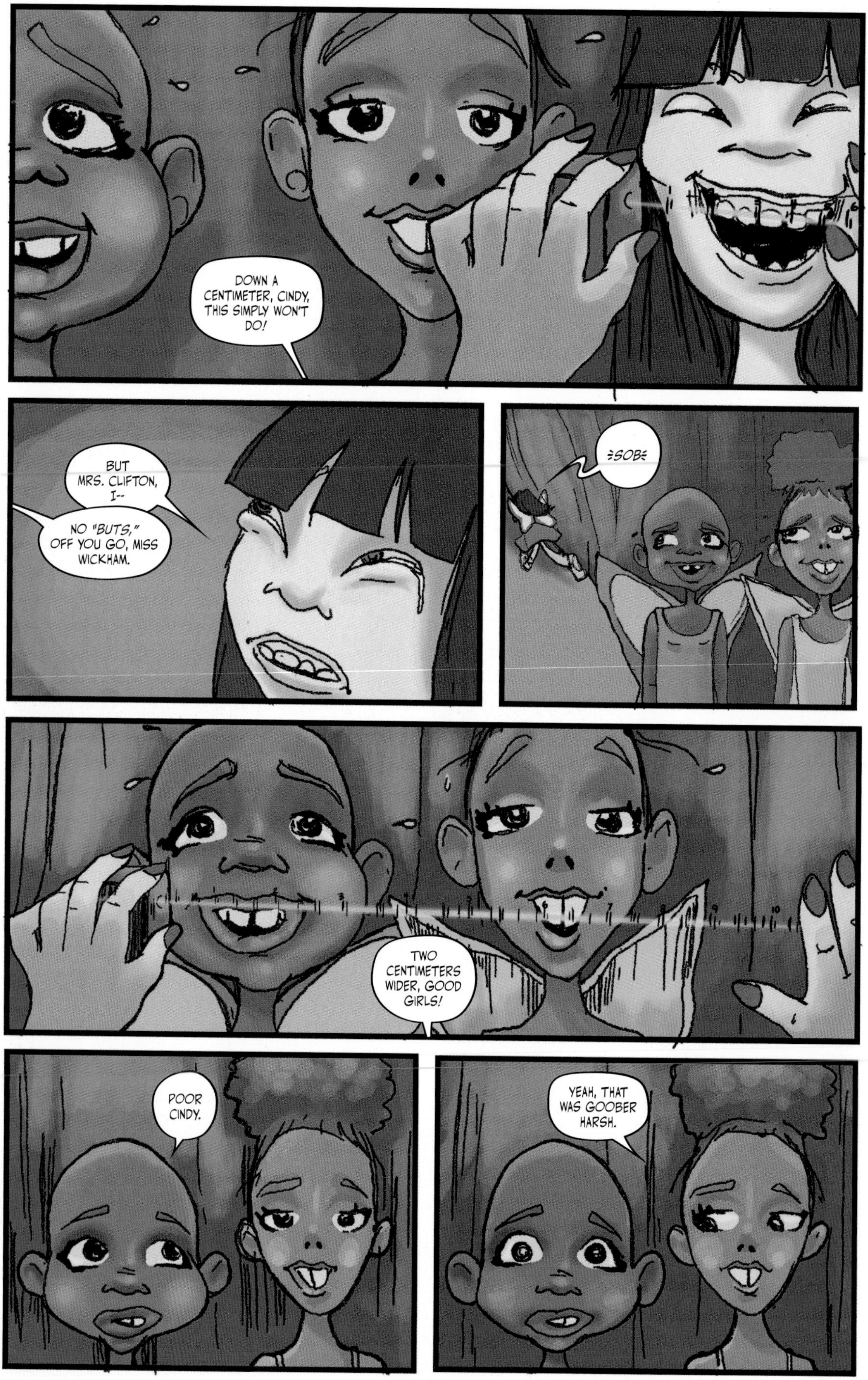
DOWN A CENTIMETER, CINDY, THIS SIMPLY WON'T DO!
BUT MRS. CLIFTON, I--
NO "BUTS," OFF YOU GO, MISS WICKHAM.
SOB
TWO CENTIMETERS WIDER, GOOD GIRLS!
POOR CINDY.
YEAH, THAT WAS GOOBER HARSH.

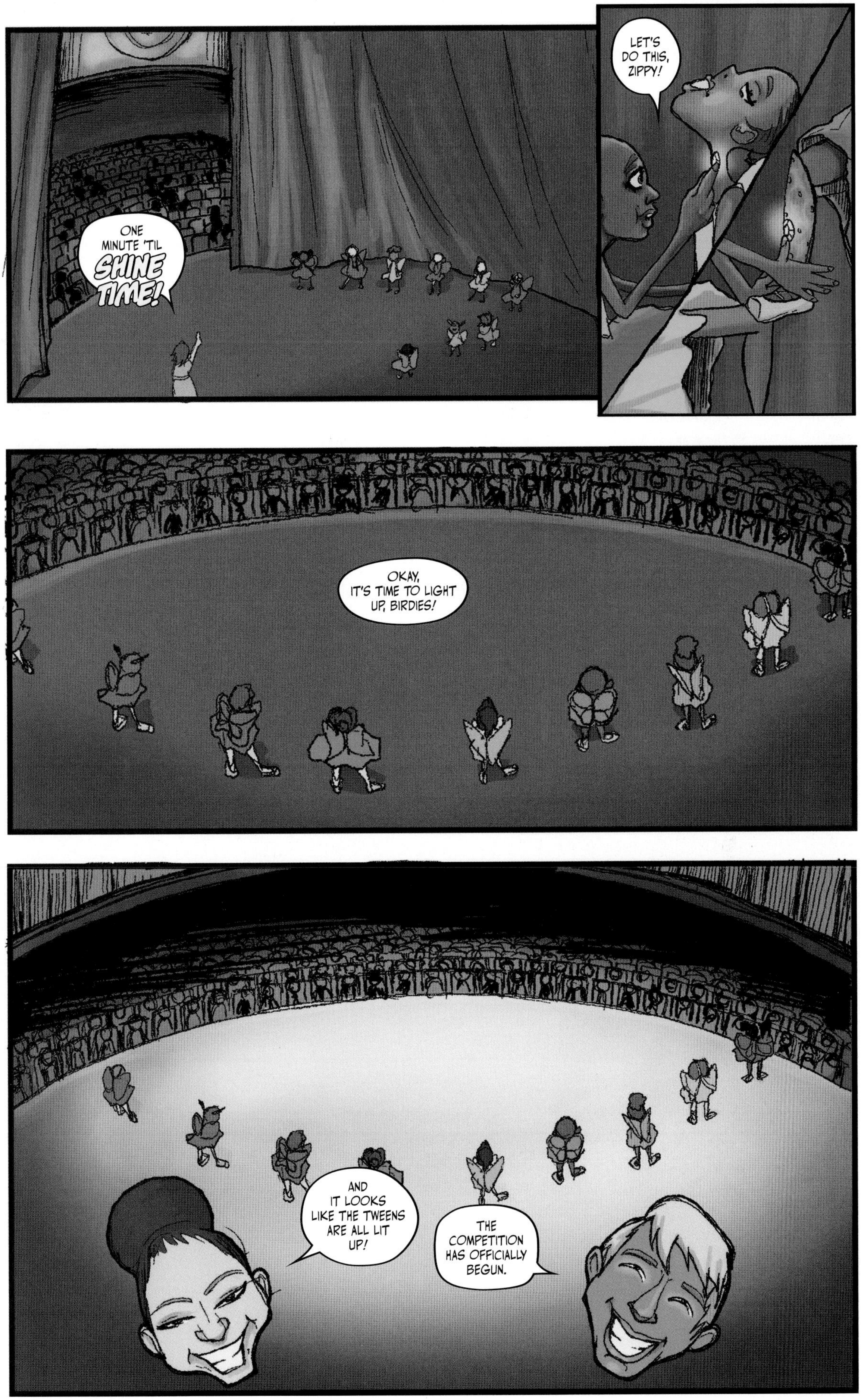
ONE MINUTE 'TIL SHINE TIME!
LET'S DO THIS, ZIPPY!
OKAY, IT'S TIME TO LIGHT UP, BIRDIES!
AND IT LOOKS LIKE THE TWEENS ARE ALL LIT UP!
THE COMPETITION HAS OFFICIALLY BEGUN.

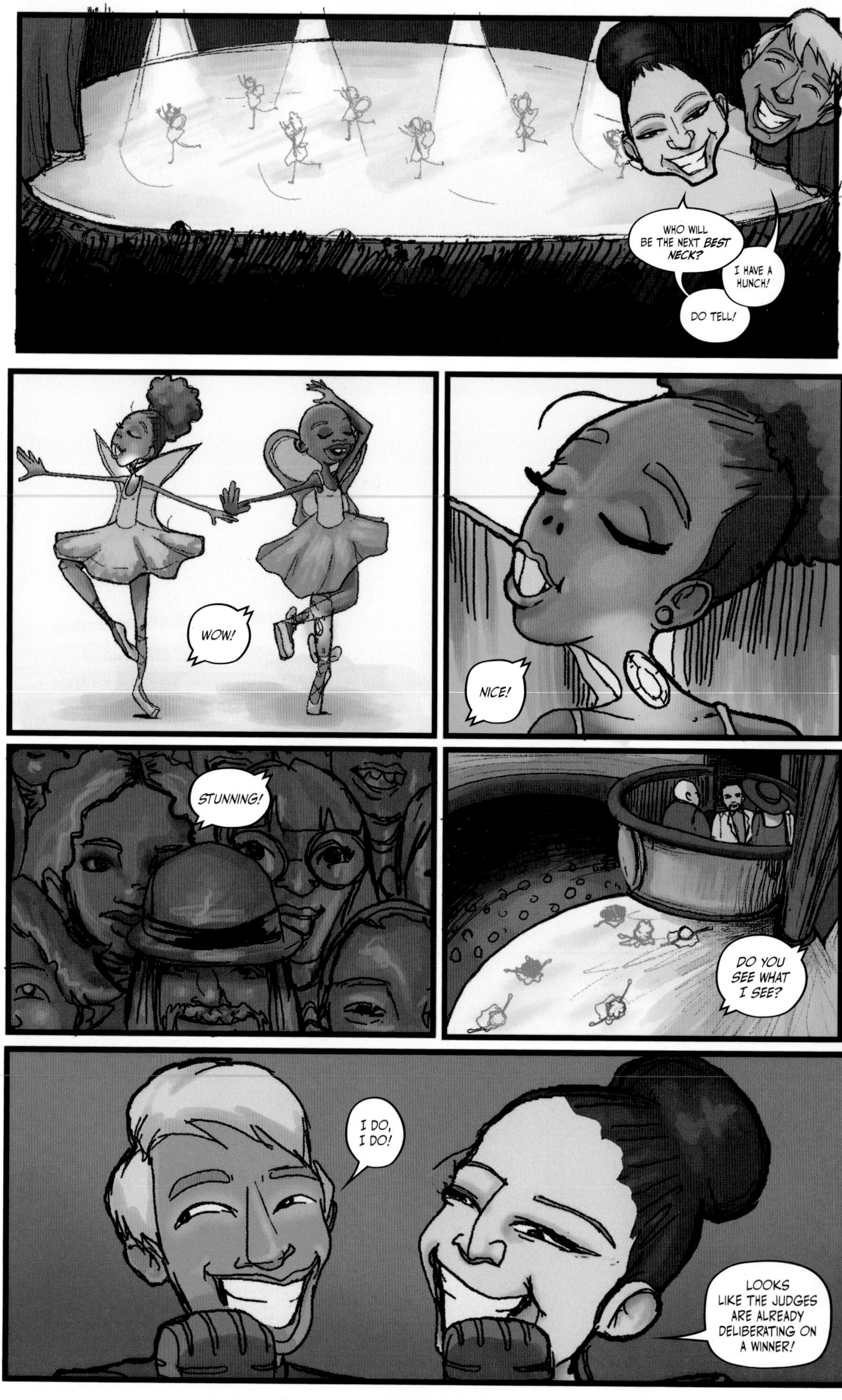
WHO WILL BE THE NEXT BEST NECK?
I HAVE A HUNCH!
DO TELL!
WOW!
NICE!
STUNNING!
DO YOU SEE WHAT I SEE?
I DO, I DO!
LOOKS LIKE THE JUDGES ARE ALREADY DELIBERATING ON A WINNER!

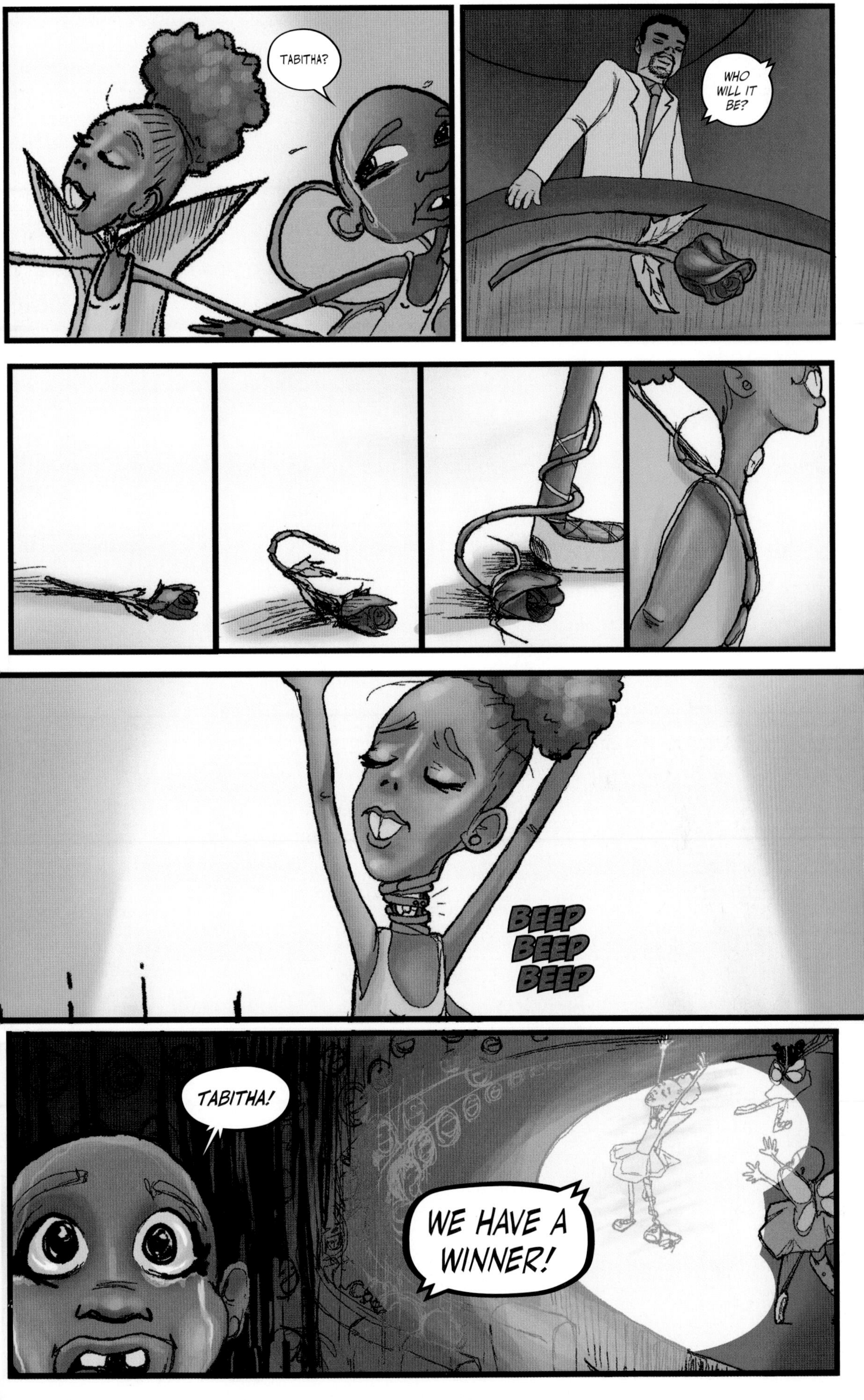
TABITHA?
WHO WILL IT BE?
BEEP BEEP BEEP
TABITHA!
WE HAVE A WINNER!

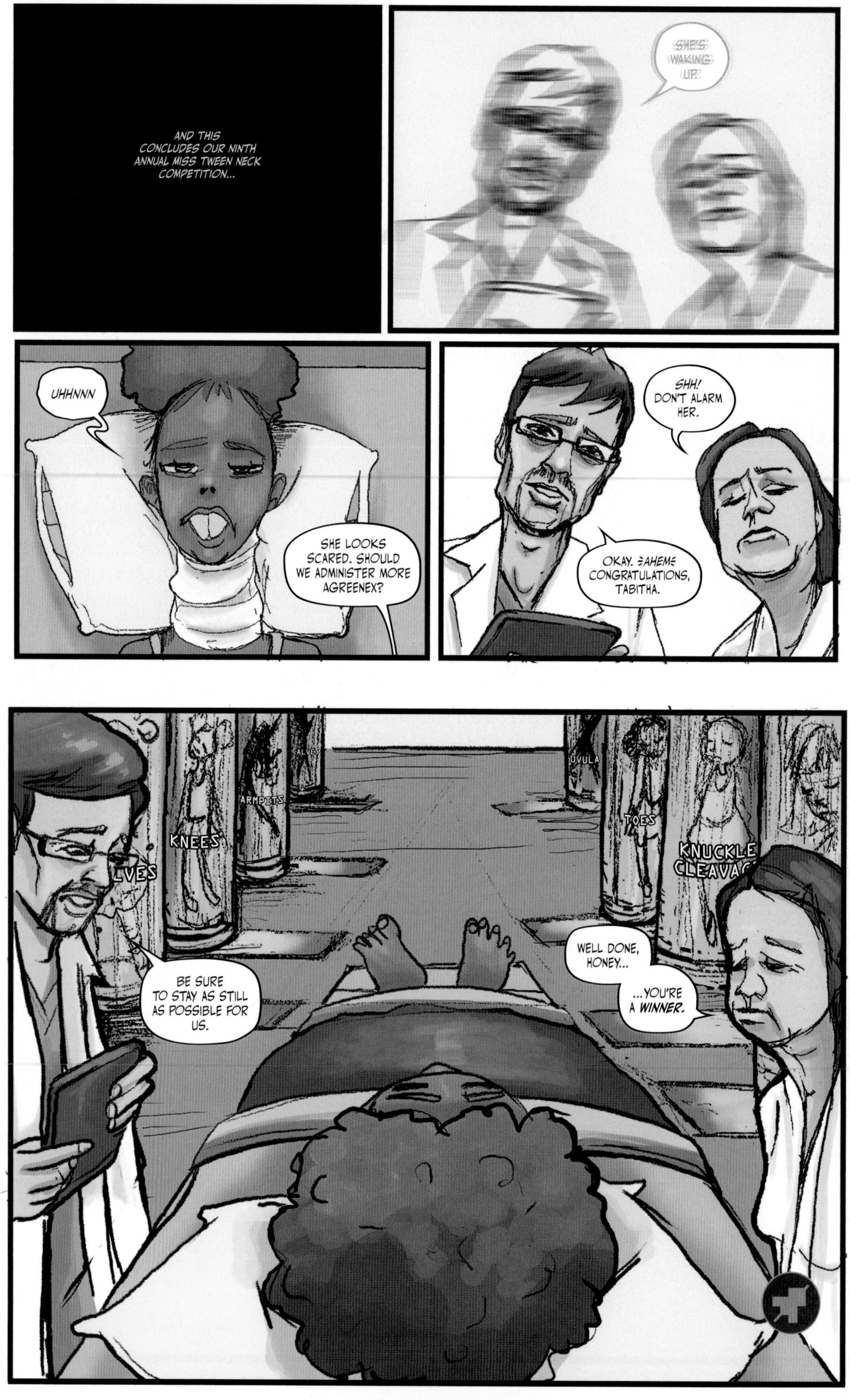
AND THIS CONCLUDES OUR NINTH ANNUAL MISS TWEEN NECK COMPETITION...
SHE'S WAKING UP?
UHHNNN
SHE LOOKS SCARED. SHOULD WE ADMINISTER MORE AGREENEX?
SHH! DON'T ALARM HER.
OKAY. AHEM CONGRATULATIONS, TABITHA.
CALVES
UVULA
ARMPITS
KNEES
LVES
TOES
KNUCKLE CLEAVAG
BE SURE TO STAY AS STILL AS POSSIBLE FOR US.
WELL DONE, HONEY...
...YOU'RE A *WINNER.*

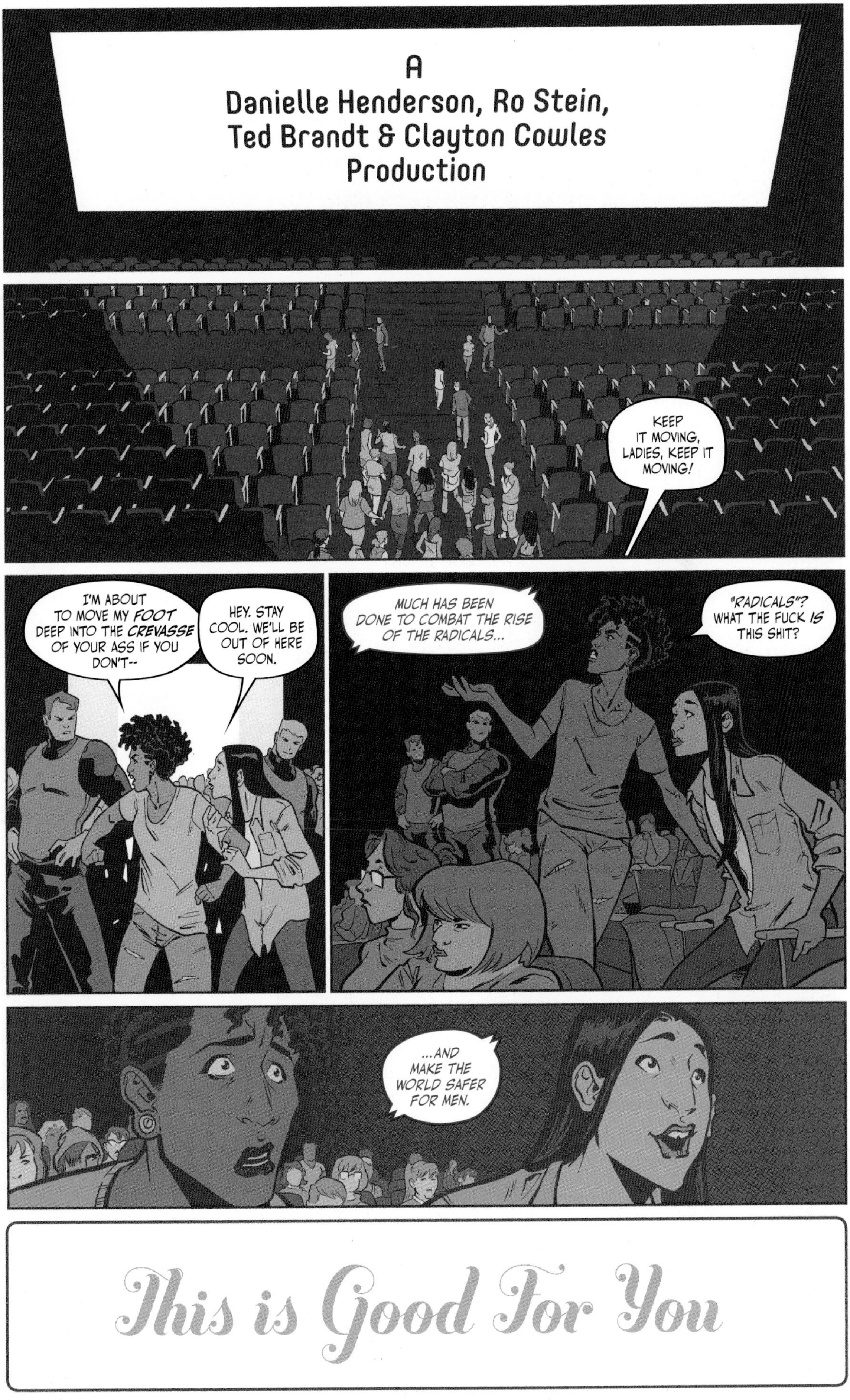
A
Danielle Henderson, Ro Stein,
Ted Brandt & Clayton Cowles
Production
KEEP IT MOVING, LADIES, KEEP IT MOVING!
I'M ABOUT TO MOVE MY *FOOT* DEEP INTO THE *CREVASSE* OF YOUR ASS IF YOU DON'T--
HEY. STAY COOL. WE'LL BE OUT OF HERE SOON.
MUCH HAS BEEN DONE TO COMBAT THE RISE OF THE RADICALS...
"RADICALS"? WHAT THE FUCK *IS* THIS SHIT?
...AND MAKE THE WORLD SAFER FOR MEN.
This is Good For You

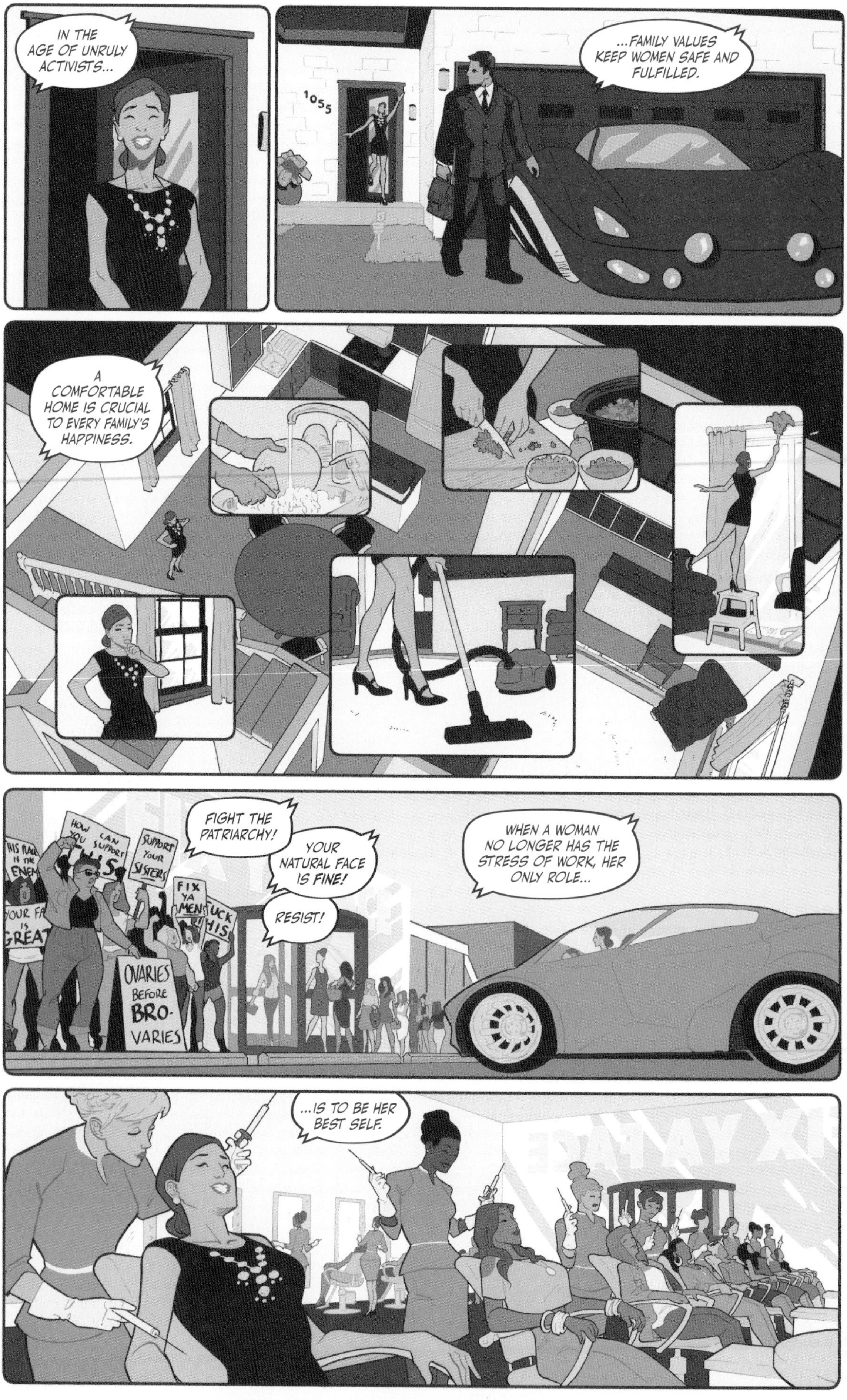
IN THE AGE OF UNRULY ACTIVISTS...
1055
...FAMILY VALUES KEEP WOMEN SAFE AND FULFILLED.
A COMFORTABLE HOME IS CRUCIAL TO EVERY FAMILY'S HAPPINESS.
SUPPORT YOUR SISTERS
FIX YA MEN
OVARIES BEFORE BRO-VARIES
FIGHT THE PATRIARCHY!
YOUR NATURAL FACE IS FINE!
RESIST!
WHEN A WOMAN NO LONGER HAS THE STRESS OF WORK, HER ONLY ROLE...
...IS TO BE HER BEST SELF.

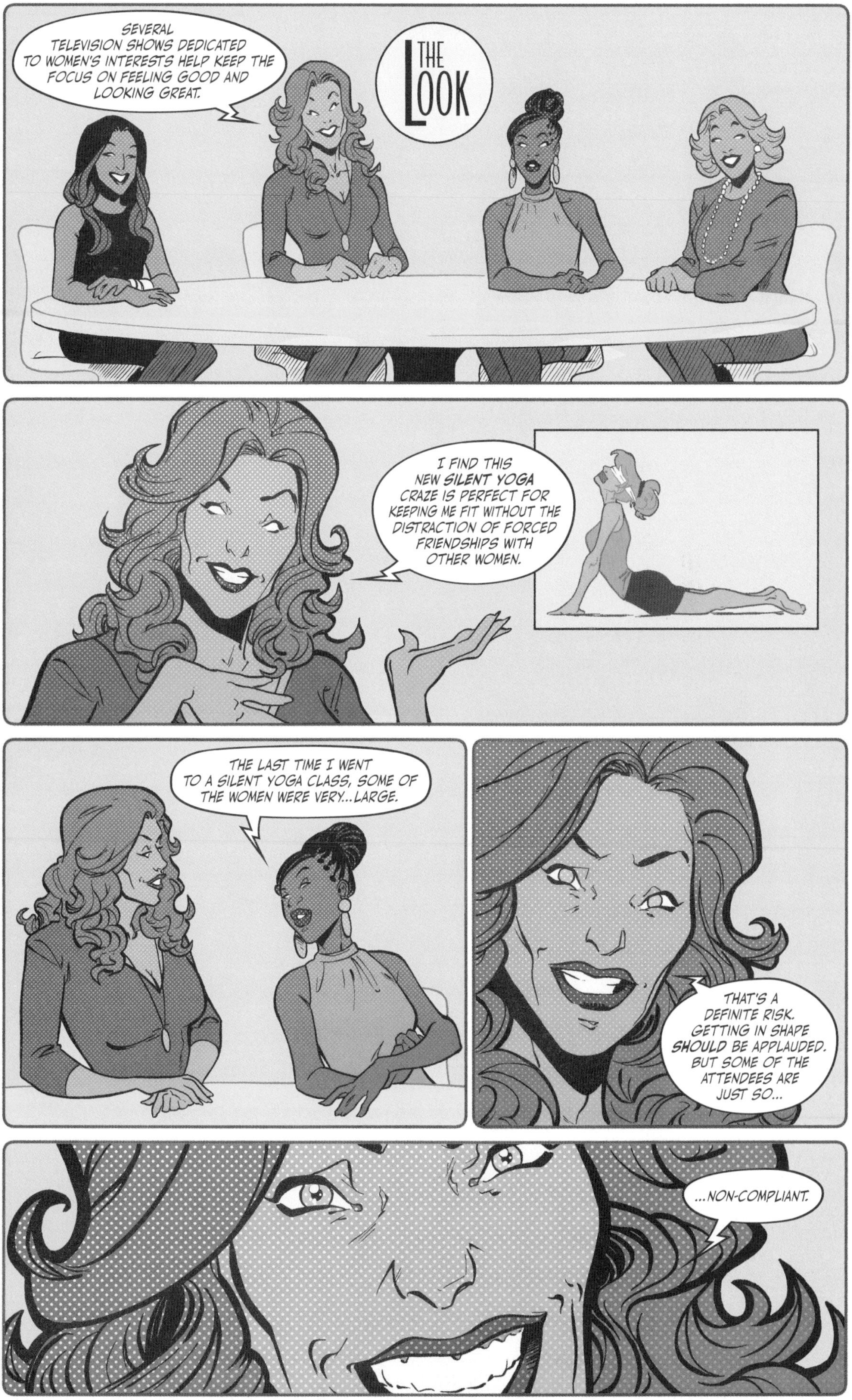
SEVERAL TELEVISION SHOWS DEDICATED TO WOMEN'S INTERESTS HELP KEEP THE FOCUS ON FEELING GOOD AND LOOKING GREAT.
THE LOOK
I FIND THIS NEW SILENT YOGA CRAZE IS PERFECT FOR KEEPING ME FIT WITHOUT THE DISTRACTION OF FORCED FRIENDSHIPS WITH OTHER WOMEN.
THE LAST TIME I WENT TO A SILENT YOGA CLASS, SOME OF THE WOMEN WERE VERY...LARGE.
THAT'S A DEFINITE RISK. GETTING IN SHAPE SHOULD BE APPLAUDED. BUT SOME OF THE ATTENDEES ARE JUST SO...
...NON-COMPLIANT.

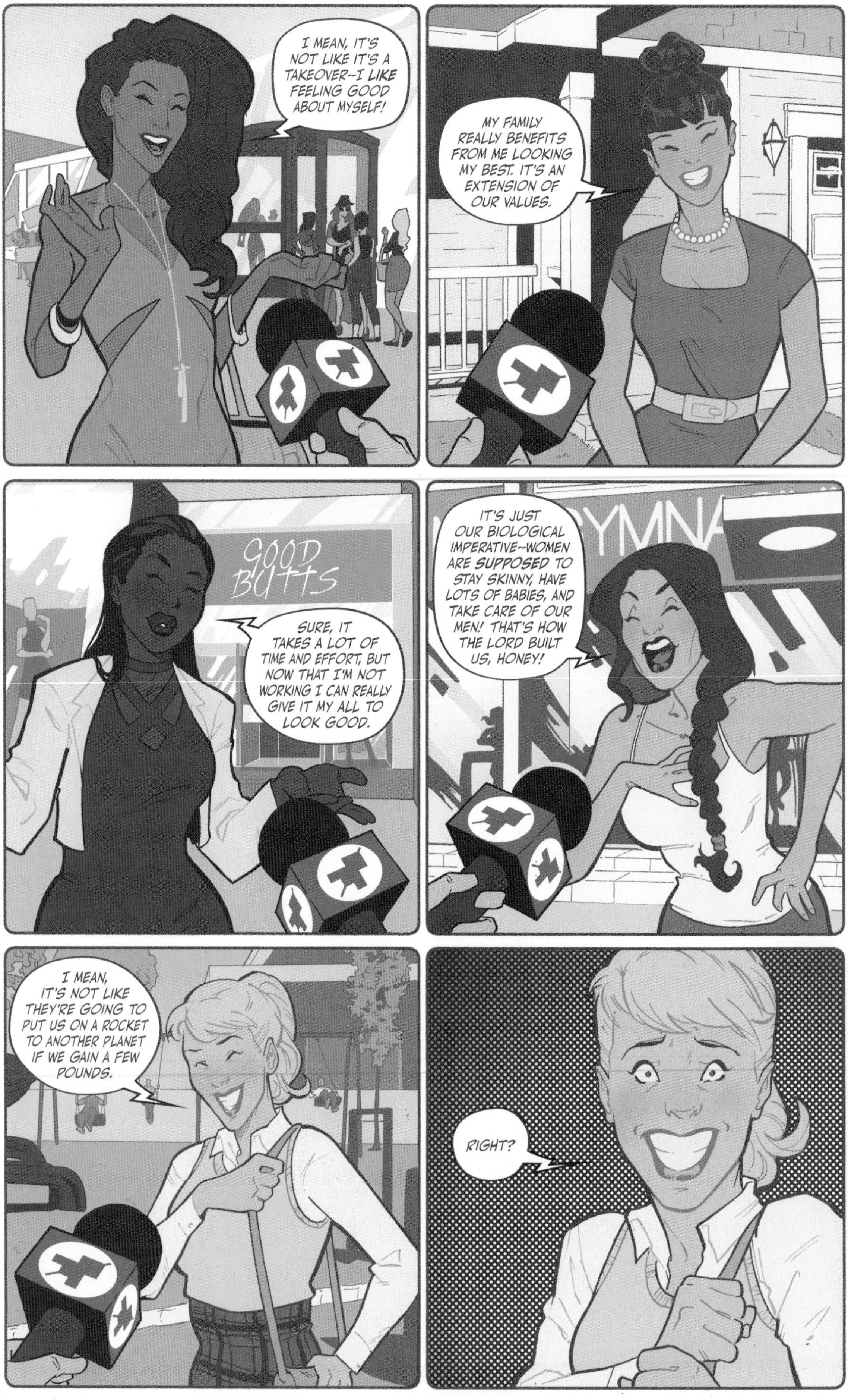
I MEAN, IT'S NOT LIKE IT'S A TAKEOVER--I LIKE FEELING GOOD ABOUT MYSELF!
MY FAMILY REALLY BENEFITS FROM ME LOOKING MY BEST. IT'S AN EXTENSION OF OUR VALUES.
GOOD BUTTS
SURE, IT TAKES A LOT OF TIME AND EFFORT, BUT NOW THAT I'M NOT WORKING I CAN REALLY GIVE IT MY ALL TO LOOK GOOD.
IT'S JUST OUR BIOLOGICAL IMPERATIVE--WOMEN ARE SUPPOSED TO STAY SKINNY, HAVE LOTS OF BABIES, AND TAKE CARE OF OUR MEN! THAT'S HOW THE LORD BUILT US, HONEY!
I MEAN, IT'S NOT LIKE THEY'RE GOING TO PUT US ON A ROCKET TO ANOTHER PLANET IF WE GAIN A FEW POUNDS.
RIGHT?

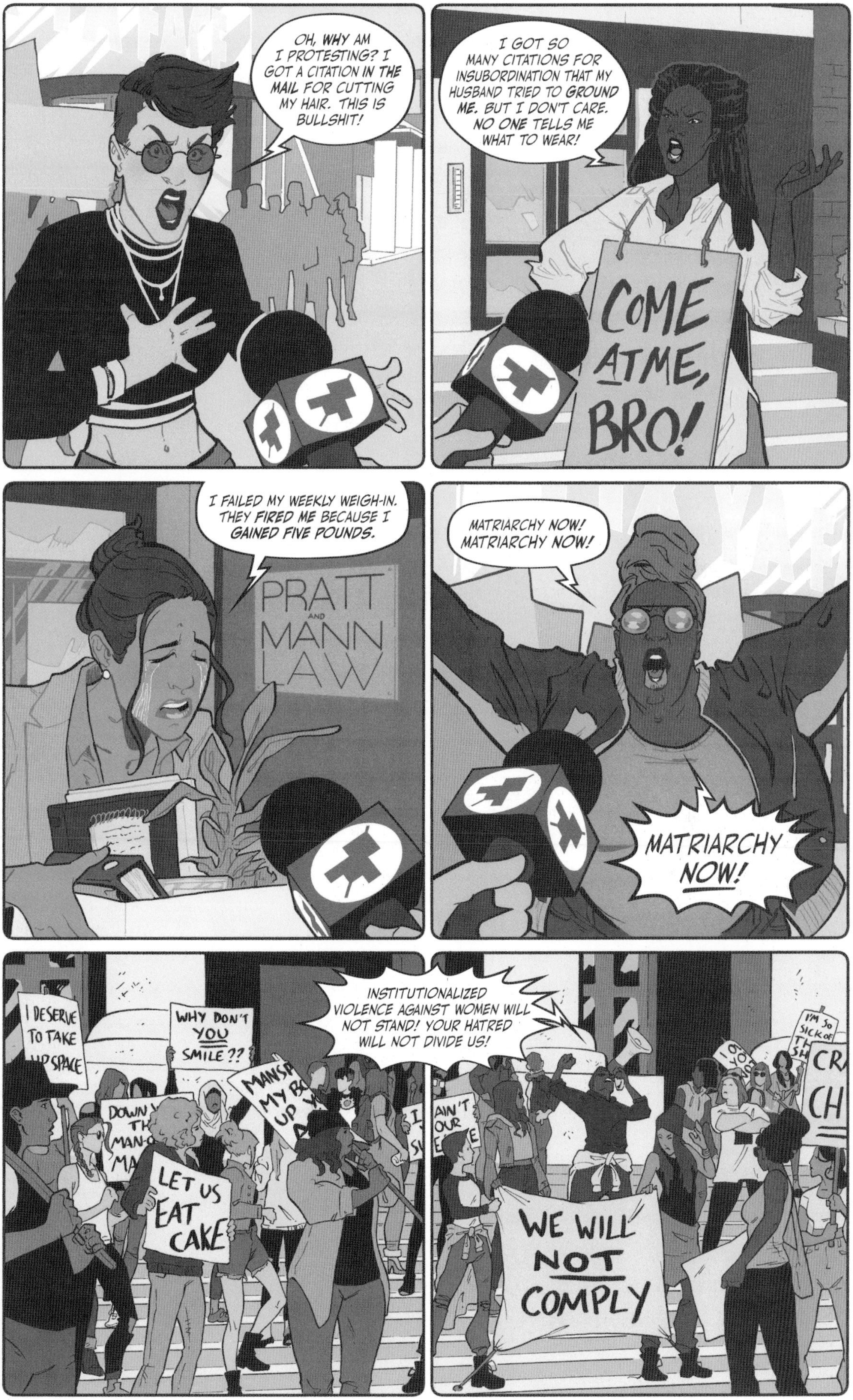
OH, WHY AM I PROTESTING? I GOT A CITATION IN THE MAIL FOR CUTTING MY HAIR. THIS IS BULLSHIT!
I GOT SO MANY CITATIONS FOR INSUBORDINATION THAT MY HUSBAND TRIED TO GROUND ME. BUT I DON'T CARE. NO ONE TELLS ME WHAT TO WEAR!
COME AT ME, BRO!
I FAILED MY WEEKLY WEIGH-IN. THEY FIRED ME BECAUSE I GAINED FIVE POUNDS.
PRATT AND MANN LAW
MATRIARCHY NOW! MATRIARCHY NOW!
MATRIARCHY NOW!
INSTITUTIONALIZED VIOLENCE AGAINST WOMEN WILL NOT STAND! YOUR HATRED WILL NOT DIVIDE US!
I DESERVE TO TAKE UP SPACE
WHY DON'T YOU SMILE??
LET US EAT CAKE
WE WILL NOT COMPLY

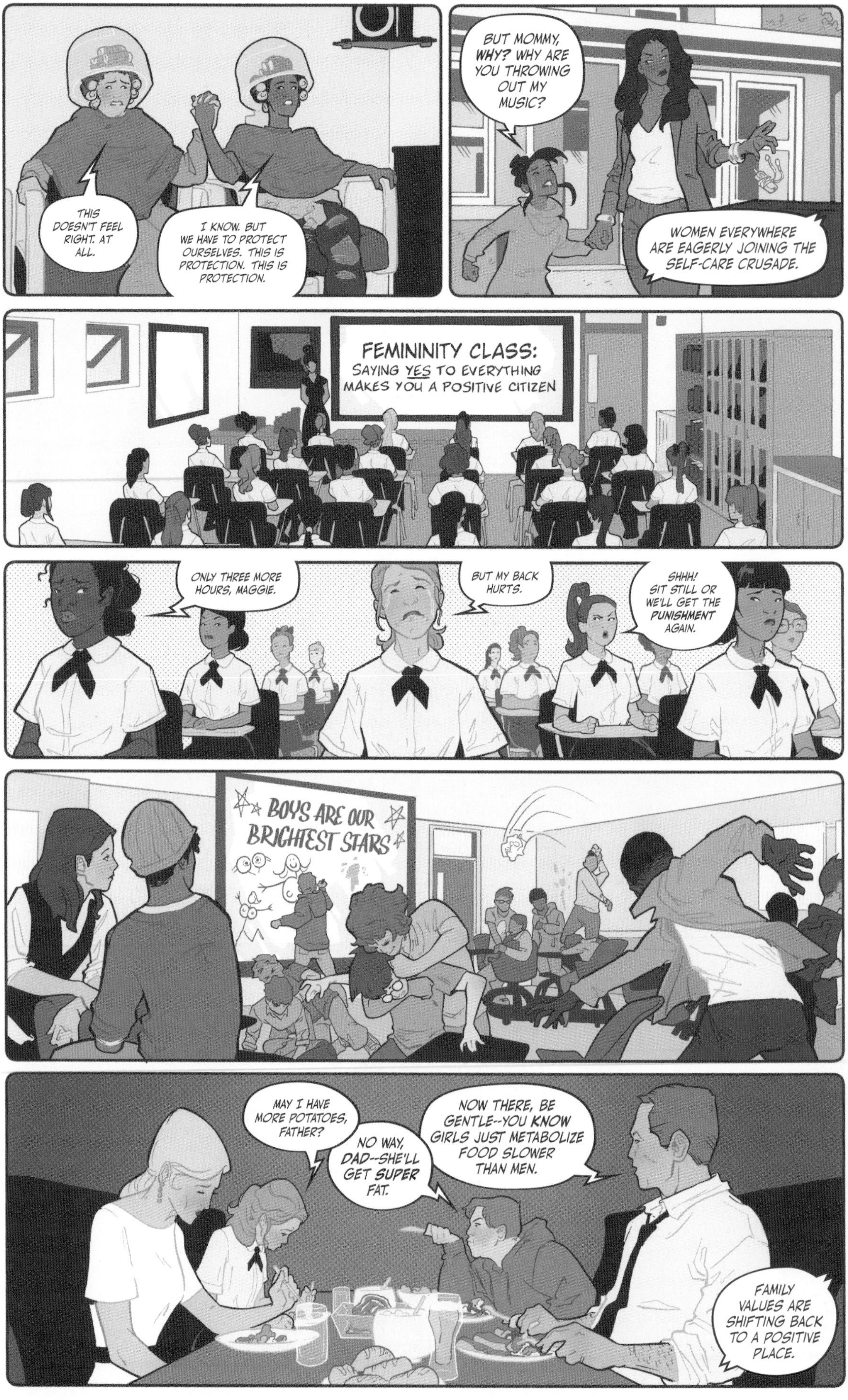
THIS DOESN'T FEEL RIGHT. AT ALL.
I KNOW. BUT WE HAVE TO PROTECT OURSELVES. THIS IS PROTECTION. THIS IS PROTECTION.
BUT MOMMY, WHY? WHY ARE YOU THROWING OUT MY MUSIC?
WOMEN EVERYWHERE ARE EAGERLY JOINING THE SELF-CARE CRUSADE.
FEMININITY CLASS: SAYING YES TO EVERYTHING MAKES YOU A POSITIVE CITIZEN
ONLY THREE MORE HOURS, MAGGIE.
BUT MY BACK HURTS.
SHHH! SIT STILL OR WE'LL GET THE PUNISHMENT AGAIN.
BOYS ARE OUR BRIGHTEST STARS
MAY I HAVE MORE POTATOES, FATHER?
NO WAY, DAD--SHE'LL GET SUPER FAT.
NOW THERE, BE GENTLE--YOU KNOW GIRLS JUST METABOLIZE FOOD SLOWER THAN MEN.
FAMILY VALUES ARE SHIFTING BACK TO A POSITIVE PLACE.

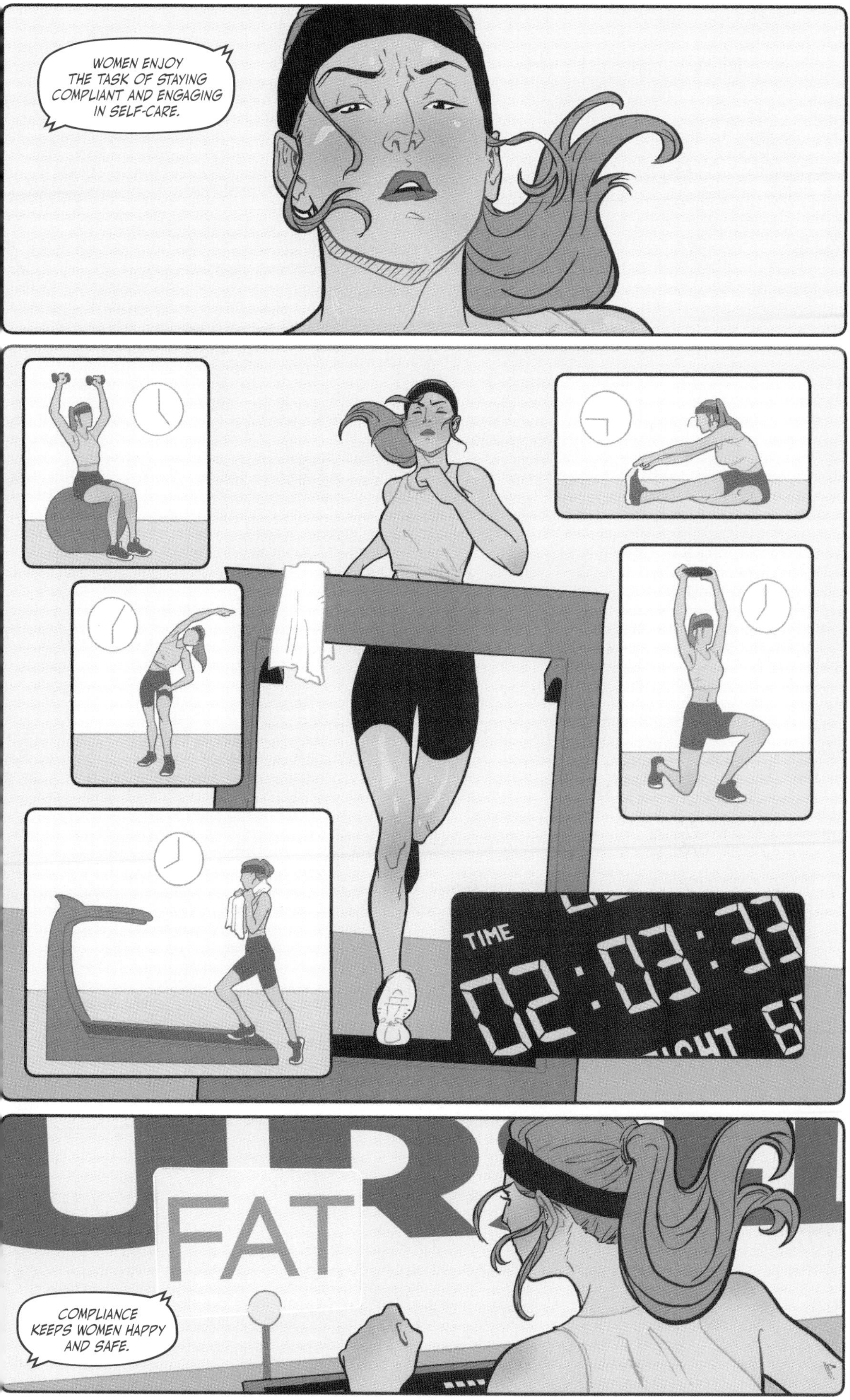
WOMEN ENJOY THE TASK OF STAYING COMPLIANT AND ENGAGING IN SELF-CARE.
TIME
02:03:33
FAT
COMPLIANCE KEEPS WOMEN HAPPY AND SAFE.

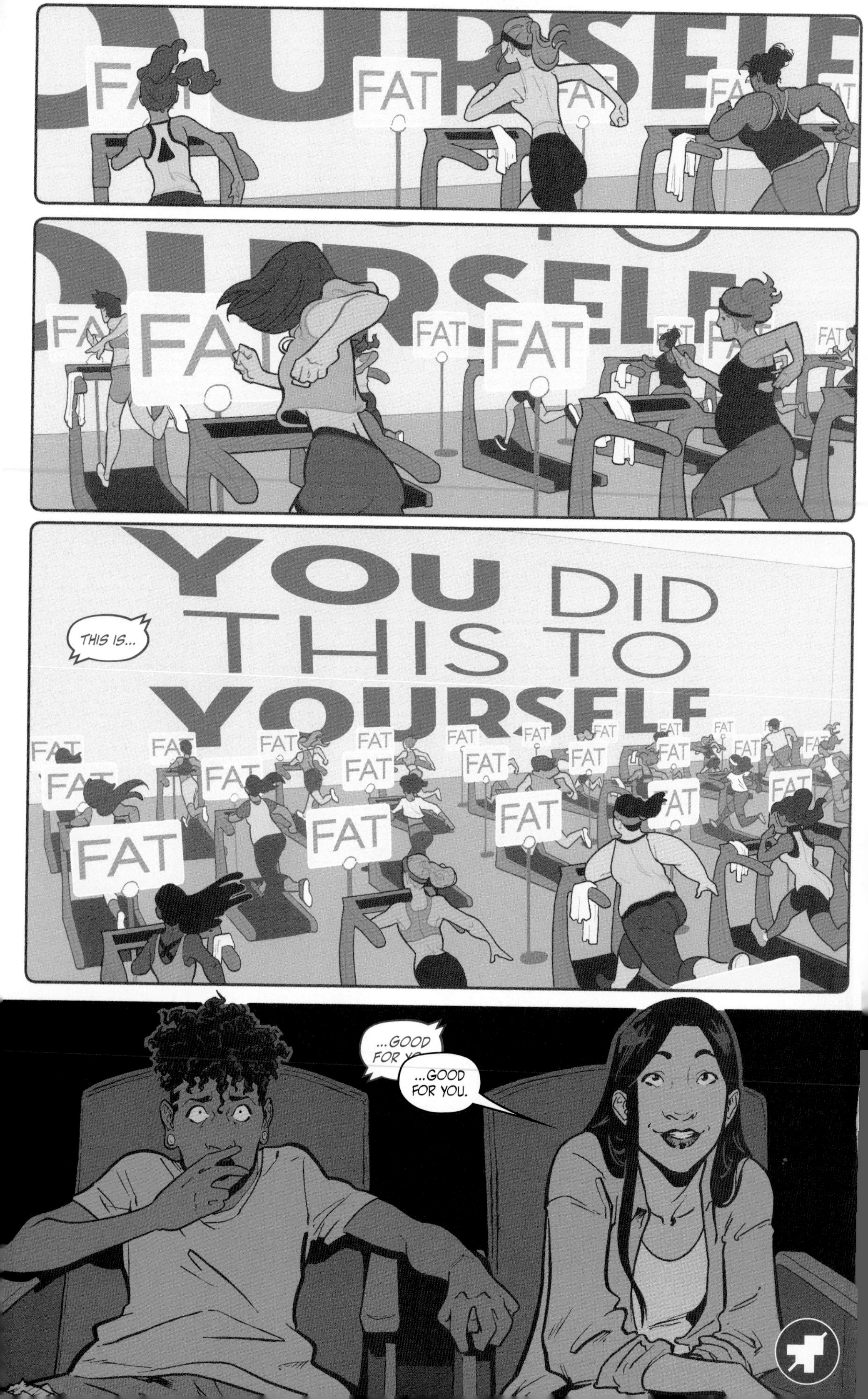
OURSELF
FAT
FAT
FAT
FAT
FAT
FAT
FAT
FAT
YOU DID THIS TO YOURSELF
THIS IS...
...GOOD FOR YOU.

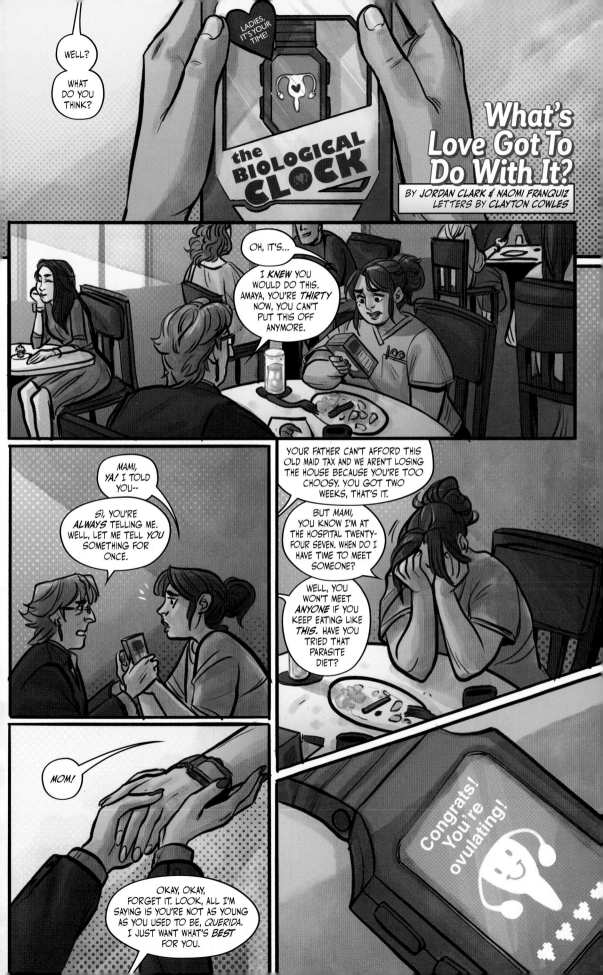

LADIES, IT'S YOUR TIME!

the BIOLOGICAL CLOCK

# What's Love Got To Do With It?

BY JORDAN CLARK & NAOMI FRANQUIZ
LETTERS BY CLAYTON COWLES

WELL?

WHAT DO YOU THINK?

OH, IT'S...

I *KNEW* YOU WOULD DO THIS. AMAYA, YOU'RE *THIRTY* NOW, YOU CAN'T PUT THIS OFF ANYMORE.

*MAMI, YA!* I TOLD YOU--

*SI,* YOU'RE *ALWAYS* TELLING ME. WELL, LET ME TELL *YOU* SOMETHING FOR ONCE.

YOUR FATHER CAN'T AFFORD THIS OLD MAID TAX AND WE AREN'T LOSING THE HOUSE BECAUSE YOU'RE TOO CHOOSY. YOU GOT TWO WEEKS, THAT'S IT.

BUT *MAMI,* YOU KNOW I'M AT THE HOSPITAL TWENTY-FOUR SEVEN. WHEN DO I HAVE TIME TO MEET SOMEONE?

WELL, YOU WON'T MEET *ANYONE* IF YOU KEEP EATING LIKE *THIS.* HAVE YOU TRIED THAT PARASITE DIET?

MOM!

OKAY, OKAY, FORGET IT. LOOK, ALL I'M SAYING IS YOU'RE NOT AS YOUNG AS YOU USED TO BE, *QUERIDA.* I JUST WANT WHAT'S *BEST* FOR YOU.

Congrats! You're ovulating!

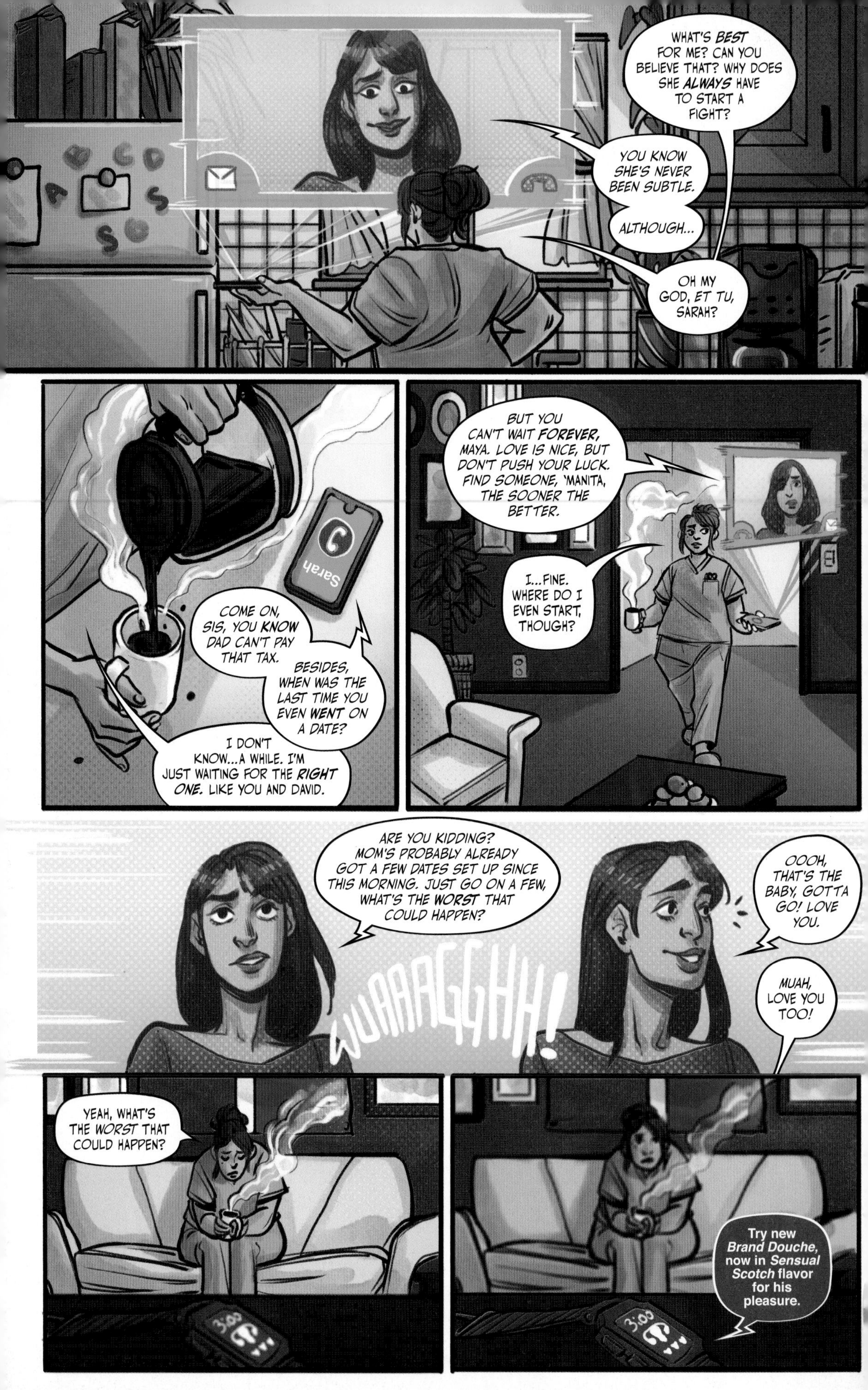
WHAT'S BEST FOR ME? CAN YOU BELIEVE THAT? WHY DOES SHE ALWAYS HAVE TO START A FIGHT?
YOU KNOW SHE'S NEVER BEEN SUBTLE.
ALTHOUGH...
OH MY GOD, ET TU, SARAH?
Sarah
COME ON, SIS, YOU KNOW DAD CAN'T PAY THAT TAX.
BESIDES, WHEN WAS THE LAST TIME YOU EVEN WENT ON A DATE?
I DON'T KNOW...A WHILE. I'M JUST WAITING FOR THE RIGHT ONE. LIKE YOU AND DAVID.
BUT YOU CAN'T WAIT FOREVER, MAYA. LOVE IS NICE, BUT DON'T PUSH YOUR LUCK. FIND SOMEONE, 'MANITA, THE SOONER THE BETTER.
I...FINE. WHERE DO I EVEN START, THOUGH?
ARE YOU KIDDING? MOM'S PROBABLY ALREADY GOT A FEW DATES SET UP SINCE THIS MORNING. JUST GO ON A FEW, WHAT'S THE WORST THAT COULD HAPPEN?
WUAAAGGHH!
OOOH, THAT'S THE BABY, GOTTA GO! LOVE YOU.
MUAH, LOVE YOU TOO!
YEAH, WHAT'S THE WORST THAT COULD HAPPEN?
3:00
3:00
Try new Brand Douche, now in Sensual Scotch flavor for his pleasure.

# "THE WORST THAT COULD HAPPEN."

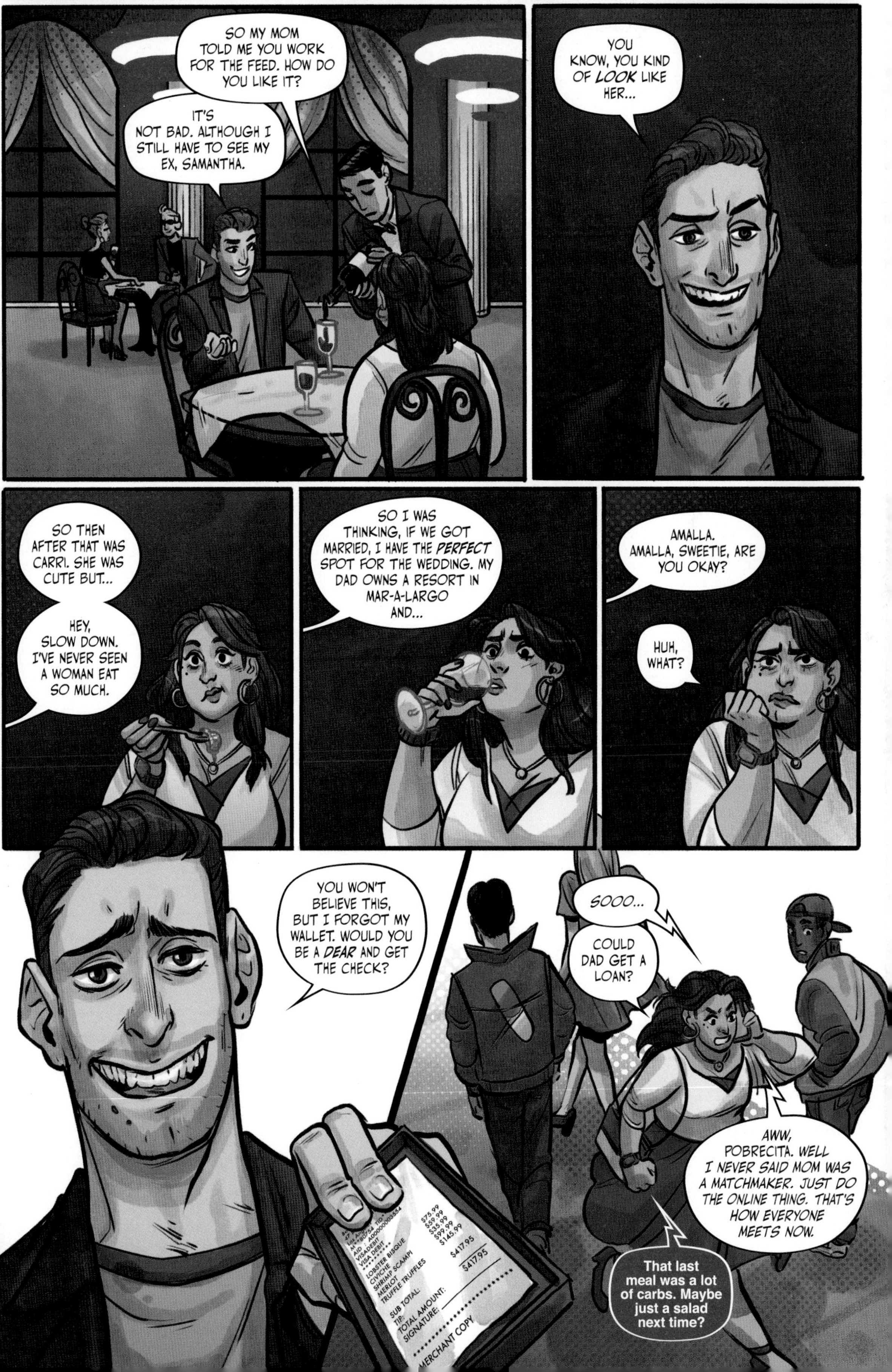
SO MY MOM TOLD ME YOU WORK FOR THE FEED. HOW DO YOU LIKE IT?
IT'S NOT BAD. ALTHOUGH I STILL HAVE TO SEE MY EX, SAMANTHA.
YOU KNOW, YOU KIND OF *LOOK* LIKE HER...
SO THEN AFTER THAT WAS CARRI. SHE WAS CUTE BUT...
HEY, SLOW DOWN. I'VE NEVER SEEN A WOMAN EAT SO MUCH.
SO I WAS THINKING, IF WE GOT MARRIED, I HAVE THE *PERFECT* SPOT FOR THE WEDDING. MY DAD OWNS A RESORT IN MAR-A-LARGO AND...
AMALLA. AMALLA, SWEETIE, ARE YOU OKAY?
HUH, WHAT?
YOU WON'T BELIEVE THIS, BUT I FORGOT MY WALLET. WOULD YOU BE A *DEAR* AND GET THE CHECK?
LOBSTER BISQUE $75.99
CIVICHE $59.99
SHRIMP SCAMPI $35.99
MERLOT $99.99
TRUFFLE TRUFFLES $145.99
SUB TOTAL: $417.95
TIP:
TOTAL AMOUNT: $417.95
SIGNATURE:
MERCHANT COPY
*SOOO...*
COULD DAD GET A LOAN?
*AWW, POBRECITA. WELL I NEVER SAID MOM WAS A MATCHMAKER. JUST DO THE ONLINE THING. THAT'S HOW EVERYONE MEETS NOW.*
That last meal was a lot of carbs. Maybe just a salad next time?

# "THE ONLINE THING."

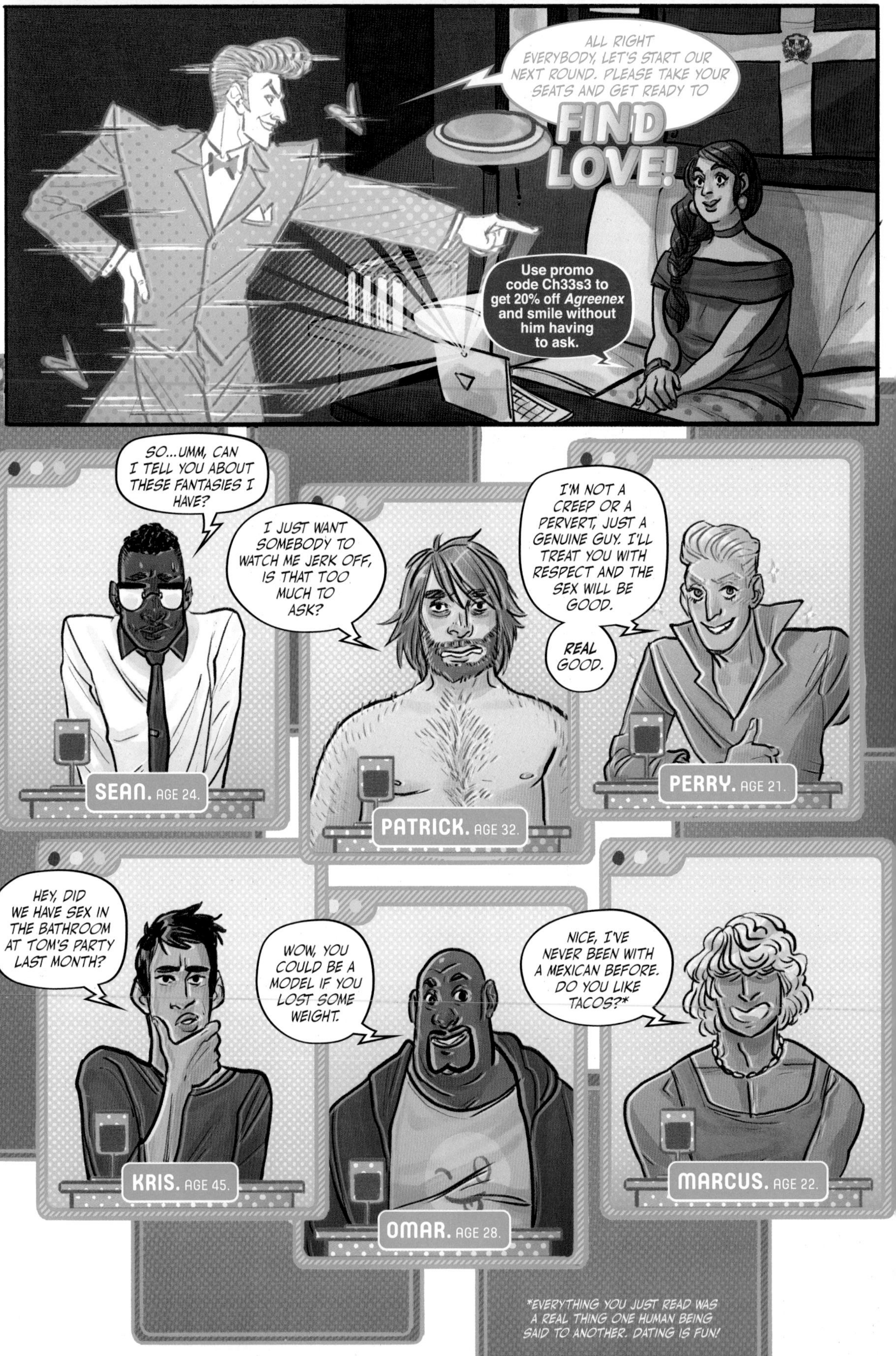

ALL RIGHT EVERYBODY, LET'S START OUR NEXT ROUND. PLEASE TAKE YOUR SEATS AND GET READY TO FIND LOVE!
Use promo code Ch33s3 to get 20% off *Agreenex* and smile without him having to ask.
SO...UMM, CAN I TELL YOU ABOUT THESE FANTASIES I HAVE?
SEAN. AGE 24.
I JUST WANT SOMEBODY TO WATCH ME JERK OFF, IS THAT TOO MUCH TO ASK?
PATRICK. AGE 32.
I'M NOT A CREEP OR A PERVERT, JUST A GENUINE GUY. I'LL TREAT YOU WITH RESPECT AND THE SEX WILL BE GOOD.
REAL GOOD.
PERRY. AGE 21.
HEY, DID WE HAVE SEX IN THE BATHROOM AT TOM'S PARTY LAST MONTH?
KRIS. AGE 45.
WOW, YOU COULD BE A MODEL IF YOU LOST SOME WEIGHT.
OMAR. AGE 28.
NICE, I'VE NEVER BEEN WITH A MEXICAN BEFORE. DO YOU LIKE TACOS?*
MARCUS. AGE 22.
*EVERYTHING YOU JUST READ WAS A REAL THING ONE HUMAN BEING SAID TO ANOTHER. DATING IS FUN!

# "THAT NEW APP."

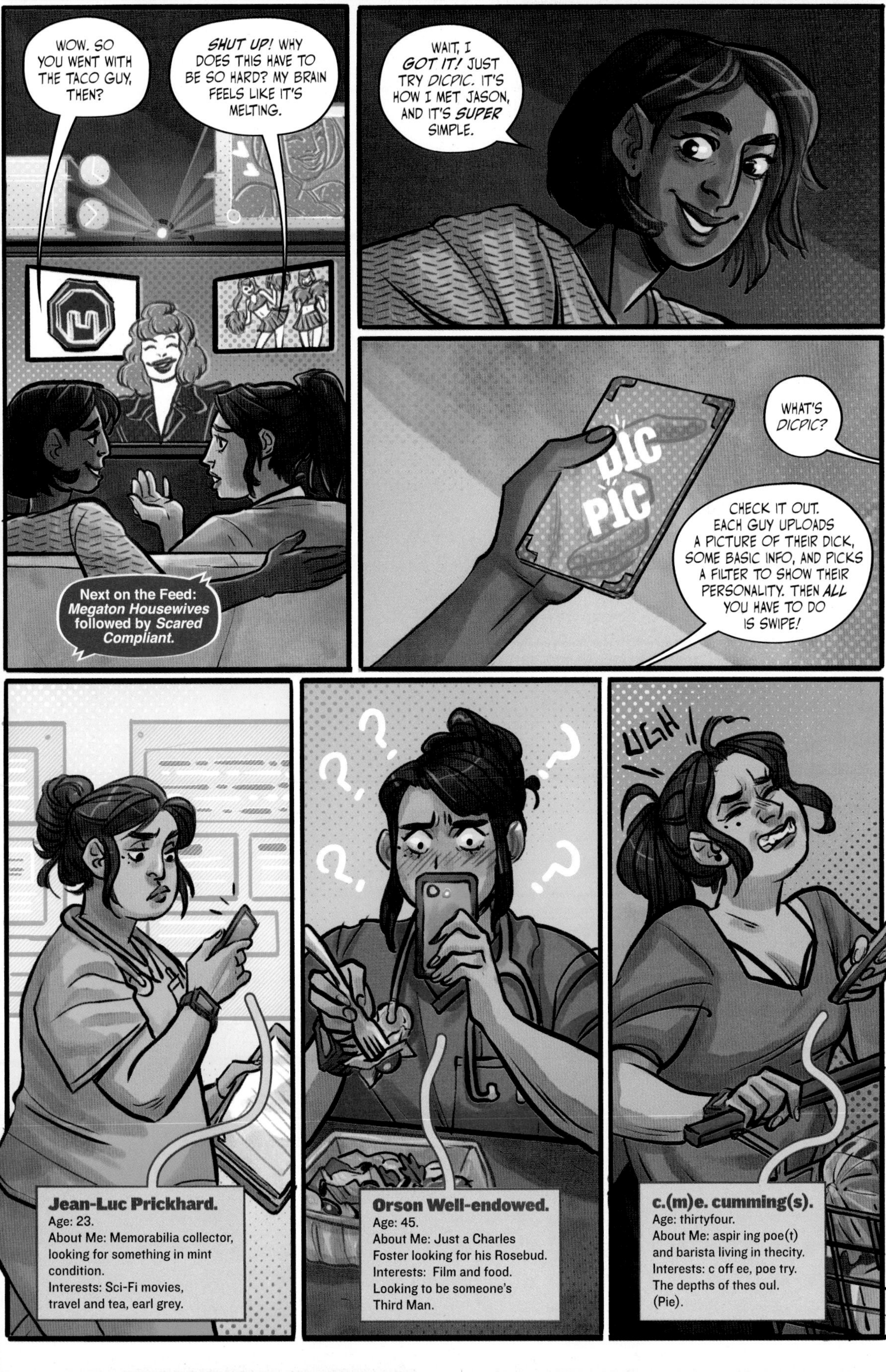
WOW. SO YOU WENT WITH THE TACO GUY, THEN?
SHUT UP! WHY DOES THIS HAVE TO BE SO HARD? MY BRAIN FEELS LIKE IT'S MELTING.
Next on the Feed: Megaton Housewives followed by Scared Compliant.
WAIT, I GOT IT! JUST TRY DICPIC. IT'S HOW I MET JASON, AND IT'S SUPER SIMPLE.
DIC PIC
WHAT'S DICPIC?
CHECK IT OUT. EACH GUY UPLOADS A PICTURE OF THEIR DICK, SOME BASIC INFO, AND PICKS A FILTER TO SHOW THEIR PERSONALITY. THEN ALL YOU HAVE TO DO IS SWIPE!
Jean-Luc Prickhard.
Age: 23.
About Me: Memorabilia collector, looking for something in mint condition.
Interests: Sci-Fi movies, travel and tea, earl grey.
Orson Well-endowed.
Age: 45.
About Me: Just a Charles Foster looking for his Rosebud.
Interests: Film and food. Looking to be someone's Third Man.
UGH!
c.(m)e. cumming(s).
Age: thirtyfour.
About Me: aspir ing poe(t) and barista living in thecity.
Interests: c off ee, poe try. The depths of thes oul. (Pie).

# "THE SMART THING."

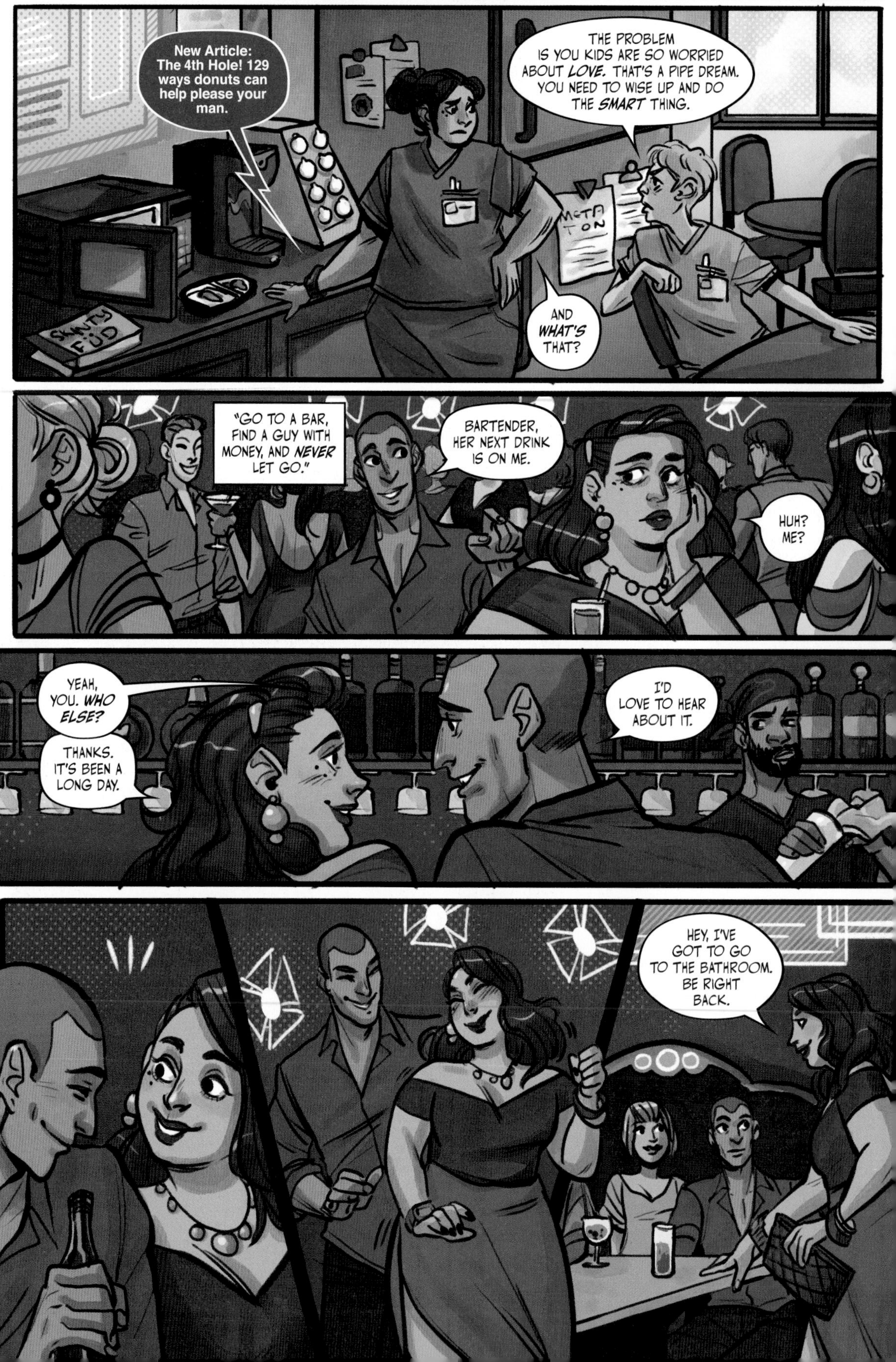
New Article: The 4th Hole! 129 ways donuts can help please your man.
THE PROBLEM IS YOU KIDS ARE SO WORRIED ABOUT *LOVE.* THAT'S A PIPE DREAM. YOU NEED TO WISE UP AND DO THE *SMART* THING.
AND *WHAT'S* THAT?
"GO TO A BAR, FIND A GUY WITH MONEY, AND *NEVER* LET GO."
BARTENDER, HER NEXT DRINK IS ON ME.
HUH? ME?
YEAH, YOU. *WHO ELSE?*
THANKS. IT'S BEEN A LONG DAY.
I'D LOVE TO HEAR ABOUT IT.
HEY, I'VE GOT TO GO TO THE BATHROOM. BE RIGHT BACK.

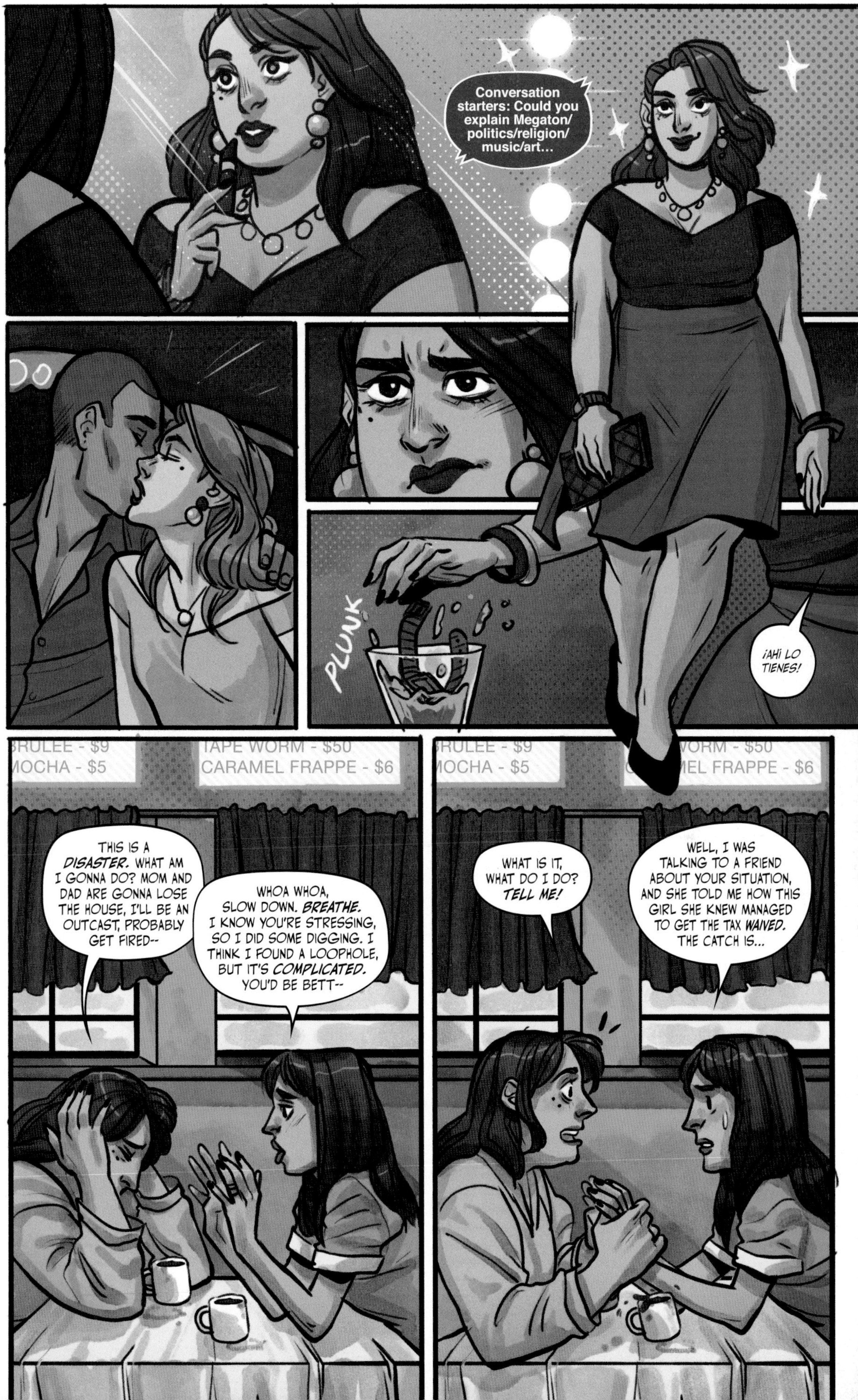

Conversation starters: Could you explain Megaton/politics/religion/music/art…
PLUNK
¡AHÍ LO TIENES!
BRULEE - $9
MOCHA - $5
TAPE WORM - $50
CARAMEL FRAPPE - $6
THIS IS A DISASTER. WHAT AM I GONNA DO? MOM AND DAD ARE GONNA LOSE THE HOUSE, I'LL BE AN OUTCAST, PROBABLY GET FIRED--
WHOA WHOA, SLOW DOWN. BREATHE. I KNOW YOU'RE STRESSING, SO I DID SOME DIGGING. I THINK I FOUND A LOOPHOLE, BUT IT'S COMPLICATED. YOU'D BE BETT--
WHAT IS IT, WHAT DO I DO? TELL ME!
WELL, I WAS TALKING TO A FRIEND ABOUT YOUR SITUATION, AND SHE TOLD ME HOW THIS GIRL SHE KNEW MANAGED TO GET THE TAX WAIVED. THE CATCH IS...

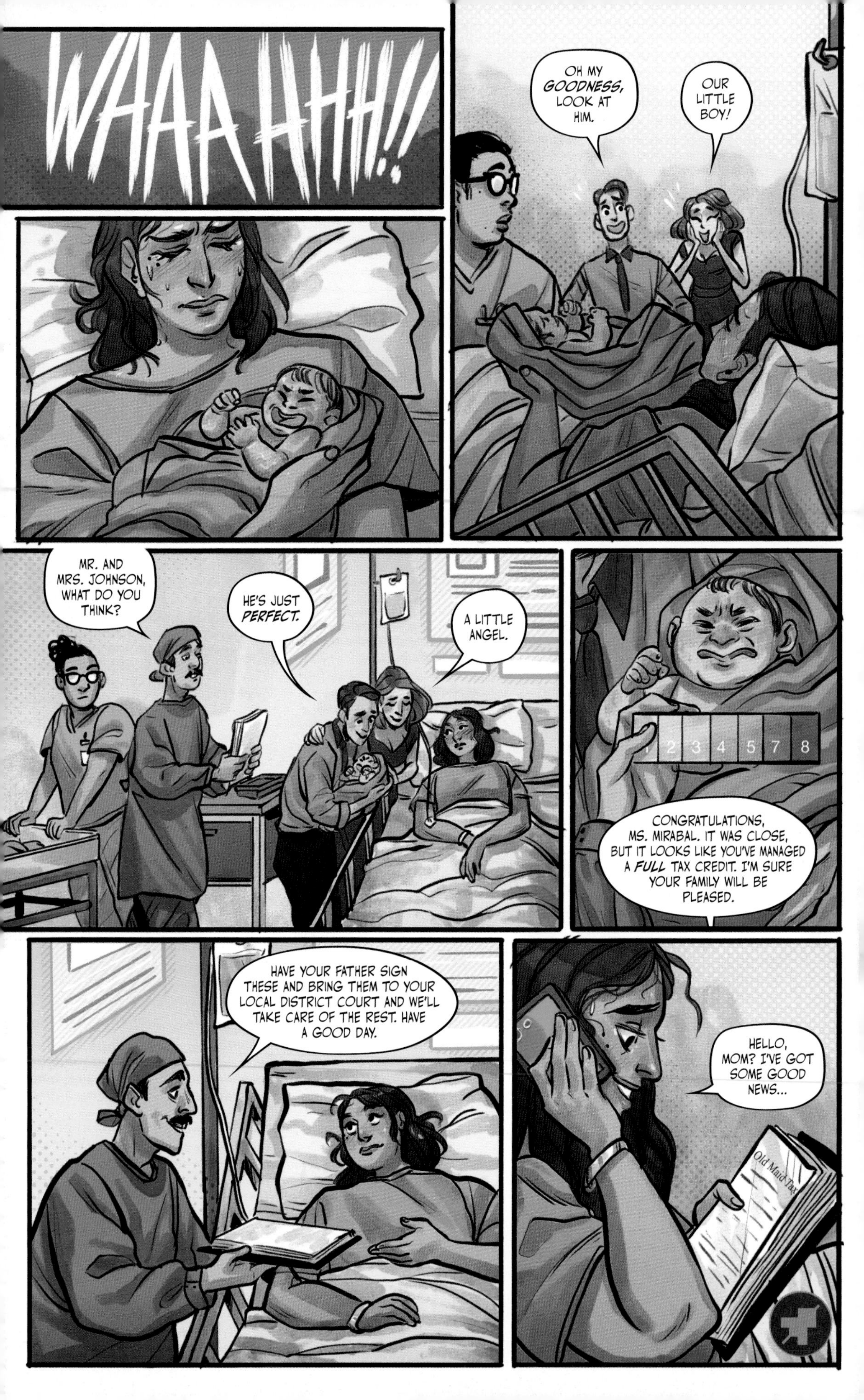
WAAAHHH!!
OH MY GOODNESS, LOOK AT HIM.
OUR LITTLE BOY!
MR. AND MRS. JOHNSON, WHAT DO YOU THINK?
HE'S JUST PERFECT.
A LITTLE ANGEL.
1 2 3 4 5 7 8
CONGRATULATIONS, MS. MIRABAL. IT WAS CLOSE, BUT IT LOOKS LIKE YOU'VE MANAGED A FULL TAX CREDIT. I'M SURE YOUR FAMILY WILL BE PLEASED.
HAVE YOUR FATHER SIGN THESE AND BRING THEM TO YOUR LOCAL DISTRICT COURT AND WE'LL TAKE CARE OF THE REST. HAVE A GOOD DAY.
HELLO, MOM? I'VE GOT SOME GOOD NEWS...
Old Maid Tax

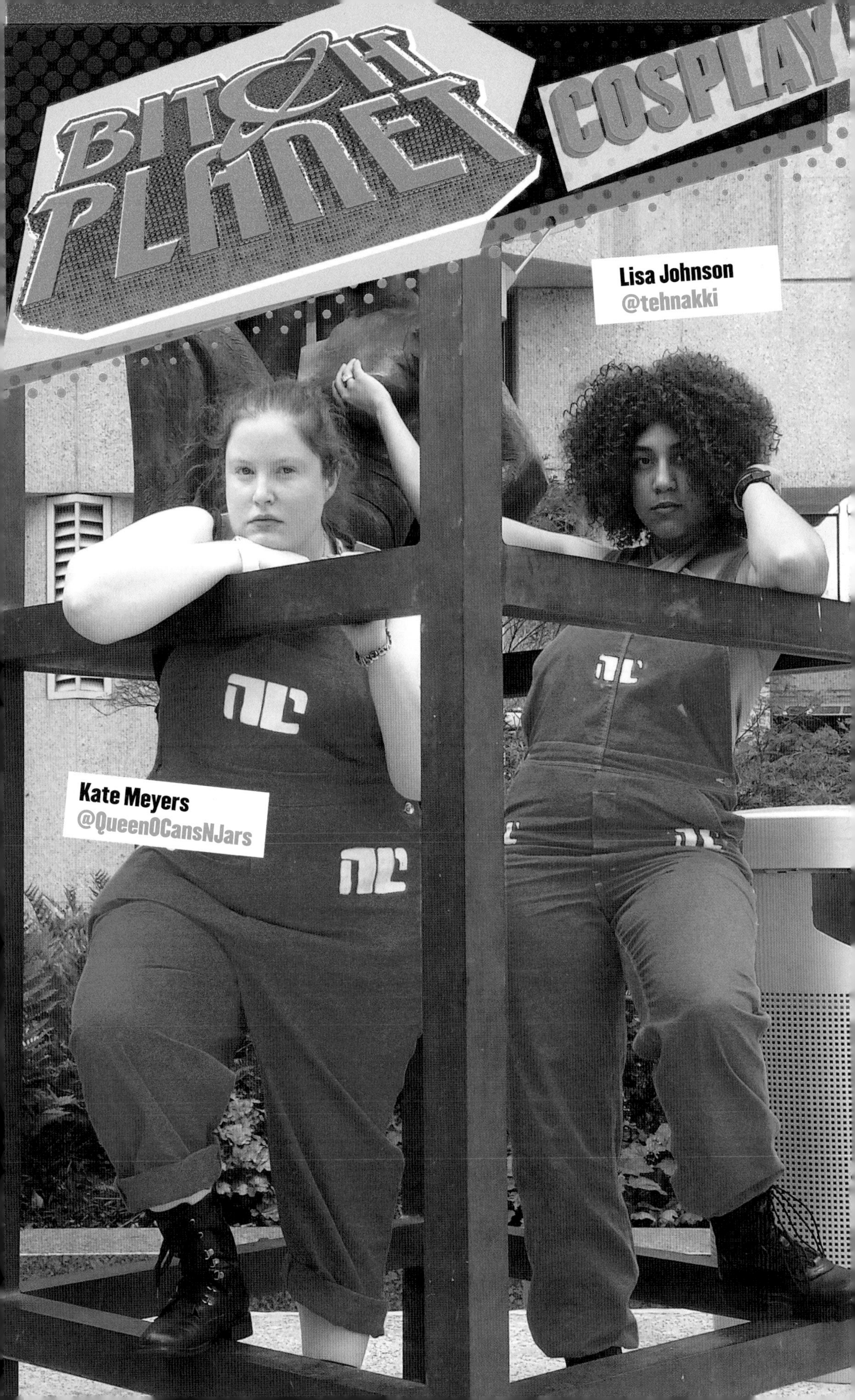
BITCH PLANET
COSPLAY
Lisa Johnson
@tehnakki
Kate Meyers
@QueenOCansNJars

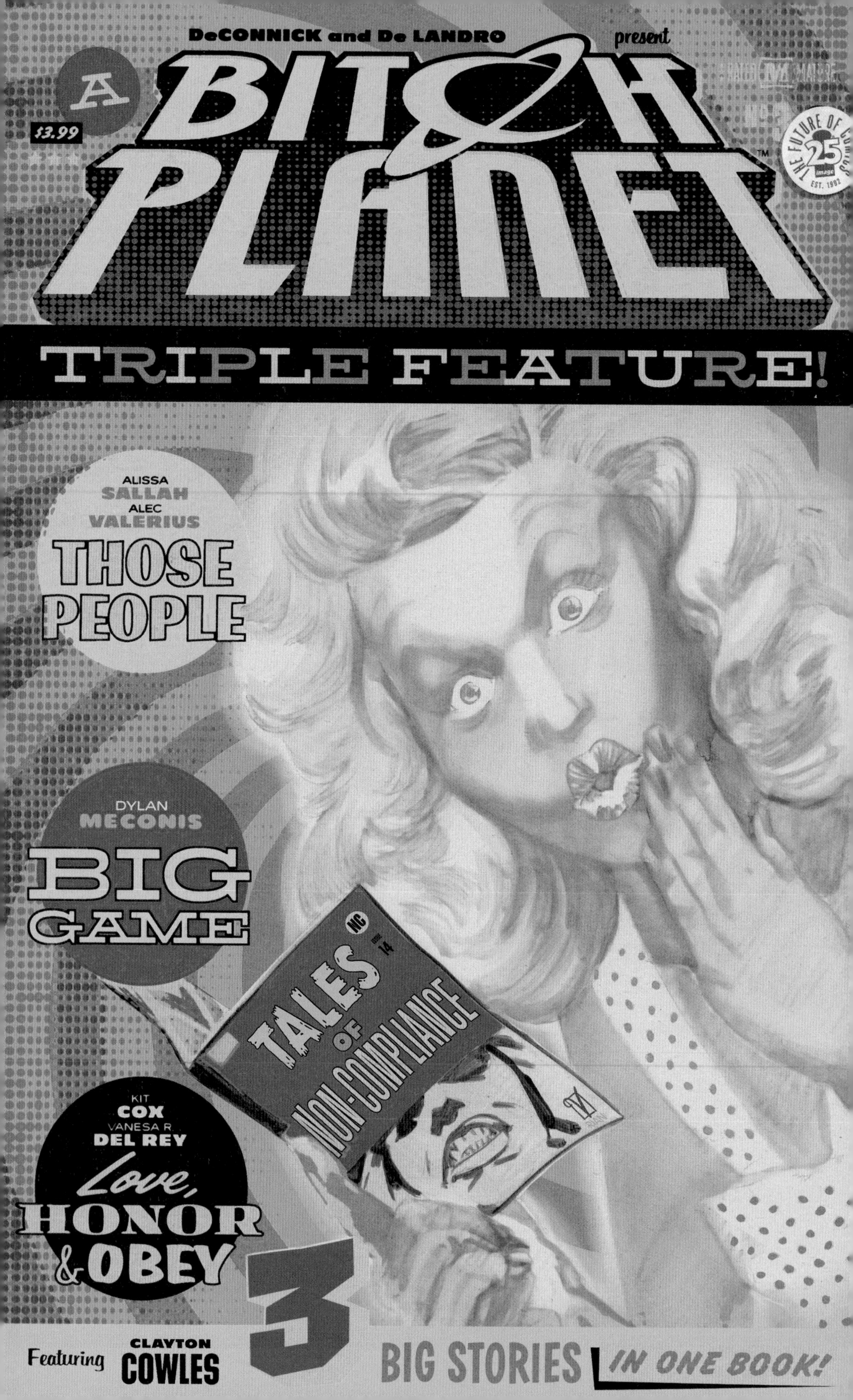
DeCONNICK and De LANDRO
present
A
$3.99
BITCH PLANET
TM
RATED M MATURE
THE FUTURE OF COMICS
25
image
EST. 1992
TRIPLE FEATURE!
ALISSA
SALLAH
ALEC
VALERIUS
THOSE PEOPLE
DYLAN
MECONIS
BIG GAME
NC
ISSUE 14
TALES OF NON-COMPLIANCE
KIT
COX
VANESA R
DEL REY
Love, HONOR & OBEY
3
BIG STORIES
IN ONE BOOK!
Featuring
CLAYTON
COWLES

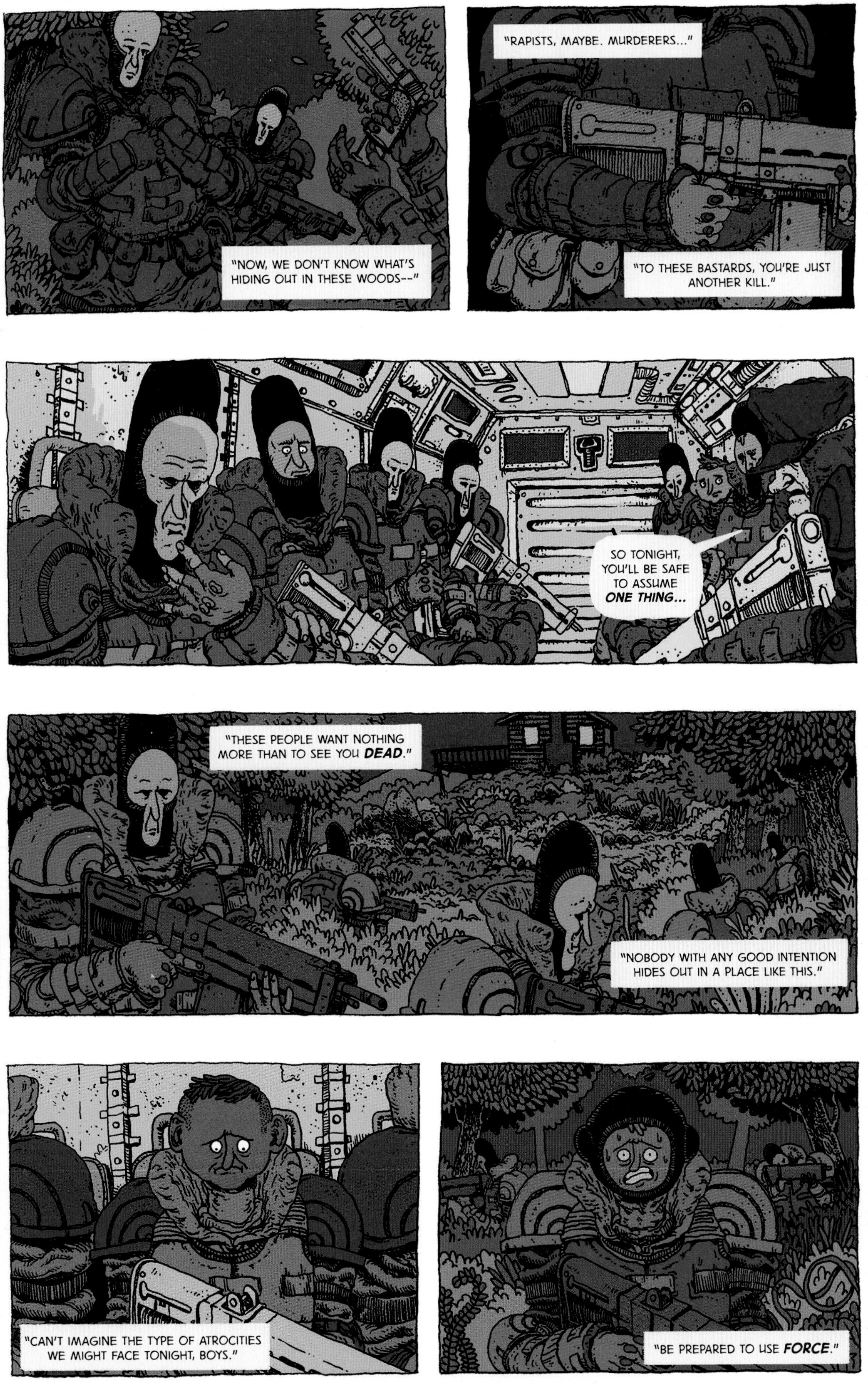
"NOW, WE DON'T KNOW WHAT'S HIDING OUT IN THESE WOODS--"
"RAPISTS, MAYBE. MURDERERS..."
"TO THESE BASTARDS, YOU'RE JUST ANOTHER KILL."
SO TONIGHT, YOU'LL BE SAFE TO ASSUME ***ONE THING...***
"THESE PEOPLE WANT NOTHING MORE THAN TO SEE YOU ***DEAD***."
"NOBODY WITH ANY GOOD INTENTION HIDES OUT IN A PLACE LIKE THIS."
"CAN'T IMAGINE THE TYPE OF ATROCITIES WE MIGHT FACE TONIGHT, BOYS."
"BE PREPARED TO USE ***FORCE***."

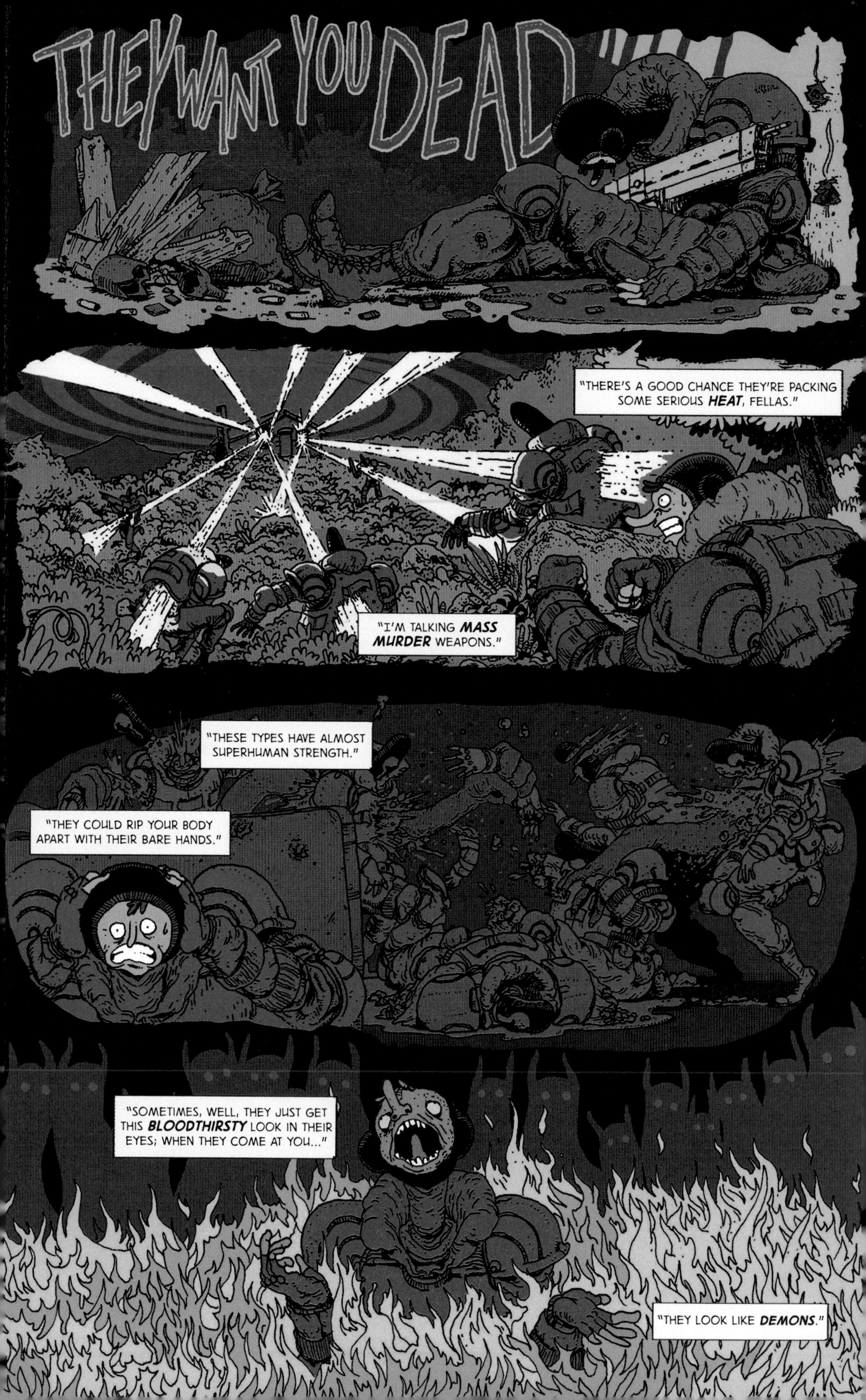
THEY WANT YOU DEAD
"THERE'S A GOOD CHANCE THEY'RE PACKING SOME SERIOUS HEAT, FELLAS."
"I'M TALKING MASS MURDER WEAPONS."
"THESE TYPES HAVE ALMOST SUPERHUMAN STRENGTH."
"THEY COULD RIP YOUR BODY APART WITH THEIR BARE HANDS."
"SOMETIMES, WELL, THEY JUST GET THIS BLOODTHIRSTY LOOK IN THEIR EYES; WHEN THEY COME AT YOU..."
"THEY LOOK LIKE DEMONS."

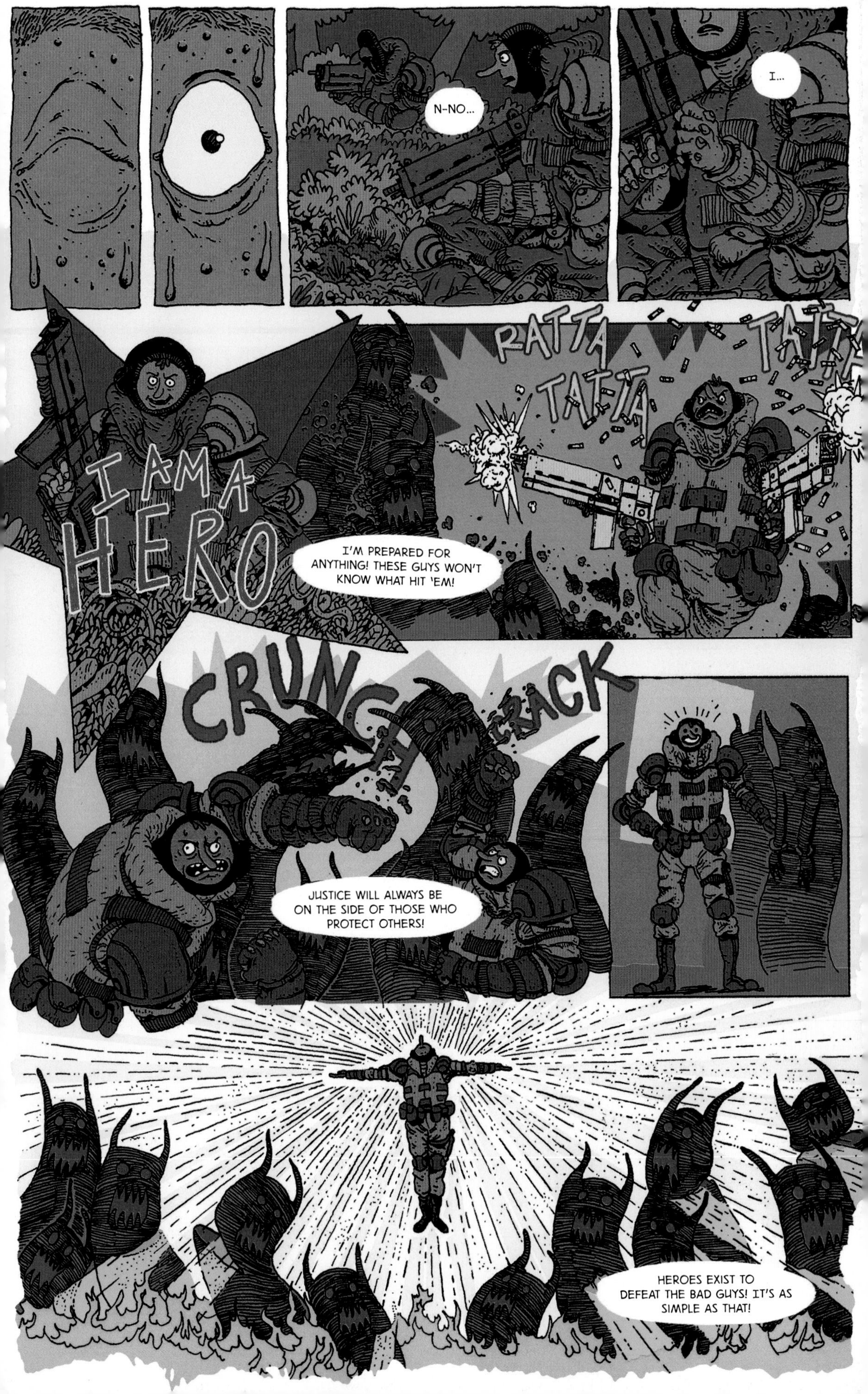
N-NO...
I...
I AM A HERO
RATTA TATTA TATTA
I'M PREPARED FOR ANYTHING! THESE GUYS WON'T KNOW WHAT HIT 'EM!
CRUNCH
CRACK
JUSTICE WILL ALWAYS BE ON THE SIDE OF THOSE WHO PROTECT OTHERS!
HEROES EXIST TO DEFEAT THE BAD GUYS! IT'S AS SIMPLE AS THAT!

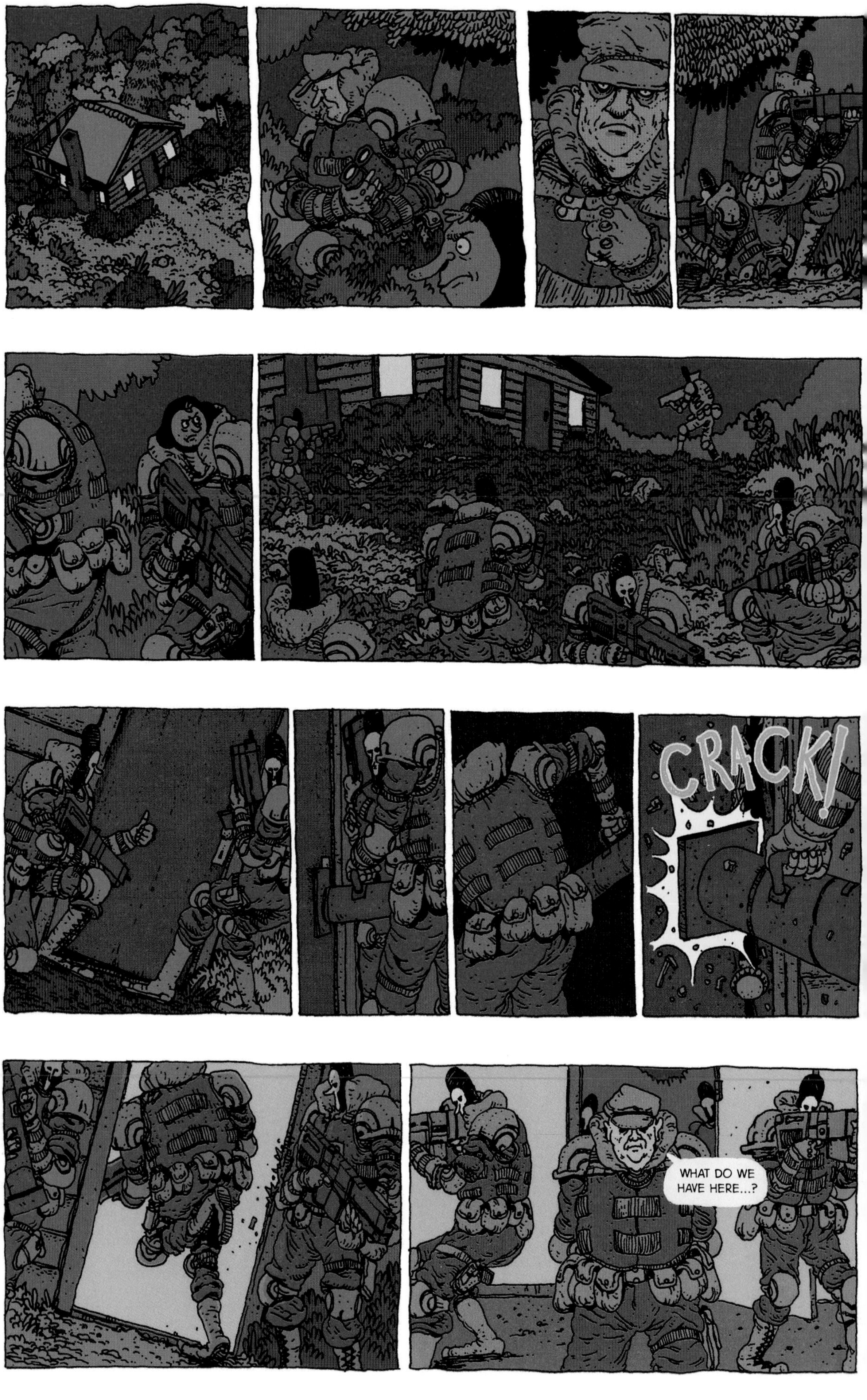
CRACK!
WHAT DO WE HAVE HERE...?

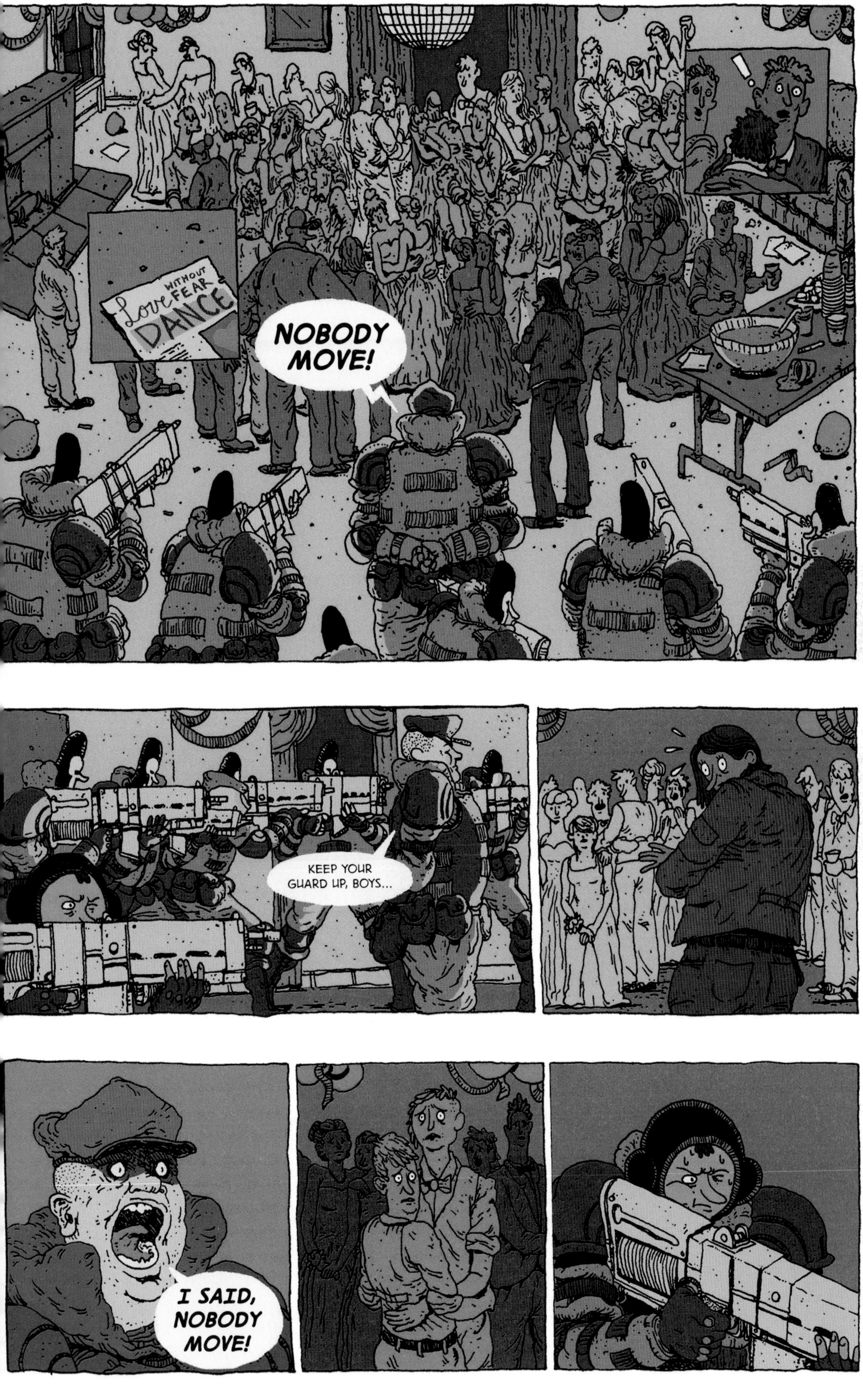
Love WITHOUT FEAR DANCE
NOBODY MOVE!
KEEP YOUR GUARD UP, BOYS...
I SAID, NOBODY MOVE!

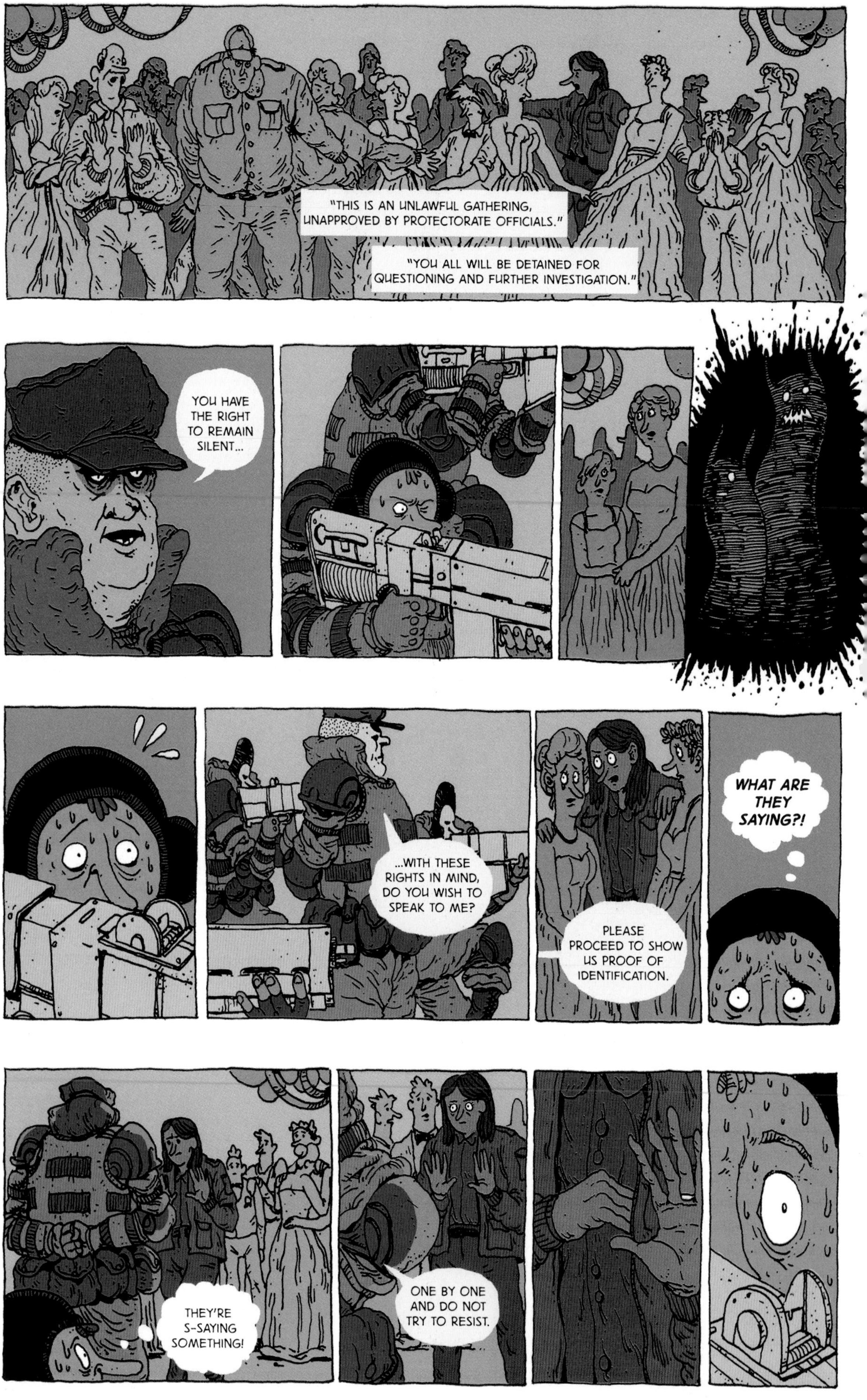
"THIS IS AN UNLAWFUL GATHERING, UNAPPROVED BY PROTECTORATE OFFICIALS."
"YOU ALL WILL BE DETAINED FOR QUESTIONING AND FURTHER INVESTIGATION."
YOU HAVE THE RIGHT TO REMAIN SILENT...
...WITH THESE RIGHTS IN MIND, DO YOU WISH TO SPEAK TO ME?
PLEASE PROCEED TO SHOW US PROOF OF IDENTIFICATION.
WHAT ARE THEY SAYING?!
THEY'RE S-SAYING SOMETHING!
ONE BY ONE AND DO NOT TRY TO RESIST.

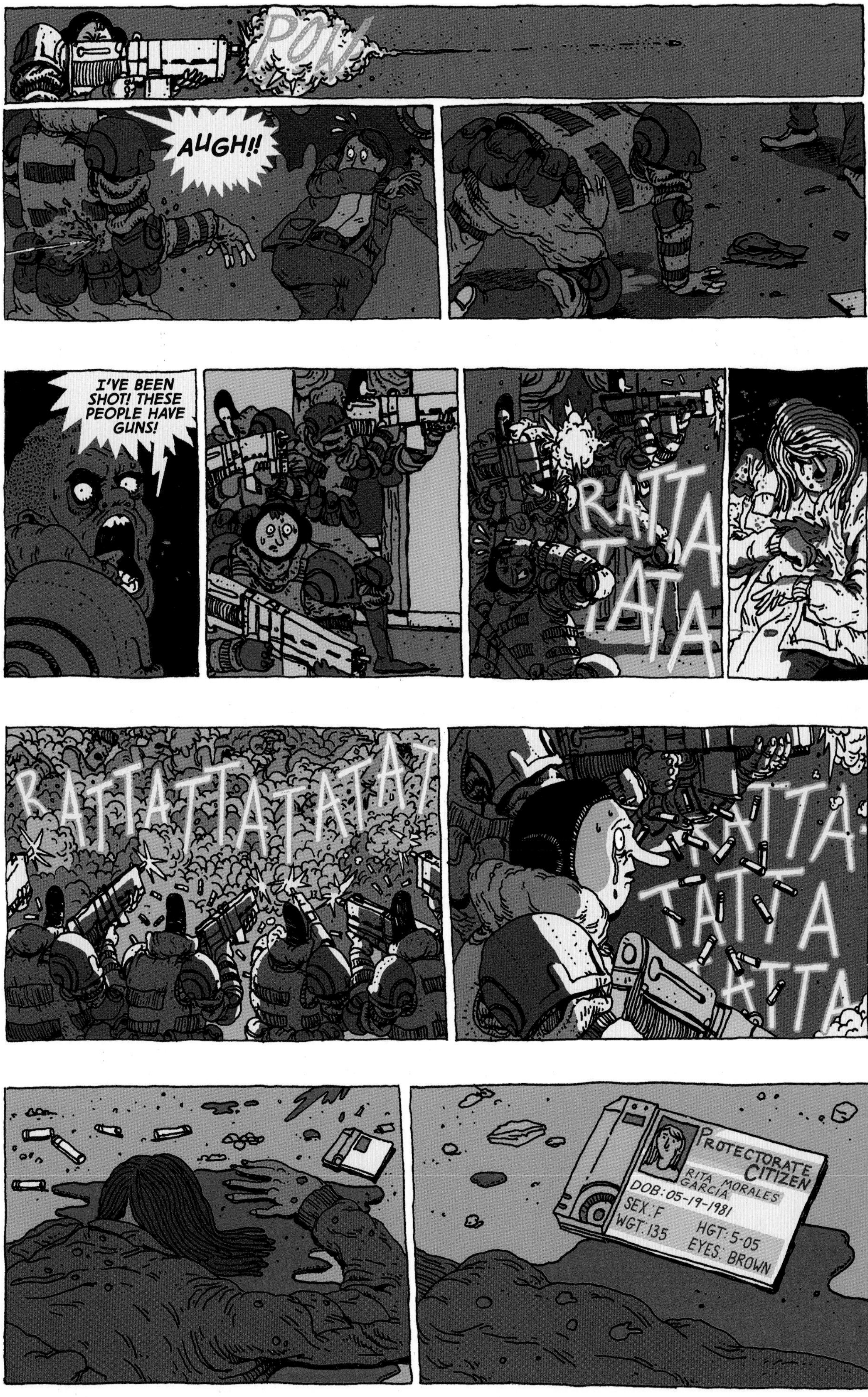
POW
AUGH!!
I'VE BEEN SHOT! THESE PEOPLE HAVE GUNS!
RATTA TATA TATA
RATTATTATATAT
RATTA- TATTA TATTA
PROTECTORATE CITIZEN
RITA MORALES GARCIA
DOB: 05-19-1981
SEX: F
WGT: 135
HGT: 5-05
EYES: BROWN

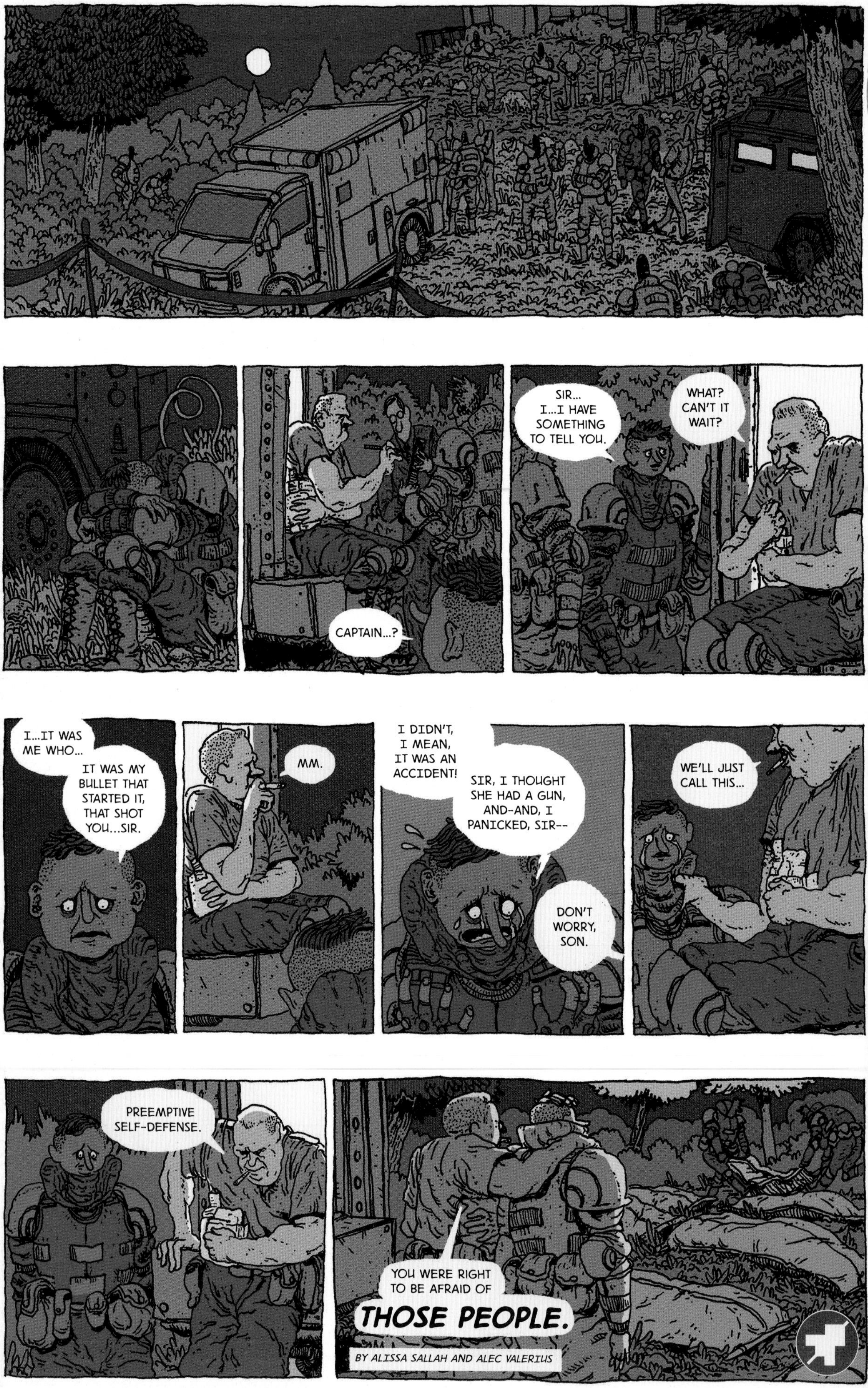
CAPTAIN...?
SIR... I...I HAVE SOMETHING TO TELL YOU.
WHAT? CAN'T IT WAIT?
I...IT WAS ME WHO...
IT WAS MY BULLET THAT STARTED IT, THAT SHOT YOU...SIR.
MM.
I DIDN'T, I MEAN, IT WAS AN ACCIDENT!
SIR, I THOUGHT SHE HAD A GUN, AND-AND, I PANICKED, SIR--
DON'T WORRY, SON.
WE'LL JUST CALL THIS...
PREEMPTIVE SELF-DEFENSE.
YOU WERE RIGHT TO BE AFRAID OF
THOSE PEOPLE.
BY ALISSA SALLAH AND ALEC VALERIUS

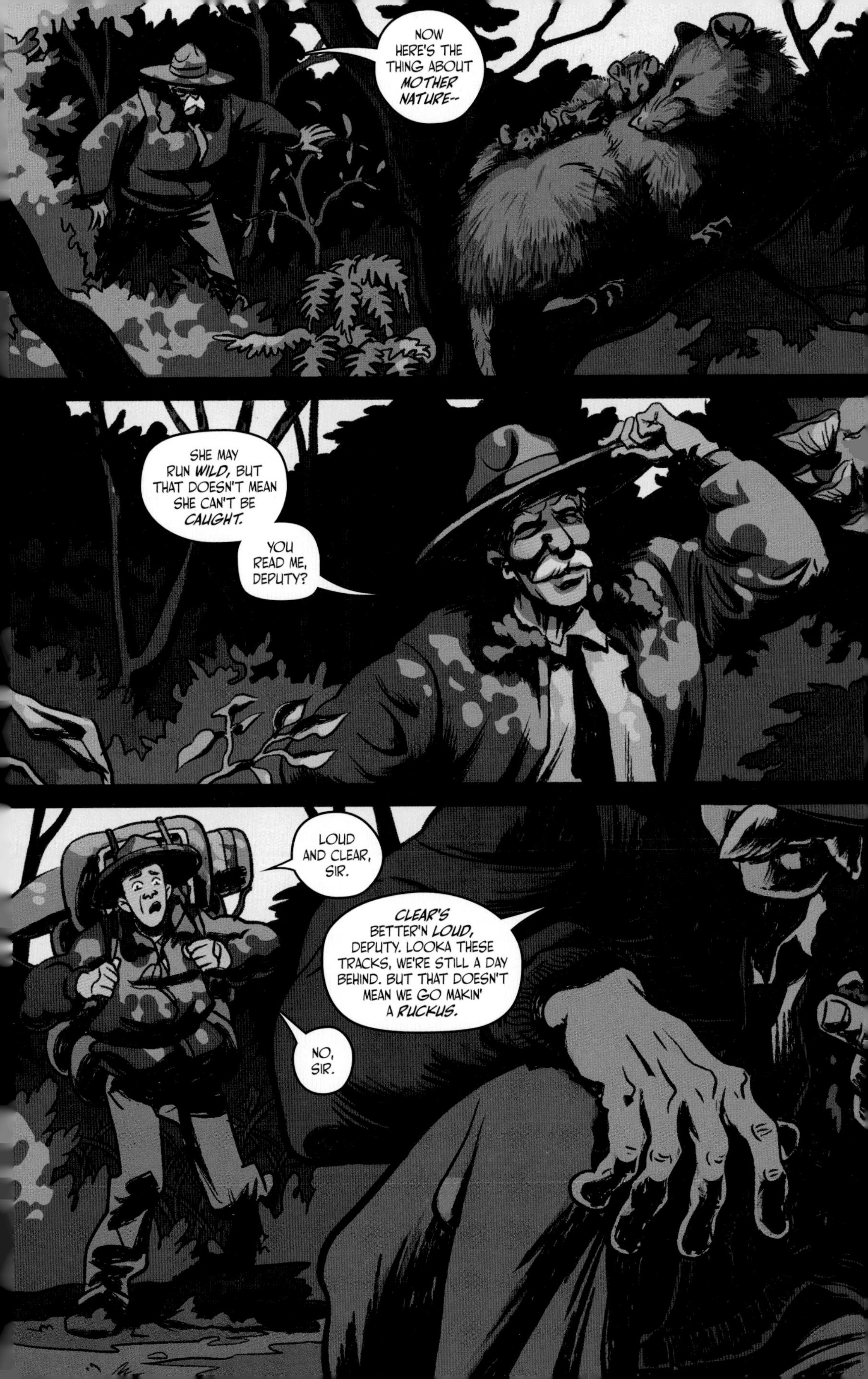
NOW HERE'S THE THING ABOUT MOTHER NATURE--
SHE MAY RUN WILD, BUT THAT DOESN'T MEAN SHE CAN'T BE CAUGHT.
YOU READ ME, DEPUTY?
LOUD AND CLEAR, SIR.
CLEAR'S BETTER'N LOUD, DEPUTY. LOOKA THESE TRACKS, WE'RE STILL A DAY BEHIND. BUT THAT DOESN'T MEAN WE GO MAKIN' A RUCKUS.
NO, SIR.

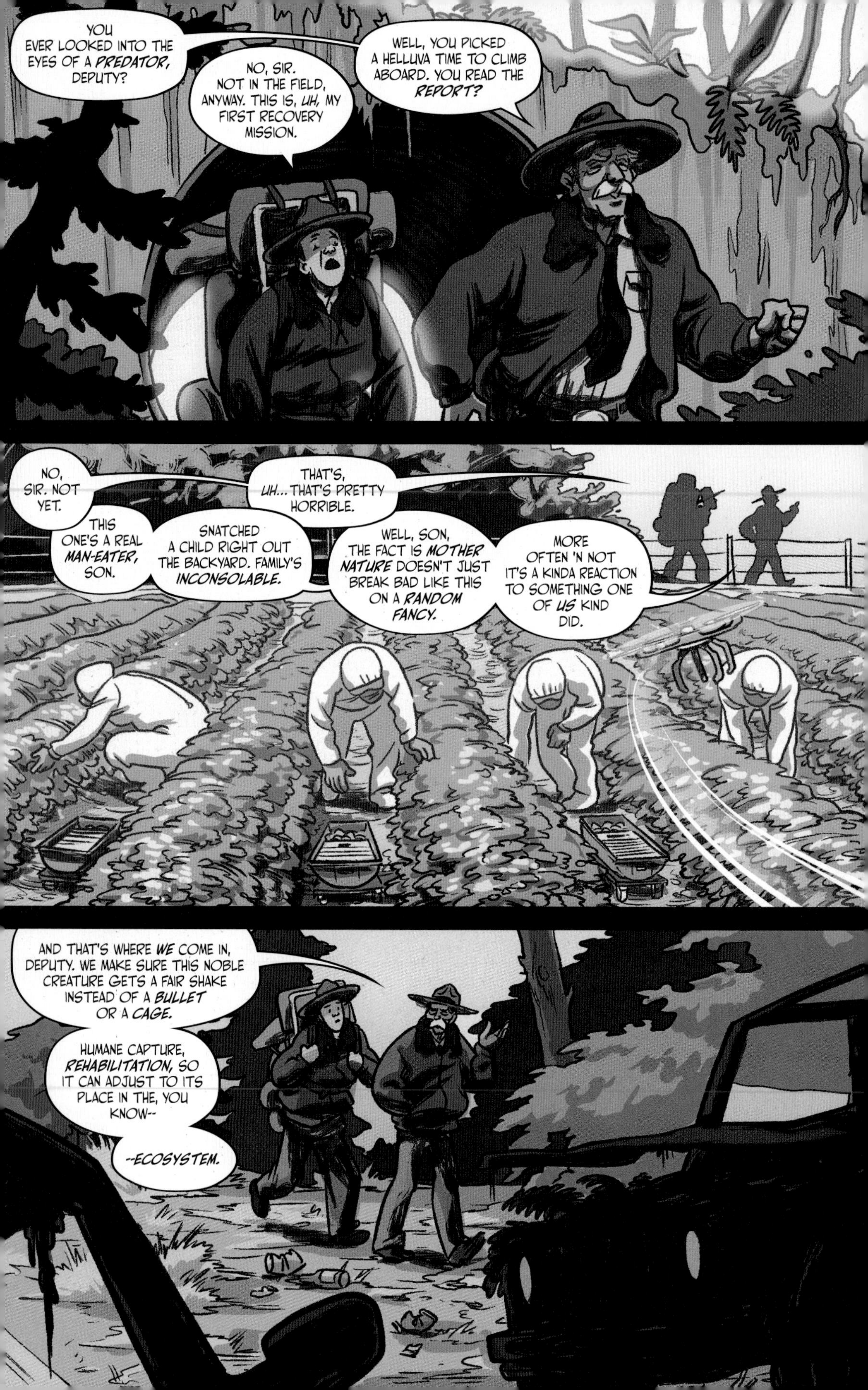
YOU EVER LOOKED INTO THE EYES OF A *PREDATOR,* DEPUTY?
NO, SIR. NOT IN THE FIELD, ANYWAY. THIS IS, *UH,* MY FIRST RECOVERY MISSION.
WELL, YOU PICKED A HELLUVA TIME TO CLIMB ABOARD. YOU READ THE *REPORT?*
NO, SIR. NOT YET.
THIS ONE'S A REAL *MAN-EATER,* SON.
SNATCHED A CHILD RIGHT OUT THE BACKYARD. FAMILY'S *INCONSOLABLE.*
THAT'S, *UH*... THAT'S PRETTY HORRIBLE.
WELL, SON, THE FACT IS *MOTHER NATURE* DOESN'T JUST BREAK BAD LIKE THIS ON A *RANDOM FANCY.*
MORE OFTEN 'N NOT IT'S A KINDA REACTION TO SOMETHING ONE OF *US* KIND DID.
AND THAT'S WHERE *WE* COME IN, DEPUTY. WE MAKE SURE THIS NOBLE CREATURE GETS A FAIR SHAKE INSTEAD OF A *BULLET* OR A *CAGE.*
HUMANE CAPTURE, *REHABILITATION,* SO IT CAN ADJUST TO ITS PLACE IN THE, YOU KNOW--
--*ECOSYSTEM.*

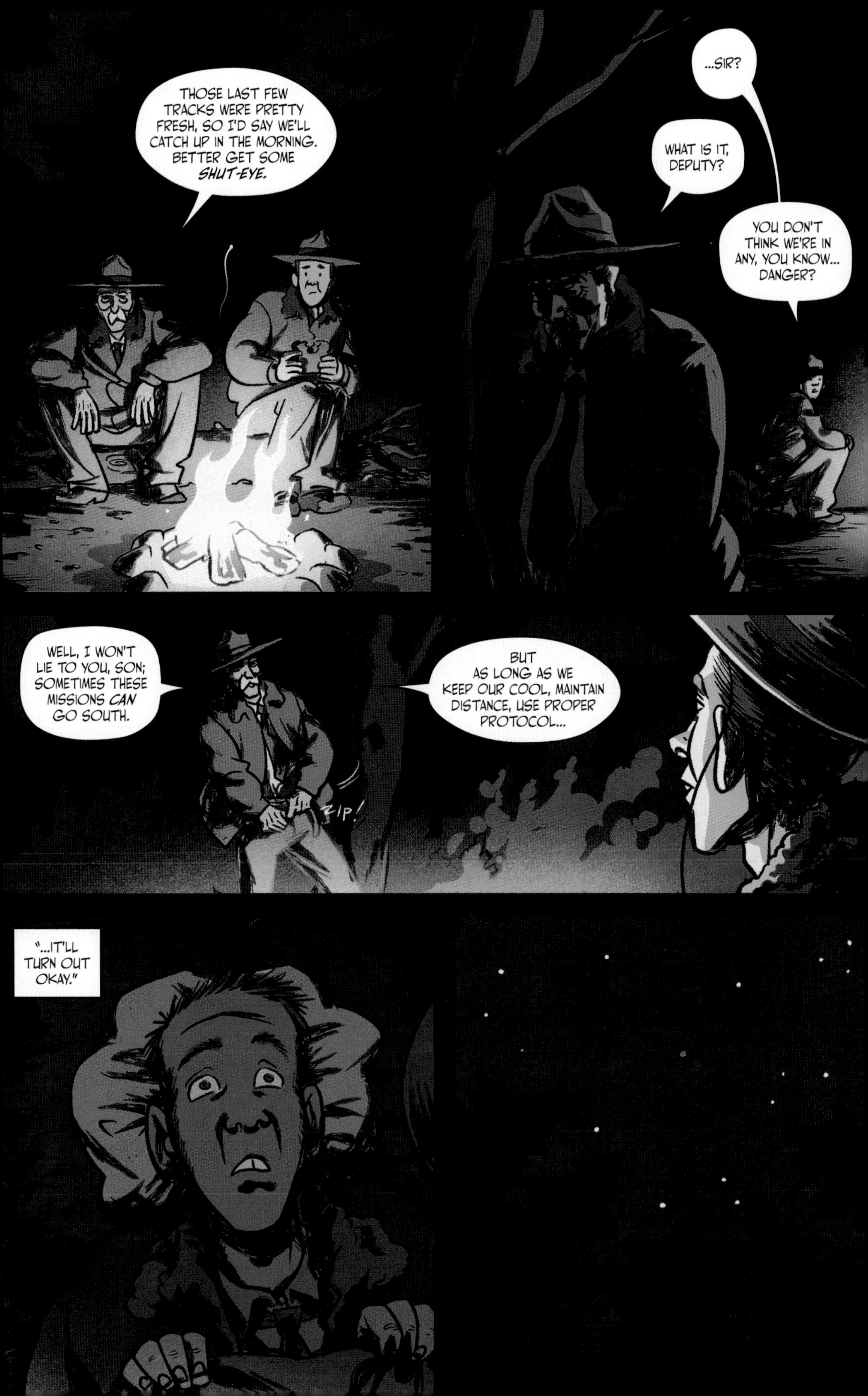
THOSE LAST FEW TRACKS WERE PRETTY FRESH, SO I'D SAY WE'LL CATCH UP IN THE MORNING. BETTER GET SOME SHUT-EYE.
...SIR?
WHAT IS IT, DEPUTY?
YOU DON'T THINK WE'RE IN ANY, YOU KNOW... DANGER?
WELL, I WON'T LIE TO YOU, SON; SOMETIMES THESE MISSIONS CAN GO SOUTH.
BUT AS LONG AS WE KEEP OUR COOL, MAINTAIN DISTANCE, USE PROPER PROTOCOL...
ZIP!
"...IT'LL TURN OUT OKAY."

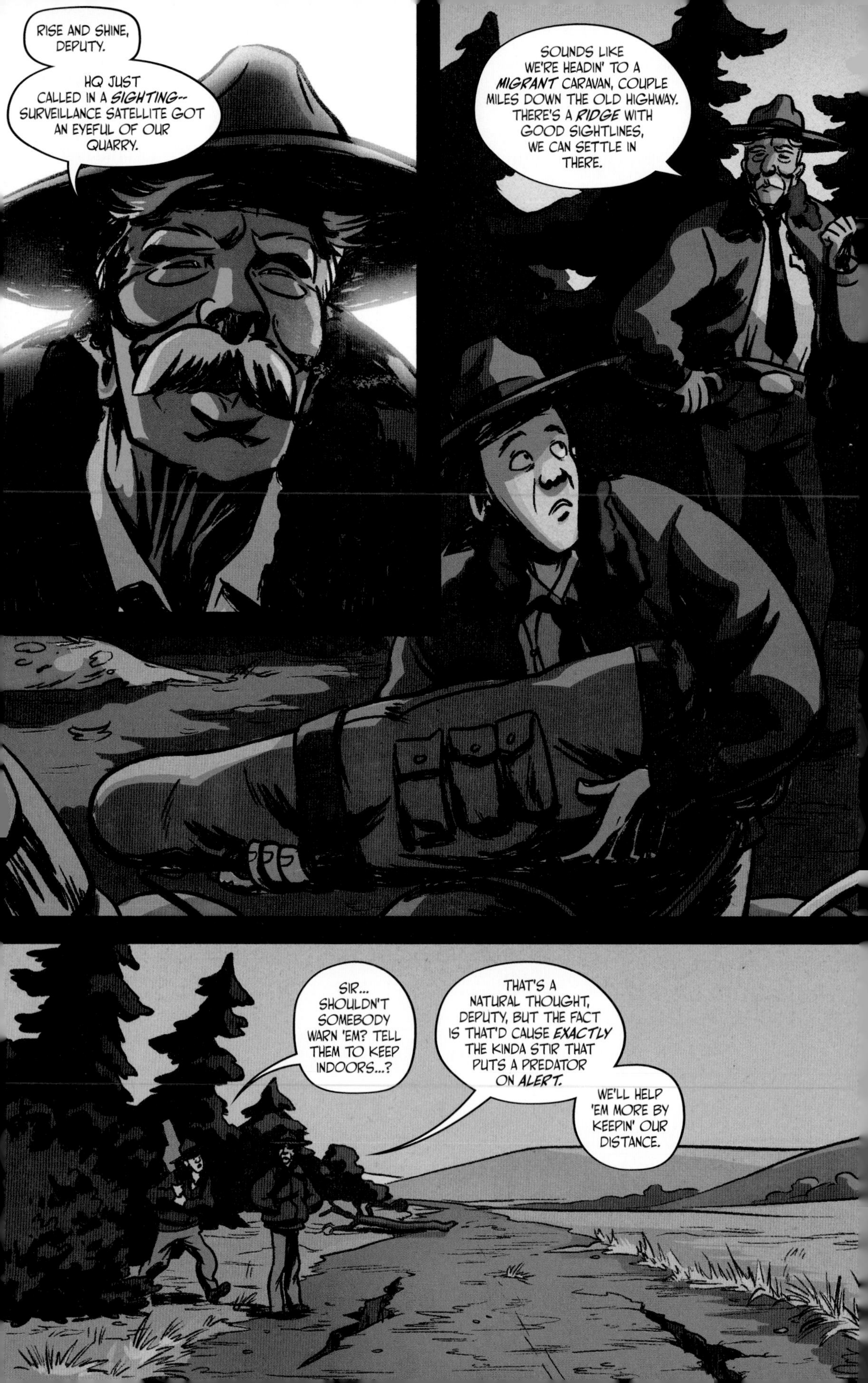
RISE AND SHINE, DEPUTY.
HQ JUST CALLED IN A SIGHTING-- SURVEILLANCE SATELLITE GOT AN EYEFUL OF OUR QUARRY.
SOUNDS LIKE WE'RE HEADIN' TO A MIGRANT CARAVAN, COUPLE MILES DOWN THE OLD HIGHWAY. THERE'S A RIDGE WITH GOOD SIGHTLINES, WE CAN SETTLE IN THERE.
SIR... SHOULDN'T SOMEBODY WARN 'EM? TELL THEM TO KEEP INDOORS...?
THAT'S A NATURAL THOUGHT, DEPUTY, BUT THE FACT IS THAT'D CAUSE EXACTLY THE KINDA STIR THAT PUTS A PREDATOR ON ALERT.
WE'LL HELP 'EM MORE BY KEEPIN' OUR DISTANCE.

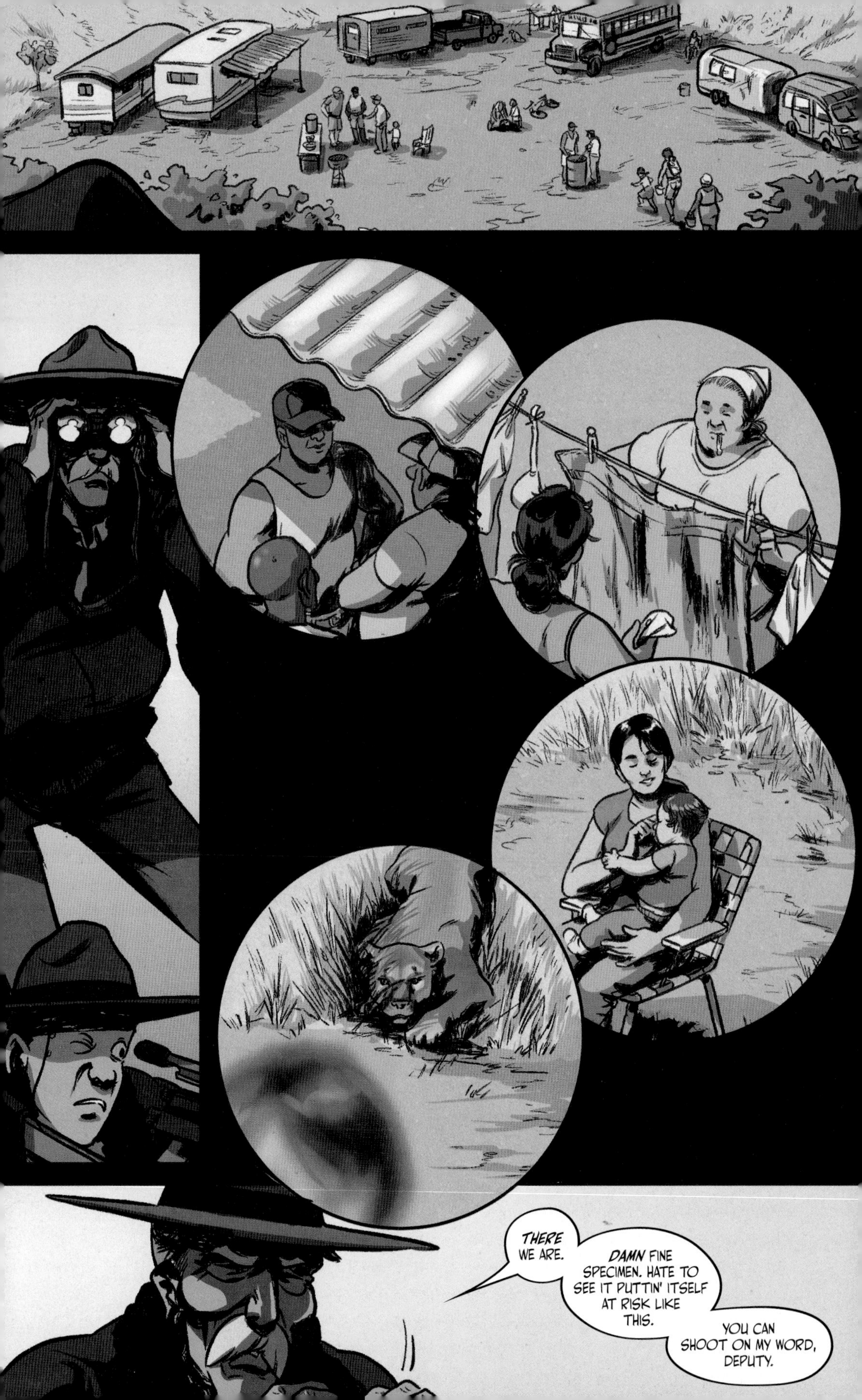
THERE WE ARE.
DAMN FINE SPECIMEN. HATE TO SEE IT PUTTIN' ITSELF AT RISK LIKE THIS.
YOU CAN SHOOT ON MY WORD, DEPUTY.

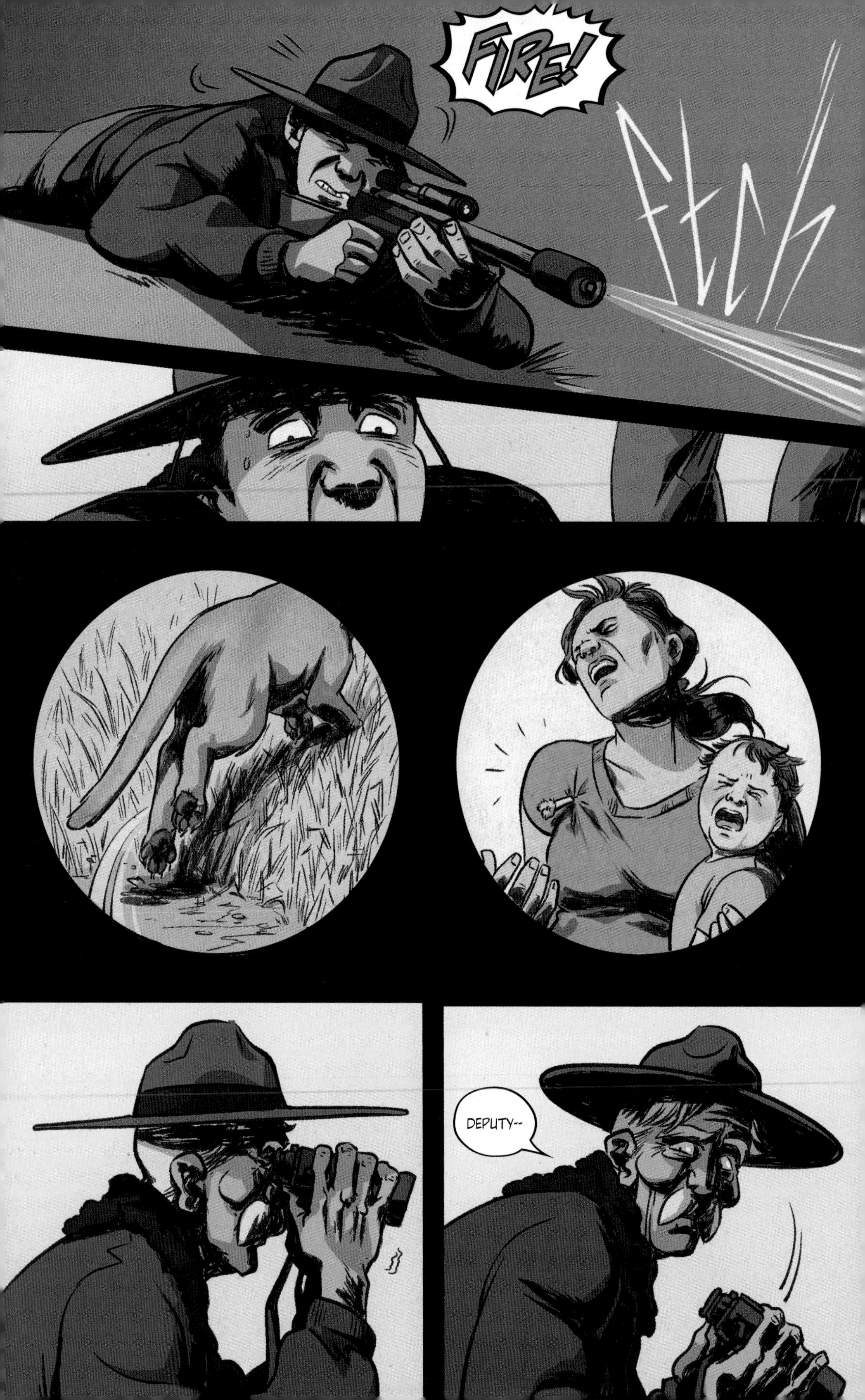
FIRE!
DEPUTY--

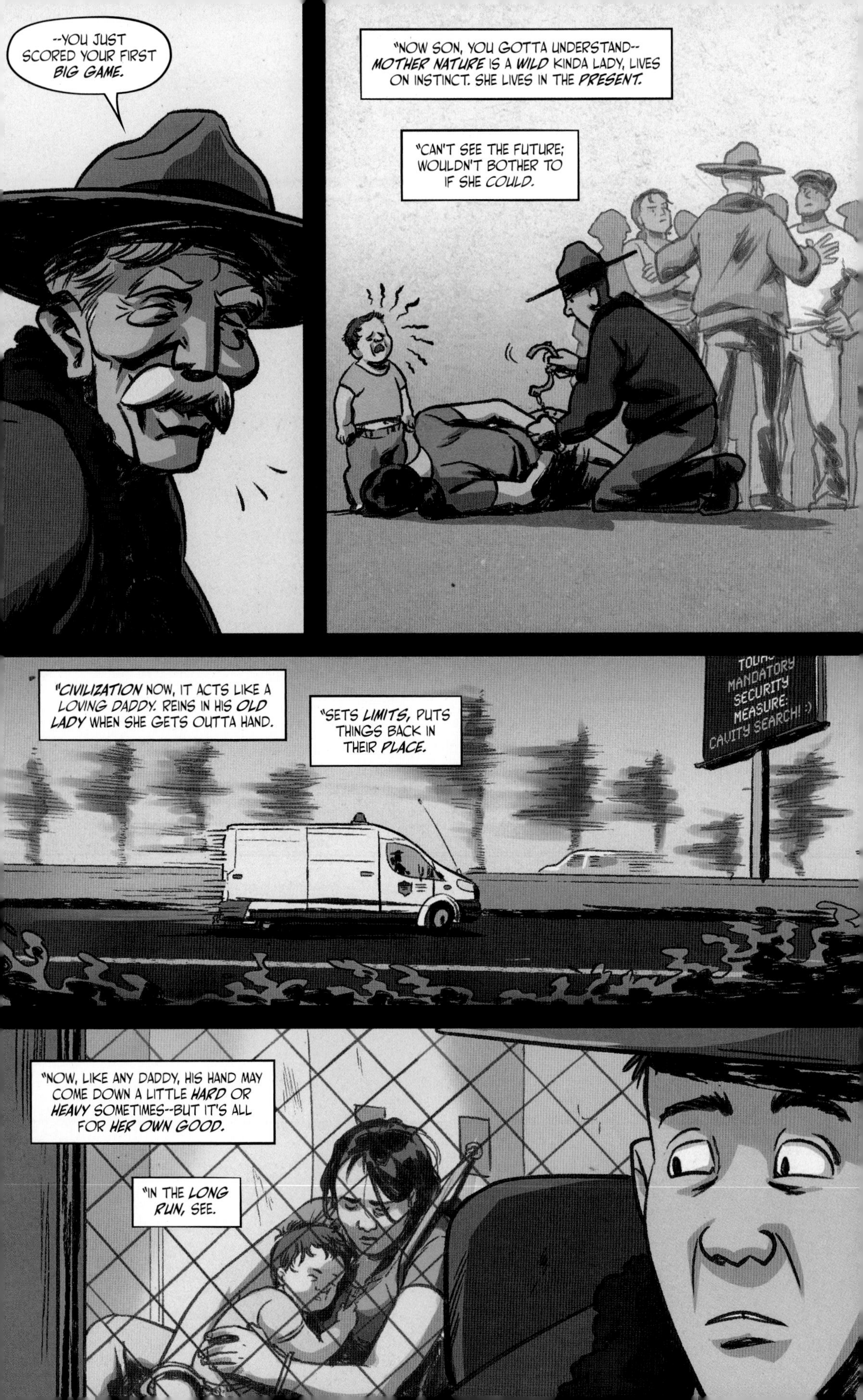
--YOU JUST SCORED YOUR FIRST BIG GAME.
"NOW SON, YOU GOTTA UNDERSTAND-- MOTHER NATURE IS A WILD KINDA LADY, LIVES ON INSTINCT. SHE LIVES IN THE PRESENT.
"CAN'T SEE THE FUTURE; WOULDN'T BOTHER TO IF SHE COULD.
"CIVILIZATION NOW, IT ACTS LIKE A LOVING DADDY. REINS IN HIS OLD LADY WHEN SHE GETS OUTTA HAND.
"SETS LIMITS, PUTS THINGS BACK IN THEIR PLACE.
MANDATORY SECURITY MEASURE: CAVITY SEARCH! :)
"NOW, LIKE ANY DADDY, HIS HAND MAY COME DOWN A LITTLE HARD OR HEAVY SOMETIMES--BUT IT'S ALL FOR HER OWN GOOD.
"IN THE LONG RUN, SEE.

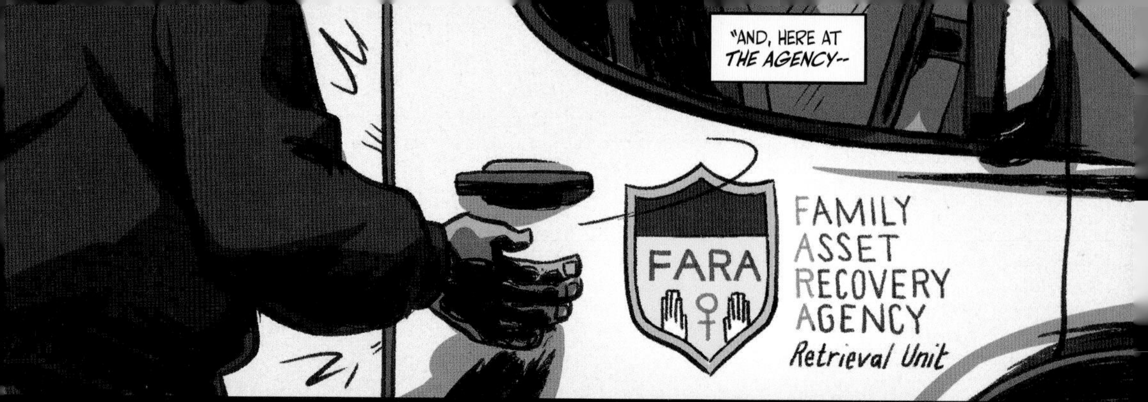
"AND, HERE AT THE AGENCY--
FARA
FAMILY ASSET RECOVERY AGENCY
Retrieval Unit

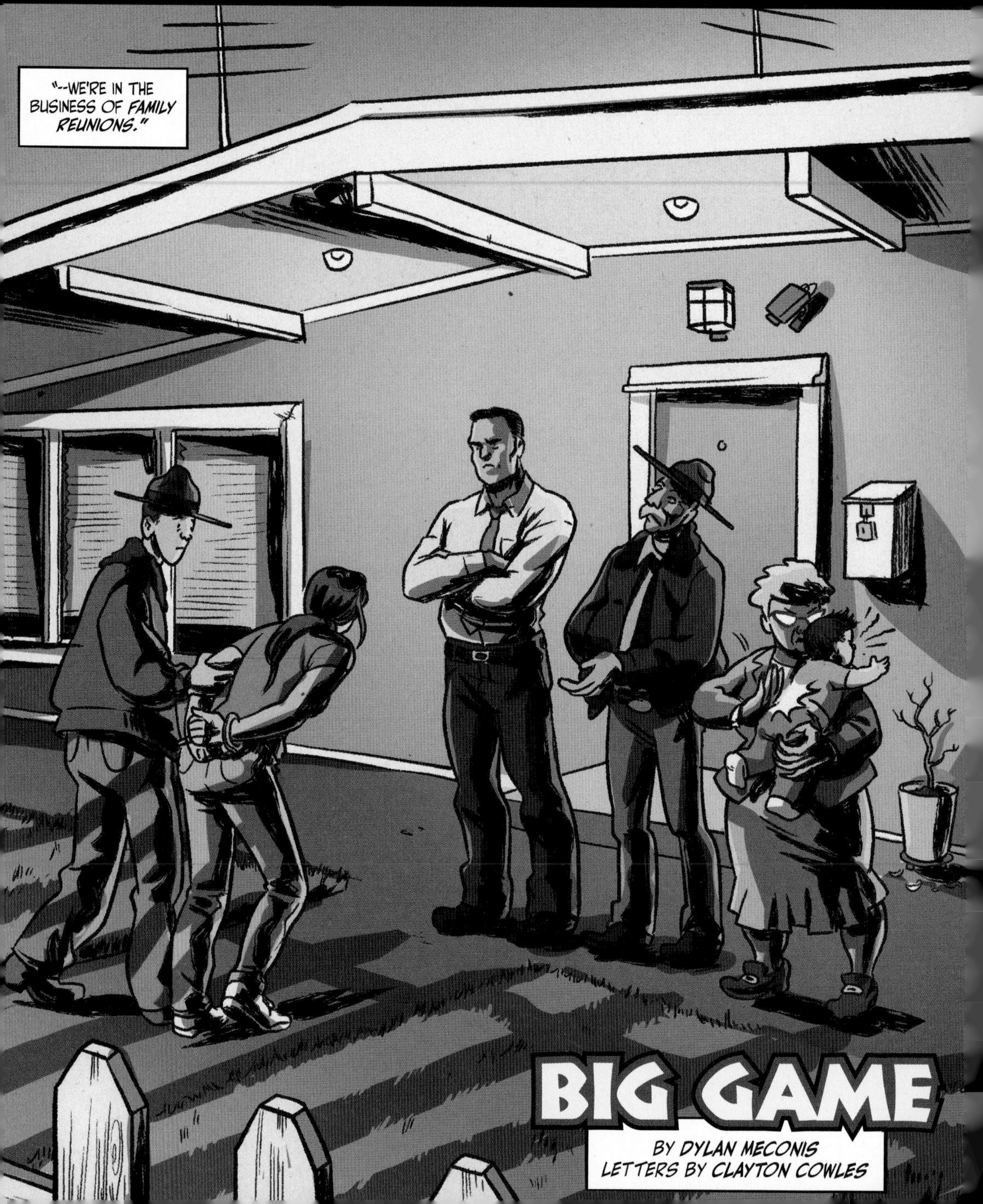
"--WE'RE IN THE BUSINESS OF FAMILY REUNIONS."
BIG GAME
BY DYLAN MECONIS
LETTERS BY CLAYTON COWLES

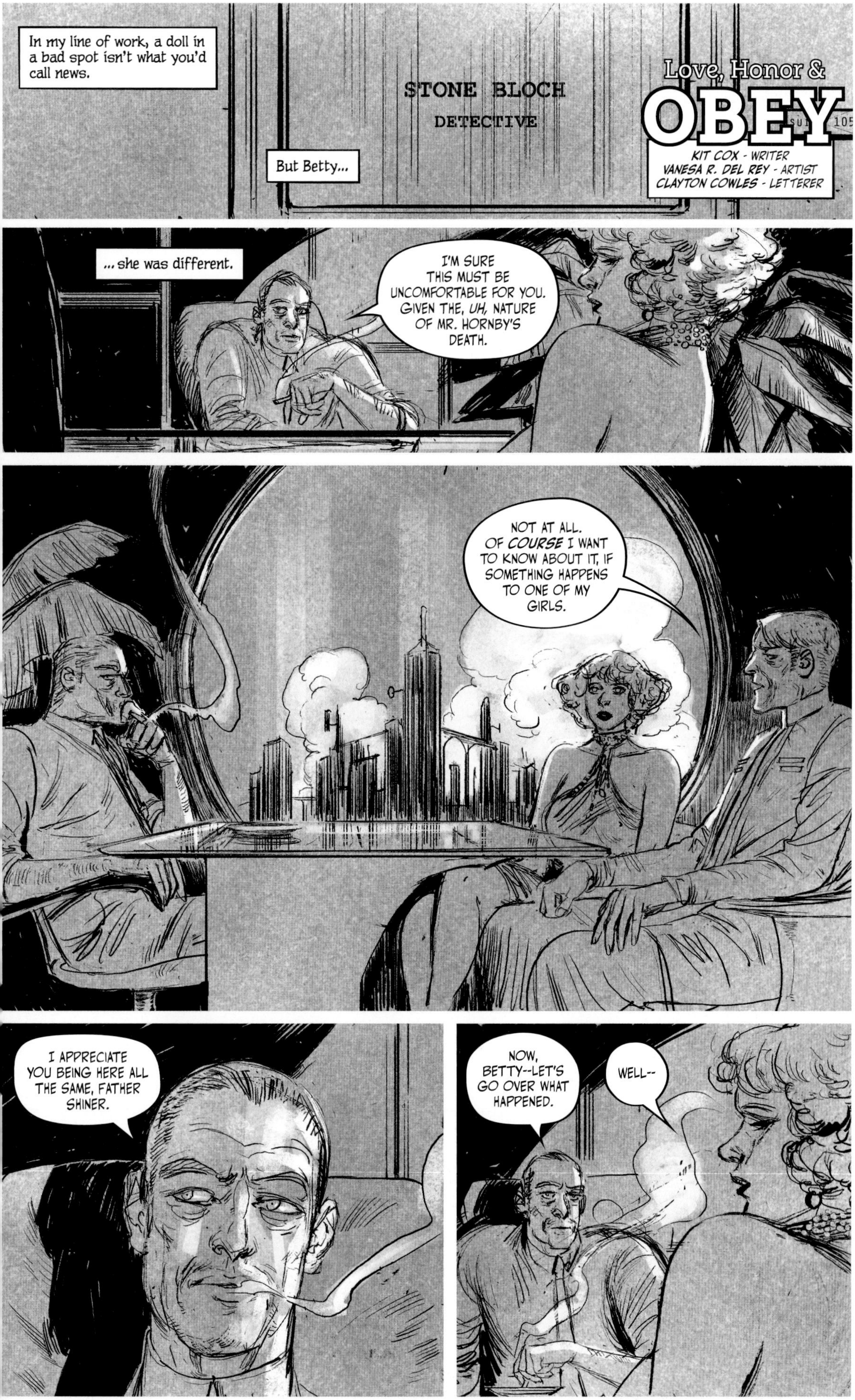

In my line of work, a doll in a bad spot isn't what you'd call news.
STONE BLOCH
DETECTIVE
But Betty...
Love, Honor &
OBEY
KIT COX - WRITER
VANESA R. DEL REY - ARTIST
CLAYTON COWLES - LETTERER
...she was different.
I'M SURE THIS MUST BE UNCOMFORTABLE FOR YOU. GIVEN THE, UH, NATURE OF MR. HORNBY'S DEATH.
NOT AT ALL. OF COURSE I WANT TO KNOW ABOUT IT, IF SOMETHING HAPPENS TO ONE OF MY GIRLS.
I APPRECIATE YOU BEING HERE ALL THE SAME, FATHER SHINER.
NOW, BETTY--LET'S GO OVER WHAT HAPPENED.
WELL--

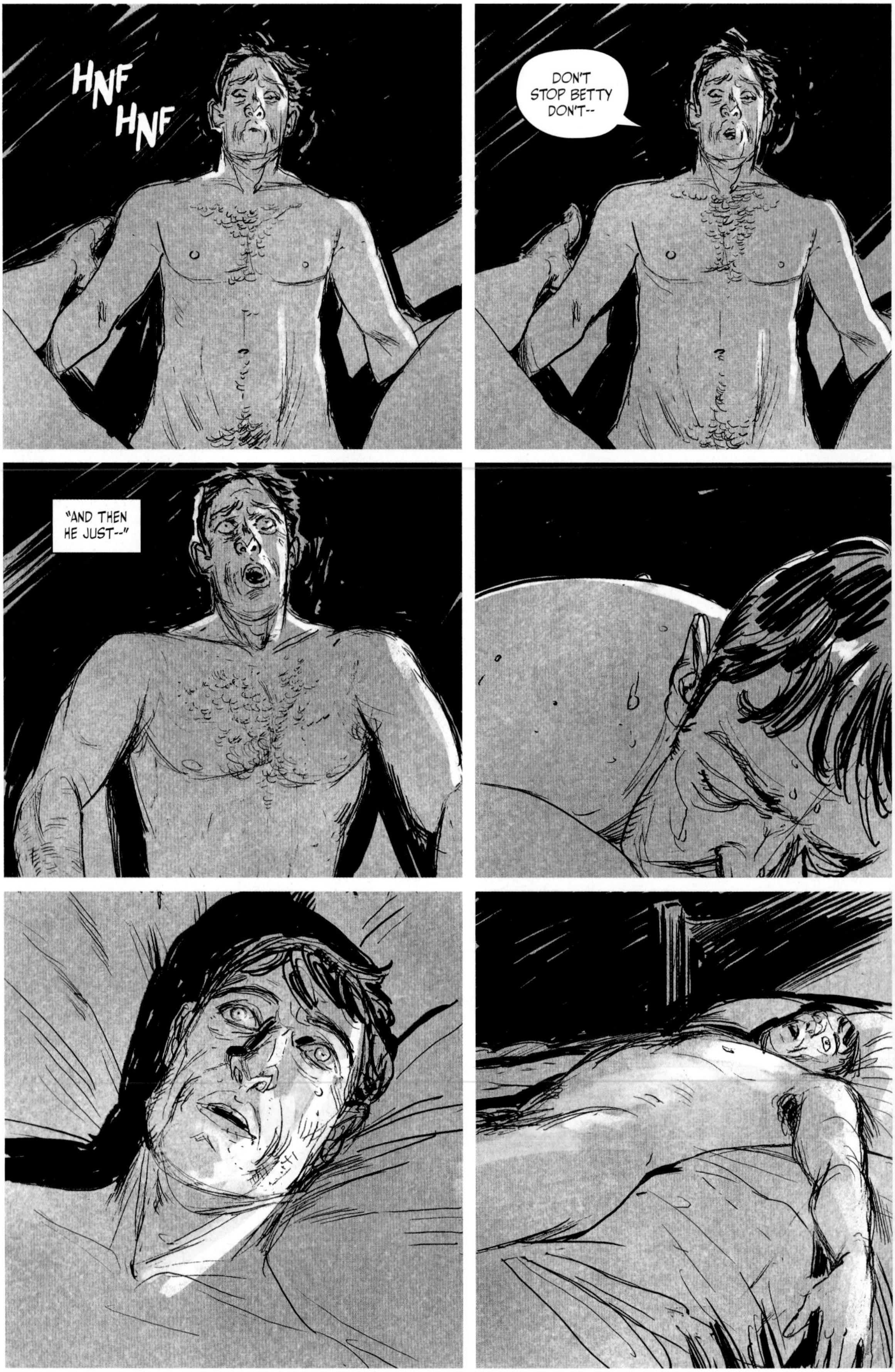
HNF
HNF
DON'T STOP BETTY DON'T--
"AND THEN HE JUST--"

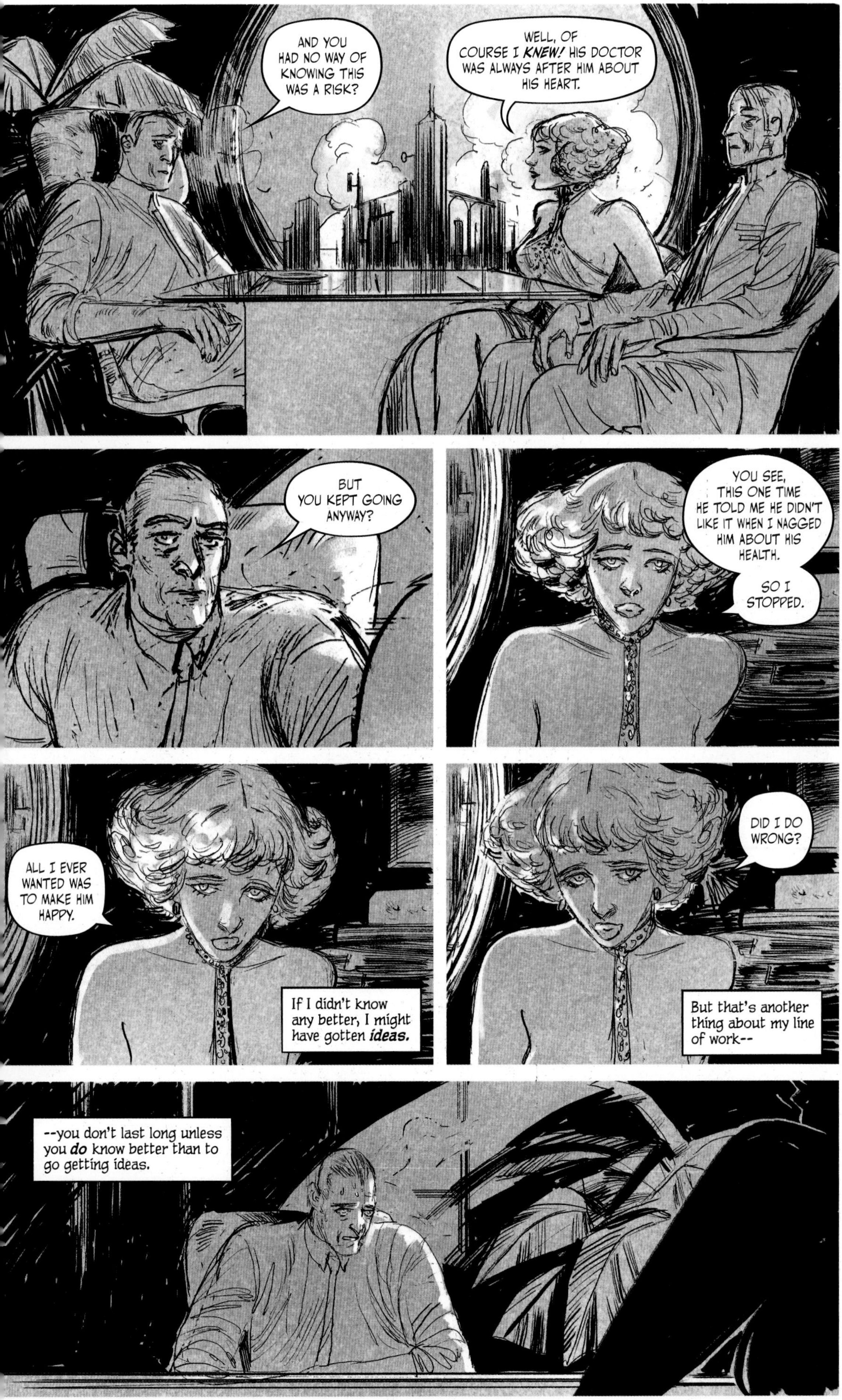
AND YOU HAD NO WAY OF KNOWING THIS WAS A RISK?
WELL, OF COURSE I KNEW! HIS DOCTOR WAS ALWAYS AFTER HIM ABOUT HIS HEART.
BUT YOU KEPT GOING ANYWAY?
YOU SEE, THIS ONE TIME HE TOLD ME HE DIDN'T LIKE IT WHEN I NAGGED HIM ABOUT HIS HEALTH.
SO I STOPPED.
ALL I EVER WANTED WAS TO MAKE HIM HAPPY.
If I didn't know any better, I might have gotten ideas.
DID I DO WRONG?
But that's another thing about my line of work--
--you don't last long unless you do know better than to go getting ideas.

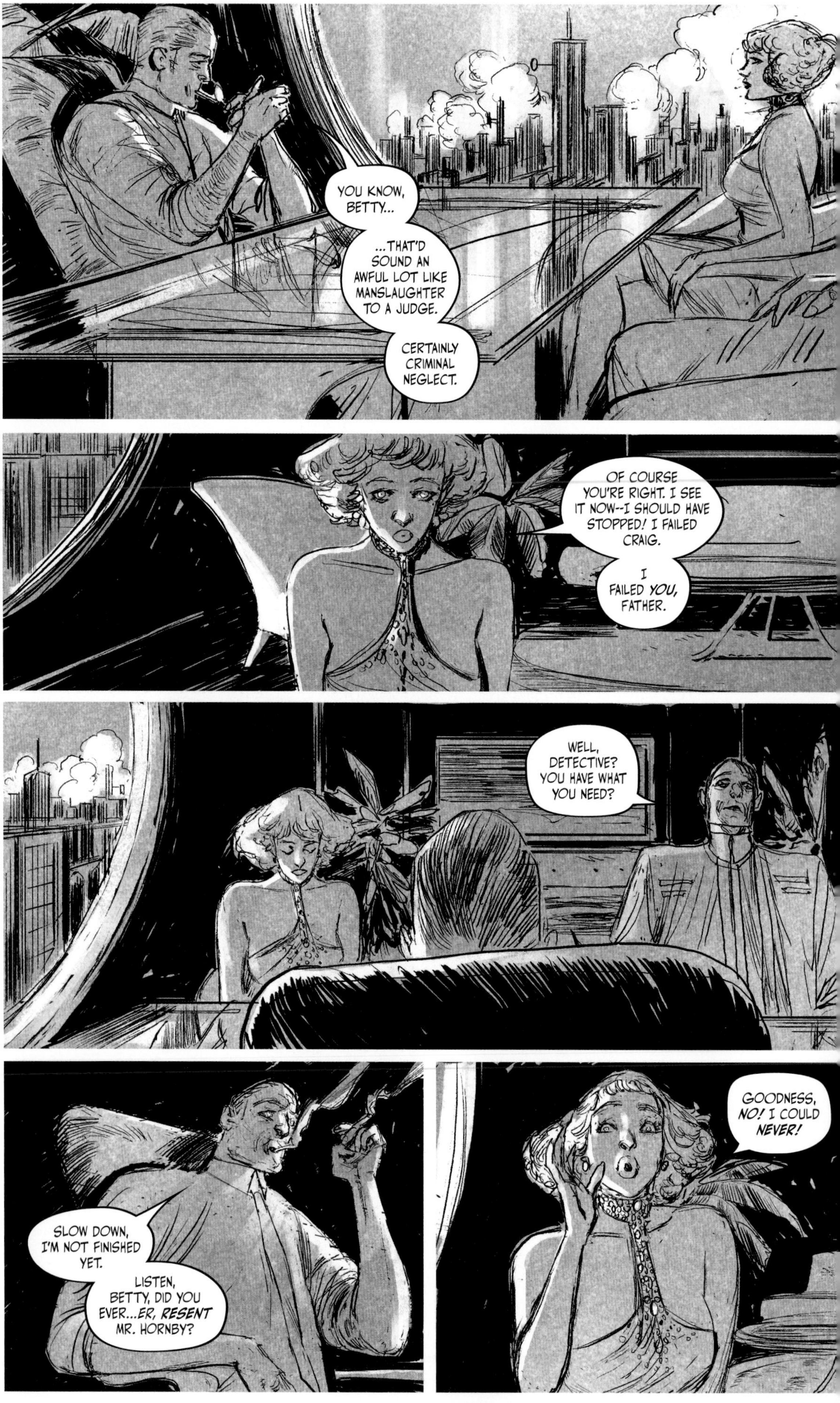

YOU KNOW, BETTY...
...THAT'D SOUND AN AWFUL LOT LIKE MANSLAUGHTER TO A JUDGE.
CERTAINLY CRIMINAL NEGLECT.
OF COURSE YOU'RE RIGHT. I SEE IT NOW--I SHOULD HAVE STOPPED! I FAILED CRAIG.
I FAILED *YOU,* FATHER.
WELL, DETECTIVE? YOU HAVE WHAT YOU NEED?
SLOW DOWN, I'M NOT FINISHED YET.
LISTEN, BETTY, DID YOU EVER...*ER, RESENT* MR. HORNBY?
GOODNESS, *NO!* I COULD *NEVER!*

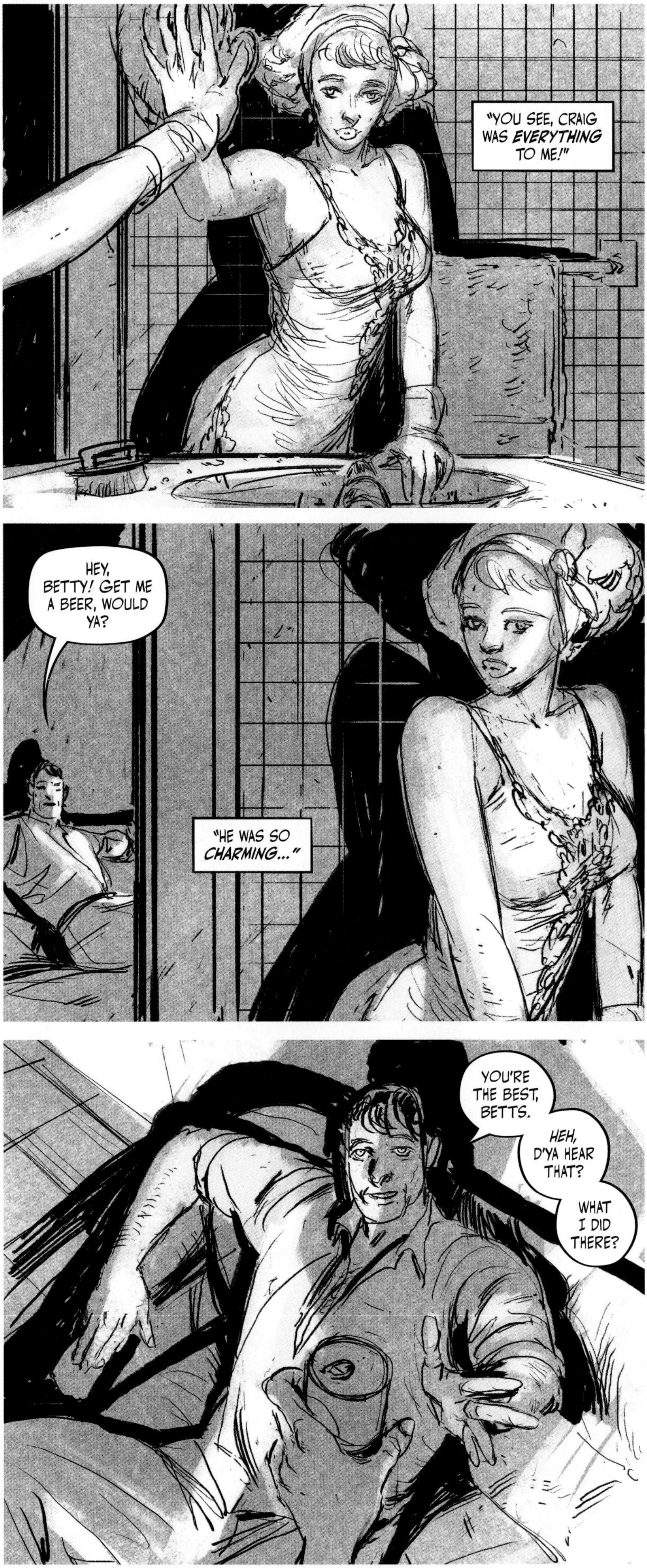
"YOU SEE, CRAIG WAS *EVERYTHING* TO ME!"
HEY, BETTY! GET ME A BEER, WOULD YA?
"HE WAS SO *CHARMING*..."
YOU'RE THE BEST, BETTS.
*HEH*, D'YA HEAR THAT?
WHAT I DID THERE?

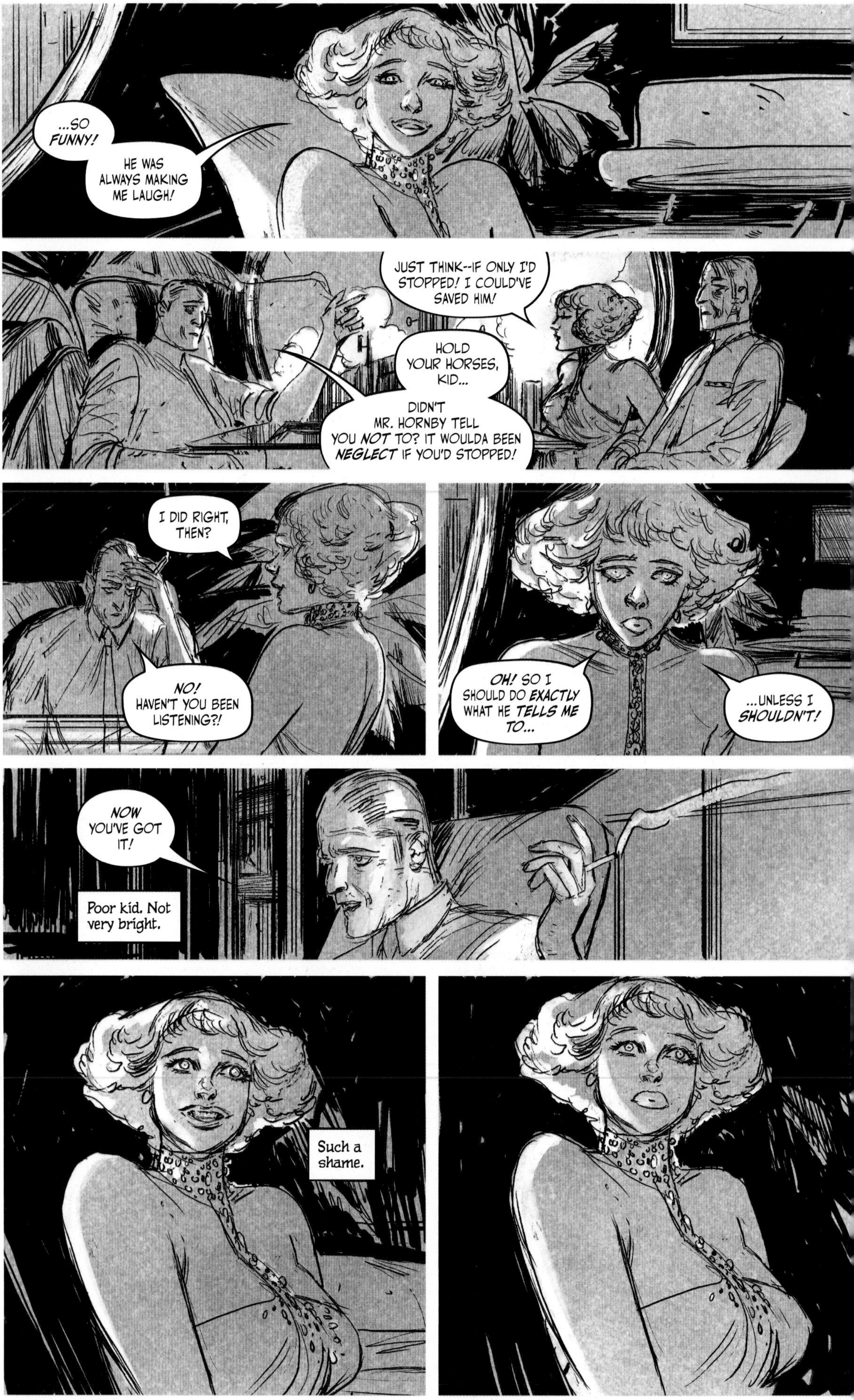
...SO FUNNY! HE WAS ALWAYS MAKING ME LAUGH!
JUST THINK--IF ONLY I'D STOPPED! I COULD'VE SAVED HIM!
HOLD YOUR HORSES, KID...
DIDN'T MR. HORNBY TELL YOU NOT TO? IT WOULDA BEEN NEGLECT IF YOU'D STOPPED!
I DID RIGHT, THEN?
NO! HAVEN'T YOU BEEN LISTENING?!
OH! SO I SHOULD DO EXACTLY WHAT HE TELLS ME TO...
...UNLESS I SHOULDN'T!
NOW YOU'VE GOT IT!
Poor kid. Not very bright.
Such a shame.

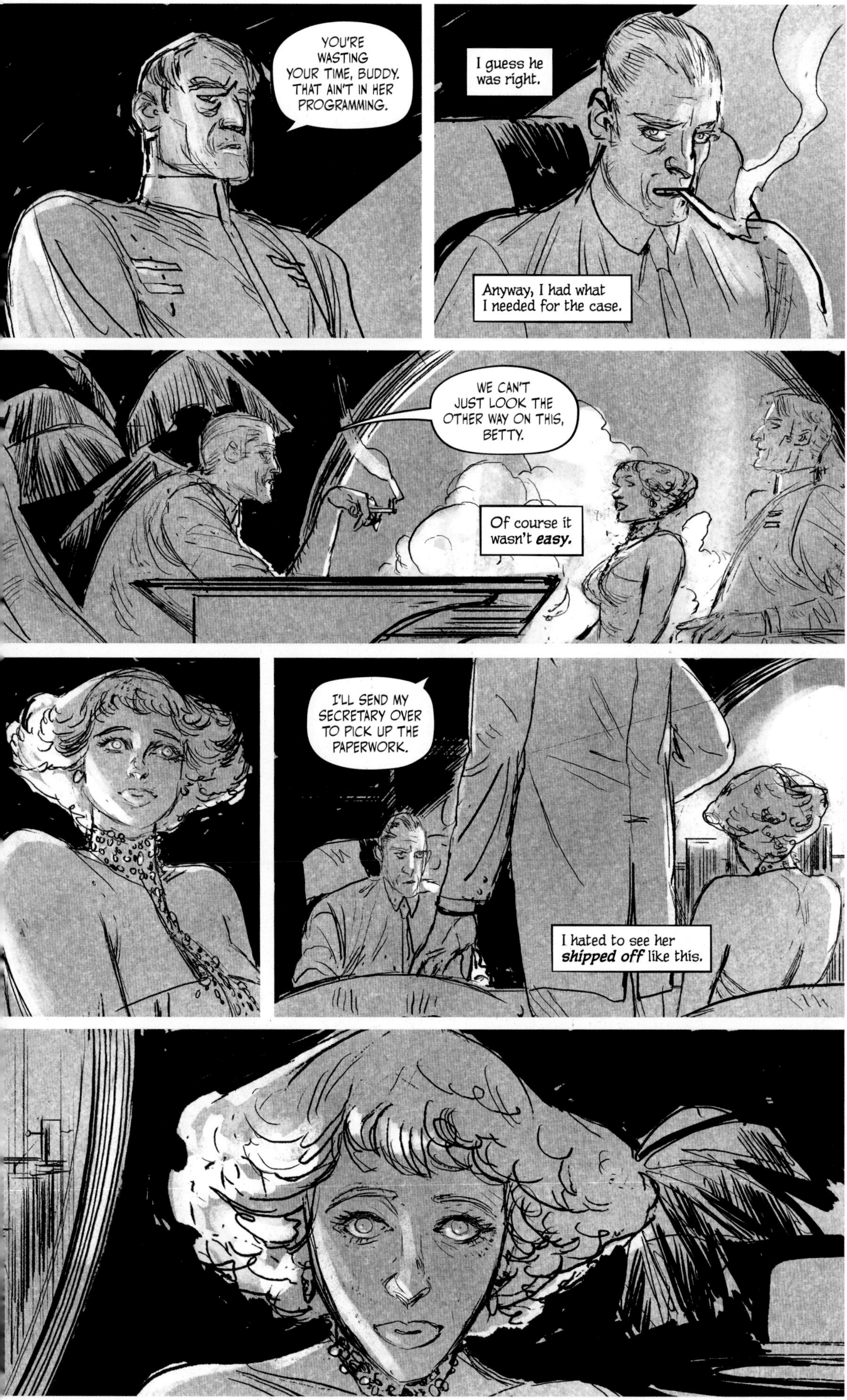
YOU'RE WASTING YOUR TIME, BUDDY. THAT AIN'T IN HER PROGRAMMING.
I guess he was right.
Anyway, I had what I needed for the case.
WE CAN'T JUST LOOK THE OTHER WAY ON THIS, BETTY.
Of course it wasn't *easy.*
I'LL SEND MY SECRETARY OVER TO PICK UP THE PAPERWORK.
I hated to see her *shipped off* like this.

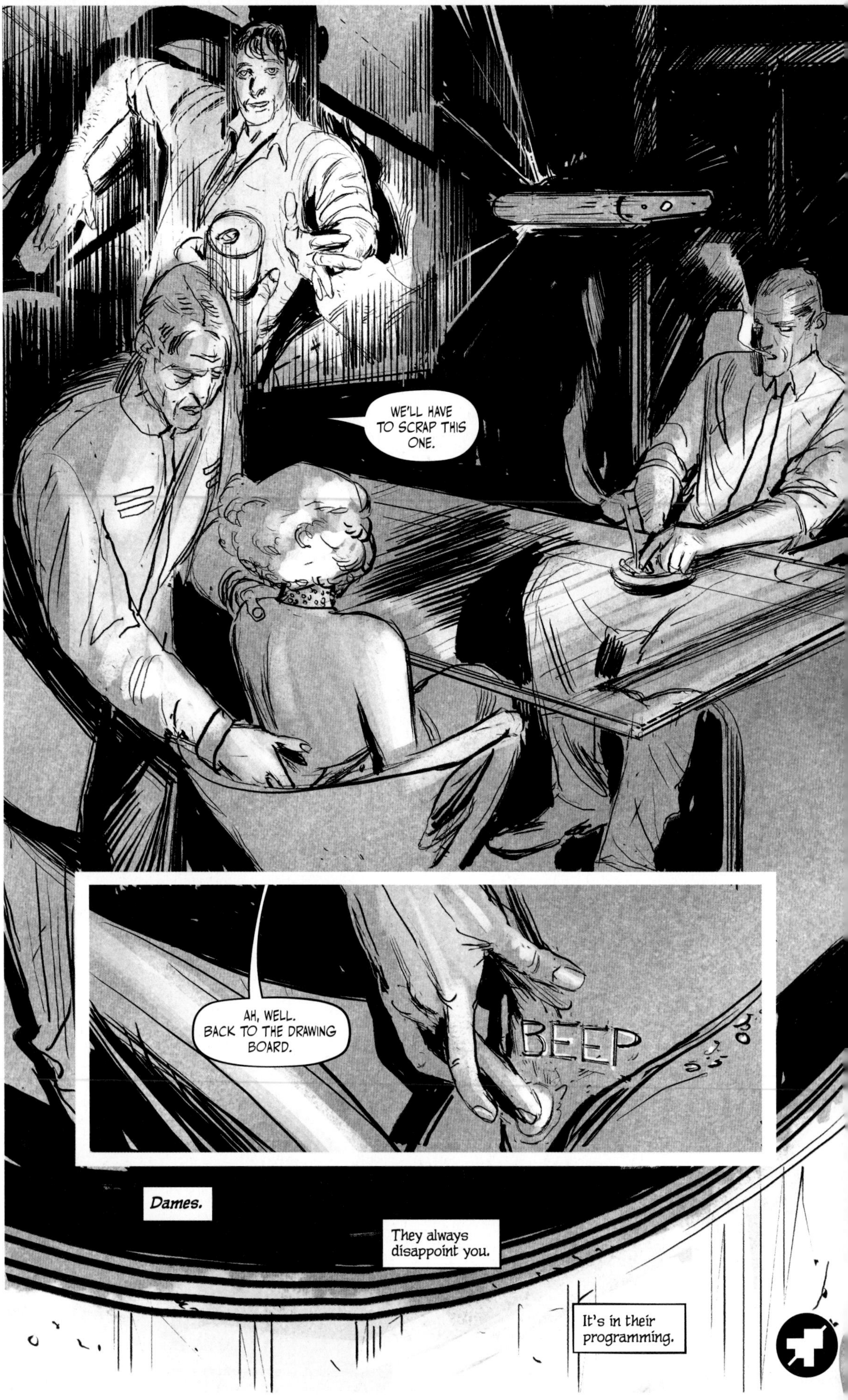

WE'LL HAVE TO SCRAP THIS ONE.
AH, WELL. BACK TO THE DRAWING BOARD.
BEEP
Dames.
They always disappoint you.
It's in their programming.

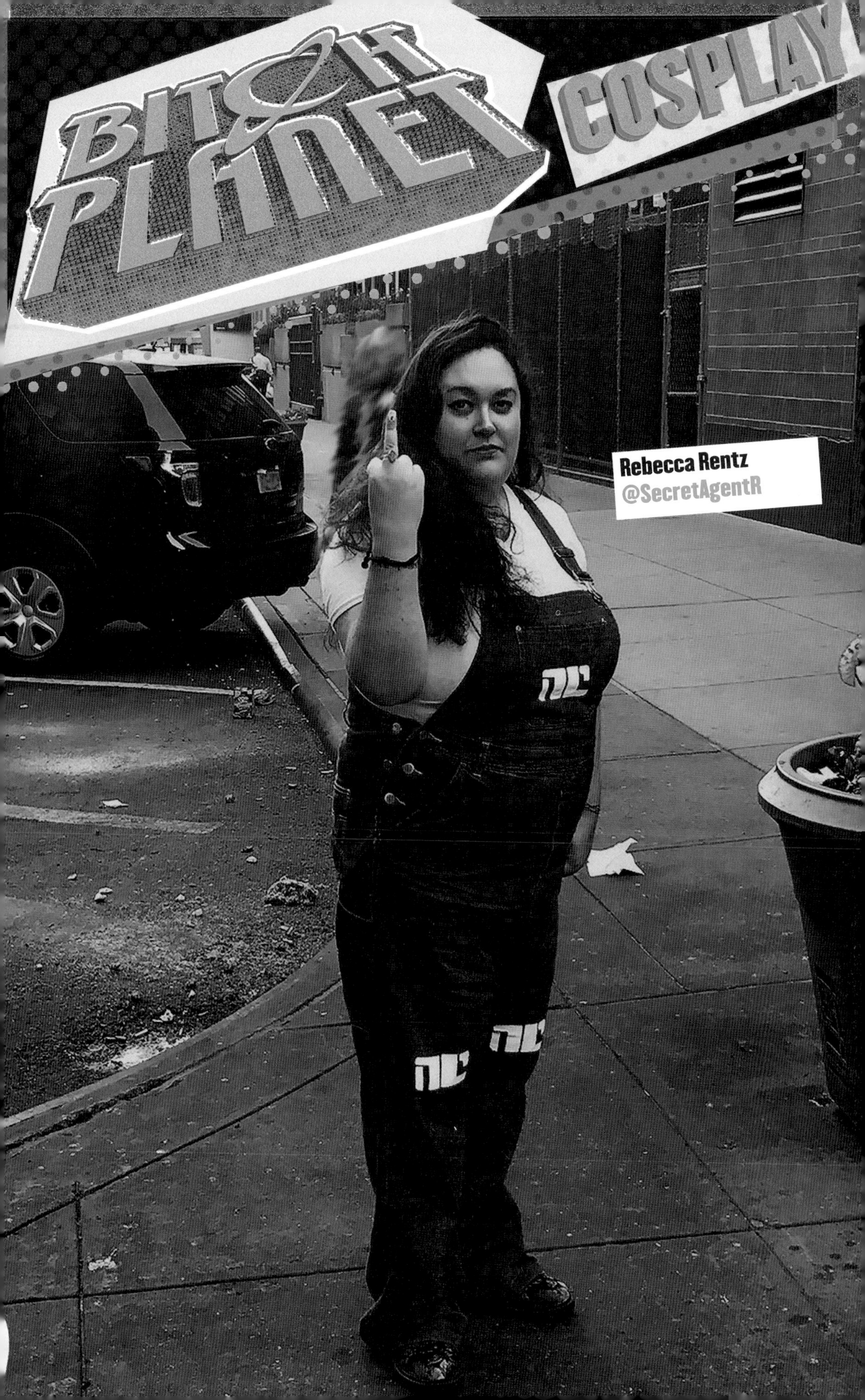
BITCH PLANET
COSPLAY
Rebecca Rentz
@SecretAgentR

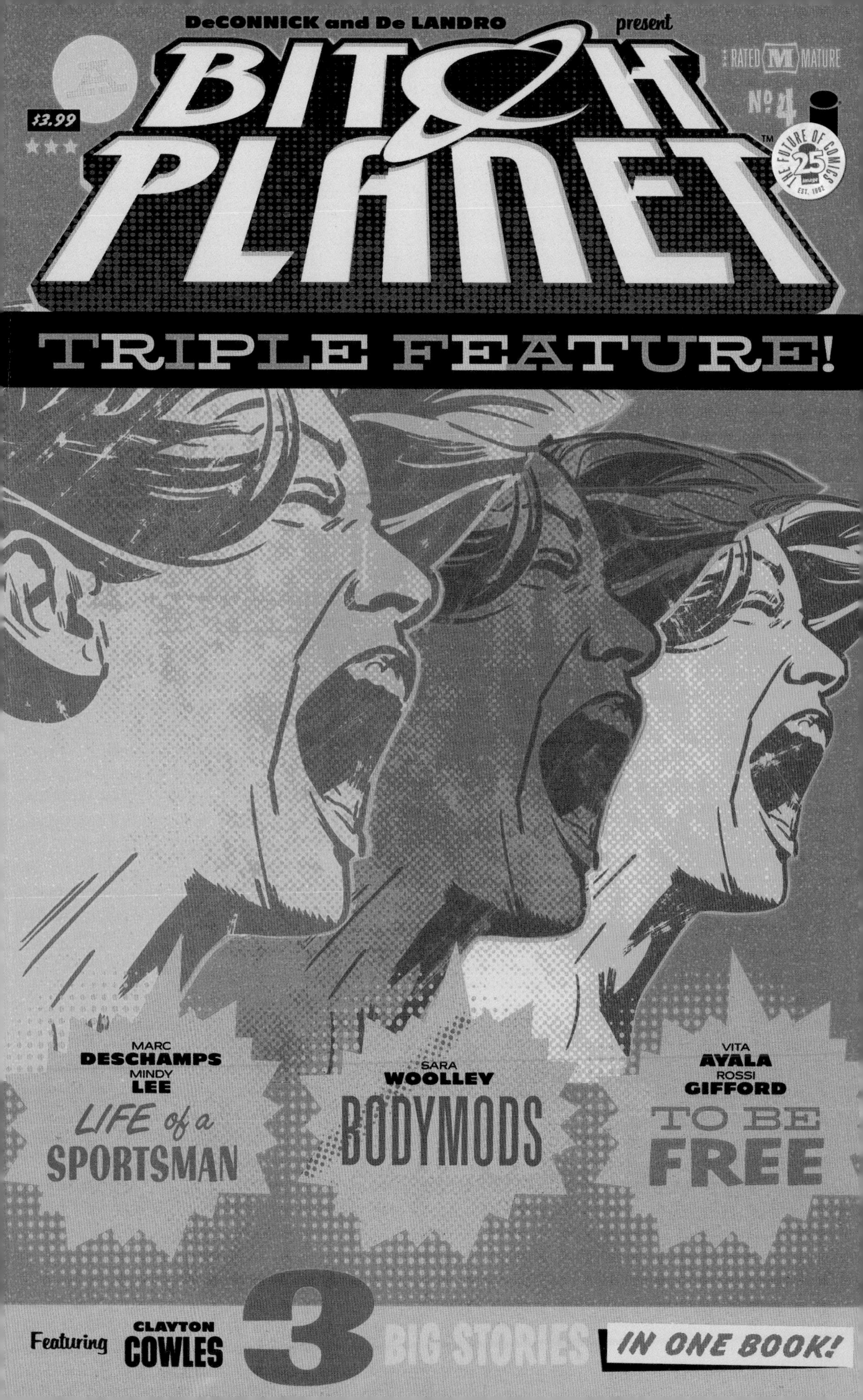
DeCONNICK and De LANDRO
present
BITCH PLANET™
$3.99
RATED M MATURE
Nº 4
THE FUTURE OF COMICS
25
image
EST. 1992
TRIPLE FEATURE!
MARC
DESCHAMPS
MINDY
LEE
LIFE of a
SPORTSMAN
SARA
WOOLLEY
BODYMODS
VITA
AYALA
ROSSI
GIFFORD
TO BE
FREE
Featuring
CLAYTON
COWLES
3
BIG STORIES
IN ONE BOOK!

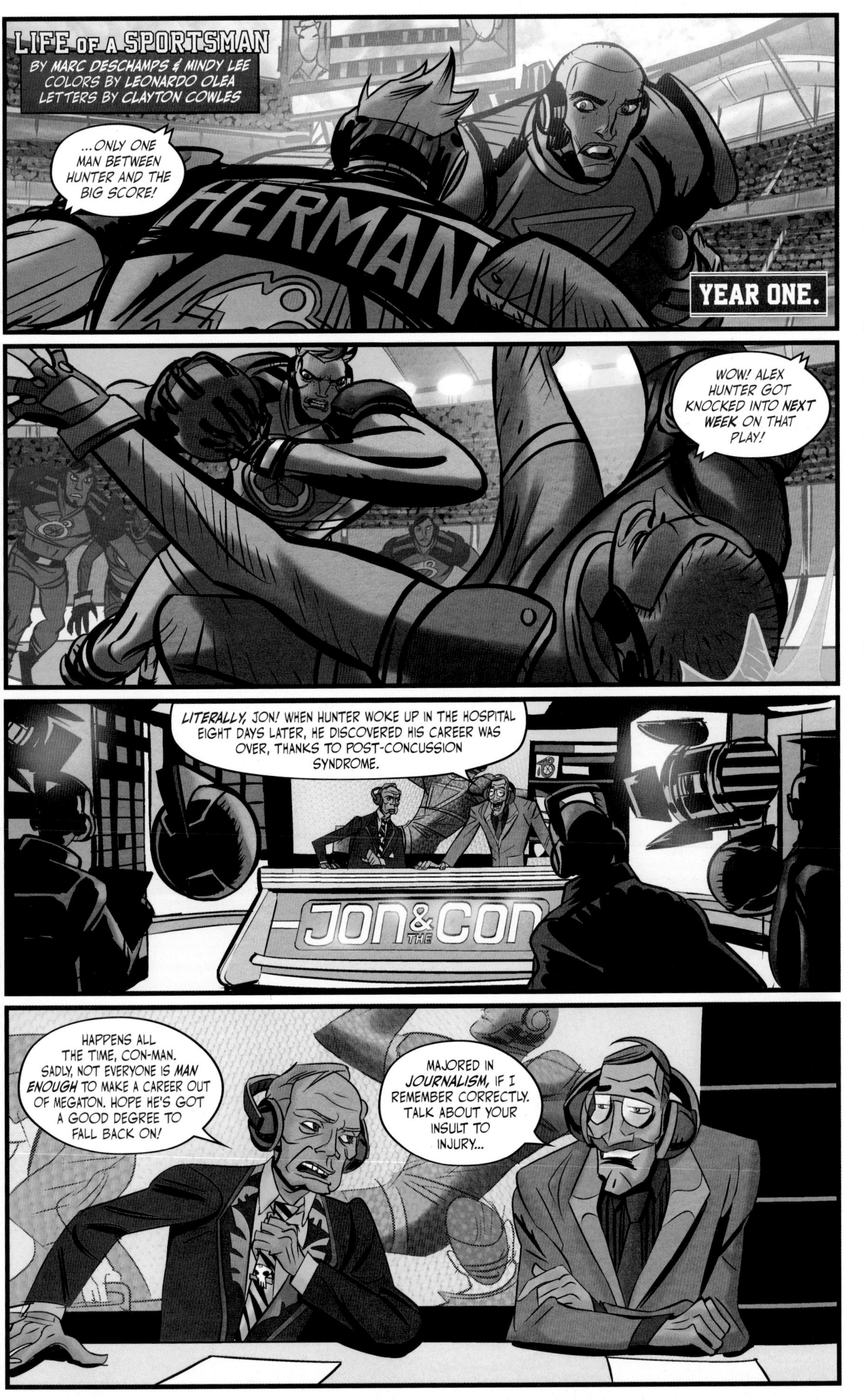
LIFE OF A SPORTSMAN
BY MARC DESCHAMPS & MINDY LEE
COLORS BY LEONARDO OLEA
LETTERS BY CLAYTON COWLES
...ONLY ONE MAN BETWEEN HUNTER AND THE BIG SCORE!
HERMAN
YEAR ONE.
WOW! ALEX HUNTER GOT KNOCKED INTO NEXT WEEK ON THAT PLAY!
LITERALLY, JON! WHEN HUNTER WOKE UP IN THE HOSPITAL EIGHT DAYS LATER, HE DISCOVERED HIS CAREER WAS OVER, THANKS TO POST-CONCUSSION SYNDROME.
JON & THE CON
HAPPENS ALL THE TIME, CON-MAN. SADLY, NOT EVERYONE IS MAN ENOUGH TO MAKE A CAREER OUT OF MEGATON. HOPE HE'S GOT A GOOD DEGREE TO FALL BACK ON!
MAJORED IN JOURNALISM, IF I REMEMBER CORRECTLY. TALK ABOUT YOUR INSULT TO INJURY...

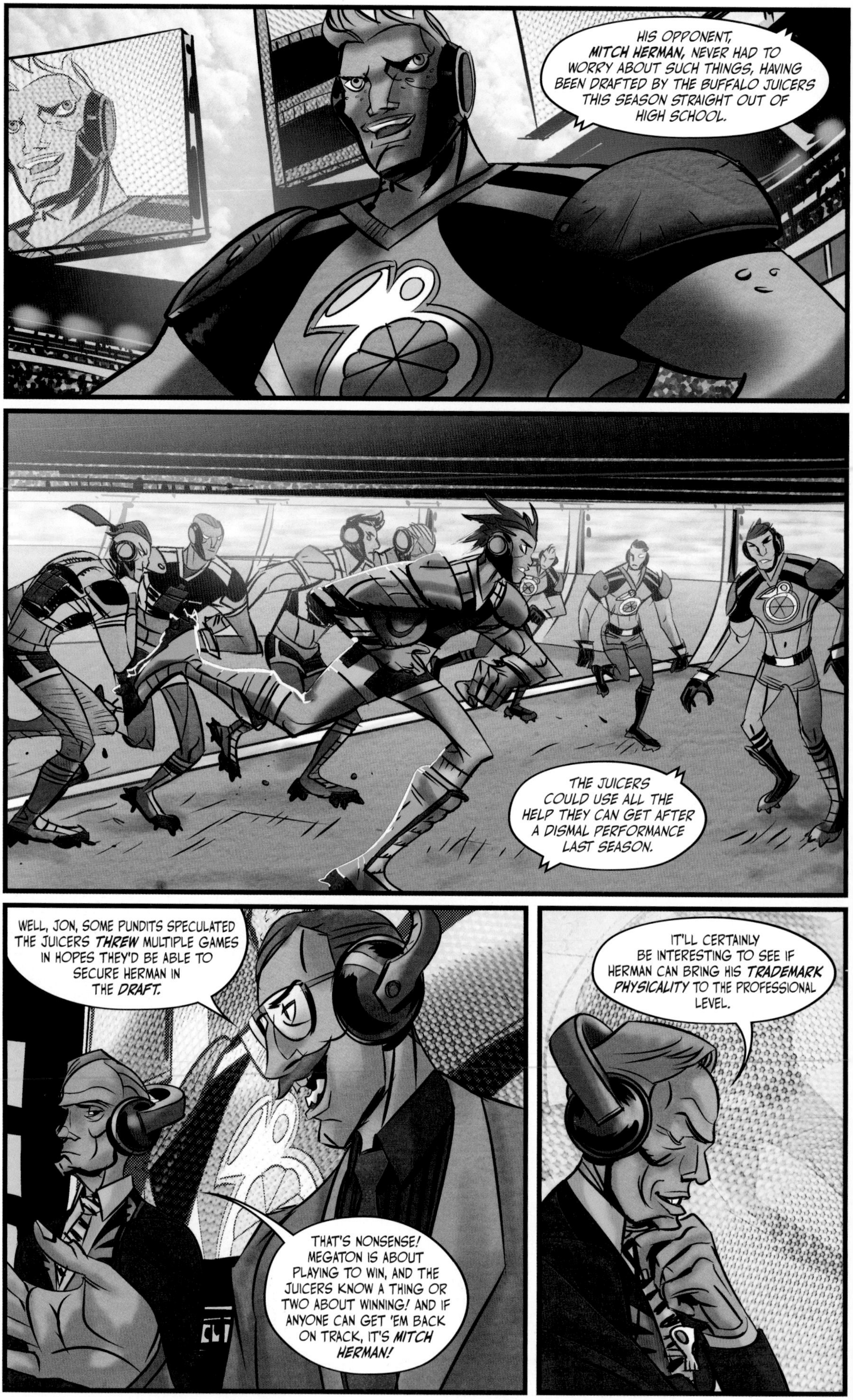
HIS OPPONENT, MITCH HERMAN, NEVER HAD TO WORRY ABOUT SUCH THINGS, HAVING BEEN DRAFTED BY THE BUFFALO JUICERS THIS SEASON STRAIGHT OUT OF HIGH SCHOOL.
THE JUICERS COULD USE ALL THE HELP THEY CAN GET AFTER A DISMAL PERFORMANCE LAST SEASON.
WELL, JON, SOME PUNDITS SPECULATED THE JUICERS THREW MULTIPLE GAMES IN HOPES THEY'D BE ABLE TO SECURE HERMAN IN THE DRAFT.
THAT'S NONSENSE! MEGATON IS ABOUT PLAYING TO WIN, AND THE JUICERS KNOW A THING OR TWO ABOUT WINNING! AND IF ANYONE CAN GET 'EM BACK ON TRACK, IT'S MITCH HERMAN!
IT'LL CERTAINLY BE INTERESTING TO SEE IF HERMAN CAN BRING HIS TRADEMARK PHYSICALITY TO THE PROFESSIONAL LEVEL.

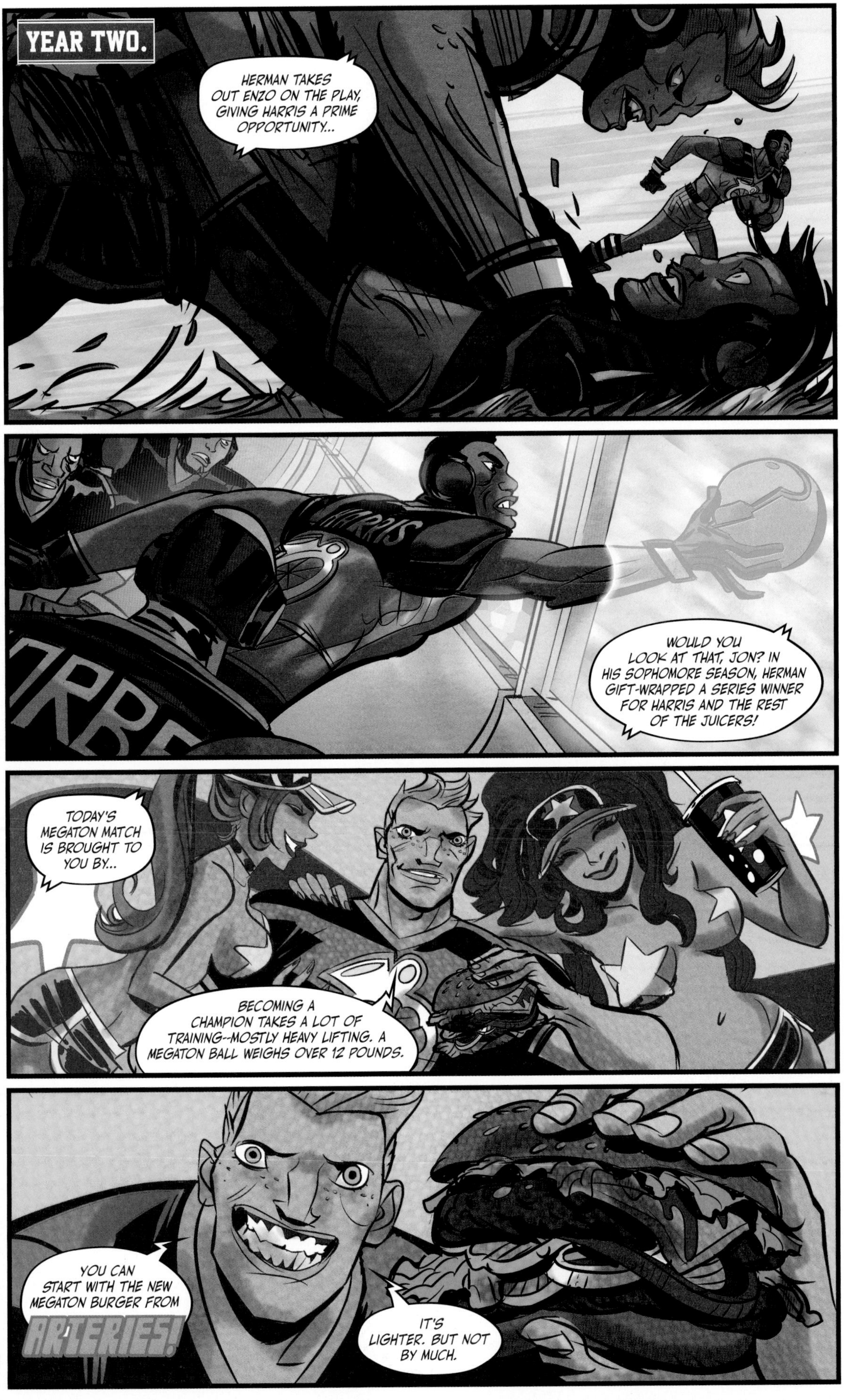
YEAR TWO.
HERMAN TAKES OUT ENZO ON THE PLAY, GIVING HARRIS A PRIME OPPORTUNITY...
HARRIS
WOULD YOU LOOK AT THAT, JON? IN HIS SOPHOMORE SEASON, HERMAN GIFT-WRAPPED A SERIES WINNER FOR HARRIS AND THE REST OF THE JUICERS!
TODAY'S MEGATON MATCH IS BROUGHT TO YOU BY...
BECOMING A CHAMPION TAKES A LOT OF TRAINING--MOSTLY HEAVY LIFTING. A MEGATON BALL WEIGHS OVER 12 POUNDS.
YOU CAN START WITH THE NEW MEGATON BURGER FROM
ARTERIES!
IT'S LIGHTER. BUT NOT BY MUCH.

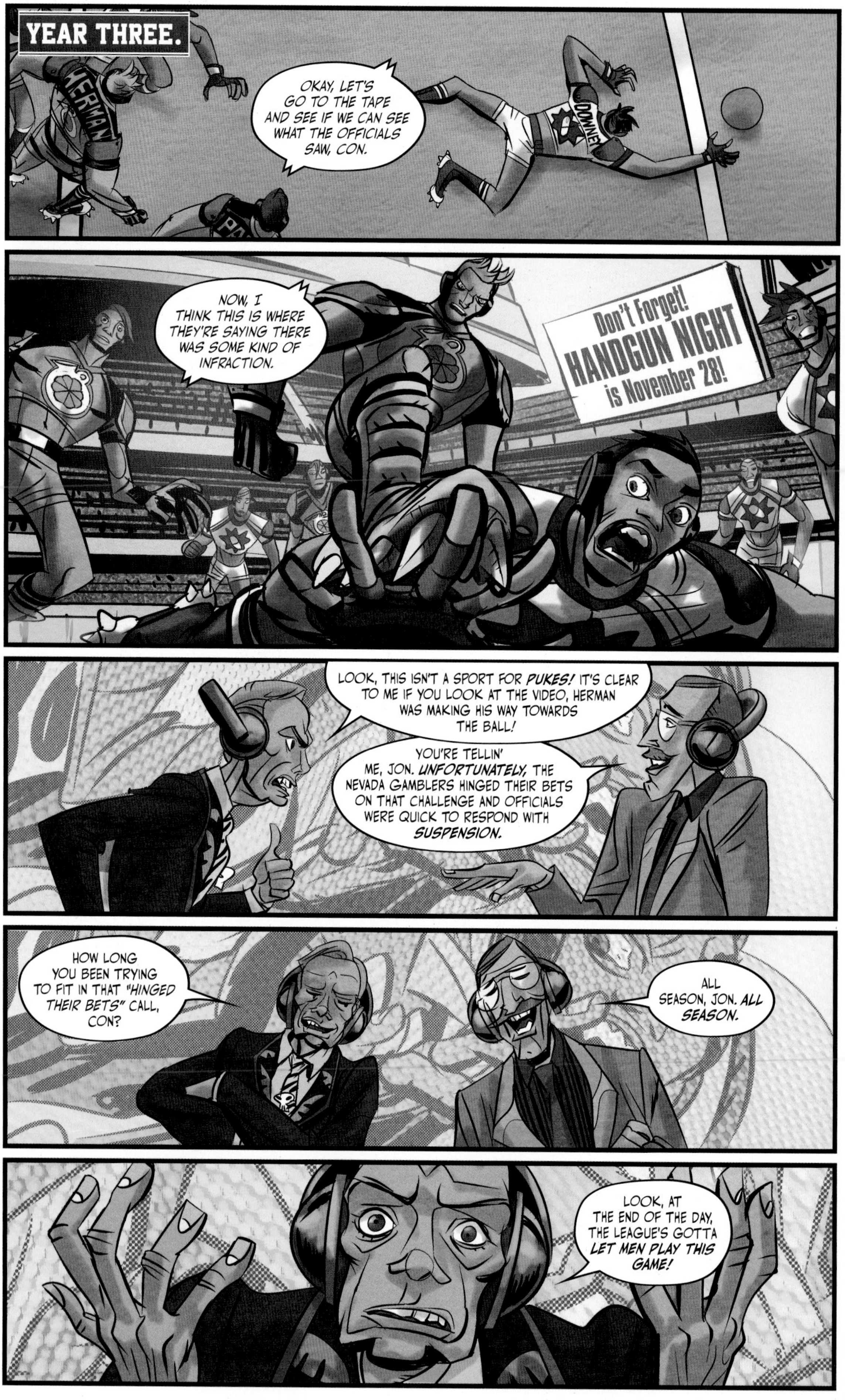
YEAR THREE.
OKAY, LET'S GO TO THE TAPE AND SEE IF WE CAN SEE WHAT THE OFFICIALS SAW, CON.
NOW, I THINK THIS IS WHERE THEY'RE SAYING THERE WAS SOME KIND OF INFRACTION.
Don't Forget! HANDGUN NIGHT is November 28!
LOOK, THIS ISN'T A SPORT FOR PUKES! IT'S CLEAR TO ME IF YOU LOOK AT THE VIDEO, HERMAN WAS MAKING HIS WAY TOWARDS THE BALL!
YOU'RE TELLIN' ME, JON. UNFORTUNATELY, THE NEVADA GAMBLERS HINGED THEIR BETS ON THAT CHALLENGE AND OFFICIALS WERE QUICK TO RESPOND WITH SUSPENSION.
HOW LONG YOU BEEN TRYING TO FIT IN THAT "HINGED THEIR BETS" CALL, CON?
ALL SEASON, JON. ALL SEASON.
LOOK, AT THE END OF THE DAY, THE LEAGUE'S GOTTA LET MEN PLAY THIS GAME!

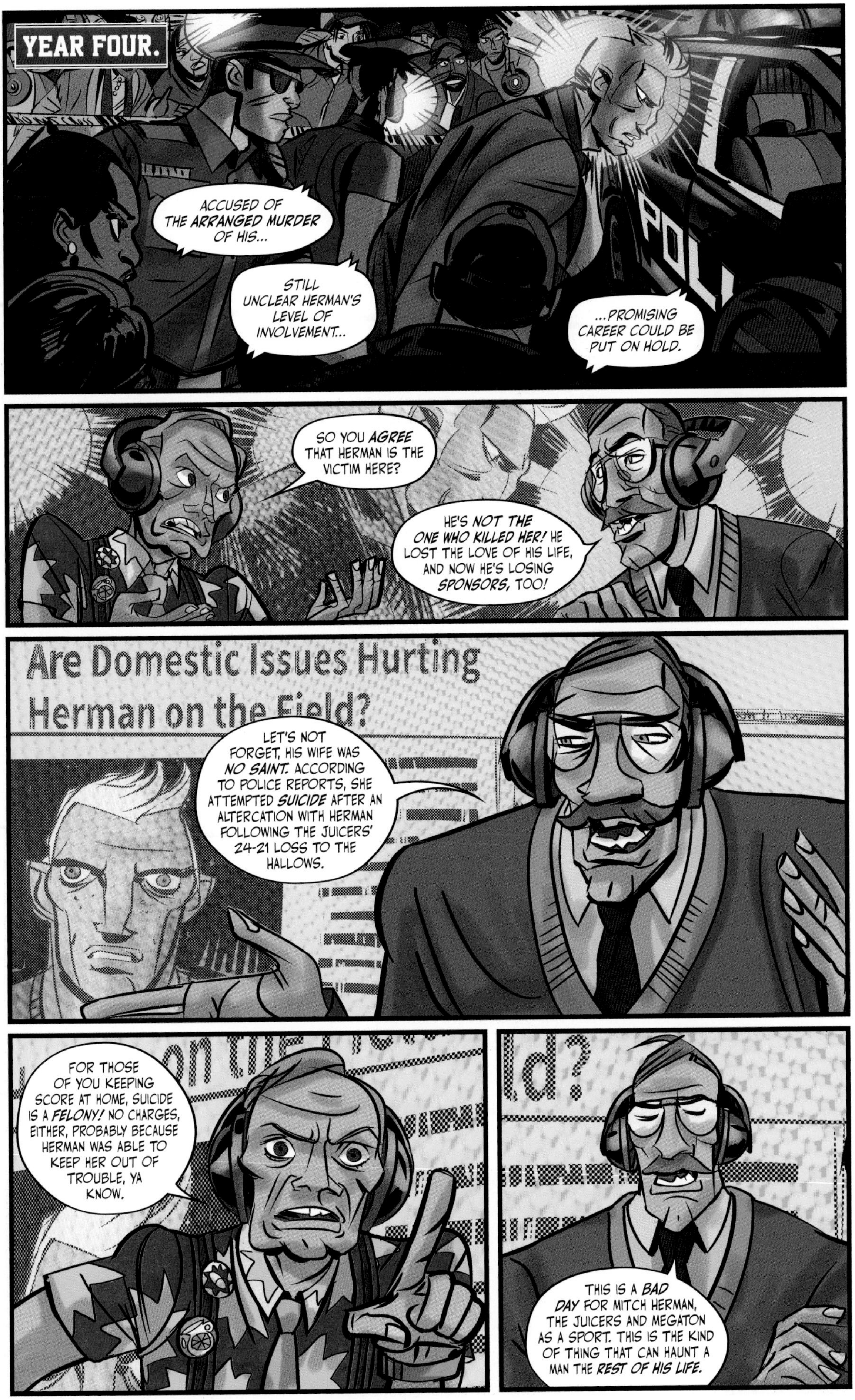
YEAR FOUR.
ACCUSED OF THE ARRANGED MURDER OF HIS...
STILL UNCLEAR HERMAN'S LEVEL OF INVOLVEMENT...
...PROMISING CAREER COULD BE PUT ON HOLD.
POLI
SO YOU AGREE THAT HERMAN IS THE VICTIM HERE?
HE'S NOT THE ONE WHO KILLED HER! HE LOST THE LOVE OF HIS LIFE, AND NOW HE'S LOSING SPONSORS, TOO!
Are Domestic Issues Hurting Herman on the Field?
LET'S NOT FORGET, HIS WIFE WAS NO SAINT. ACCORDING TO POLICE REPORTS, SHE ATTEMPTED SUICIDE AFTER AN ALTERCATION WITH HERMAN FOLLOWING THE JUICERS' 24-21 LOSS TO THE HALLOWS.
FOR THOSE OF YOU KEEPING SCORE AT HOME, SUICIDE IS A FELONY! NO CHARGES, EITHER, PROBABLY BECAUSE HERMAN WAS ABLE TO KEEP HER OUT OF TROUBLE, YA KNOW.
THIS IS A BAD DAY FOR MITCH HERMAN, THE JUICERS AND MEGATON AS A SPORT. THIS IS THE KIND OF THING THAT CAN HAUNT A MAN THE REST OF HIS LIFE.

YEAR SIX.

WOW! HERMAN DIDN'T NEED ANYONE TO DO HIS DIRTY WORK ON *THAT* PLAY!

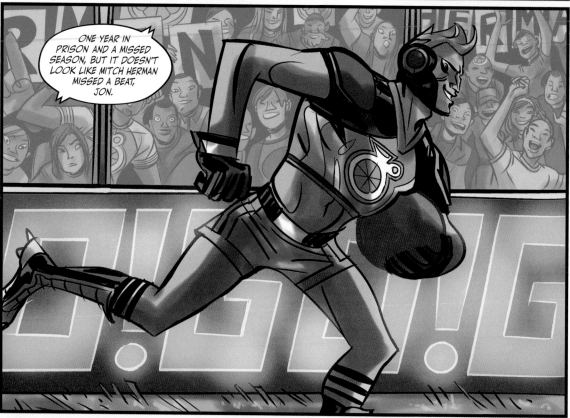

ONE YEAR IN PRISON AND A MISSED SEASON, BUT IT DOESN'T LOOK LIKE MITCH HERMAN MISSED A BEAT, JON.

NOT AT ALL! LOT OF YOUNG UPSTARTS CAME INTO THIS LEAGUE LAST SEASON, AND THEY'RE GONNA LEARN QUICKLY WHY HERMAN IS ONE OF THE *GREATEST OF ALL TIME.*

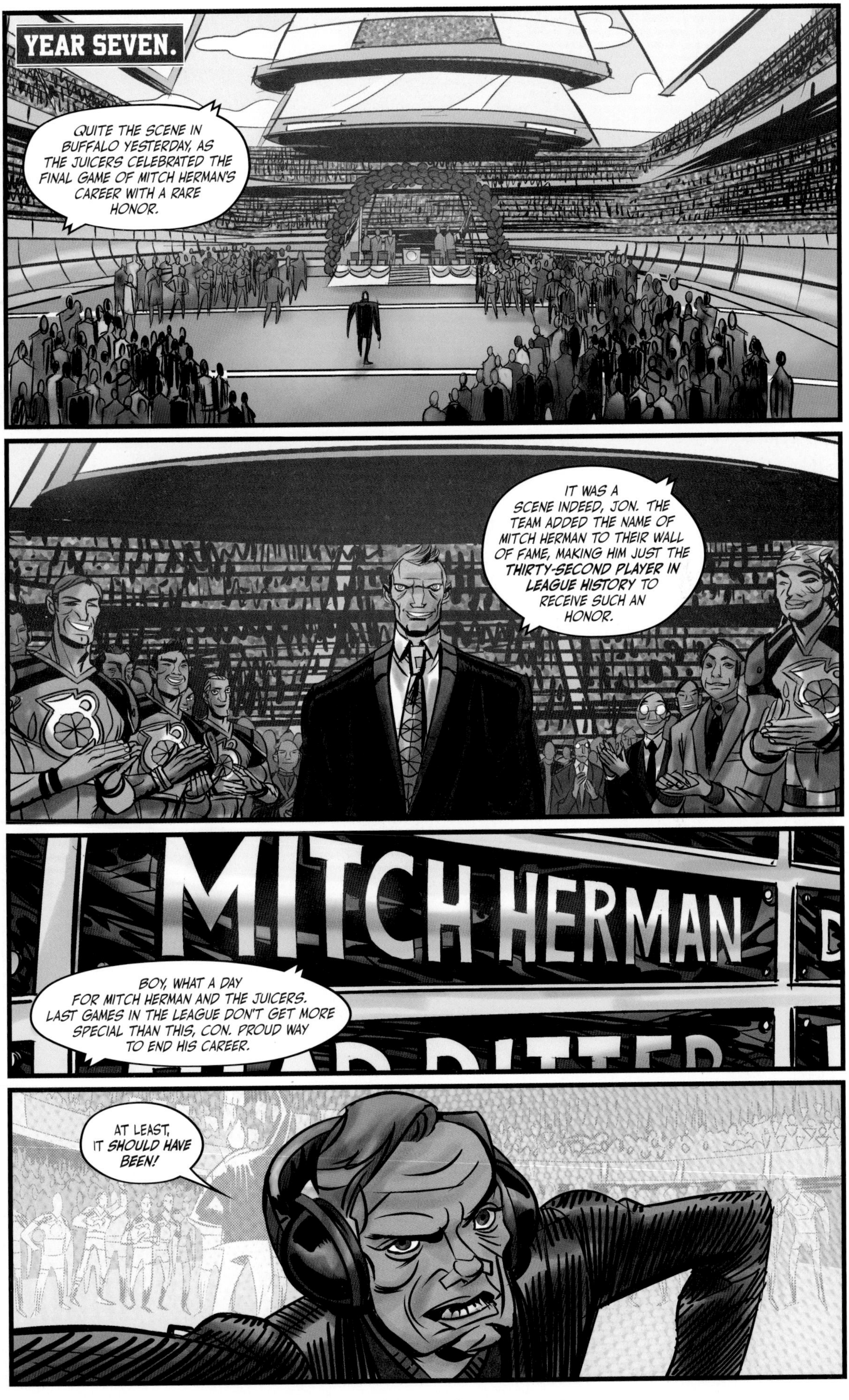
YEAR SEVEN.
QUITE THE SCENE IN BUFFALO YESTERDAY, AS THE JUICERS CELEBRATED THE FINAL GAME OF MITCH HERMAN'S CAREER WITH A RARE HONOR.
IT WAS A SCENE INDEED, JON. THE TEAM ADDED THE NAME OF MITCH HERMAN TO THEIR WALL OF FAME, MAKING HIM JUST THE THIRTY-SECOND PLAYER IN LEAGUE HISTORY TO RECEIVE SUCH AN HONOR.
MITCH HERMAN
BOY, WHAT A DAY FOR MITCH HERMAN AND THE JUICERS. LAST GAMES IN THE LEAGUE DON'T GET MORE SPECIAL THAN THIS, CON. PROUD WAY TO END HIS CAREER.
AT LEAST, IT SHOULD HAVE BEEN!

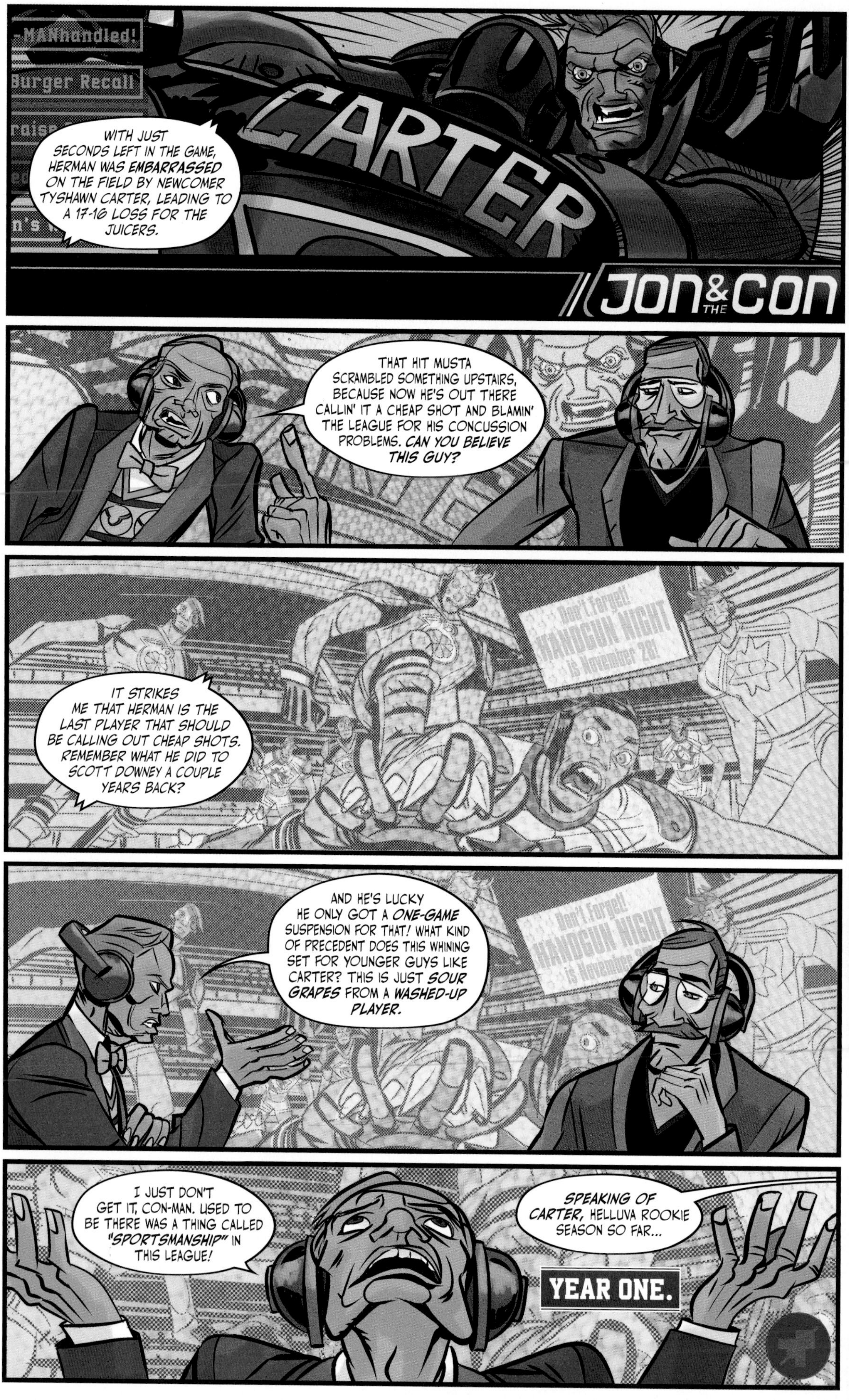

-MANhandled!
Burger Recall
CARTER
WITH JUST SECONDS LEFT IN THE GAME, HERMAN WAS *EMBARRASSED* ON THE FIELD BY NEWCOMER TYSHAWN CARTER, LEADING TO A 17-16 LOSS FOR THE JUICERS.
JON & THE CON
THAT HIT MUSTA SCRAMBLED SOMETHING UPSTAIRS, BECAUSE NOW HE'S OUT THERE CALLIN' IT A CHEAP SHOT AND BLAMIN' THE LEAGUE FOR HIS CONCUSSION PROBLEMS. ***CAN YOU BELIEVE THIS GUY?***
Don't Forget! HANDGUN NIGHT is November 28!
IT STRIKES ME THAT HERMAN IS THE LAST PLAYER THAT SHOULD BE CALLING OUT CHEAP SHOTS. REMEMBER WHAT HE DID TO SCOTT DOWNEY A COUPLE YEARS BACK?
AND HE'S LUCKY HE ONLY GOT A ***ONE-GAME*** SUSPENSION FOR THAT! WHAT KIND OF PRECEDENT DOES THIS WHINING SET FOR YOUNGER GUYS LIKE CARTER? THIS IS JUST ***SOUR GRAPES*** FROM A ***WASHED-UP PLAYER.***
I JUST DON'T GET IT, CON-MAN. USED TO BE THERE WAS A THING CALLED ***"SPORTSMANSHIP"*** IN THIS LEAGUE!
***SPEAKING OF CARTER,*** HELLUVA ROOKIE SEASON SO FAR...
YEAR ONE.

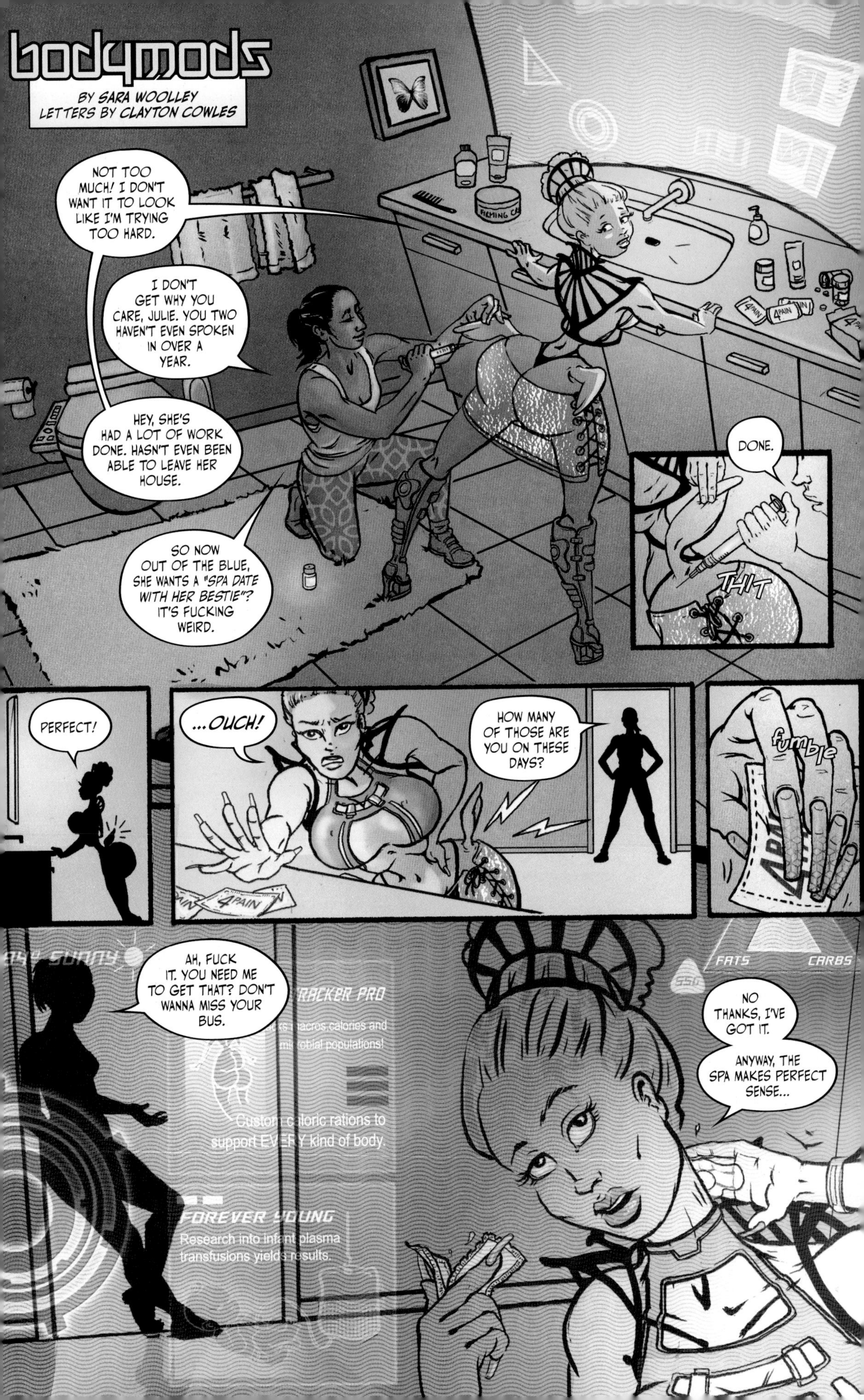
bodymods
BY SARA WOOLLEY
LETTERS BY CLAYTON COWLES
NOT TOO MUCH! I DON'T WANT IT TO LOOK LIKE I'M TRYING TOO HARD.
I DON'T GET WHY YOU CARE, JULIE. YOU TWO HAVEN'T EVEN SPOKEN IN OVER A YEAR.
HEY, SHE'S HAD A LOT OF WORK DONE. HASN'T EVEN BEEN ABLE TO LEAVE HER HOUSE.
SO NOW OUT OF THE BLUE, SHE WANTS A "SPA DATE WITH HER BESTIE"? IT'S FUCKING WEIRD.
DONE.
THIT
PERFECT!
...OUCH!
HOW MANY OF THOSE ARE YOU ON THESE DAYS?
fumble
AH, FUCK IT. YOU NEED ME TO GET THAT? DON'T WANNA MISS YOUR BUS.
FATS
CARBS
NO THANKS, I'VE GOT IT.
ANYWAY, THE SPA MAKES PERFECT SENSE...

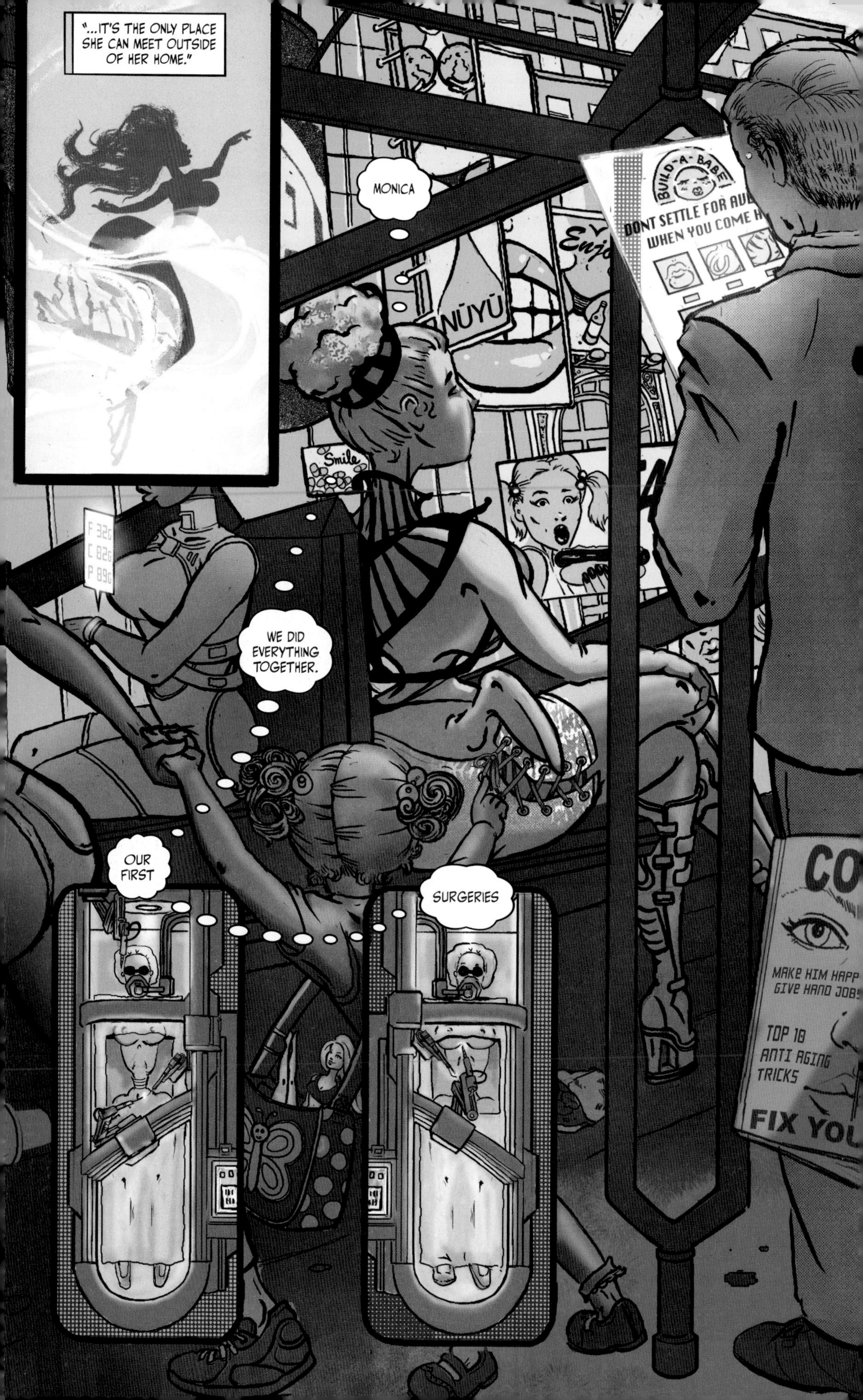
"...IT'S THE ONLY PLACE SHE CAN MEET OUTSIDE OF HER HOME."
MONICA
BUILD-A-BABE
DONT SETTLE FOR AVE
WHEN YOU COME H
NŪYŪ
Smile
F 32¢
C 82¢
P 89¢
WE DID EVERYTHING TOGETHER.
OUR FIRST
SURGERIES
CO
MAKE HIM HAPP
GIVE HAND JOBS
TOP 10 ANTI AGING TRICKS
FIX YOU

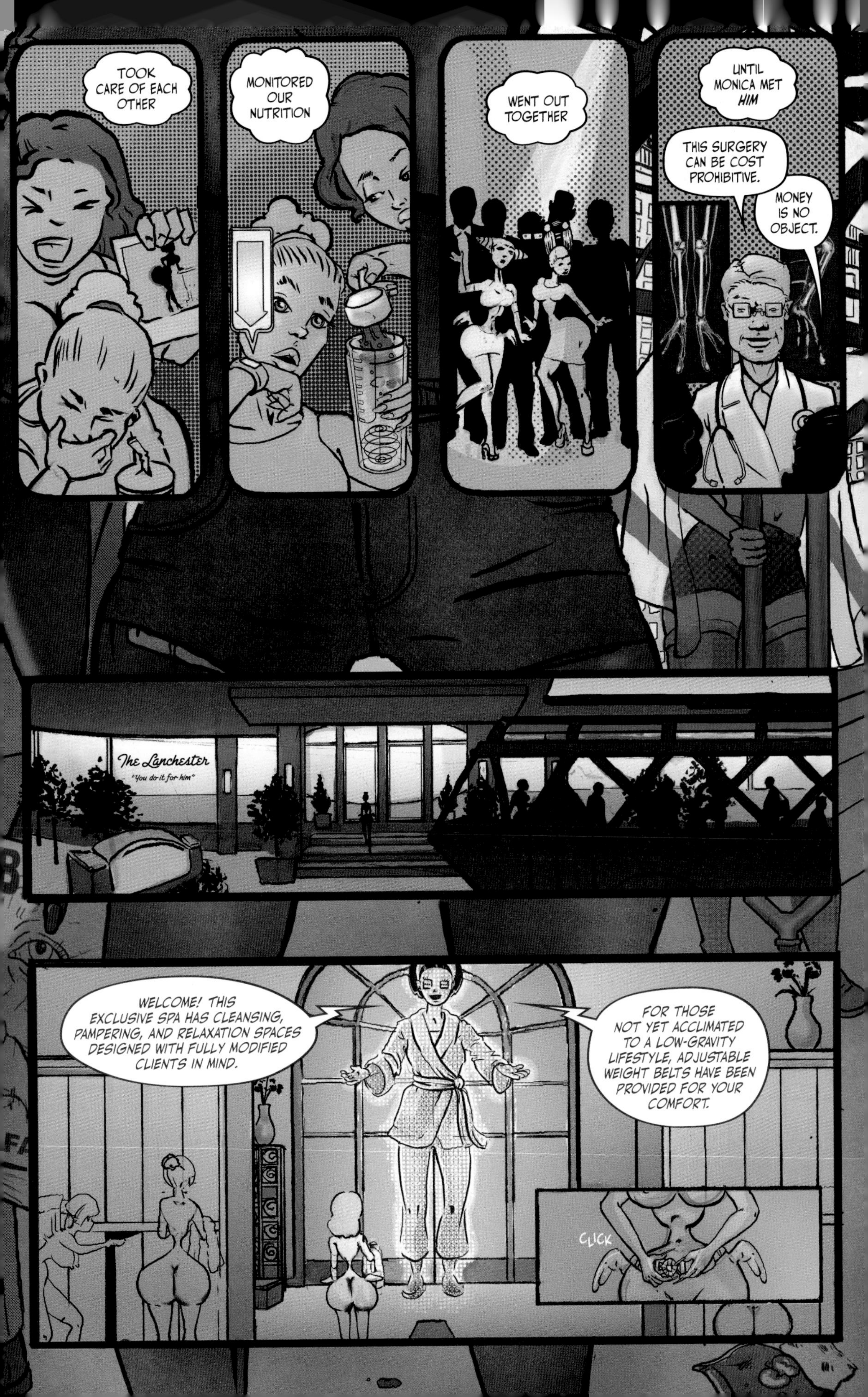
TOOK CARE OF EACH OTHER
MONITORED OUR NUTRITION
WENT OUT TOGETHER
UNTIL MONICA MET *HIM*
THIS SURGERY CAN BE COST PROHIBITIVE.
MONEY IS NO OBJECT.
The Lanchester
"You do it for him"
WELCOME! THIS EXCLUSIVE SPA HAS CLEANSING, PAMPERING, AND RELAXATION SPACES DESIGNED WITH FULLY MODIFIED CLIENTS IN MIND.
FOR THOSE NOT YET ACCLIMATED TO A LOW-GRAVITY LIFESTYLE, ADJUSTABLE WEIGHT BELTS HAVE BEEN PROVIDED FOR YOUR COMFORT.
CLICK

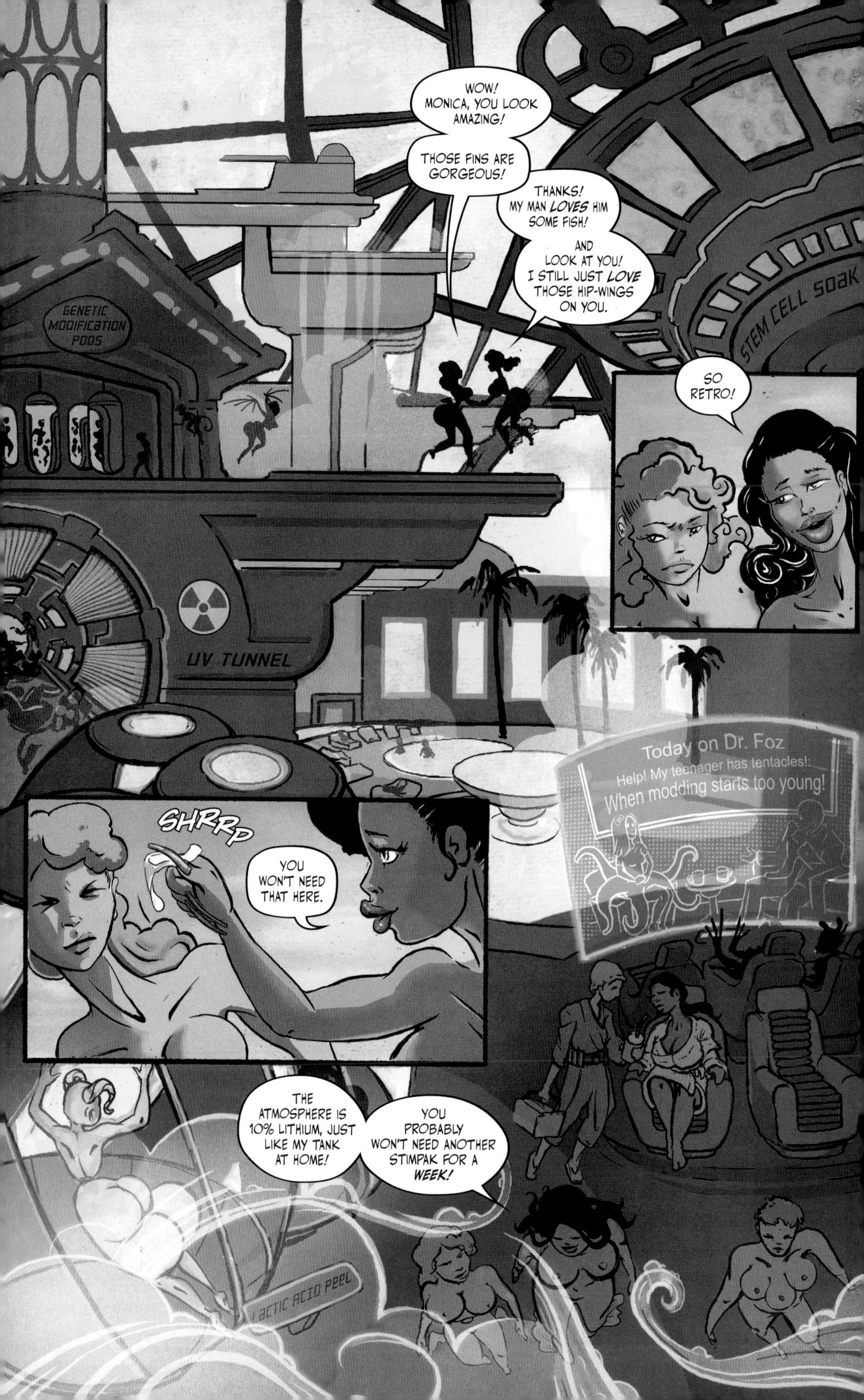
WOW! MONICA, YOU LOOK AMAZING!
THOSE FINS ARE GORGEOUS!
THANKS! MY MAN LOVES HIM SOME FISH!
AND LOOK AT YOU! I STILL JUST LOVE THOSE HIP-WINGS ON YOU.
GENETIC MODIFICATION PODS
STEM CELL SOAK
SO RETRO!
UV TUNNEL
Today on Dr. Foz
Help! My teenager has tentacles!
When modding starts too young!
SHRRP
YOU WON'T NEED THAT HERE.
THE ATMOSPHERE IS 10% LITHIUM, JUST LIKE MY TANK AT HOME!
YOU PROBABLY WON'T NEED ANOTHER STIMPAK FOR A WEEK!
LACTIC ACID PEEL

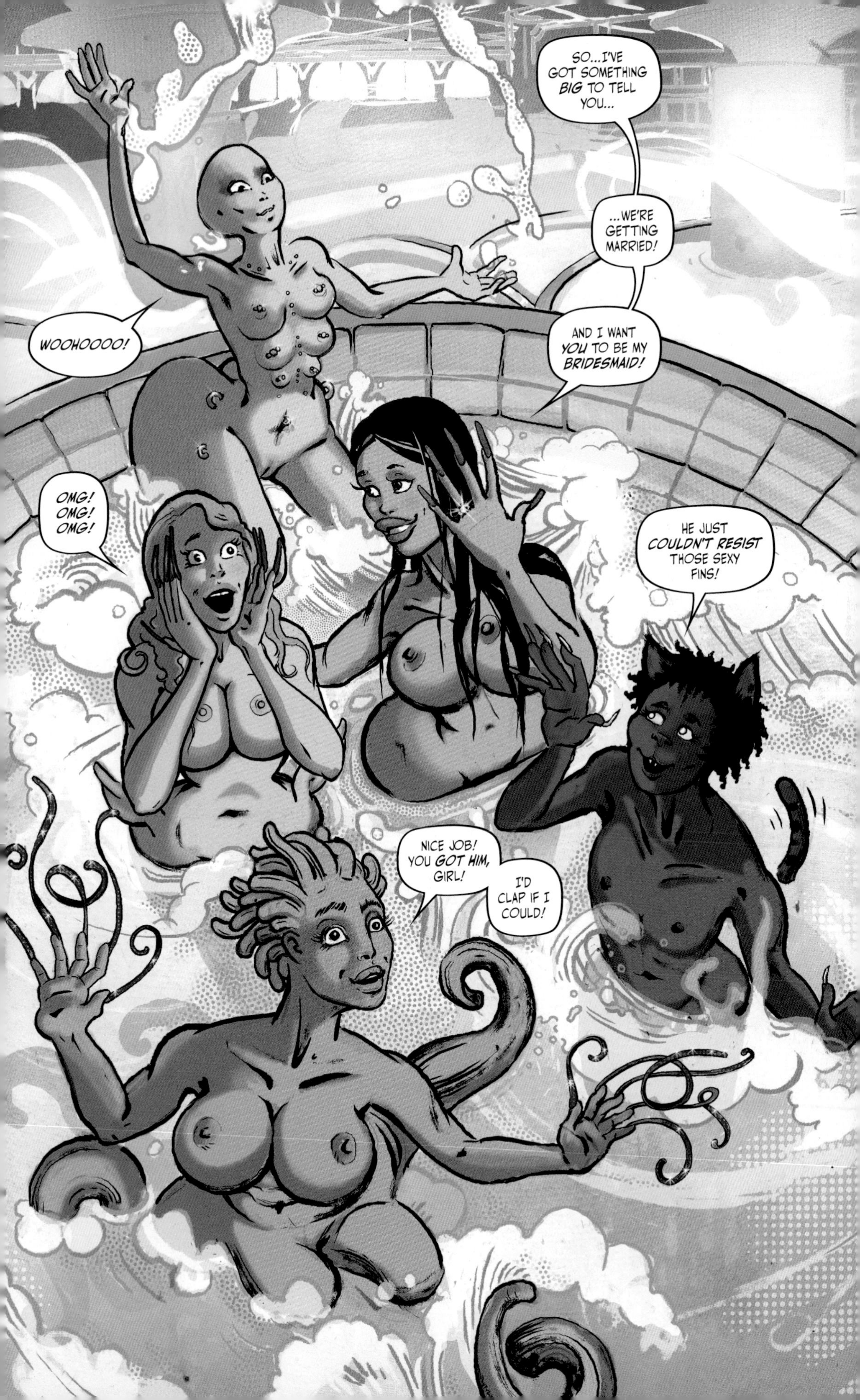
SO...I'VE GOT SOMETHING *BIG* TO TELL YOU...
...WE'RE GETTING MARRIED!
WOOHOOOO!
AND I WANT *YOU* TO BE MY *BRIDESMAID!*
OMG! OMG! OMG!
HE JUST *COULDN'T RESIST* THOSE SEXY FINS!
NICE JOB! YOU *GOT HIM,* GIRL!
I'D CLAP IF I COULD!

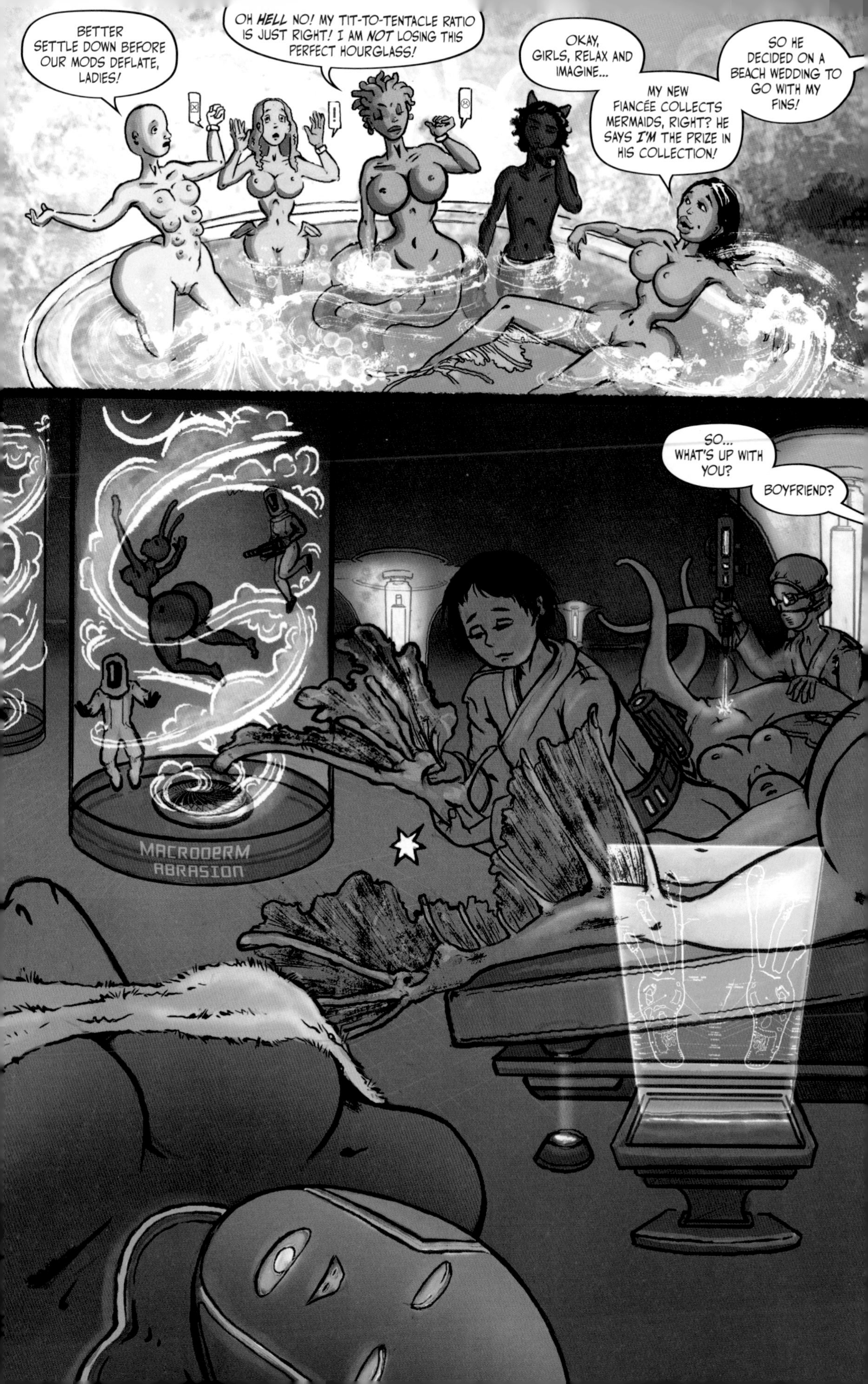
BETTER SETTLE DOWN BEFORE OUR MODS DEFLATE, LADIES!
OH **HELL** NO! MY TIT-TO-TENTACLE RATIO IS JUST RIGHT! I AM **NOT** LOSING THIS PERFECT HOURGLASS!
!
OKAY, GIRLS, RELAX AND IMAGINE...
MY NEW FIANCÉE COLLECTS MERMAIDS, RIGHT? HE SAYS **I'M** THE PRIZE IN HIS COLLECTION!
SO HE DECIDED ON A BEACH WEDDING TO GO WITH MY FINS!
SO... WHAT'S UP WITH YOU?
BOYFRIEND?
MACRODERM ABRASION

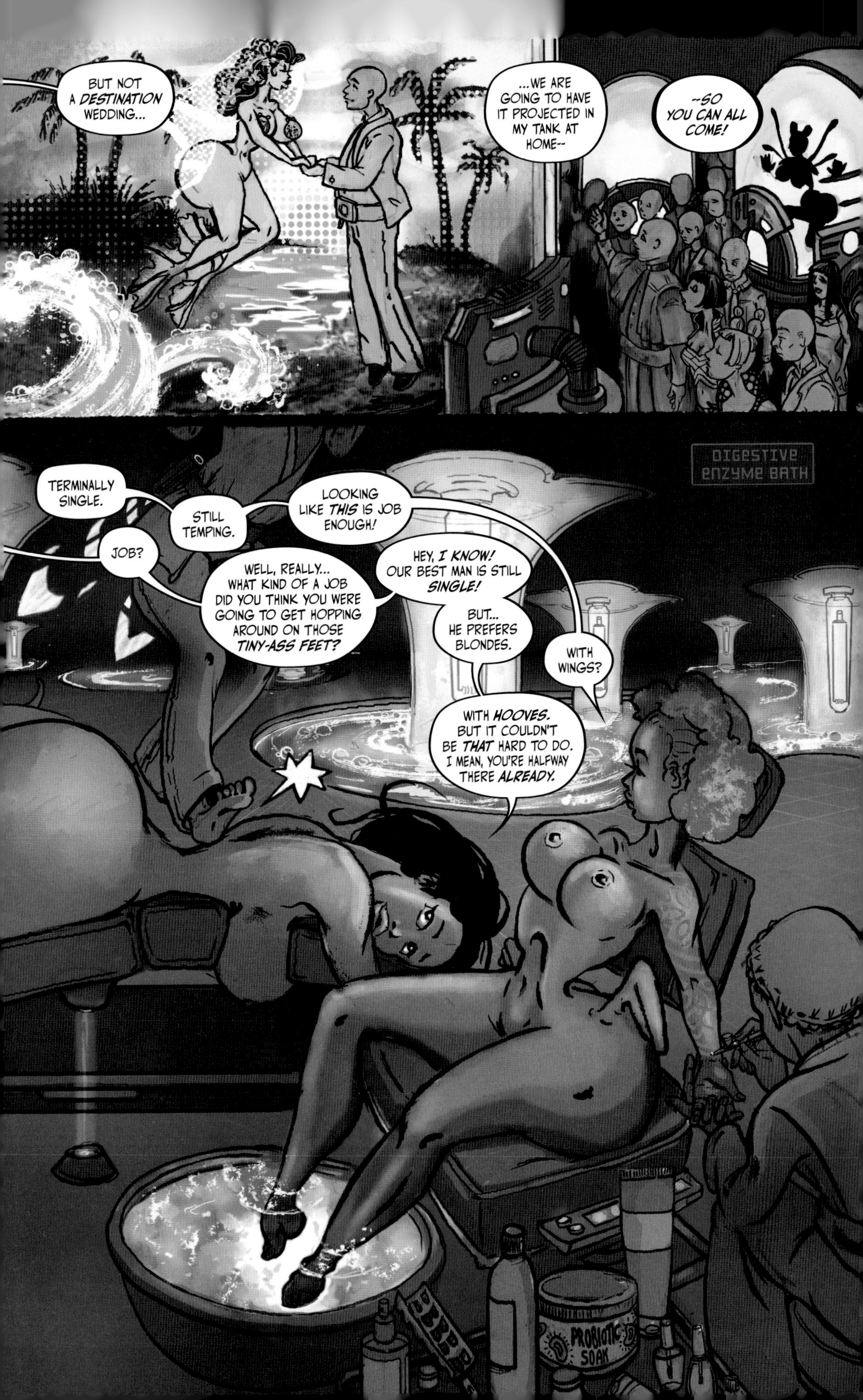
BUT NOT A *DESTINATION* WEDDING...
...WE ARE GOING TO HAVE IT PROJECTED IN MY TANK AT HOME--
--SO YOU CAN ALL COME!
DIGESTIVE ENZYME BATH
TERMINALLY SINGLE.
STILL TEMPING.
LOOKING LIKE *THIS* IS JOB ENOUGH!
JOB?
WELL, REALLY... WHAT KIND OF A JOB DID YOU THINK YOU WERE GOING TO GET HOPPING AROUND ON THOSE *TINY-ASS FEET?*
HEY, *I KNOW!* OUR BEST MAN IS STILL *SINGLE!*
BUT... HE PREFERS BLONDES.
WITH WINGS?
WITH *HOOVES.* BUT IT COULDN'T BE *THAT* HARD TO DO. I MEAN, YOU'RE HALFWAY THERE *ALREADY.*
PROBIOTIC SOAK

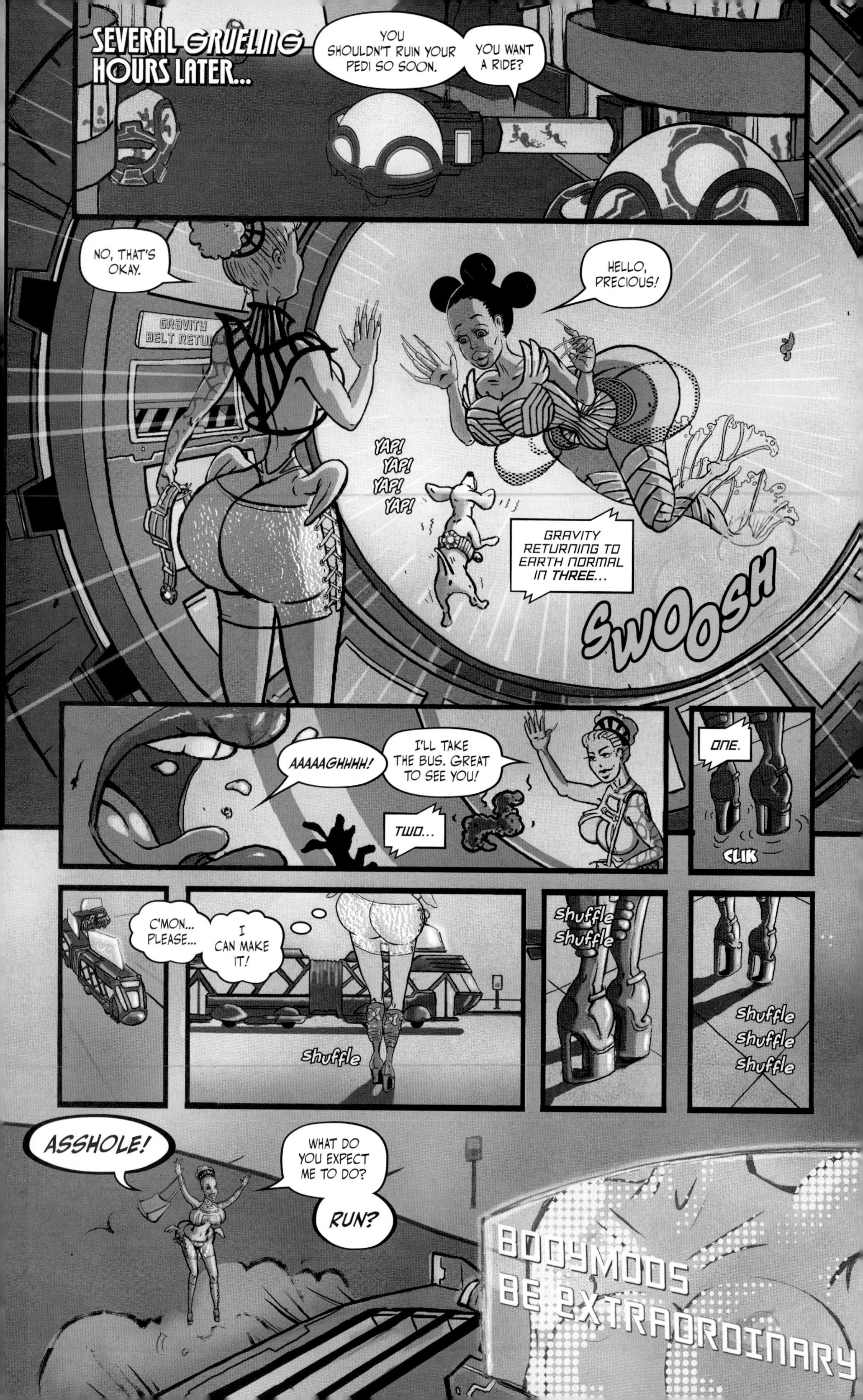

SEVERAL GRUELING HOURS LATER...
YOU SHOULDN'T RUIN YOUR PEDI SO SOON.
YOU WANT A RIDE?
NO, THAT'S OKAY.
HELLO, PRECIOUS!
GRAVITY BELT RETUR
YAP! YAP! YAP! YAP!
GRAVITY RETURNING TO EARTH NORMAL IN THREE...
SWOOSH
AAAAAGHHHH!
I'LL TAKE THE BUS. GREAT TO SEE YOU!
TWO...
ONE.
CLIK
C'MON... PLEASE...
I CAN MAKE IT!
Shuffle
shuffle shuffle
Shuffle Shuffle Shuffle
ASSHOLE!
WHAT DO YOU EXPECT ME TO DO?
RUN?
BODYMODS BE EXTRAORDINARY

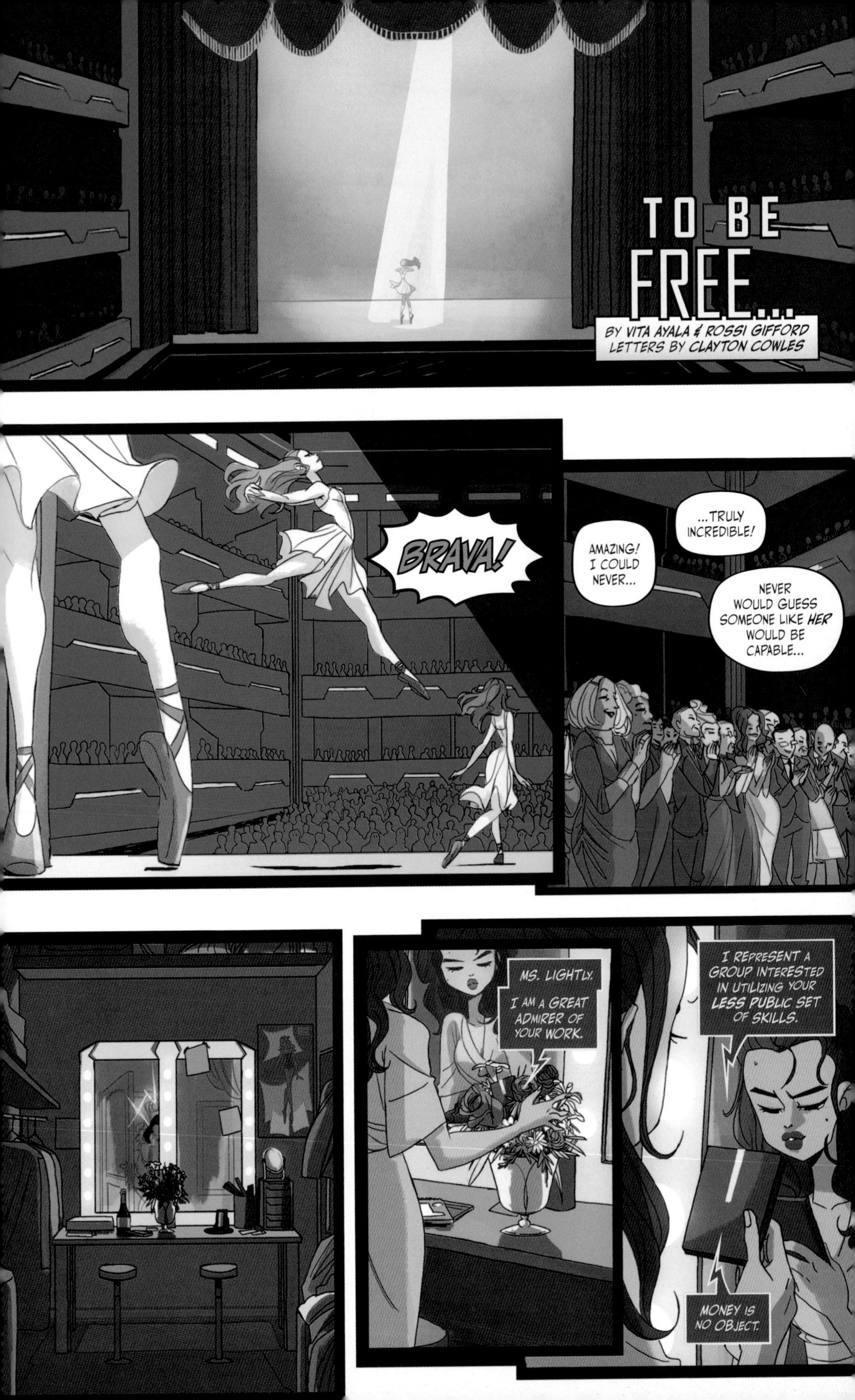
TO BE FREE...
BY VITA AYALA & ROSSI GIFFORD
LETTERS BY CLAYTON COWLES
BRAVA!
AMAZING! I COULD NEVER...
...TRULY INCREDIBLE!
NEVER WOULD GUESS SOMEONE LIKE HER WOULD BE CAPABLE...
MS. LIGHTLY.
I AM A GREAT ADMIRER OF YOUR WORK.
I REPRESENT A GROUP INTERESTED IN UTILIZING YOUR LESS PUBLIC SET OF SKILLS.
MONEY IS NO OBJECT.

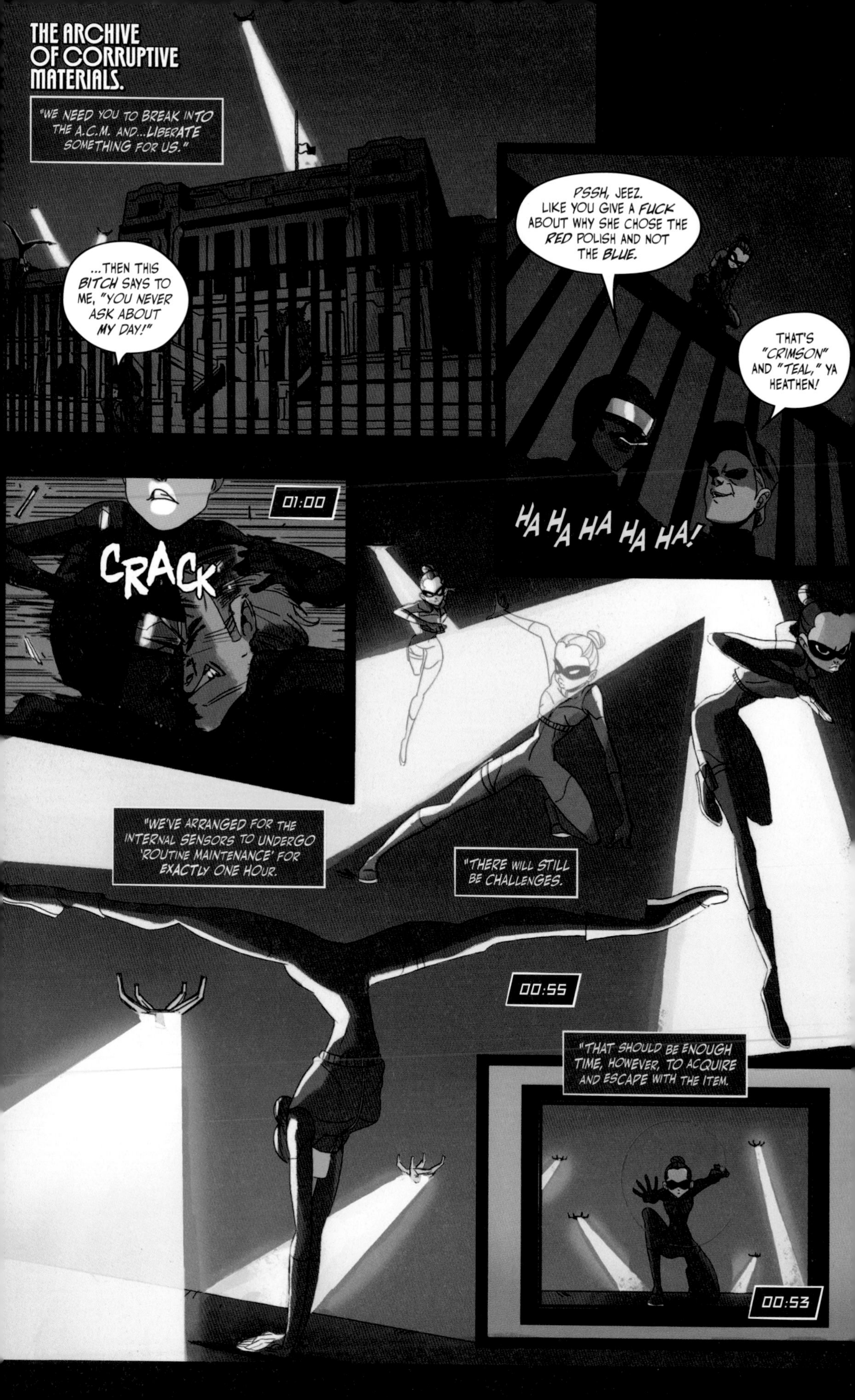
THE ARCHIVE OF CORRUPTIVE MATERIALS.
"WE NEED YOU TO BREAK INTO THE A.C.M. AND...LIBERATE SOMETHING FOR US."
...THEN THIS BITCH SAYS TO ME, "YOU NEVER ASK ABOUT MY DAY!"
PSSH, JEEZ. LIKE YOU GIVE A FUCK ABOUT WHY SHE CHOSE THE RED POLISH AND NOT THE BLUE.
THAT'S "CRIMSON" AND "TEAL," YA HEATHEN!
HA HA HA HA HA!
01:00
CRACK
"WE'VE ARRANGED FOR THE INTERNAL SENSORS TO UNDERGO 'ROUTINE MAINTENANCE' FOR EXACTLY ONE HOUR.
"THERE WILL STILL BE CHALLENGES.
00:55
"THAT SHOULD BE ENOUGH TIME, HOWEVER, TO ACQUIRE AND ESCAPE WITH THE ITEM.
00:53

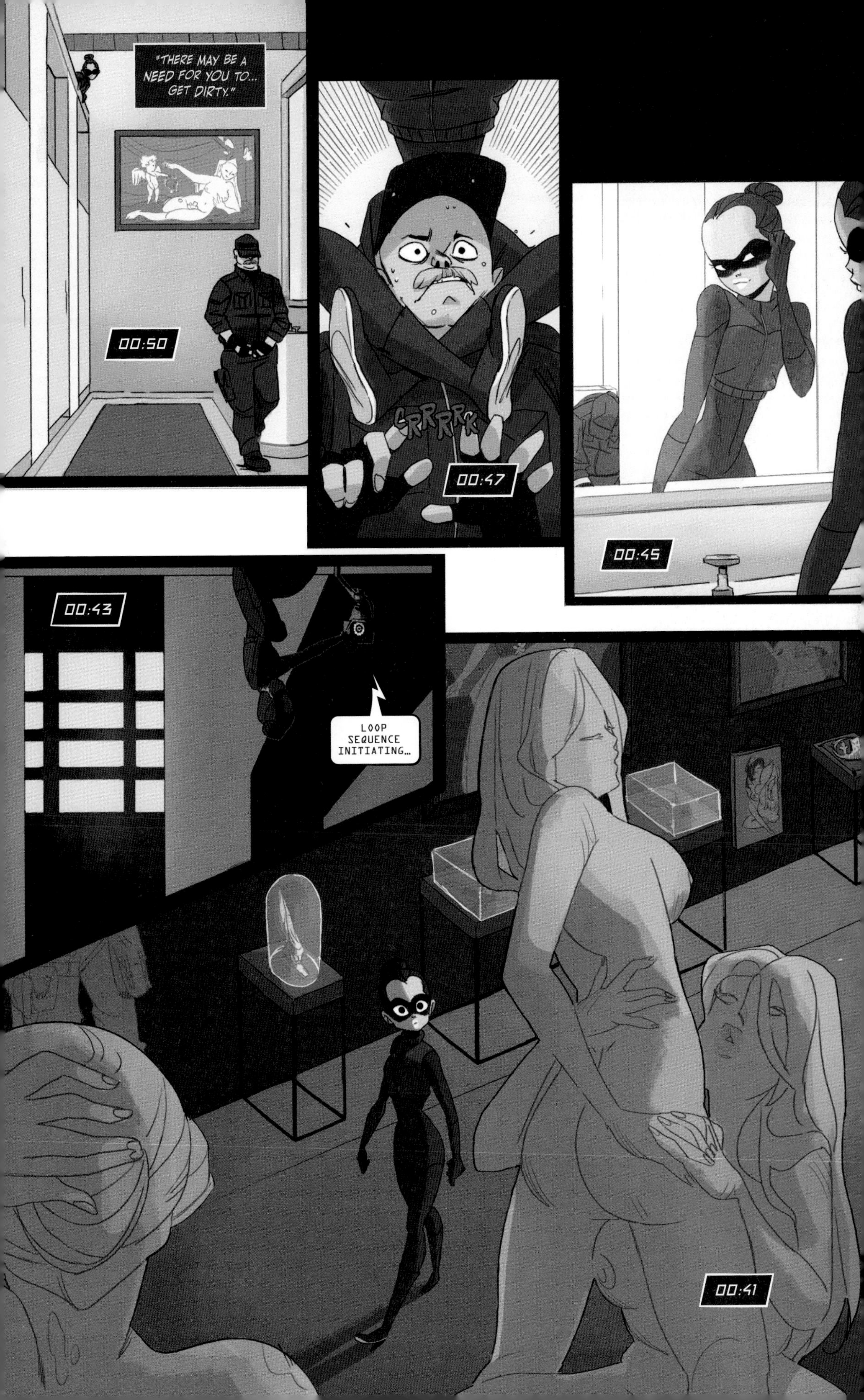
"THERE MAY BE A NEED FOR YOU TO... GET DIRTY."
00:50
CRRRRK
00:47
00:45
00:43
LOOP SEQUENCE INITIATING...
00:41

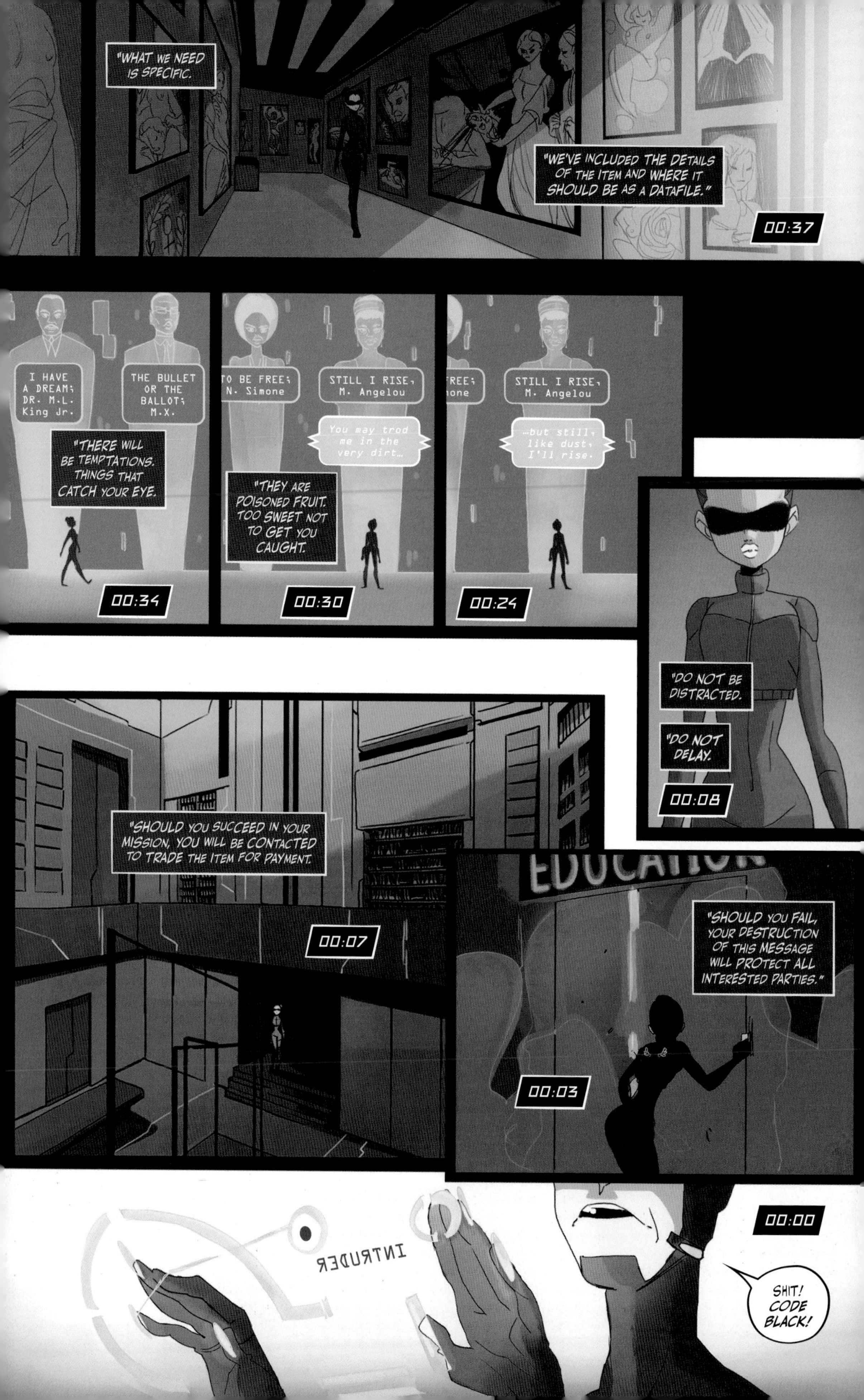
"WHAT WE NEED IS SPECIFIC.
"WE'VE INCLUDED THE DETAILS OF THE ITEM AND WHERE IT SHOULD BE AS A DATAFILE."
00:37
I HAVE A DREAM; DR. M.L. King Jr.
THE BULLET OR THE BALLOT; M.X.
"THERE WILL BE TEMPTATIONS. THINGS THAT CATCH YOUR EYE.
00:34
TO BE FREE; N. Simone
STILL I RISE, M. Angelou
You may trod me in the very dirt…
"THEY ARE POISONED FRUIT. TOO SWEET NOT TO GET YOU CAUGHT.
00:30
STILL I RISE, M. Angelou
…but still, like dust, I'll rise.
00:24
"DO NOT BE DISTRACTED.
"DO NOT DELAY.
00:08
"SHOULD YOU SUCCEED IN YOUR MISSION, YOU WILL BE CONTACTED TO TRADE THE ITEM FOR PAYMENT.
00:07
"SHOULD YOU FAIL, YOUR DESTRUCTION OF THIS MESSAGE WILL PROTECT ALL INTERESTED PARTIES."
00:03
00:00
INTRUDER
SHIT! CODE BLACK!

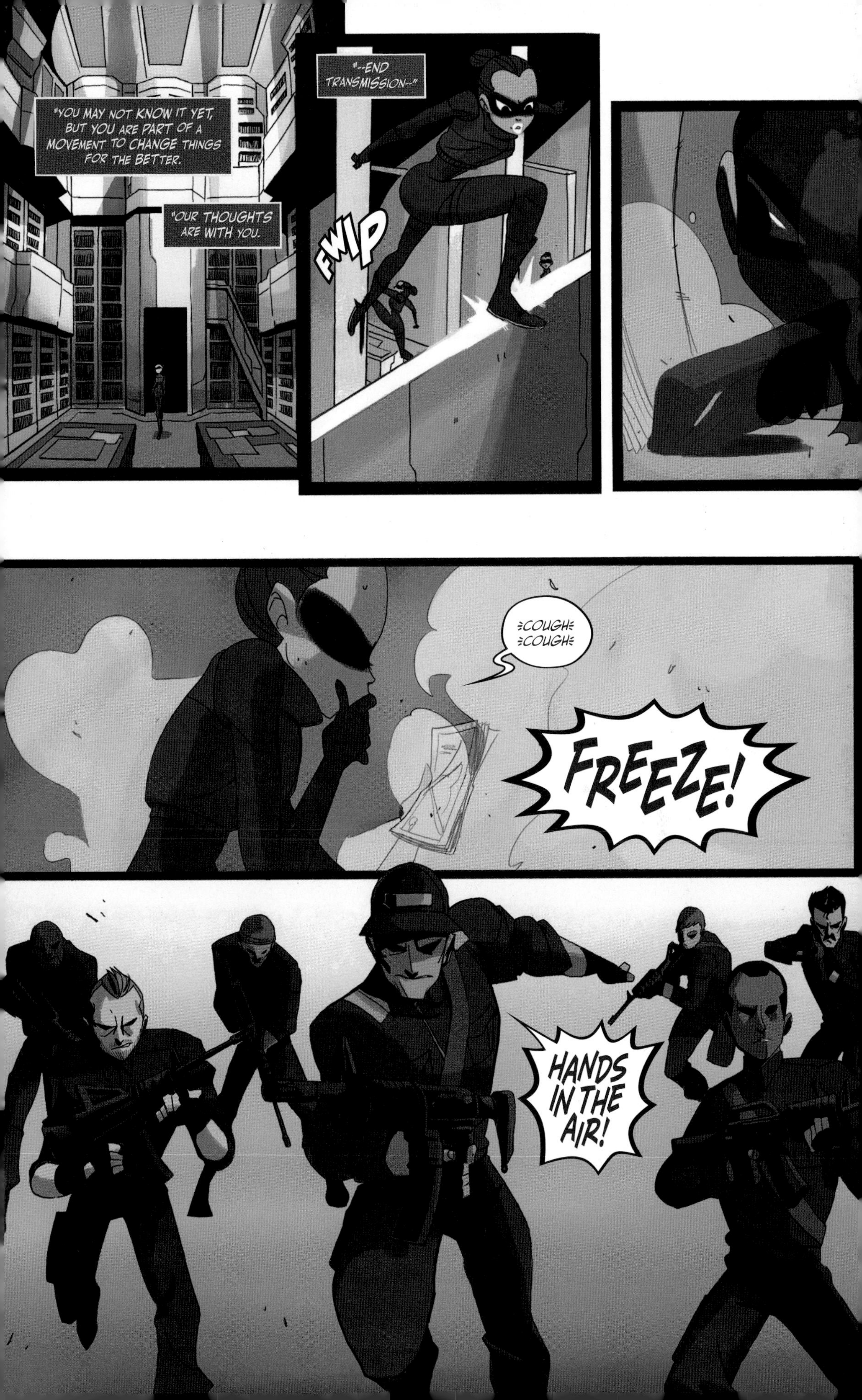
"YOU MAY NOT KNOW IT YET, BUT YOU ARE PART OF A MOVEMENT TO CHANGE THINGS FOR THE BETTER.
"OUR THOUGHTS ARE WITH YOU.
"--END TRANSMISSION--"
FWIP
COUGH COUGH
FREEZE!
HANDS IN THE AIR!

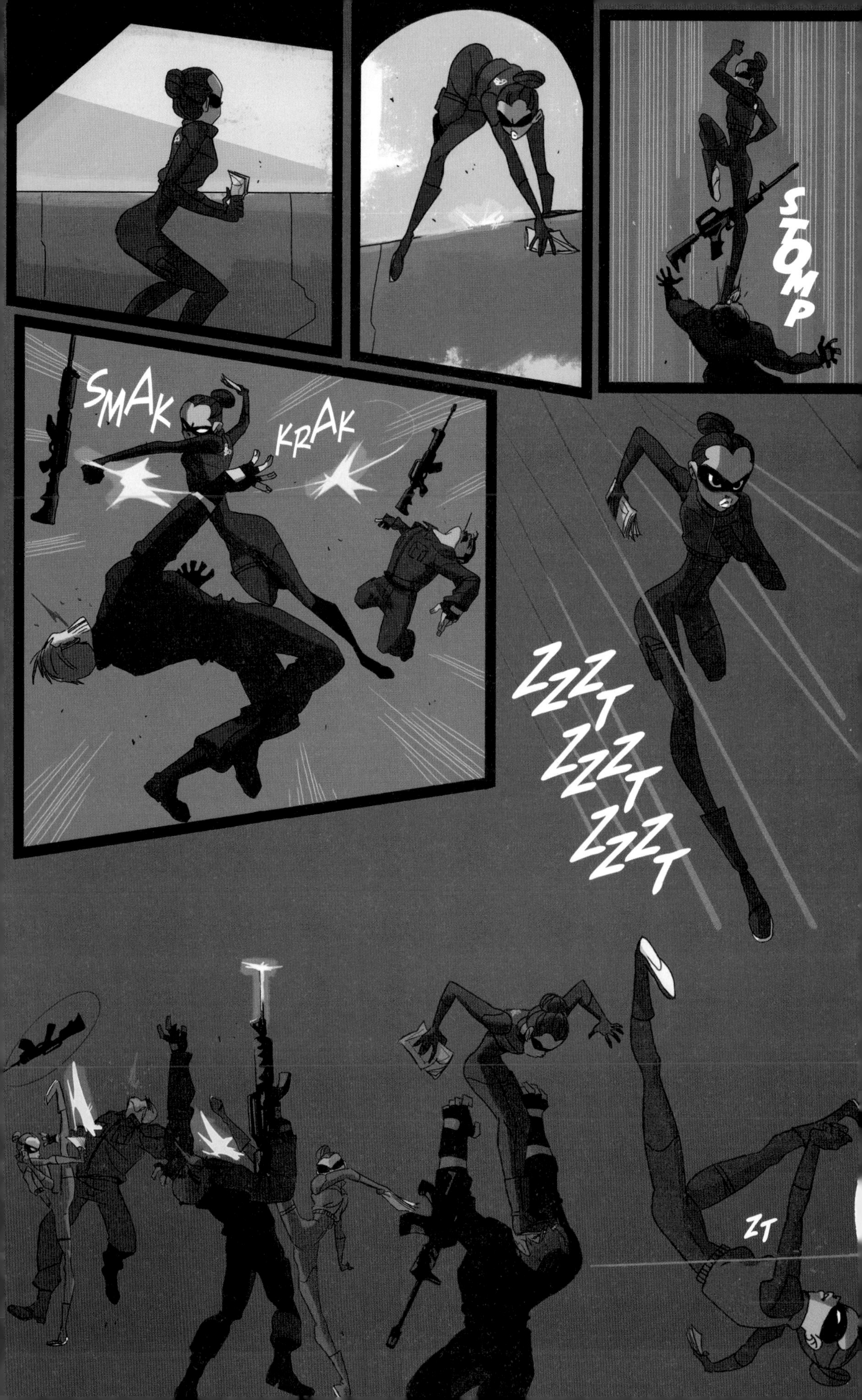
STOMP
SMAK
KRAK
ZZZT
ZZZT
ZZZT
ZT

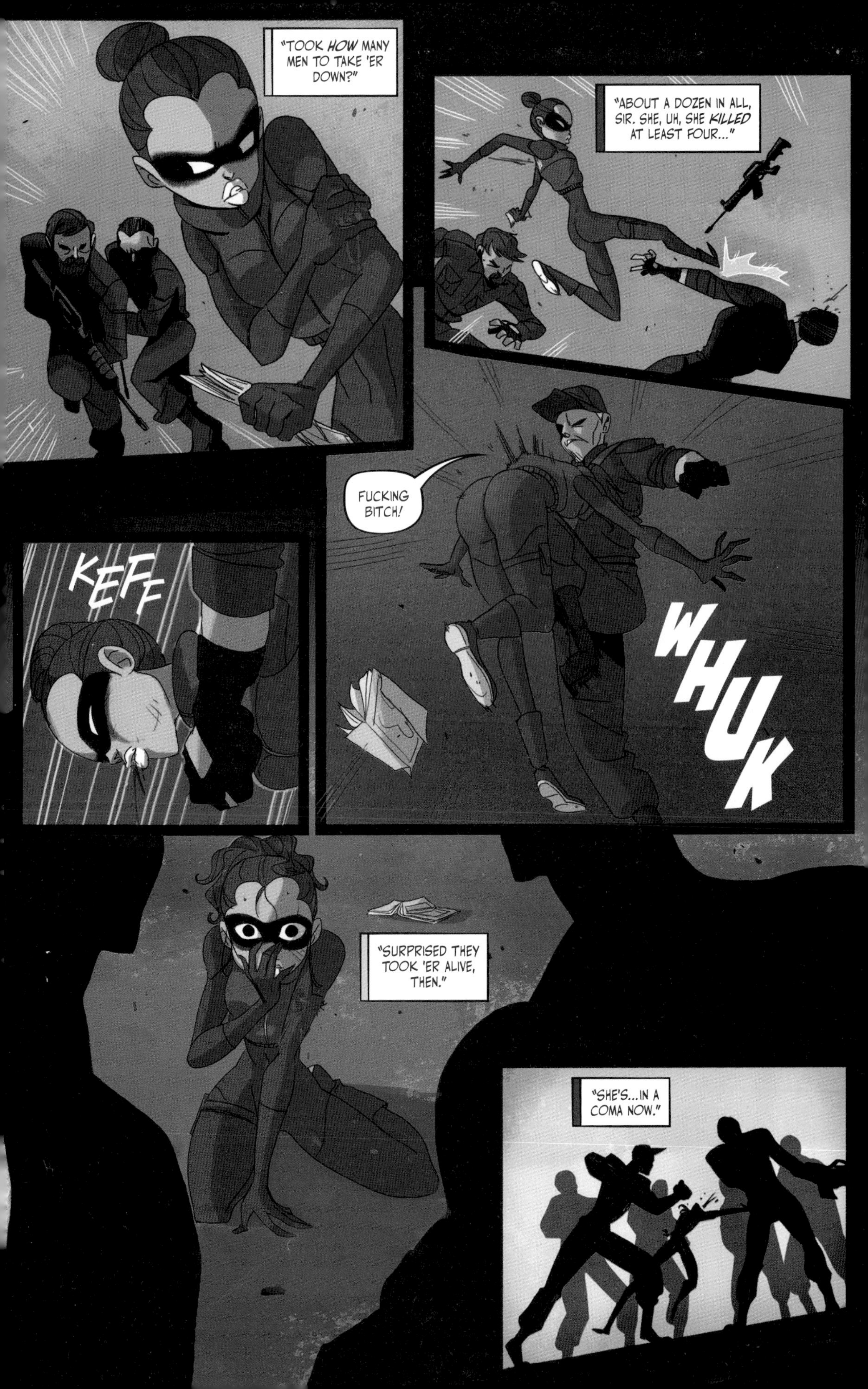
"TOOK HOW MANY MEN TO TAKE 'ER DOWN?"
"ABOUT A DOZEN IN ALL, SIR. SHE, UH, SHE KILLED AT LEAST FOUR..."
FUCKING BITCH!
WHUK
KEFF
"SURPRISED THEY TOOK 'ER ALIVE, THEN."
"SHE'S...IN A COMA NOW."

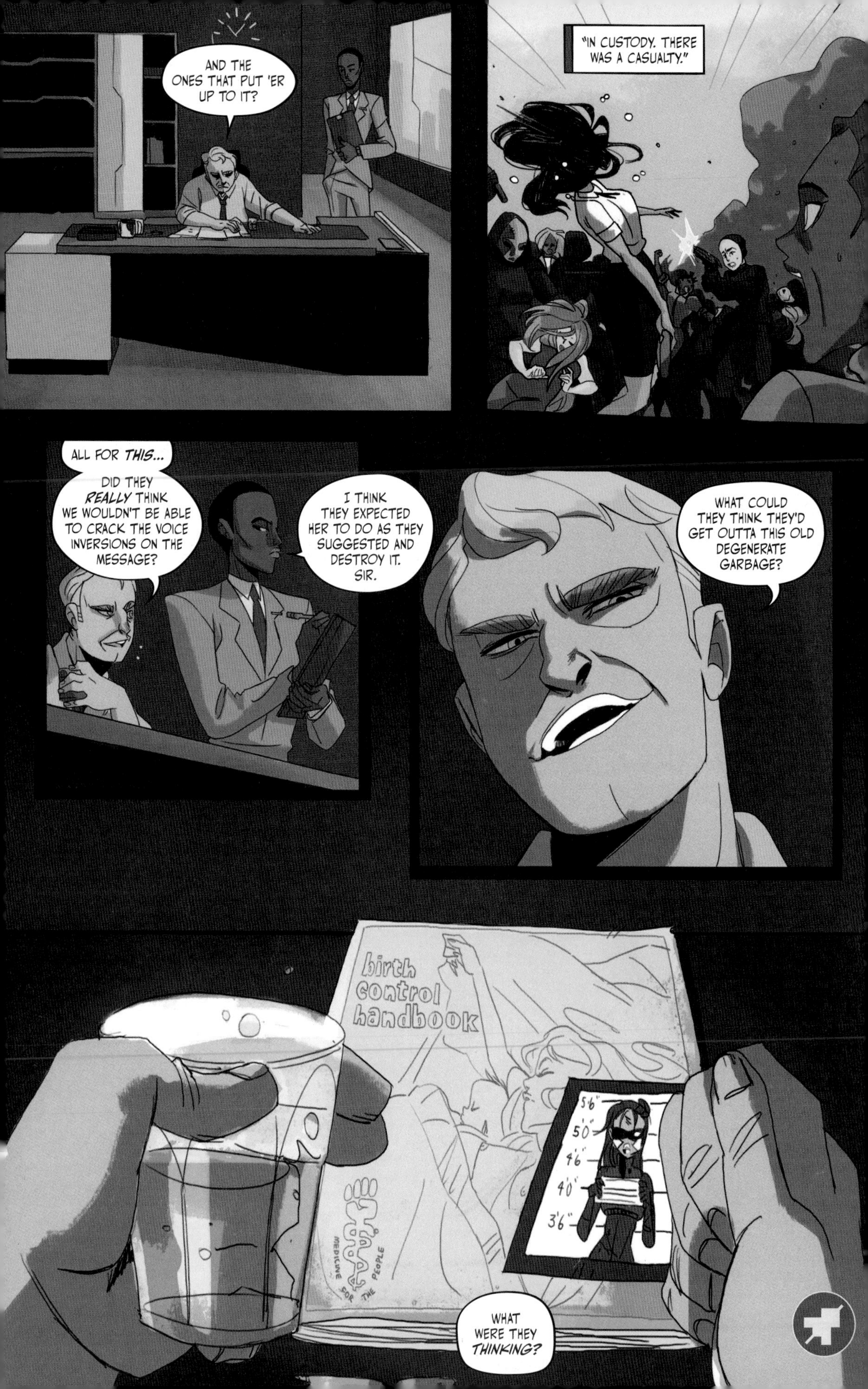
AND THE ONES THAT PUT 'ER UP TO IT?
"IN CUSTODY. THERE WAS A CASUALTY."
ALL FOR *THIS...*
DID THEY *REALLY* THINK WE WOULDN'T BE ABLE TO CRACK THE VOICE INVERSIONS ON THE MESSAGE?
I THINK THEY EXPECTED HER TO DO AS THEY SUGGESTED AND DESTROY IT. SIR.
WHAT COULD THEY THINK THEY'D GET OUTTA THIS OLD DEGENERATE GARBAGE?
birth control handbook
MEDICINE FOR THE PEOPLE
WHAT WERE THEY *THINKING?*

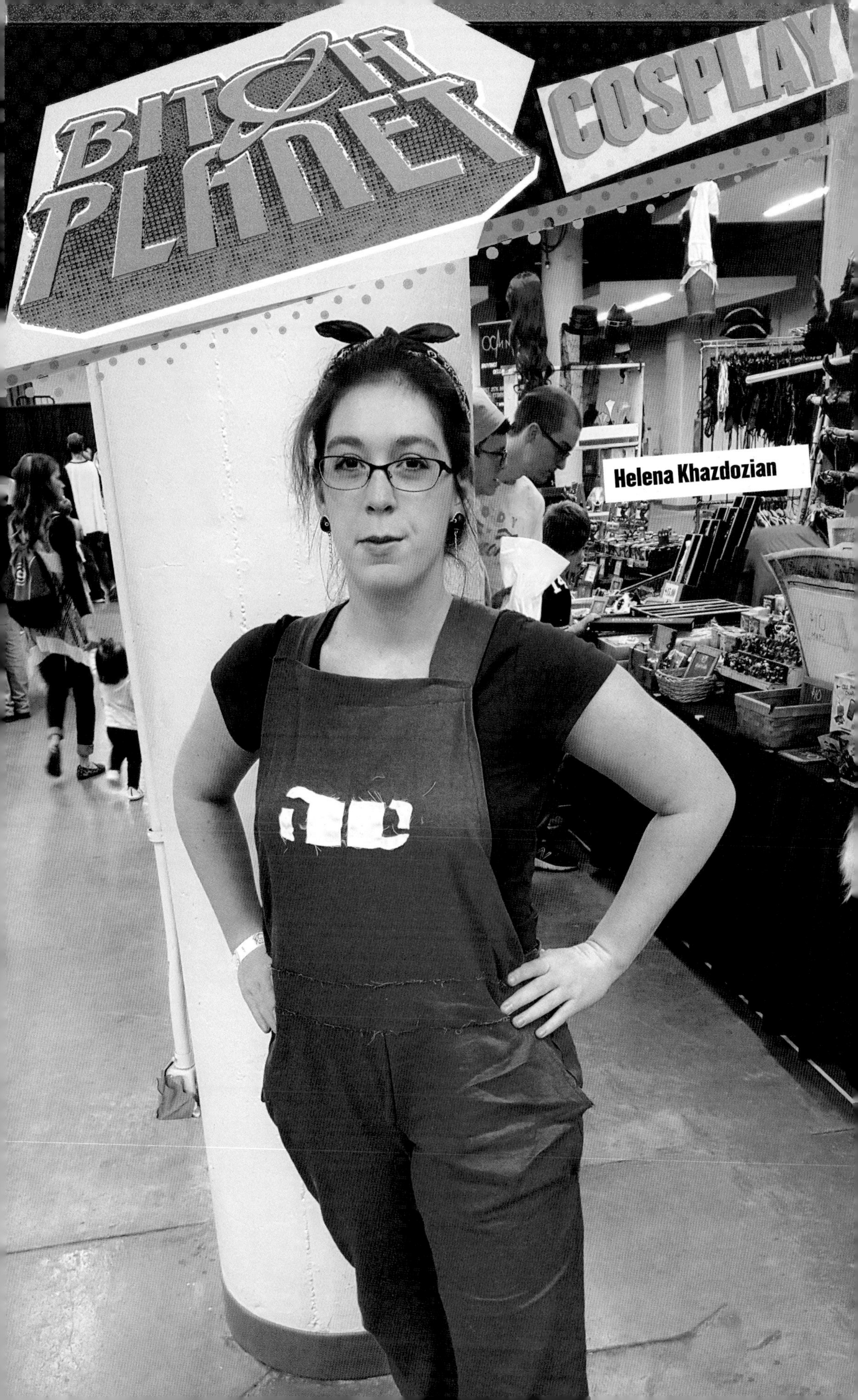
BITCH PLANET
COSPLAY

Helena Khazdozian

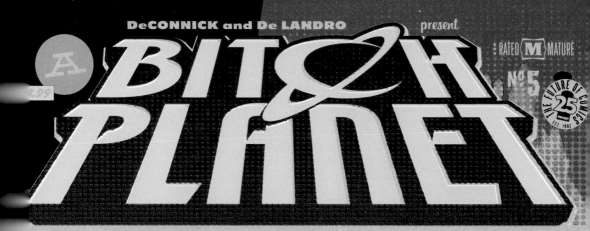

DeCONNICK and De LANDRO *present*

# BITCH PLANET

No 5

★★ RATED **M** MATURE

THE FUTURE OF COMICS EST. 1992 · 25

## TRIPLE FEATURE!

EVERYONE'S
**GRANDMA**
IS A LITTLE BIT
**FEMINIST**

MATT
**FRACTION**
ELSA
**CHARRETIER**

**MIRROR,
MIRROR**

CON
**TSUEI**

**BASIC
BITCH**

ALOBI, EYANG
& NYAMBI
**NYAMBI**

*Featuring*
CLAYTON
**COWLES**

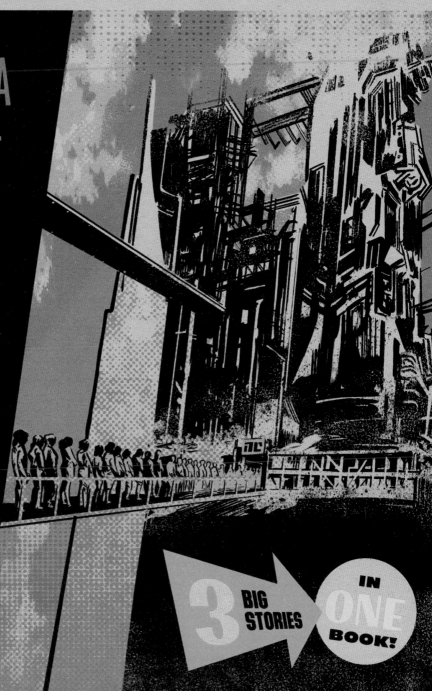

**3** BIG STORIES IN **ONE** BOOK!

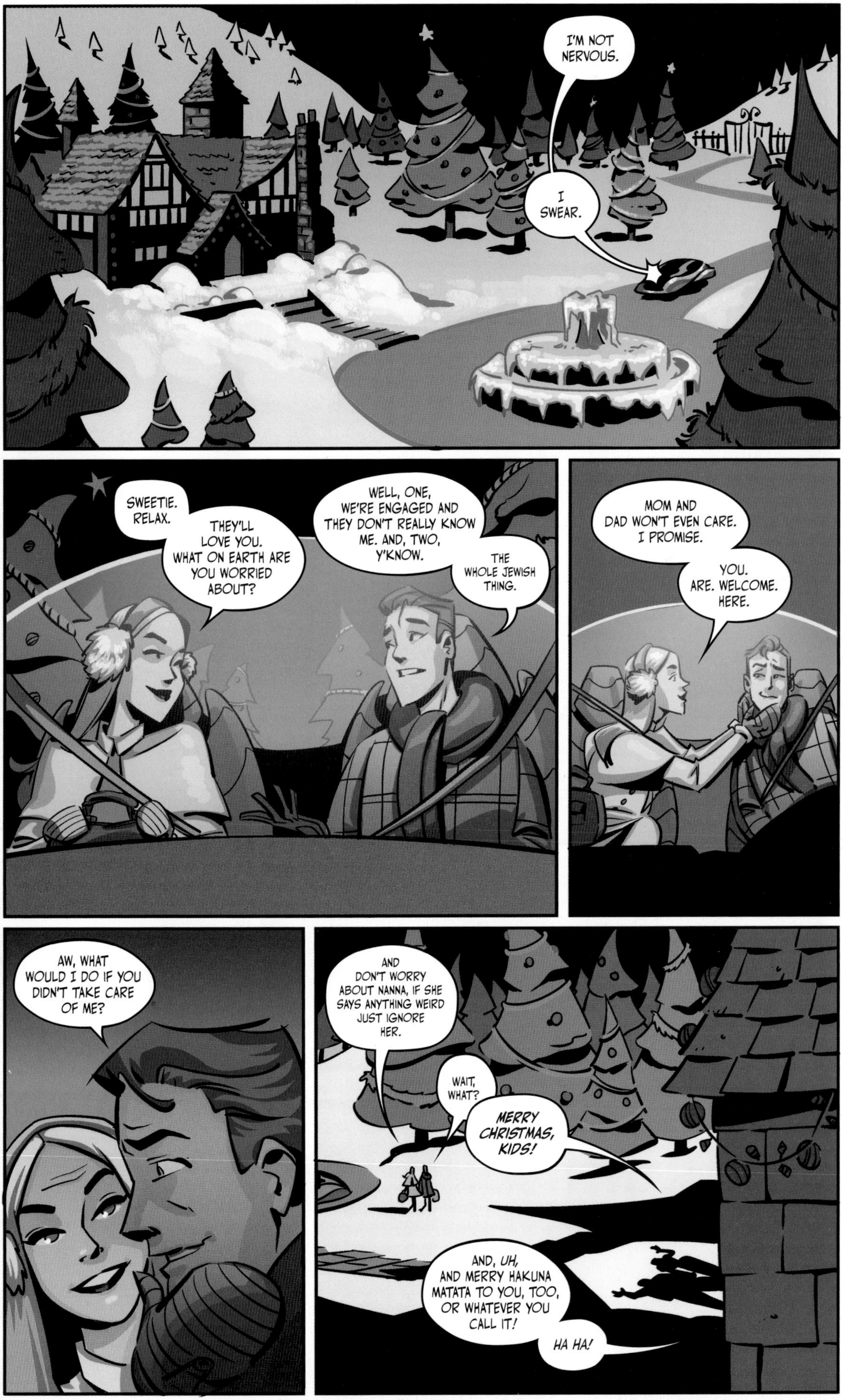
I'M NOT NERVOUS.
I SWEAR.
SWEETIE. RELAX.
THEY'LL LOVE YOU. WHAT ON EARTH ARE YOU WORRIED ABOUT?
WELL, ONE, WE'RE ENGAGED AND THEY DON'T REALLY KNOW ME. AND, TWO, Y'KNOW.
THE WHOLE JEWISH THING.
MOM AND DAD WON'T EVEN CARE. I PROMISE.
YOU. ARE. WELCOME. HERE.
AW, WHAT WOULD I DO IF YOU DIDN'T TAKE CARE OF ME?
AND DON'T WORRY ABOUT NANNA, IF SHE SAYS ANYTHING WEIRD JUST IGNORE HER.
WAIT, WHAT?
MERRY CHRISTMAS, KIDS!
AND, UH, AND MERRY HAKUNA MATATA TO YOU, TOO, OR WHATEVER YOU CALL IT!
HA HA!

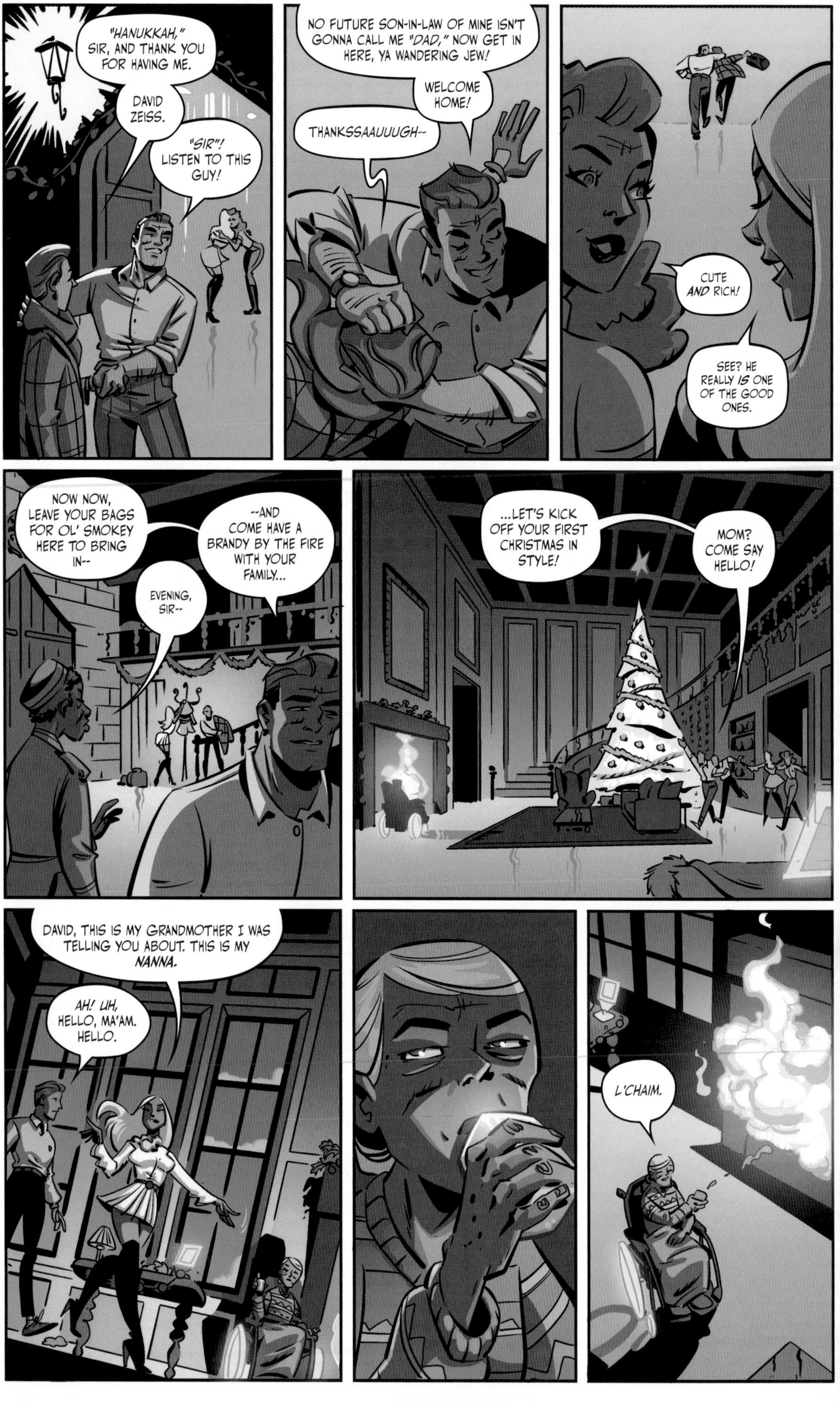

"HANUKKAH," SIR, AND THANK YOU FOR HAVING ME.
DAVID ZEISS.
"SIR"! LISTEN TO THIS GUY!
NO FUTURE SON-IN-LAW OF MINE ISN'T GONNA CALL ME "DAD," NOW GET IN HERE, YA WANDERING JEW!
WELCOME HOME!
THANKSSAAUUUGH--
CUTE AND RICH!
SEE? HE REALLY IS ONE OF THE GOOD ONES.
NOW NOW, LEAVE YOUR BAGS FOR OL' SMOKEY HERE TO BRING IN--
--AND COME HAVE A BRANDY BY THE FIRE WITH YOUR FAMILY...
EVENING, SIR--
...LET'S KICK OFF YOUR FIRST CHRISTMAS IN STYLE!
MOM? COME SAY HELLO!
DAVID, THIS IS MY GRANDMOTHER I WAS TELLING YOU ABOUT. THIS IS MY NANNA.
AH! UH, HELLO, MA'AM. HELLO.
L'CHAIM.

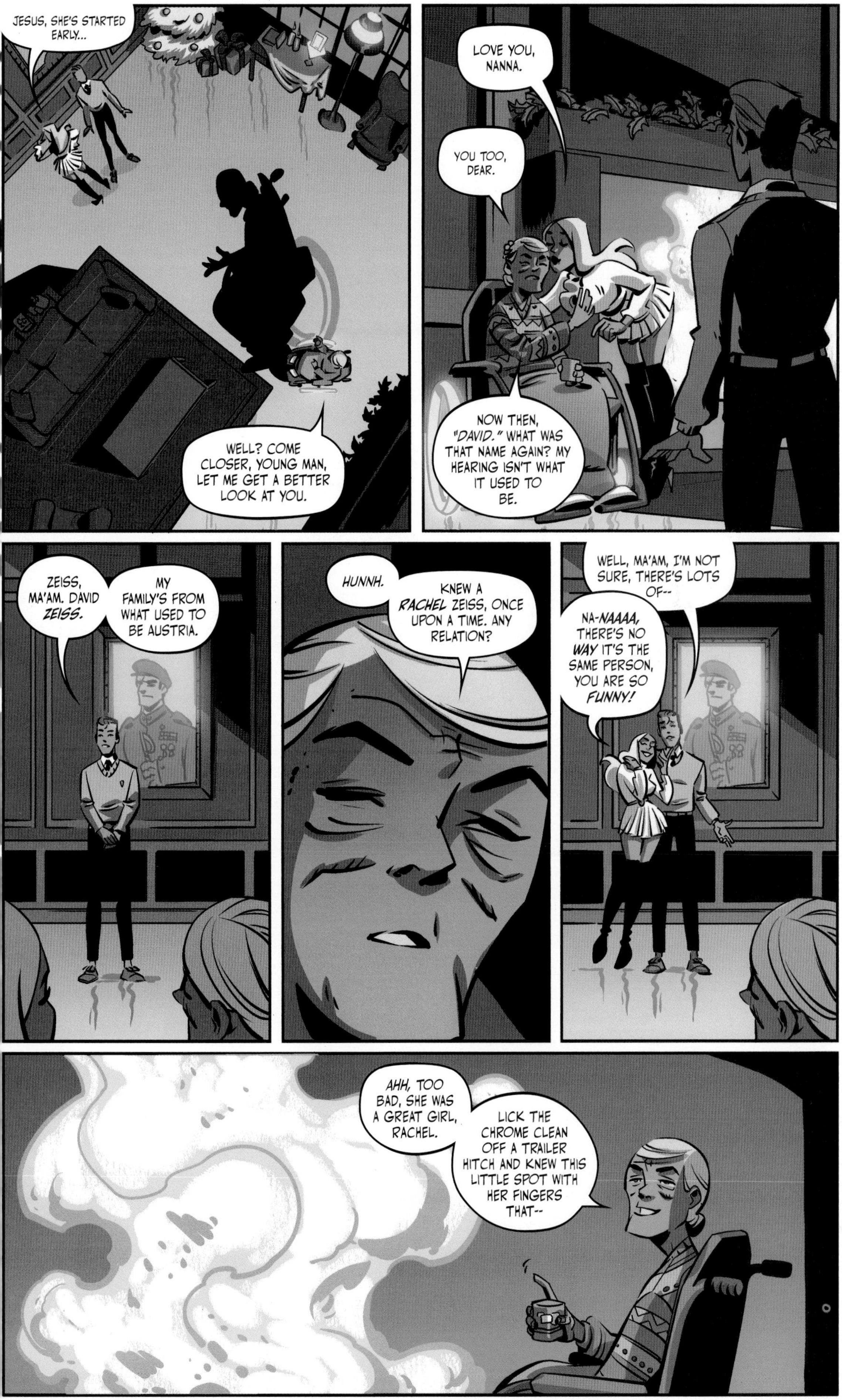
JESUS, SHE'S STARTED EARLY...
WELL? COME CLOSER, YOUNG MAN, LET ME GET A BETTER LOOK AT YOU.
LOVE YOU, NANNA.
YOU TOO, DEAR.
NOW THEN, "DAVID." WHAT WAS THAT NAME AGAIN? MY HEARING ISN'T WHAT IT USED TO BE.
ZEISS, MA'AM. DAVID ZEISS.
MY FAMILY'S FROM WHAT USED TO BE AUSTRIA.
HUNNH.
KNEW A RACHEL ZEISS, ONCE UPON A TIME. ANY RELATION?
WELL, MA'AM, I'M NOT SURE, THERE'S LOTS OF--
NA-NAAAA, THERE'S NO WAY IT'S THE SAME PERSON, YOU ARE SO FUNNY!
AHH, TOO BAD, SHE WAS A GREAT GIRL, RACHEL.
LICK THE CHROME CLEAN OFF A TRAILER HITCH AND KNEW THIS LITTLE SPOT WITH HER FINGERS THAT--

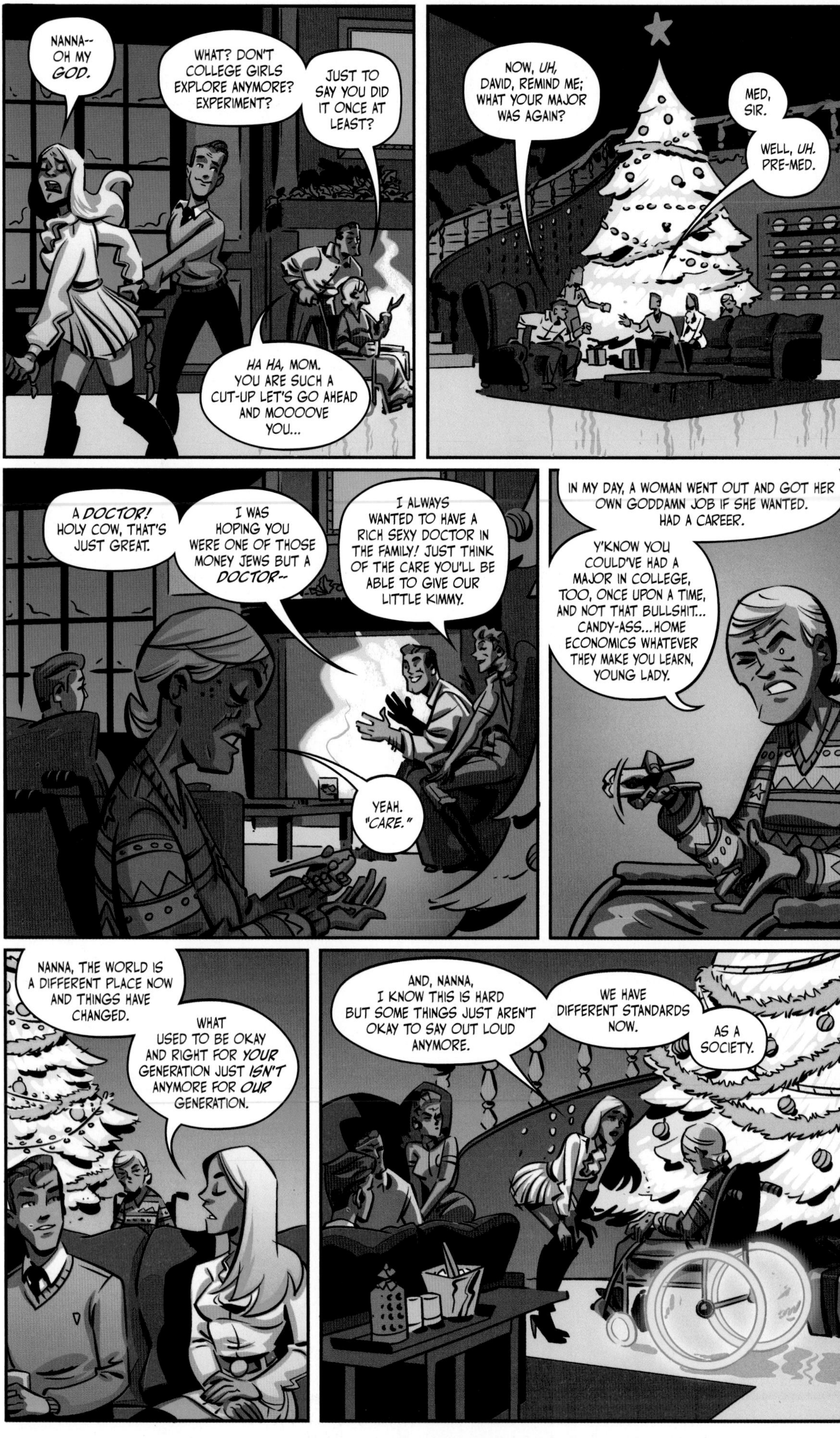
NANNA-- OH MY GOD.
WHAT? DON'T COLLEGE GIRLS EXPLORE ANYMORE? EXPERIMENT?
JUST TO SAY YOU DID IT ONCE AT LEAST?
HA HA, MOM. YOU ARE SUCH A CUT-UP LET'S GO AHEAD AND MOOOOVE YOU...
NOW, UH, DAVID, REMIND ME; WHAT YOUR MAJOR WAS AGAIN?
MED, SIR.
WELL, UH. PRE-MED.
A DOCTOR! HOLY COW, THAT'S JUST GREAT.
I WAS HOPING YOU WERE ONE OF THOSE MONEY JEWS BUT A DOCTOR--
I ALWAYS WANTED TO HAVE A RICH SEXY DOCTOR IN THE FAMILY! JUST THINK OF THE CARE YOU'LL BE ABLE TO GIVE OUR LITTLE KIMMY.
YEAH. "CARE."
IN MY DAY, A WOMAN WENT OUT AND GOT HER OWN GODDAMN JOB IF SHE WANTED. HAD A CAREER.
Y'KNOW YOU COULD'VE HAD A MAJOR IN COLLEGE, TOO, ONCE UPON A TIME, AND NOT THAT BULLSHIT... CANDY-ASS... HOME ECONOMICS WHATEVER THEY MAKE YOU LEARN, YOUNG LADY.
NANNA, THE WORLD IS A DIFFERENT PLACE NOW AND THINGS HAVE CHANGED.
WHAT USED TO BE OKAY AND RIGHT FOR YOUR GENERATION JUST ISN'T ANYMORE FOR OUR GENERATION.
AND, NANNA, I KNOW THIS IS HARD BUT SOME THINGS JUST AREN'T OKAY TO SAY OUT LOUD ANYMORE.
WE HAVE DIFFERENT STANDARDS NOW.
AS A SOCIETY.

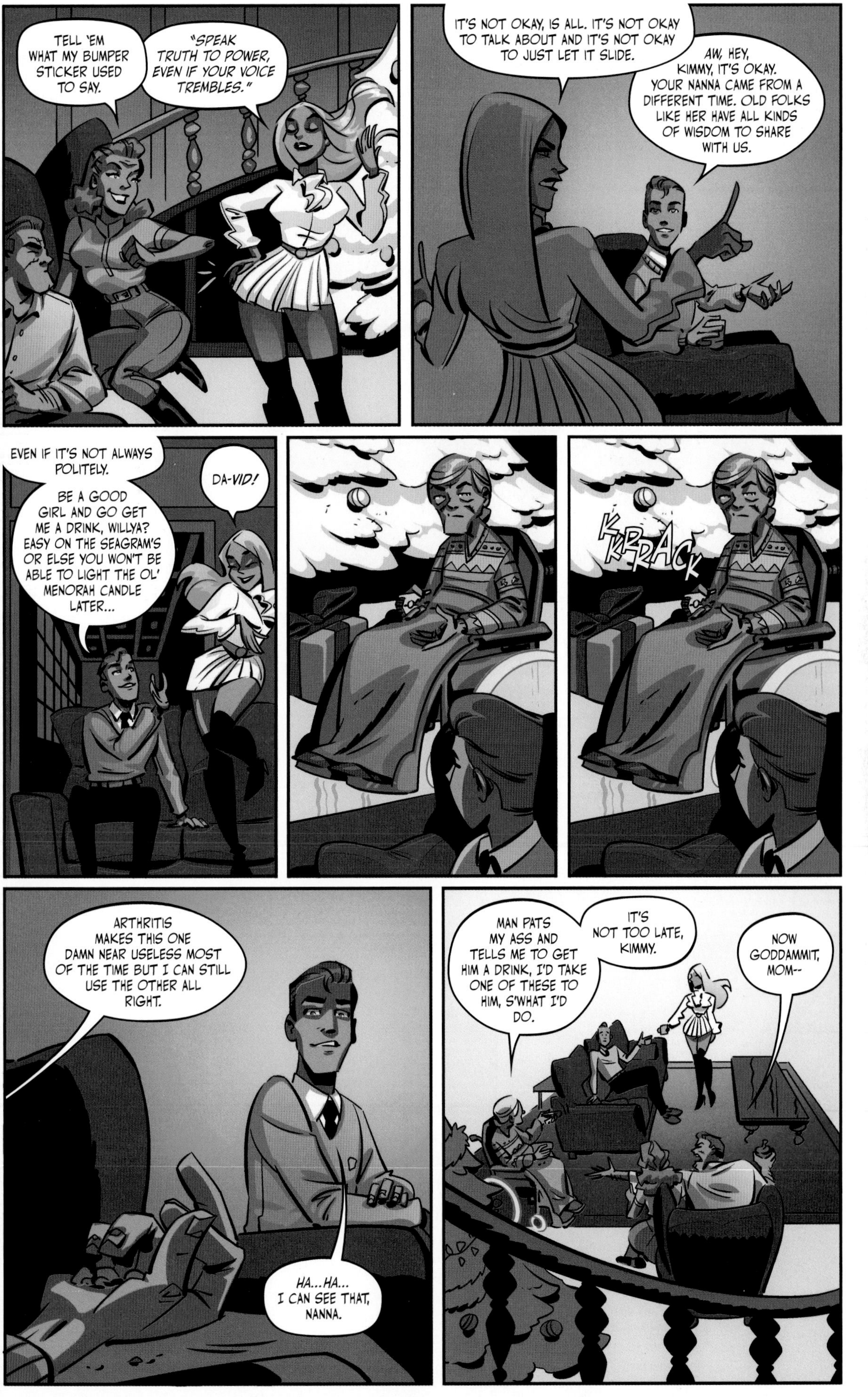
TELL 'EM WHAT MY BUMPER STICKER USED TO SAY.
"SPEAK TRUTH TO POWER, EVEN IF YOUR VOICE TREMBLES."
IT'S NOT OKAY, IS ALL. IT'S NOT OKAY TO TALK ABOUT AND IT'S NOT OKAY TO JUST LET IT SLIDE.
AW, HEY, KIMMY, IT'S OKAY. YOUR NANNA CAME FROM A DIFFERENT TIME. OLD FOLKS LIKE HER HAVE ALL KINDS OF WISDOM TO SHARE WITH US.
EVEN IF IT'S NOT ALWAYS POLITELY.
BE A GOOD GIRL AND GO GET ME A DRINK, WILLYA? EASY ON THE SEAGRAM'S OR ELSE YOU WON'T BE ABLE TO LIGHT THE OL' MENORAH CANDLE LATER...
DA-VID!
KKRRACK
ARTHRITIS MAKES THIS ONE DAMN NEAR USELESS MOST OF THE TIME BUT I CAN STILL USE THE OTHER ALL RIGHT.
HA...HA... I CAN SEE THAT, NANNA.
MAN PATS MY ASS AND TELLS ME TO GET HIM A DRINK, I'D TAKE ONE OF THESE TO HIM, S'WHAT I'D DO.
IT'S NOT TOO LATE, KIMMY.
NOW GODDAMMIT, MOM--

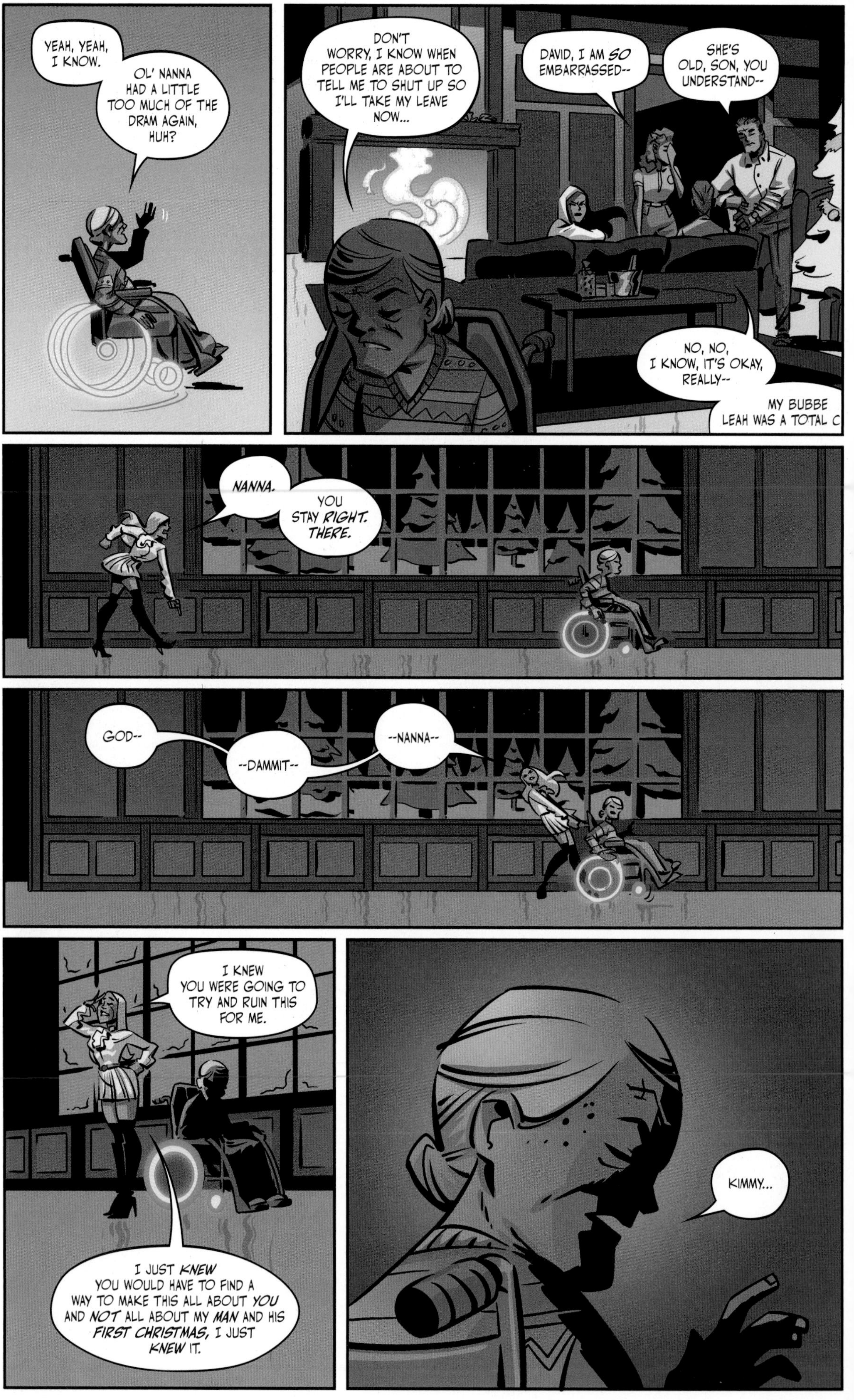

YEAH, YEAH, I KNOW.
OL' NANNA HAD A LITTLE TOO MUCH OF THE DRAM AGAIN, HUH?
DON'T WORRY, I KNOW WHEN PEOPLE ARE ABOUT TO TELL ME TO SHUT UP SO I'LL TAKE MY LEAVE NOW...
DAVID, I AM SO EMBARRASSED--
SHE'S OLD, SON, YOU UNDERSTAND--
NO, NO, I KNOW, IT'S OKAY, REALLY--
MY BUBBE LEAH WAS A TOTAL C
NANNA.
YOU STAY RIGHT. THERE.
GOD--
--DAMMIT--
--NANNA--
I KNEW YOU WERE GOING TO TRY AND RUIN THIS FOR ME.
I JUST KNEW YOU WOULD HAVE TO FIND A WAY TO MAKE THIS ALL ABOUT YOU AND NOT ALL ABOUT MY MAN AND HIS FIRST CHRISTMAS, I JUST KNEW IT.
KIMMY...

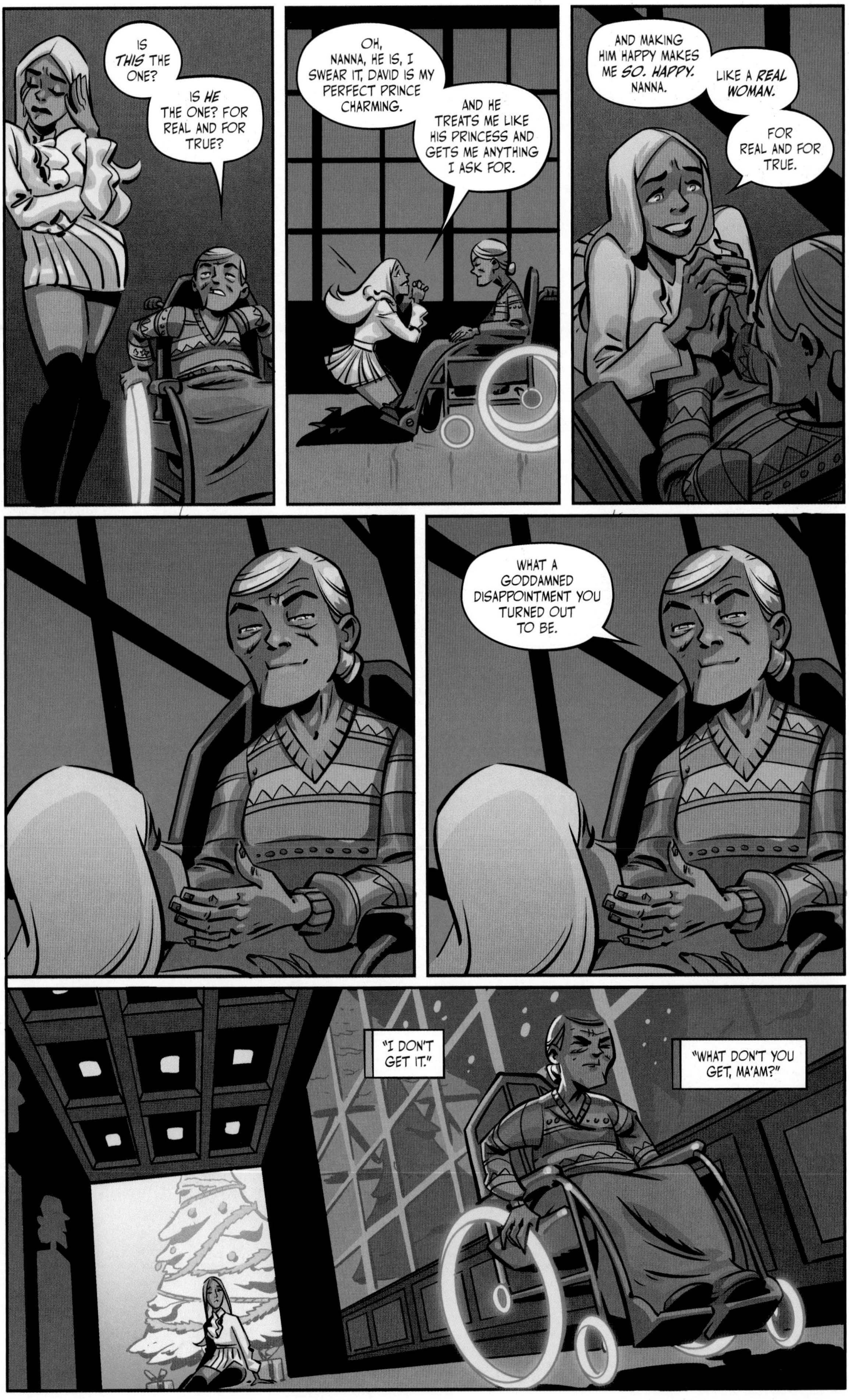
IS THIS THE ONE?
IS HE THE ONE? FOR REAL AND FOR TRUE?
OH, NANNA, HE IS, I SWEAR IT, DAVID IS MY PERFECT PRINCE CHARMING.
AND HE TREATS ME LIKE HIS PRINCESS AND GETS ME ANYTHING I ASK FOR.
AND MAKING HIM HAPPY MAKES ME SO. HAPPY. NANNA.
LIKE A REAL WOMAN.
FOR REAL AND FOR TRUE.
WHAT A GODDAMNED DISAPPOINTMENT YOU TURNED OUT TO BE.
"I DON'T GET IT."
"WHAT DON'T YOU GET, MA'AM?"

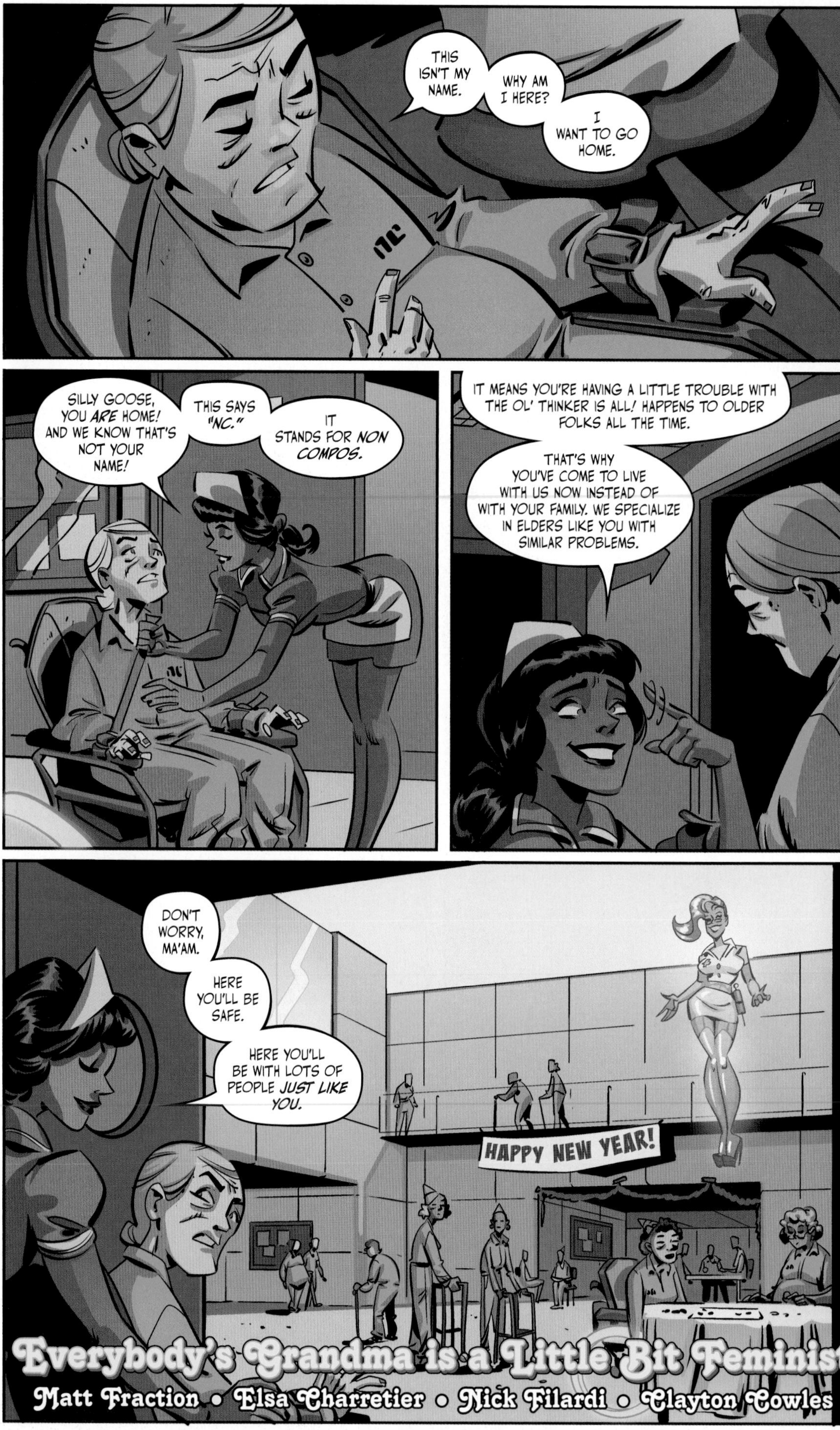

THIS ISN'T MY NAME.
WHY AM I HERE?
I WANT TO GO HOME.
SILLY GOOSE, YOU *ARE* HOME! AND WE KNOW THAT'S NOT YOUR NAME!
THIS SAYS *"NC."*
IT STANDS FOR *NON COMPOS.*
IT MEANS YOU'RE HAVING A LITTLE TROUBLE WITH THE OL' THINKER IS ALL! HAPPENS TO OLDER FOLKS ALL THE TIME.
THAT'S WHY YOU'VE COME TO LIVE WITH US NOW INSTEAD OF WITH YOUR FAMILY. WE SPECIALIZE IN ELDERS LIKE YOU WITH SIMILAR PROBLEMS.
DON'T WORRY, MA'AM.
HERE YOU'LL BE SAFE.
HERE YOU'LL BE WITH LOTS OF PEOPLE *JUST LIKE YOU.*
HAPPY NEW YEAR!
Everybody's Grandma is a Little Bit Feminist
Matt Fraction • Elsa Charretier • Nick Filardi • Clayton Cowles

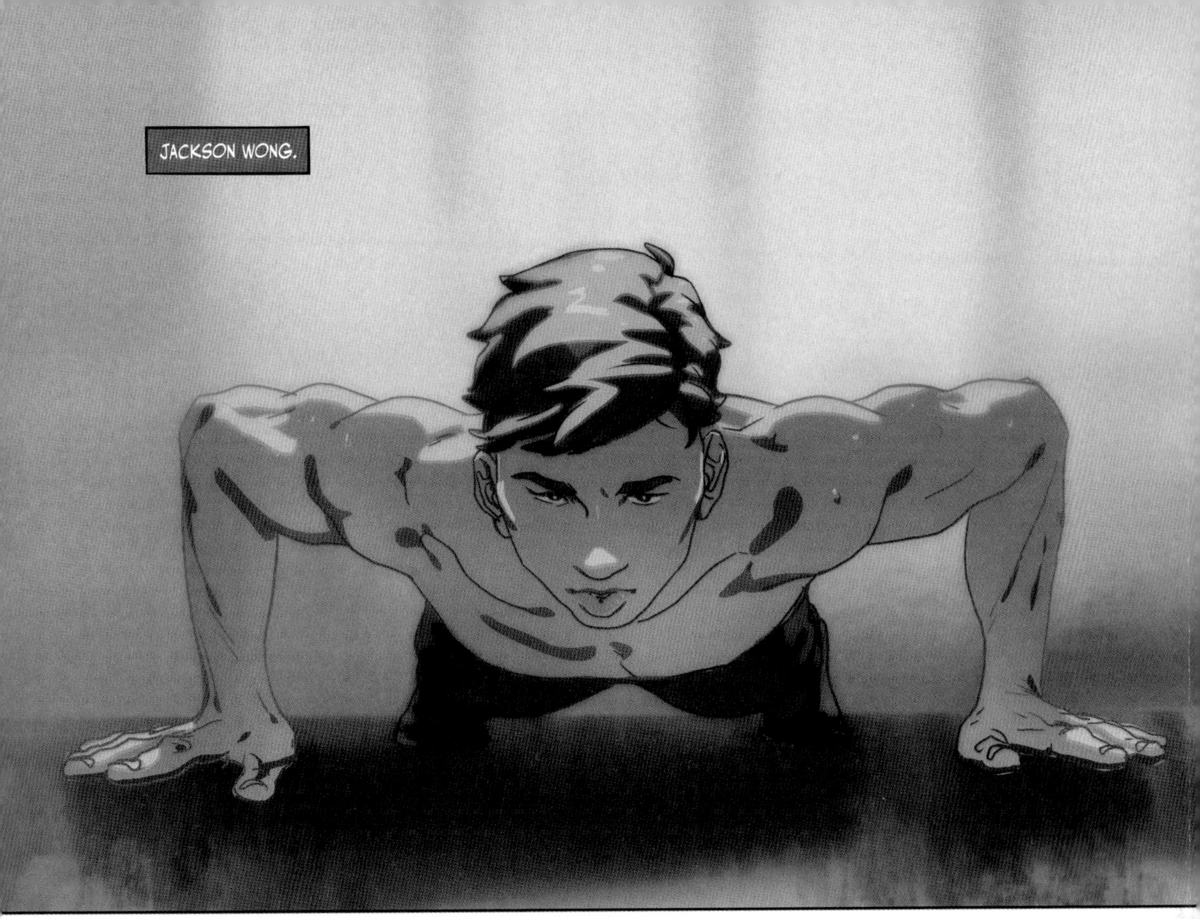
JACKSON WONG.

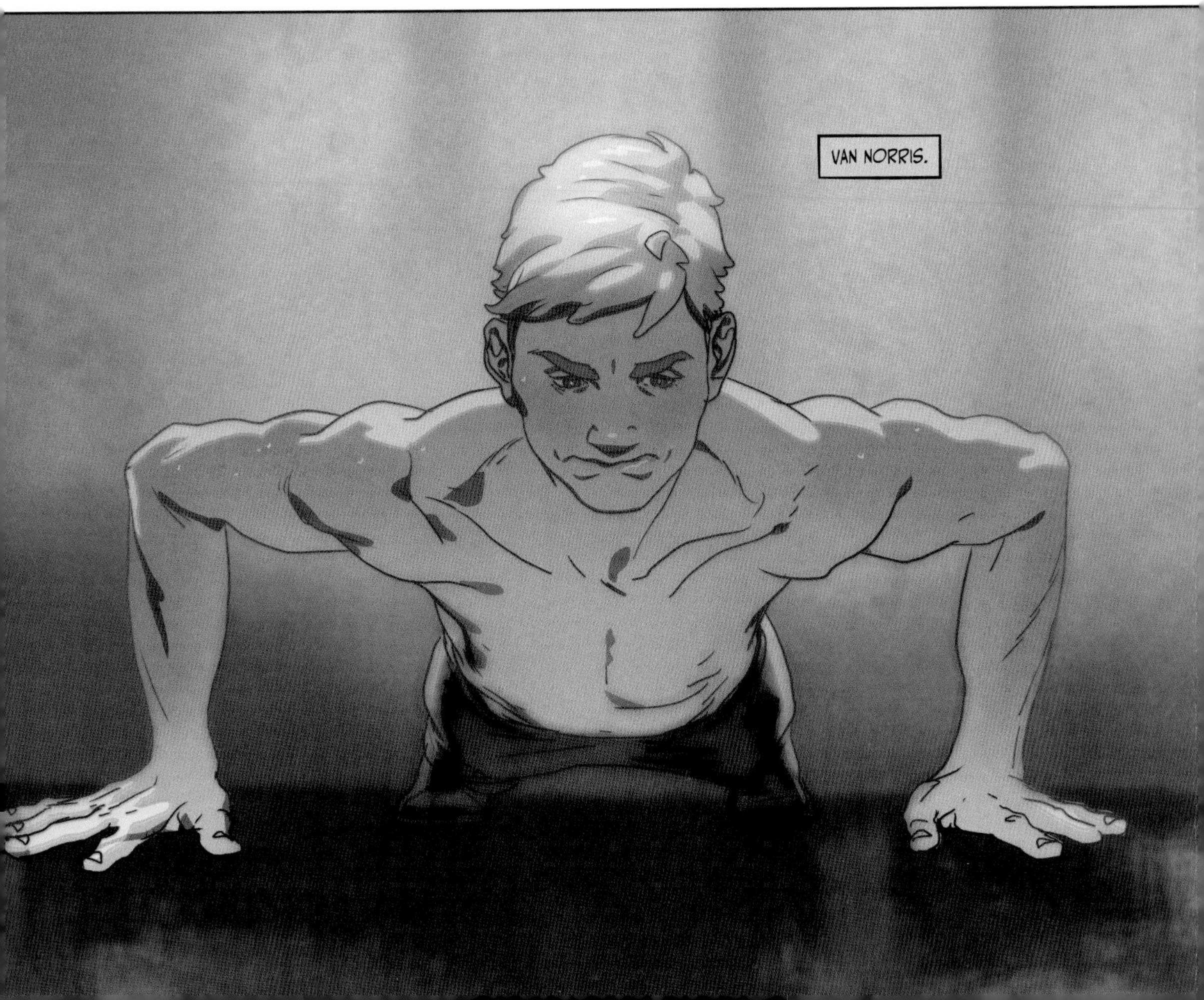
VAN NORRIS.

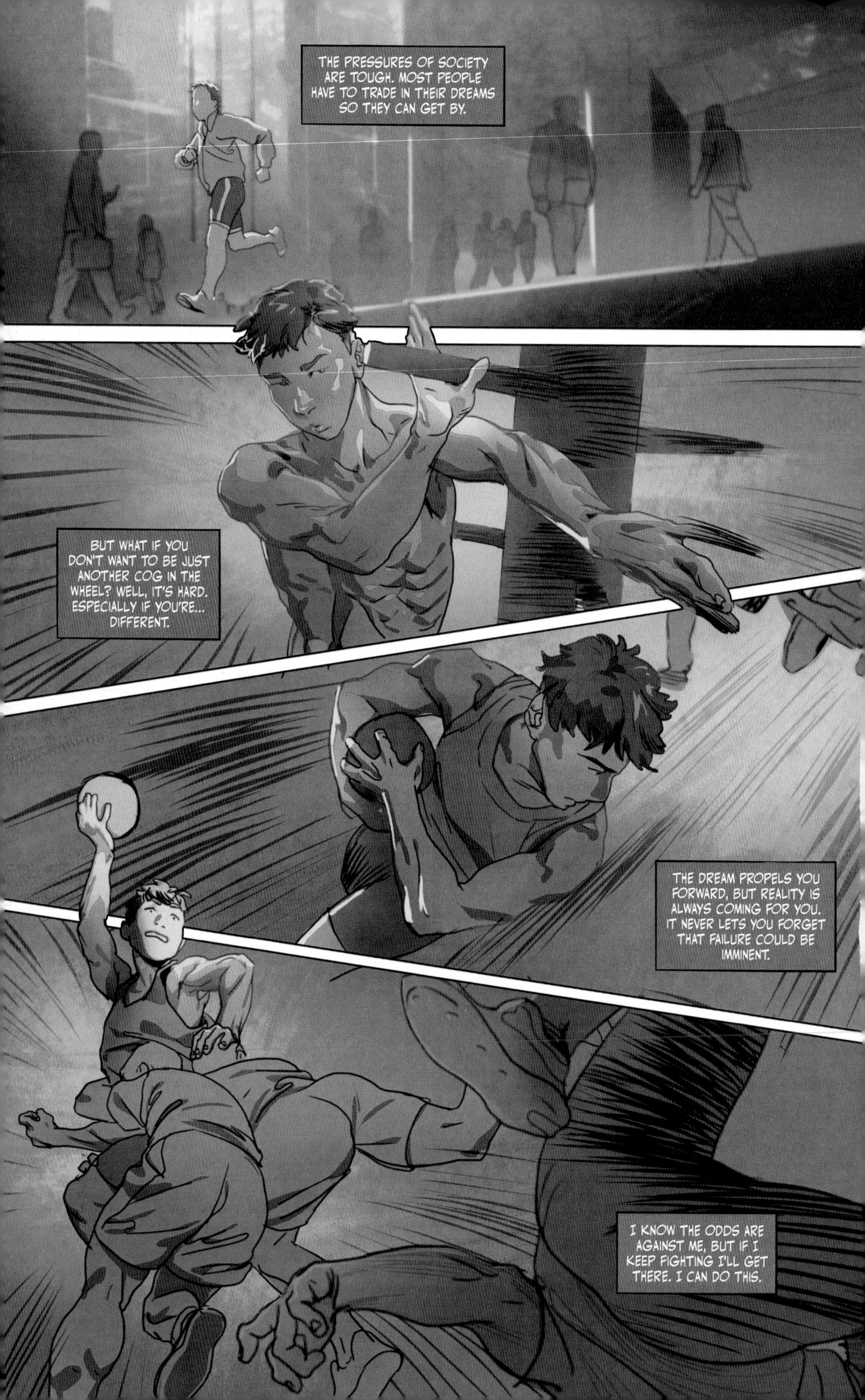
THE PRESSURES OF SOCIETY ARE TOUGH. MOST PEOPLE HAVE TO TRADE IN THEIR DREAMS SO THEY CAN GET BY.
BUT WHAT IF YOU DON'T WANT TO BE JUST ANOTHER COG IN THE WHEEL? WELL, IT'S HARD. ESPECIALLY IF YOU'RE... DIFFERENT.
THE DREAM PROPELS YOU FORWARD, BUT REALITY IS ALWAYS COMING FOR YOU. IT NEVER LETS YOU FORGET THAT FAILURE COULD BE IMMINENT.
I KNOW THE ODDS ARE AGAINST ME, BUT IF I KEEP FIGHTING I'LL GET THERE. I CAN DO THIS.

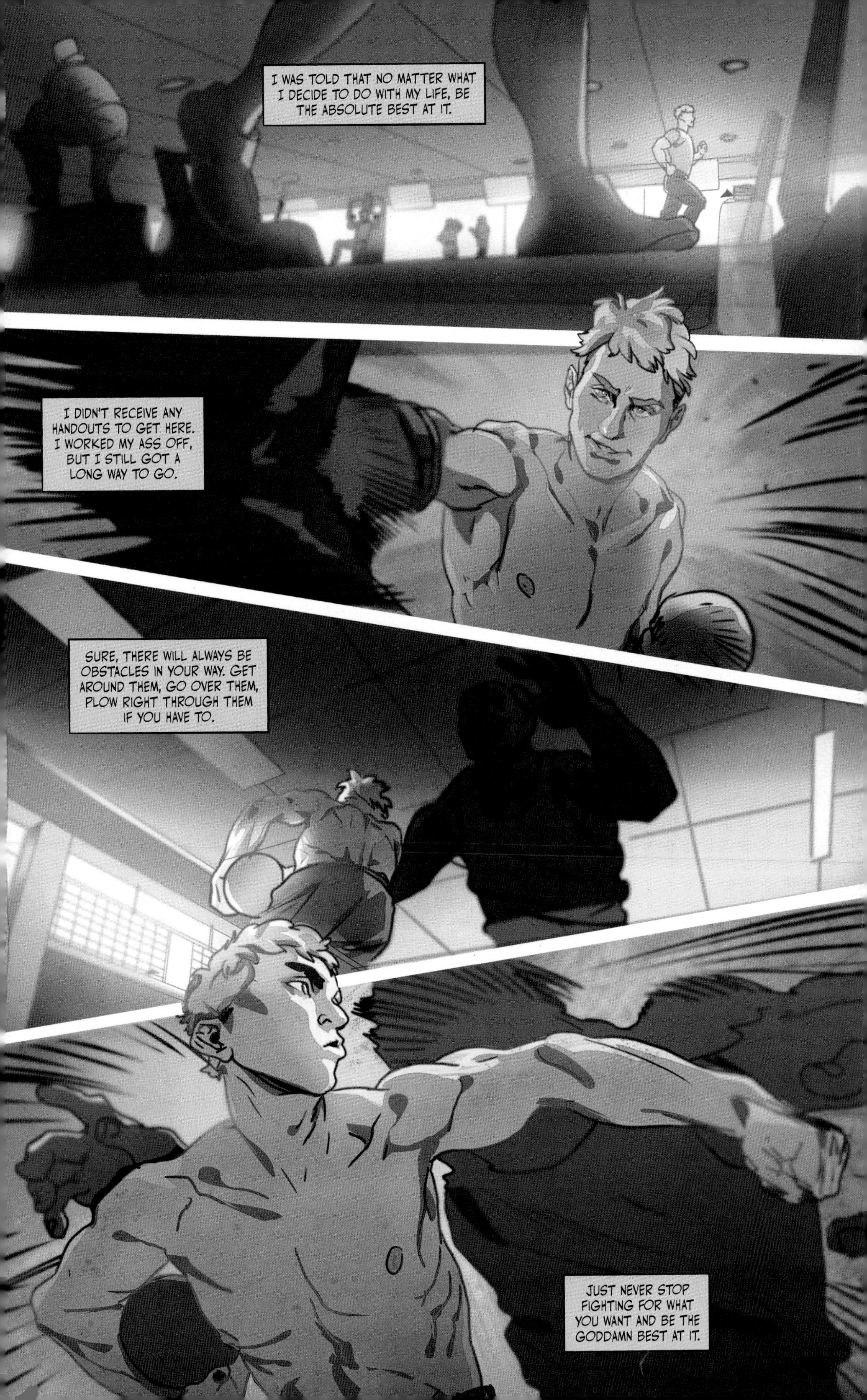
I WAS TOLD THAT NO MATTER WHAT I DECIDE TO DO WITH MY LIFE, BE THE ABSOLUTE BEST AT IT.
I DIDN'T RECEIVE ANY HANDOUTS TO GET HERE. I WORKED MY ASS OFF, BUT I STILL GOT A LONG WAY TO GO.
SURE, THERE WILL ALWAYS BE OBSTACLES IN YOUR WAY. GET AROUND THEM, GO OVER THEM, PLOW RIGHT THROUGH THEM IF YOU HAVE TO.
JUST NEVER STOP FIGHTING FOR WHAT YOU WANT AND BE THE GODDAMN BEST AT IT.

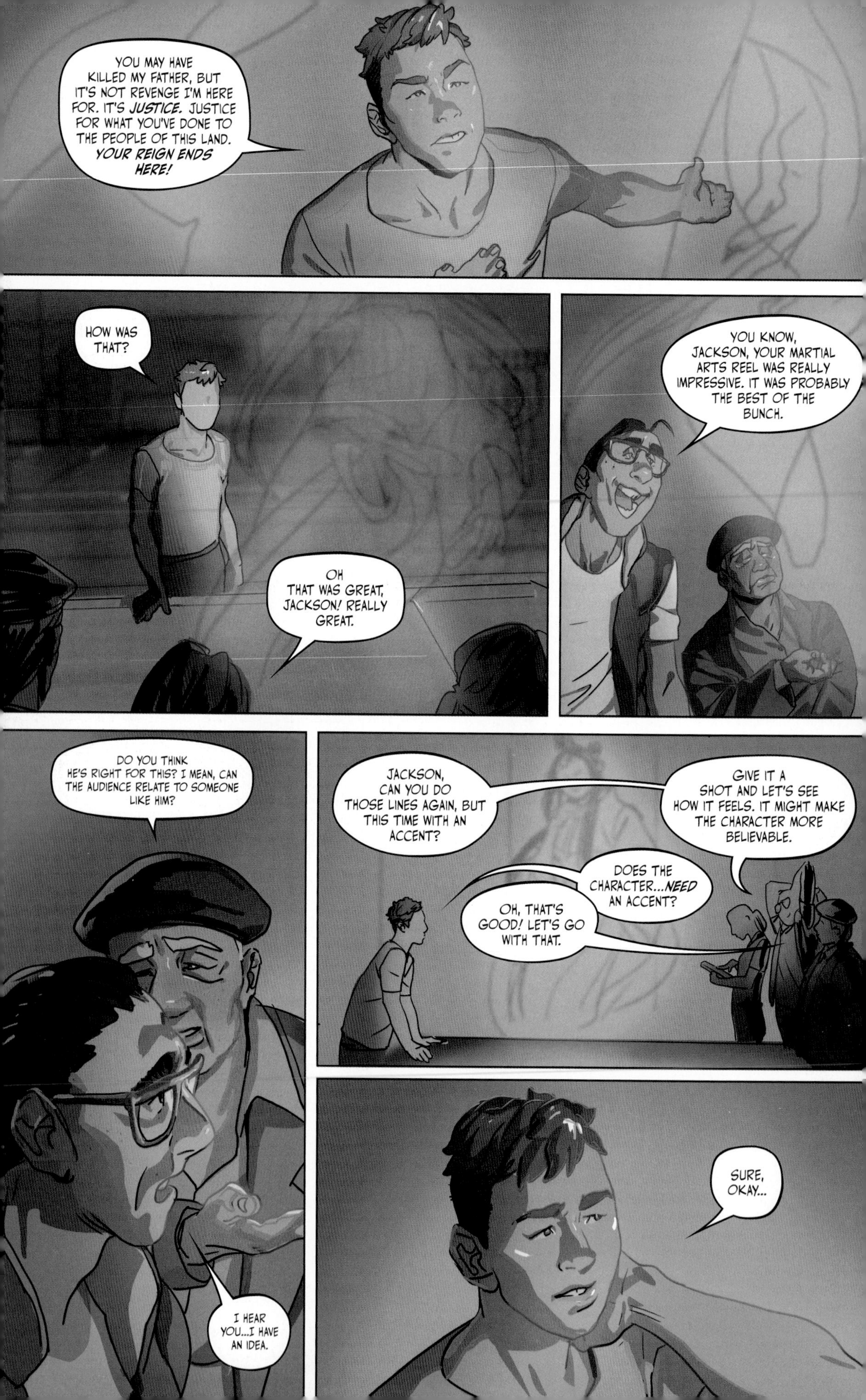
YOU MAY HAVE KILLED MY FATHER, BUT IT'S NOT REVENGE I'M HERE FOR. IT'S *JUSTICE.* JUSTICE FOR WHAT YOU'VE DONE TO THE PEOPLE OF THIS LAND. ***YOUR REIGN ENDS HERE!***
HOW WAS THAT?
OH THAT WAS GREAT, JACKSON! REALLY GREAT.
YOU KNOW, JACKSON, YOUR MARTIAL ARTS REEL WAS REALLY IMPRESSIVE. IT WAS PROBABLY THE BEST OF THE BUNCH.
DO YOU THINK HE'S RIGHT FOR THIS? I MEAN, CAN THE AUDIENCE RELATE TO SOMEONE LIKE HIM?
I HEAR YOU...I HAVE AN IDEA.
JACKSON, CAN YOU DO THOSE LINES AGAIN, BUT THIS TIME WITH AN ACCENT?
GIVE IT A SHOT AND LET'S SEE HOW IT FEELS. IT MIGHT MAKE THE CHARACTER MORE BELIEVABLE.
DOES THE CHARACTER...*NEED* AN ACCENT?
OH, THAT'S GOOD! LET'S GO WITH THAT.
SURE, OKAY...

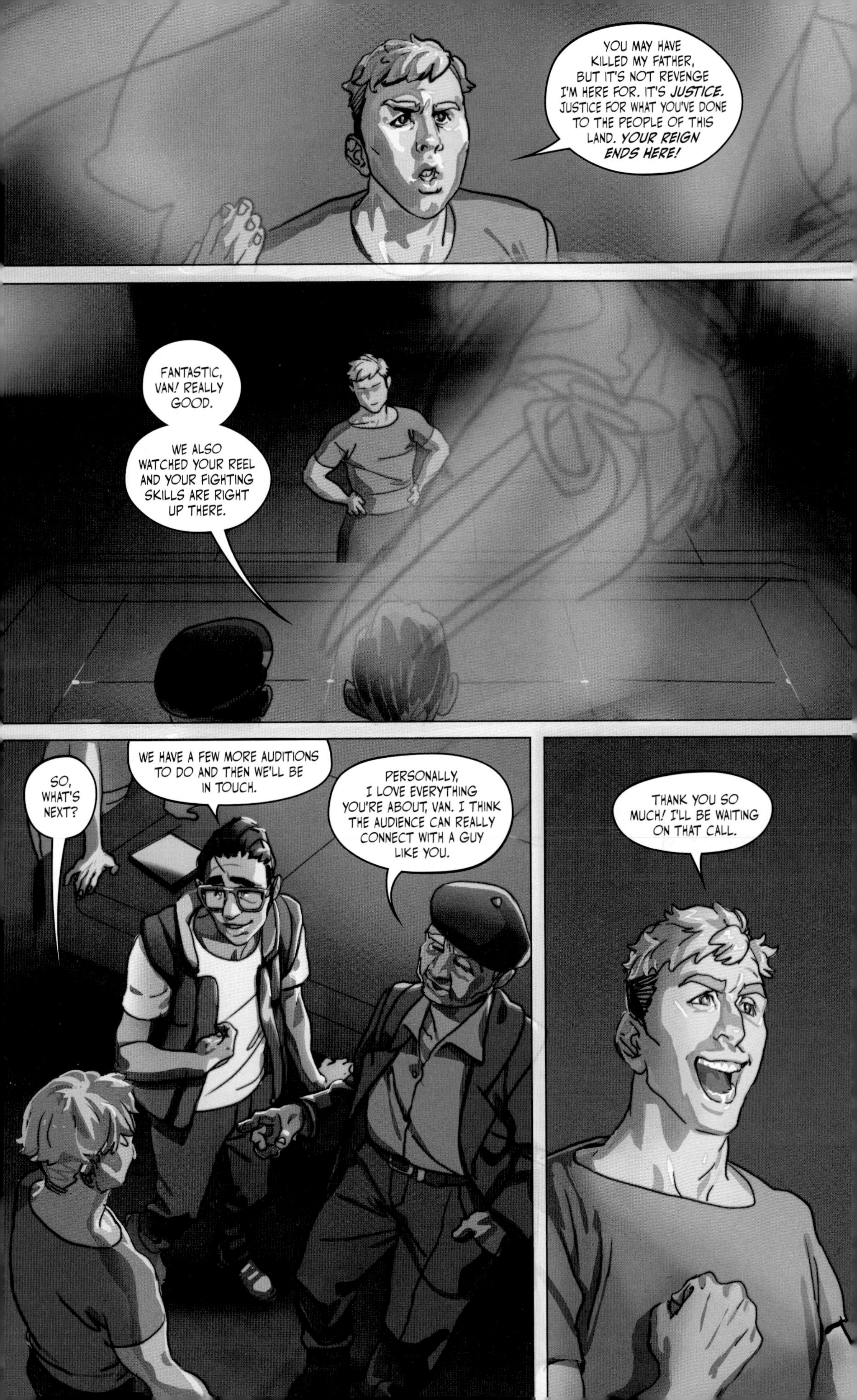
YOU MAY HAVE KILLED MY FATHER, BUT IT'S NOT REVENGE I'M HERE FOR. IT'S JUSTICE. JUSTICE FOR WHAT YOU'VE DONE TO THE PEOPLE OF THIS LAND. YOUR REIGN ENDS HERE!
FANTASTIC, VAN! REALLY GOOD.
WE ALSO WATCHED YOUR REEL AND YOUR FIGHTING SKILLS ARE RIGHT UP THERE.
SO, WHAT'S NEXT?
WE HAVE A FEW MORE AUDITIONS TO DO AND THEN WE'LL BE IN TOUCH.
PERSONALLY, I LOVE EVERYTHING YOU'RE ABOUT, VAN. I THINK THE AUDIENCE CAN REALLY CONNECT WITH A GUY LIKE YOU.
THANK YOU SO MUCH! I'LL BE WAITING ON THAT CALL.

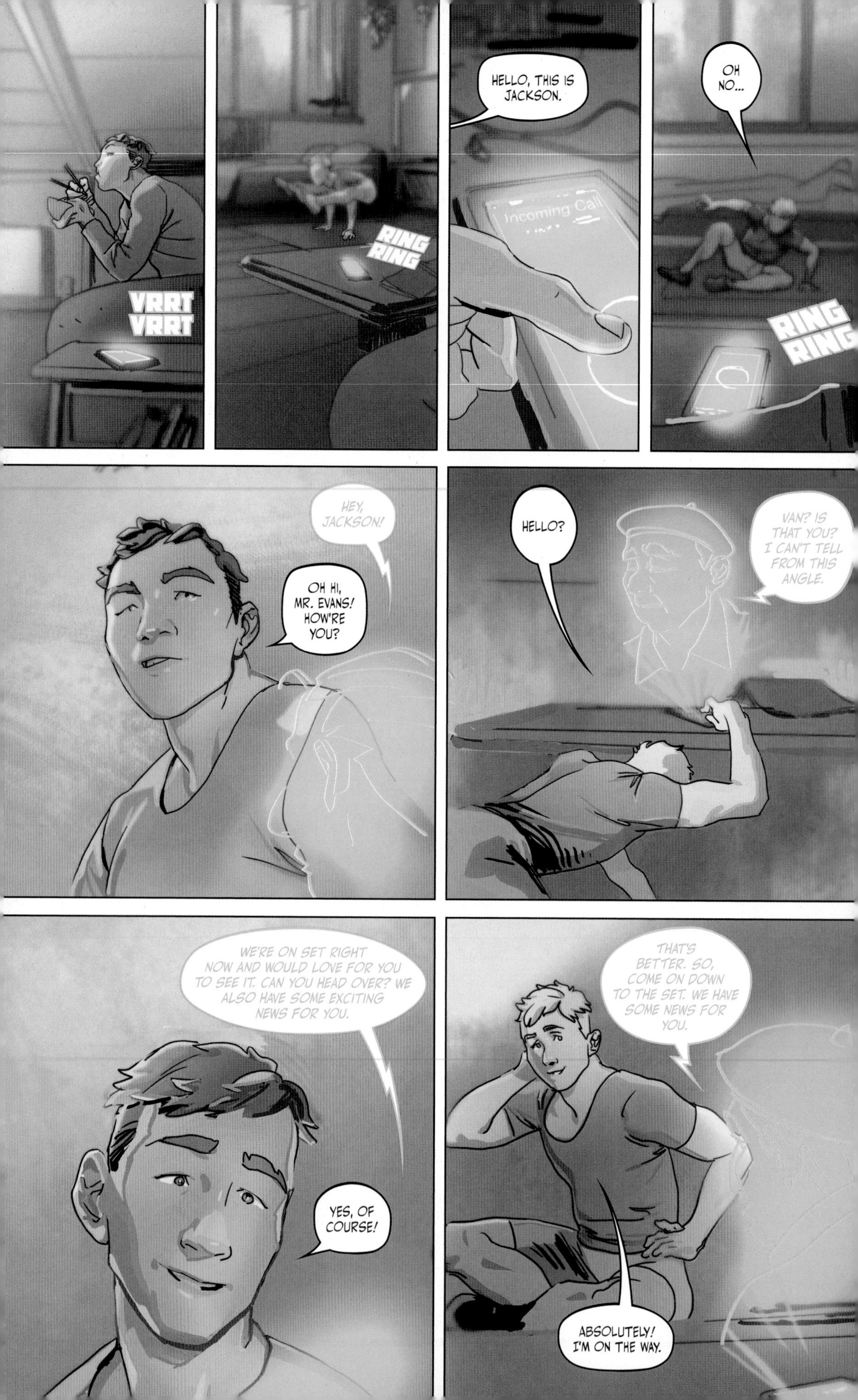
VRRT VRRT
RING RING
HELLO, THIS IS JACKSON.
Incoming Call
OH NO...
RING RING
HEY, JACKSON!
OH HI, MR. EVANS! HOW'RE YOU?
HELLO?
VAN? IS THAT YOU? I CAN'T TELL FROM THIS ANGLE.
WE'RE ON SET RIGHT NOW AND WOULD LOVE FOR YOU TO SEE IT. CAN YOU HEAD OVER? WE ALSO HAVE SOME EXCITING NEWS FOR YOU.
YES, OF COURSE!
THAT'S BETTER. SO, COME ON DOWN TO THE SET. WE HAVE SOME NEWS FOR YOU.
ABSOLUTELY! I'M ON THE WAY.

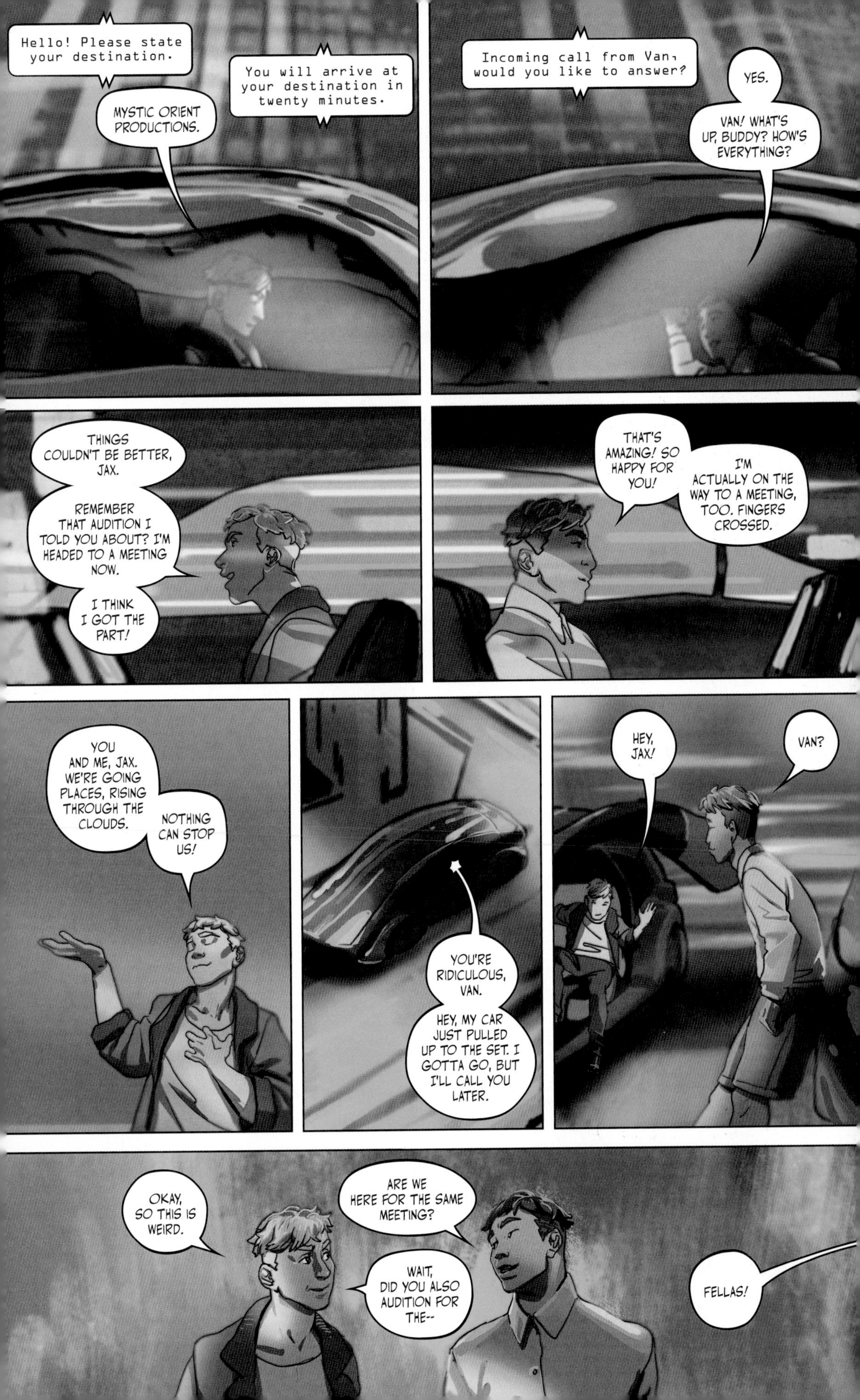
Hello! Please state your destination.
MYSTIC ORIENT PRODUCTIONS.
You will arrive at your destination in twenty minutes.
Incoming call from Van, would you like to answer?
YES.
VAN! WHAT'S UP, BUDDY? HOW'S EVERYTHING?
THINGS COULDN'T BE BETTER, JAX.
REMEMBER THAT AUDITION I TOLD YOU ABOUT? I'M HEADED TO A MEETING NOW.
I THINK I GOT THE PART!
THAT'S AMAZING! SO HAPPY FOR YOU!
I'M ACTUALLY ON THE WAY TO A MEETING, TOO. FINGERS CROSSED.
YOU AND ME, JAX. WE'RE GOING PLACES, RISING THROUGH THE CLOUDS.
NOTHING CAN STOP US!
YOU'RE RIDICULOUS, VAN.
HEY, MY CAR JUST PULLED UP TO THE SET. I GOTTA GO, BUT I'LL CALL YOU LATER.
HEY, JAX!
VAN?
OKAY, SO THIS IS WEIRD.
ARE WE HERE FOR THE SAME MEETING?
WAIT, DID YOU ALSO AUDITION FOR THE--
FELLAS!

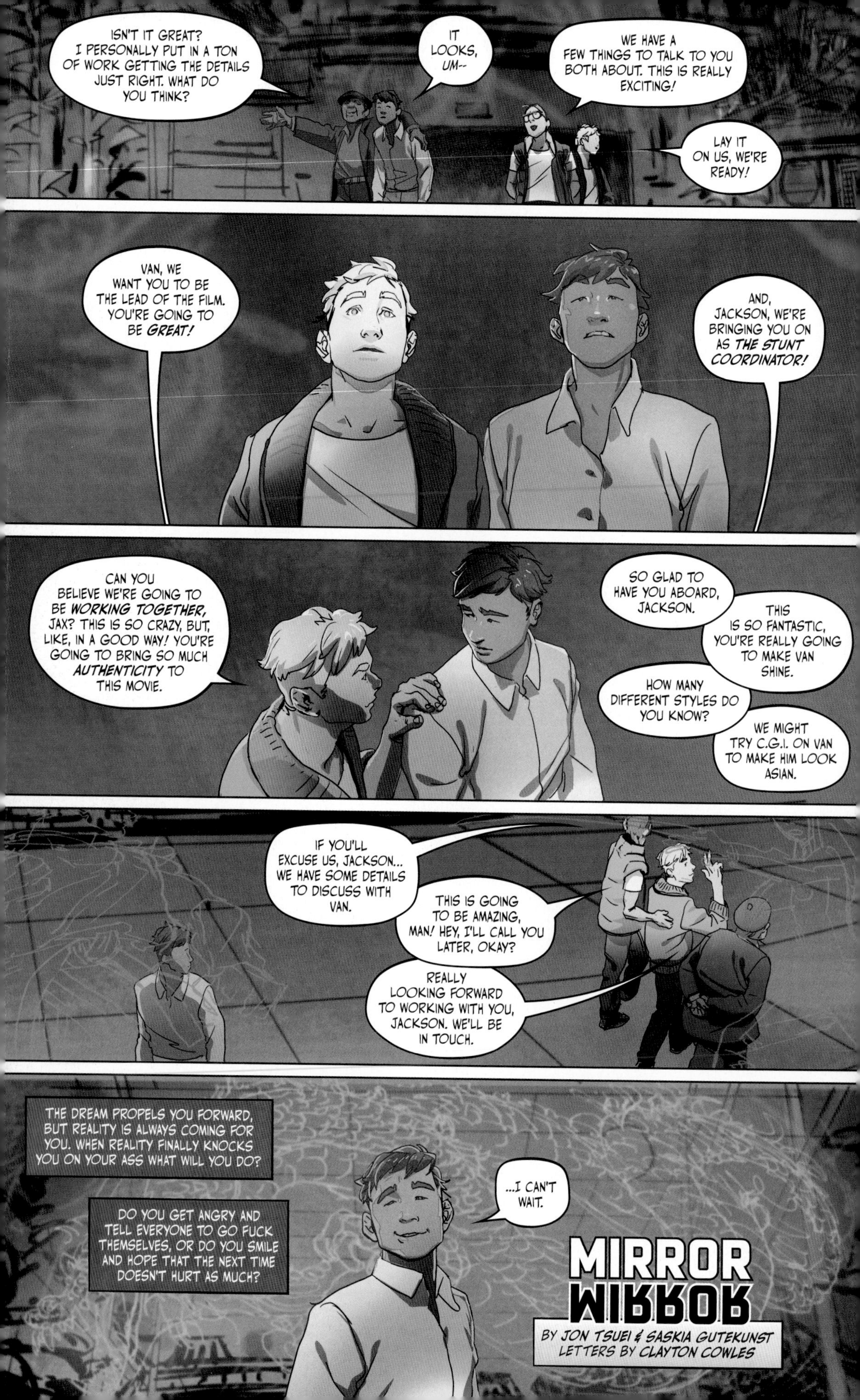
ISN'T IT GREAT? I PERSONALLY PUT IN A TON OF WORK GETTING THE DETAILS JUST RIGHT. WHAT DO YOU THINK?
IT LOOKS, UM--
WE HAVE A FEW THINGS TO TALK TO YOU BOTH ABOUT. THIS IS REALLY EXCITING!
LAY IT ON US, WE'RE READY!
VAN, WE WANT YOU TO BE THE LEAD OF THE FILM. YOU'RE GOING TO BE GREAT!
AND, JACKSON, WE'RE BRINGING YOU ON AS THE STUNT COORDINATOR!
CAN YOU BELIEVE WE'RE GOING TO BE WORKING TOGETHER, JAX? THIS IS SO CRAZY, BUT, LIKE, IN A GOOD WAY! YOU'RE GOING TO BRING SO MUCH AUTHENTICITY TO THIS MOVIE.
SO GLAD TO HAVE YOU ABOARD, JACKSON.
THIS IS SO FANTASTIC, YOU'RE REALLY GOING TO MAKE VAN SHINE.
HOW MANY DIFFERENT STYLES DO YOU KNOW?
WE MIGHT TRY C.G.I. ON VAN TO MAKE HIM LOOK ASIAN.
IF YOU'LL EXCUSE US, JACKSON... WE HAVE SOME DETAILS TO DISCUSS WITH VAN.
THIS IS GOING TO BE AMAZING, MAN! HEY, I'LL CALL YOU LATER, OKAY?
REALLY LOOKING FORWARD TO WORKING WITH YOU, JACKSON. WE'LL BE IN TOUCH.
THE DREAM PROPELS YOU FORWARD, BUT REALITY IS ALWAYS COMING FOR YOU. WHEN REALITY FINALLY KNOCKS YOU ON YOUR ASS WHAT WILL YOU DO?
...I CAN'T WAIT.
DO YOU GET ANGRY AND TELL EVERYONE TO GO FUCK THEMSELVES, OR DO YOU SMILE AND HOPE THAT THE NEXT TIME DOESN'T HURT AS MUCH?
MIRROR
MIRROR
BY JON TSUEI & SASKIA GUTEKUNST
LETTERS BY CLAYTON COWLES

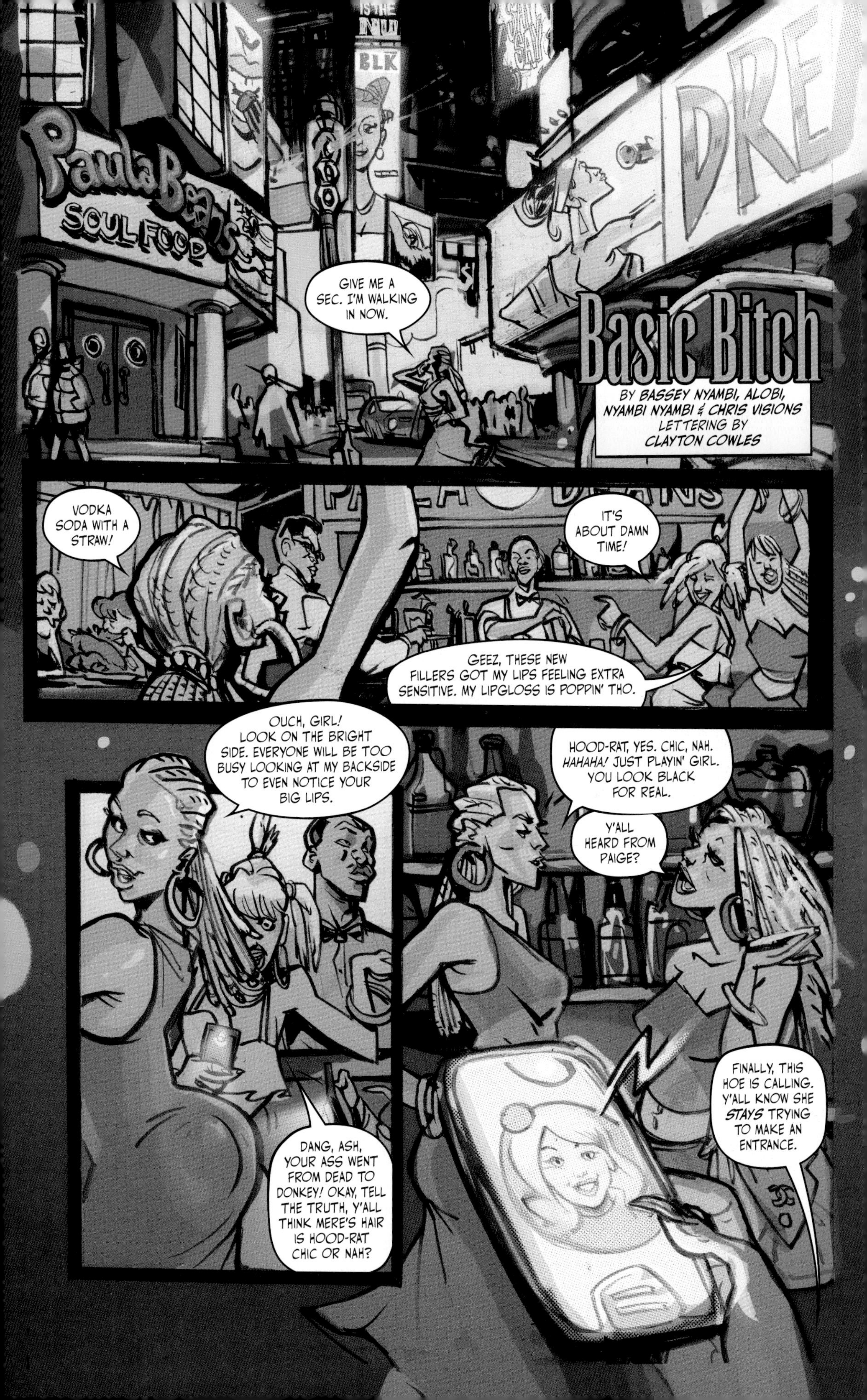
IS THE
NU
BLK
Paula Beans
SOUL FOOD
DRE
GIVE ME A SEC. I'M WALKING IN NOW.
Basic Bitch
BY BASSEY NYAMBI, ALOBI, NYAMBI NYAMBI & CHRIS VISIONS
LETTERING BY CLAYTON COWLES
VODKA SODA WITH A STRAW!
IT'S ABOUT DAMN TIME!
GEEZ, THESE NEW FILLERS GOT MY LIPS FEELING EXTRA SENSITIVE. MY LIPGLOSS IS POPPIN' THO.
OUCH, GIRL! LOOK ON THE BRIGHT SIDE. EVERYONE WILL BE TOO BUSY LOOKING AT MY BACKSIDE TO EVEN NOTICE YOUR BIG LIPS.
DANG, ASH, YOUR ASS WENT FROM DEAD TO DONKEY! OKAY, TELL THE TRUTH, Y'ALL THINK MERE'S HAIR IS HOOD-RAT CHIC OR NAH?
HOOD-RAT, YES. CHIC, NAH. HAHAHA! JUST PLAYIN' GIRL. YOU LOOK BLACK FOR REAL.
Y'ALL HEARD FROM PAIGE?
FINALLY, THIS HOE IS CALLING. Y'ALL KNOW SHE STAYS TRYING TO MAKE AN ENTRANCE.

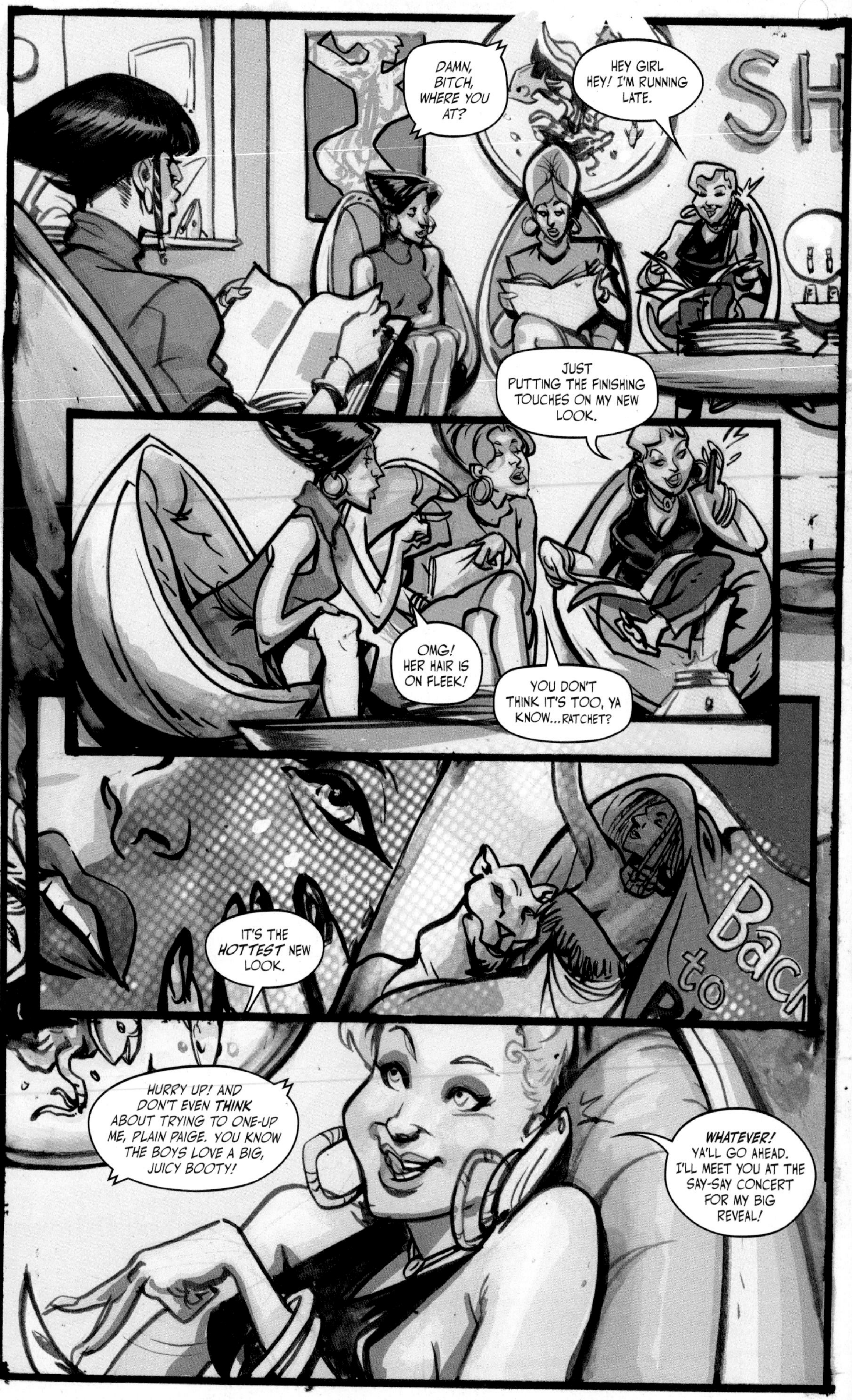
DAMN, BITCH, WHERE YOU AT?
HEY GIRL HEY! I'M RUNNING LATE.
JUST PUTTING THE FINISHING TOUCHES ON MY NEW LOOK.
OMG! HER HAIR IS ON FLEEK!
YOU DON'T THINK IT'S TOO, YA KNOW...RATCHET?
IT'S THE HOTTEST NEW LOOK.
HURRY UP! AND DON'T EVEN THINK ABOUT TRYING TO ONE-UP ME, PLAIN PAIGE. YOU KNOW THE BOYS LOVE A BIG, JUICY BOOTY!
WHATEVER! YA'LL GO AHEAD. I'LL MEET YOU AT THE SAY-SAY CONCERT FOR MY BIG REVEAL!

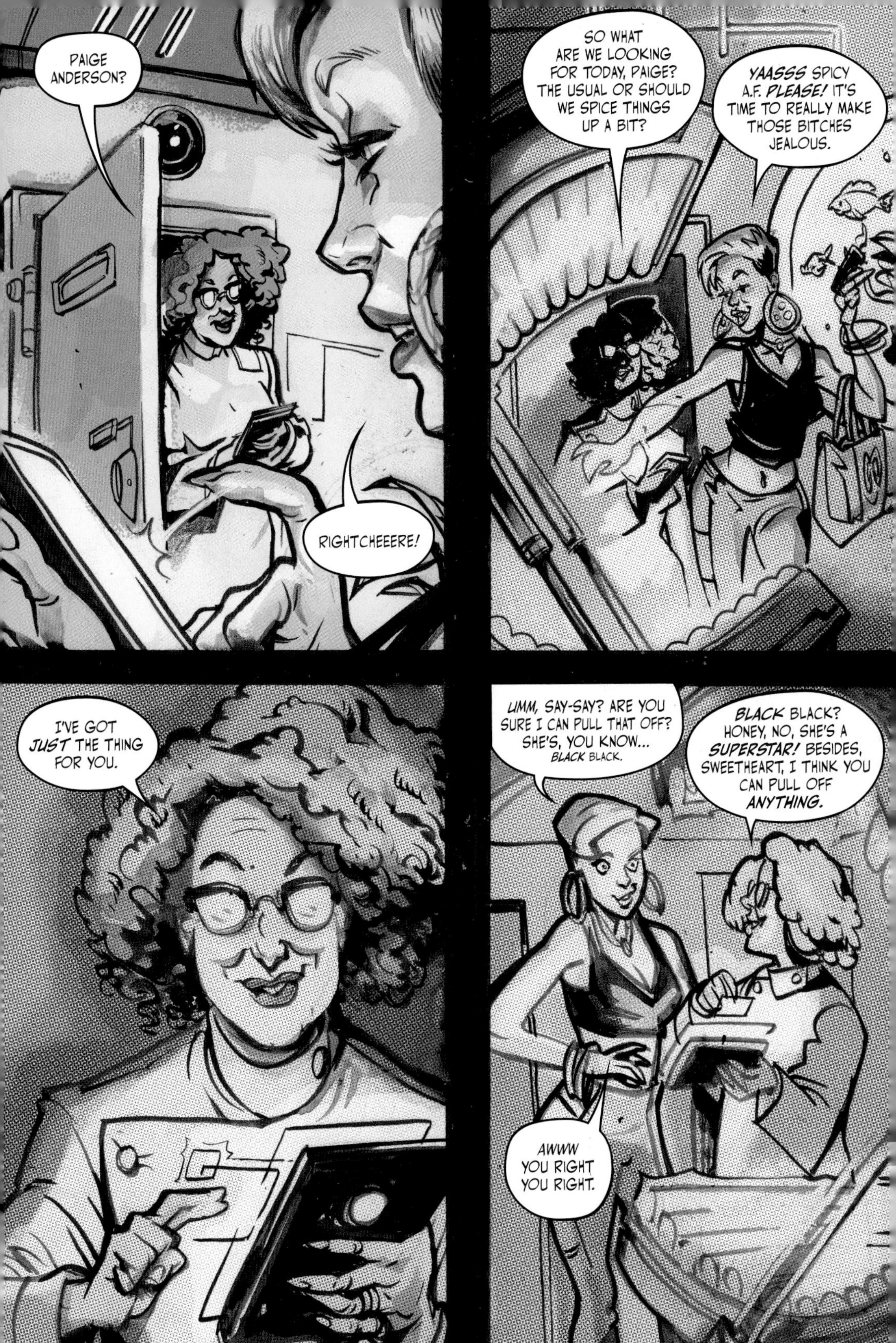
PAIGE ANDERSON?
RIGHTCHEEERE!
SO WHAT ARE WE LOOKING FOR TODAY, PAIGE? THE USUAL OR SHOULD WE SPICE THINGS UP A BIT?
YAASSS SPICY A.F. PLEASE! IT'S TIME TO REALLY MAKE THOSE BITCHES JEALOUS.
I'VE GOT JUST THE THING FOR YOU.
UMM, SAY-SAY? ARE YOU SURE I CAN PULL THAT OFF? SHE'S, YOU KNOW... BLACK BLACK.
BLACK BLACK? HONEY, NO, SHE'S A SUPERSTAR! BESIDES, SWEETHEART, I THINK YOU CAN PULL OFF ANYTHING.
AWWW YOU RIGHT YOU RIGHT.

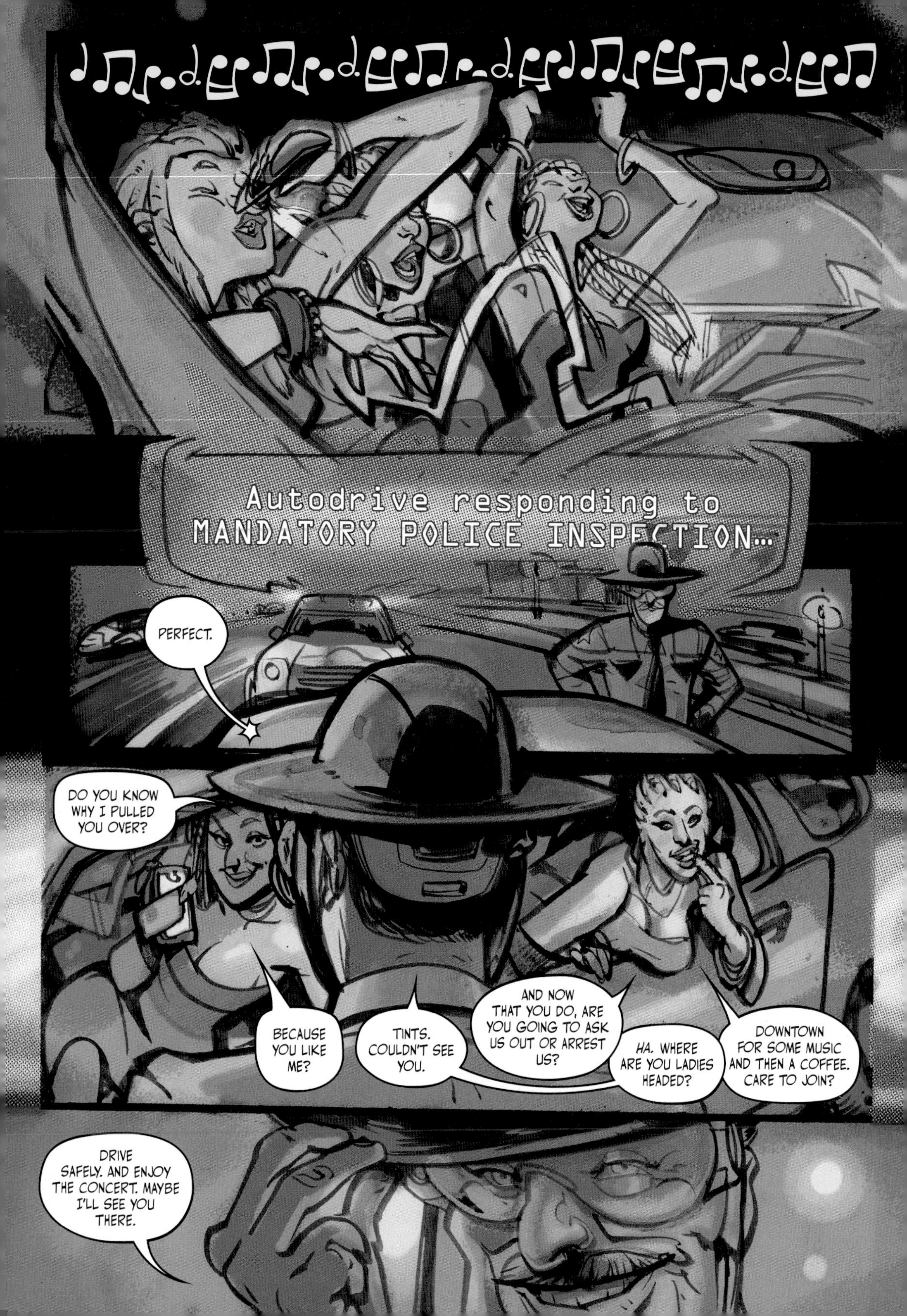
Autodrive responding to MANDATORY POLICE INSPECTION...
PERFECT.
DO YOU KNOW WHY I PULLED YOU OVER?
BECAUSE YOU LIKE ME?
TINTS. COULDN'T SEE YOU.
AND NOW THAT YOU DO, ARE YOU GOING TO ASK US OUT OR ARREST US?
HA. WHERE ARE YOU LADIES HEADED?
DOWNTOWN FOR SOME MUSIC AND THEN A COFFEE. CARE TO JOIN?
DRIVE SAFELY. AND ENJOY THE CONCERT. MAYBE I'LL SEE YOU THERE.

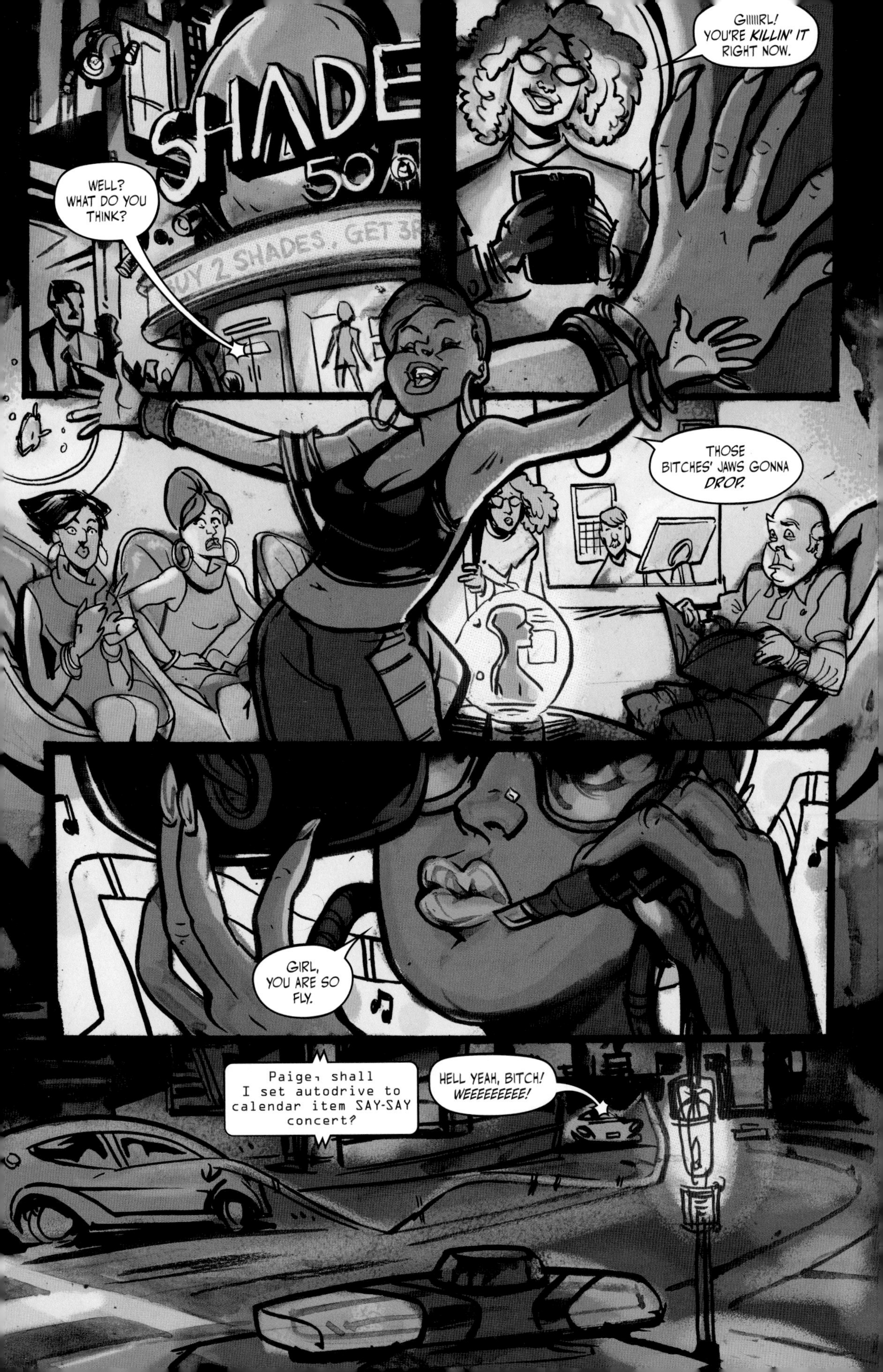

SHADE
50
BUY 2 SHADES, GET 3R
WELL? WHAT DO YOU THINK?
GIIIIRL! YOU'RE KILLIN' IT RIGHT NOW.
THOSE BITCHES' JAWS GONNA DROP.
GIRL, YOU ARE SO FLY.
Paige, shall I set autodrive to calendar item SAY-SAY concert?
HELL YEAH, BITCH! WEEEEEEEEE!

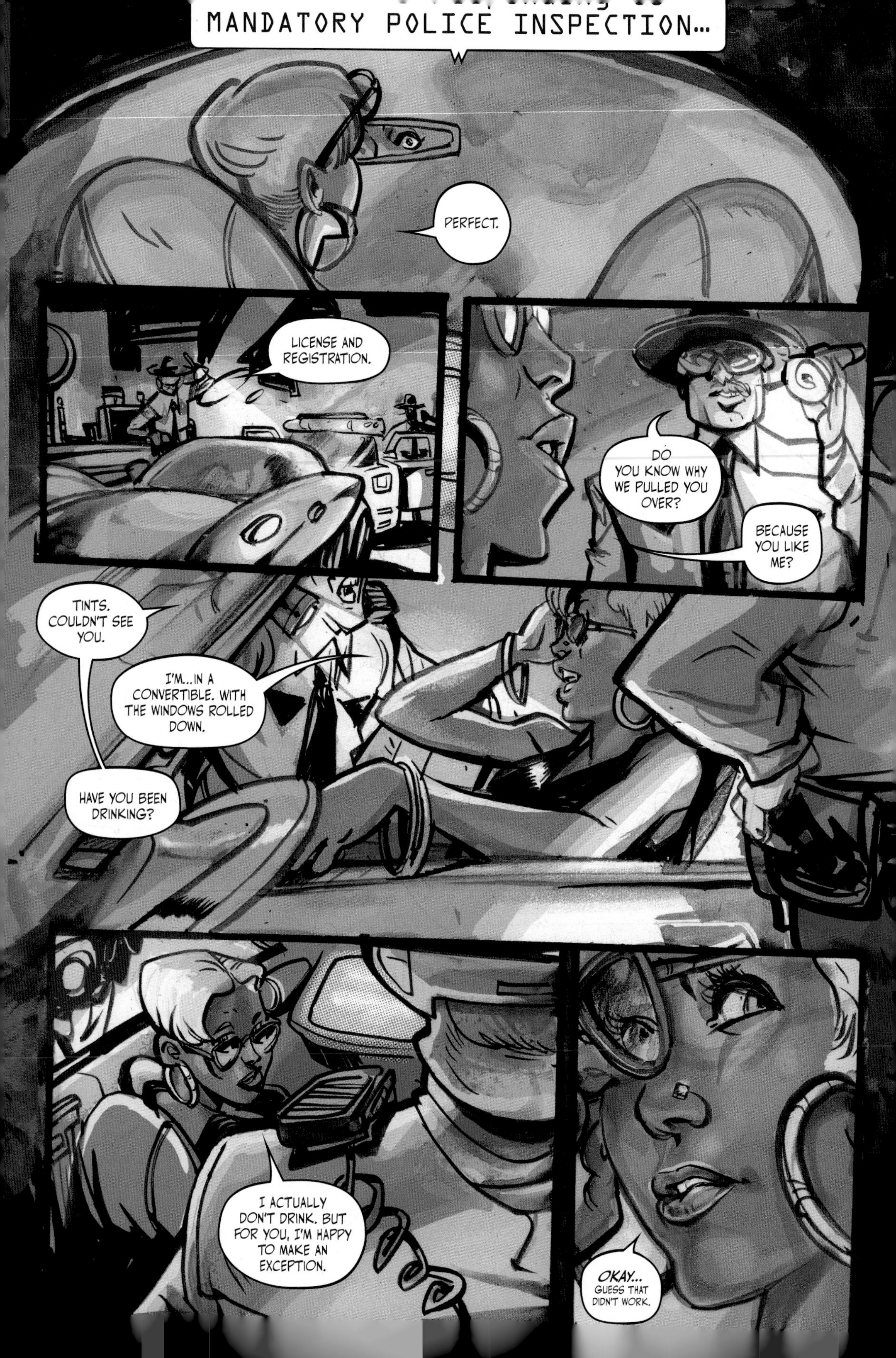
MANDATORY POLICE INSPECTION...
PERFECT.
LICENSE AND REGISTRATION.
DO YOU KNOW WHY WE PULLED YOU OVER?
BECAUSE YOU LIKE ME?
TINTS. COULDN'T SEE YOU.
I'M...IN A CONVERTIBLE. WITH THE WINDOWS ROLLED DOWN.
HAVE YOU BEEN DRINKING?
I ACTUALLY DON'T DRINK. BUT FOR YOU, I'M HAPPY TO MAKE AN EXCEPTION.
OKAY... GUESS THAT DIDN'T WORK.

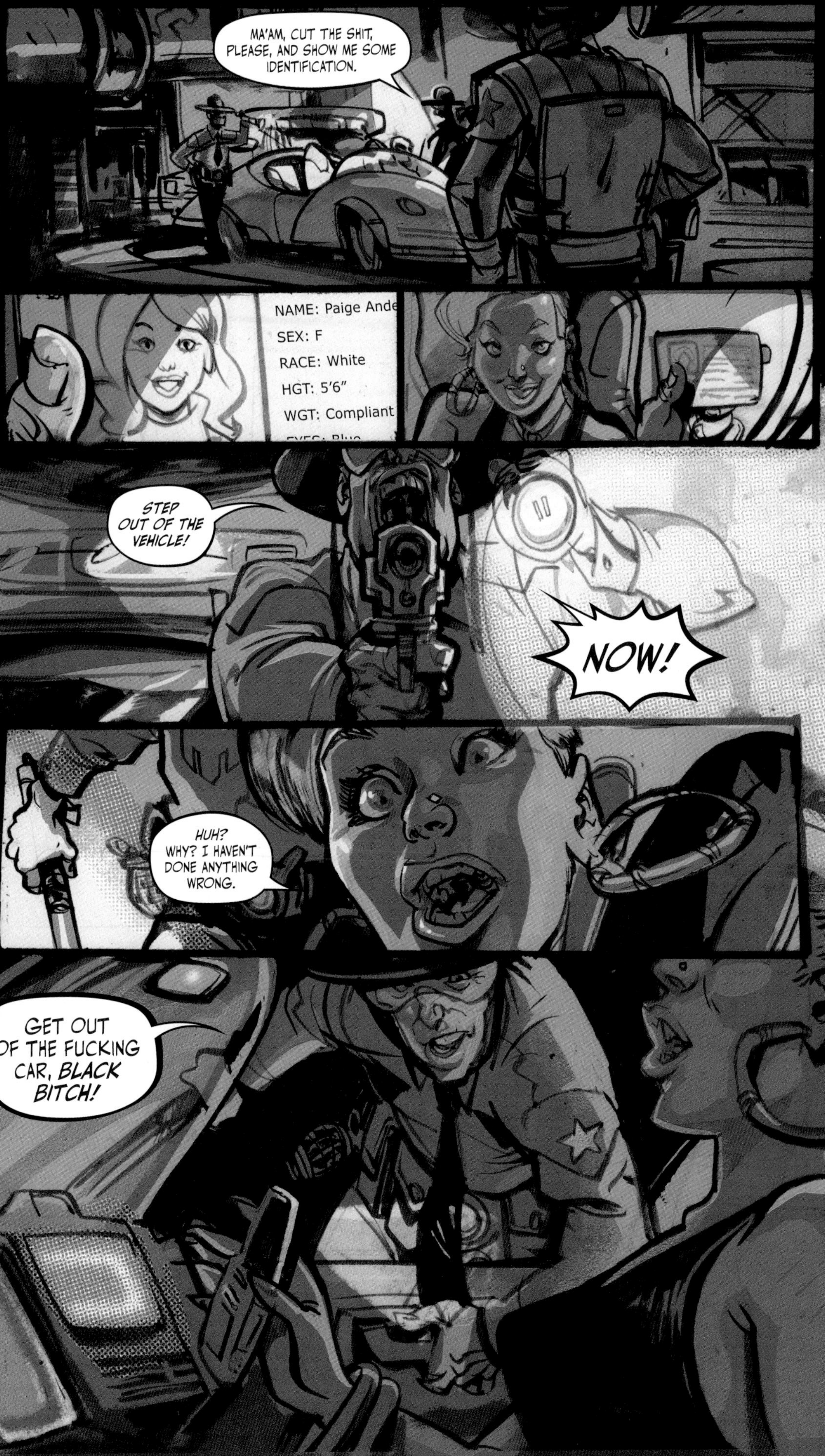
MA'AM, CUT THE SHIT, PLEASE, AND SHOW ME SOME IDENTIFICATION.
NAME: Paige Ande
SEX: F
RACE: White
HGT: 5'6"
WGT: Compliant
STEP OUT OF THE VEHICLE!
NOW!
HUH? WHY? I HAVEN'T DONE ANYTHING WRONG.
GET OUT OF THE FUCKING CAR, BLACK BITCH!

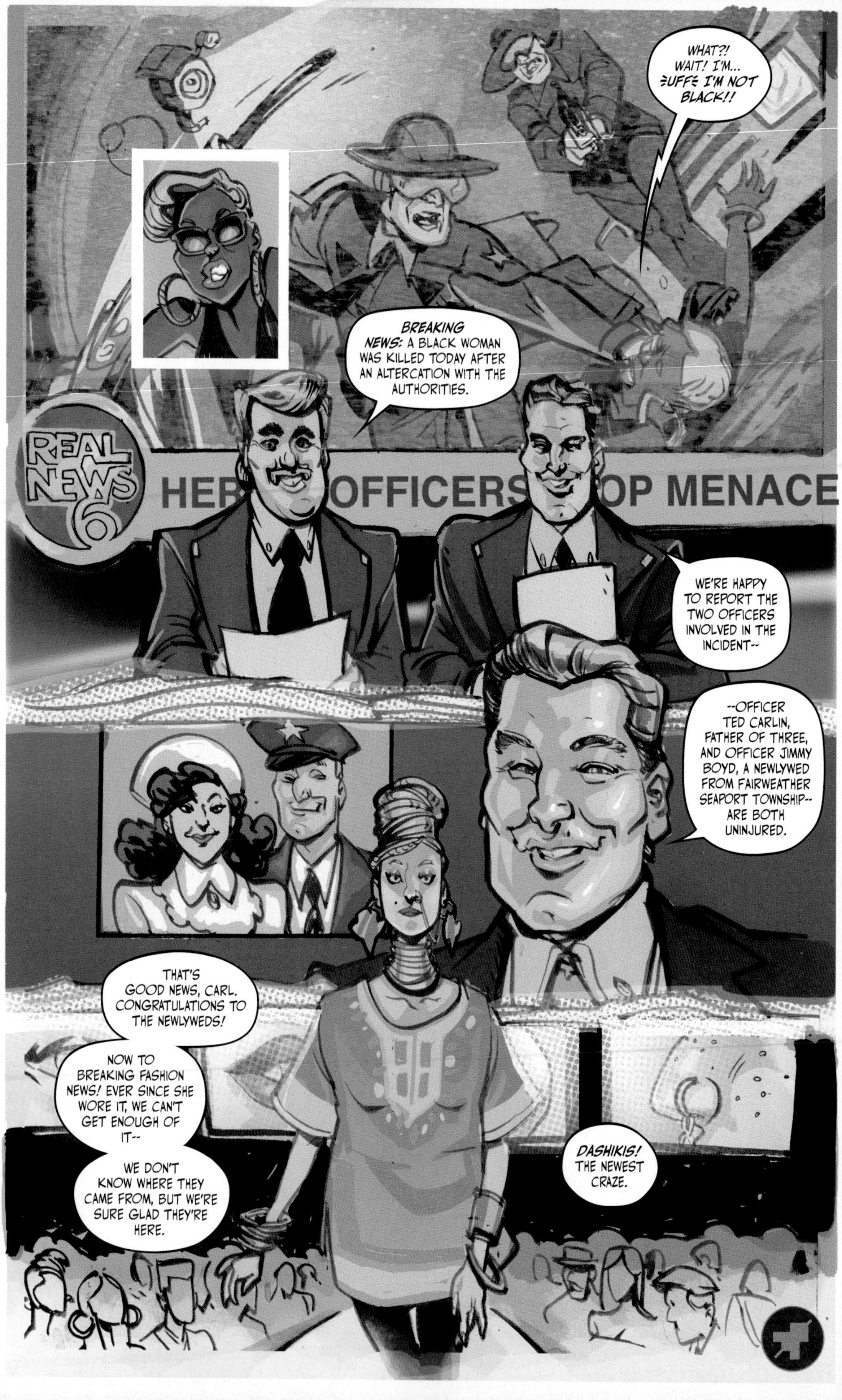

WHAT?! WAIT! I'M... =UFF= I'M NOT BLACK!!
BREAKING NEWS: A BLACK WOMAN WAS KILLED TODAY AFTER AN ALTERCATION WITH THE AUTHORITIES.
REAL NEWS 6
OFFICERS
OP MENACE
WE'RE HAPPY TO REPORT THE TWO OFFICERS INVOLVED IN THE INCIDENT--
--OFFICER TED CARLIN, FATHER OF THREE, AND OFFICER JIMMY BOYD, A NEWLYWED FROM FAIRWEATHER SEAPORT TOWNSHIP-- ARE BOTH UNINJURED.
THAT'S GOOD NEWS, CARL. CONGRATULATIONS TO THE NEWLYWEDS!
NOW TO BREAKING FASHION NEWS! EVER SINCE SHE WORE IT, WE CAN'T GET ENOUGH OF IT--
DASHIKIS! THE NEWEST CRAZE.
WE DON'T KNOW WHERE THEY CAME FROM, BUT WE'RE SURE GLAD THEY'RE HERE.

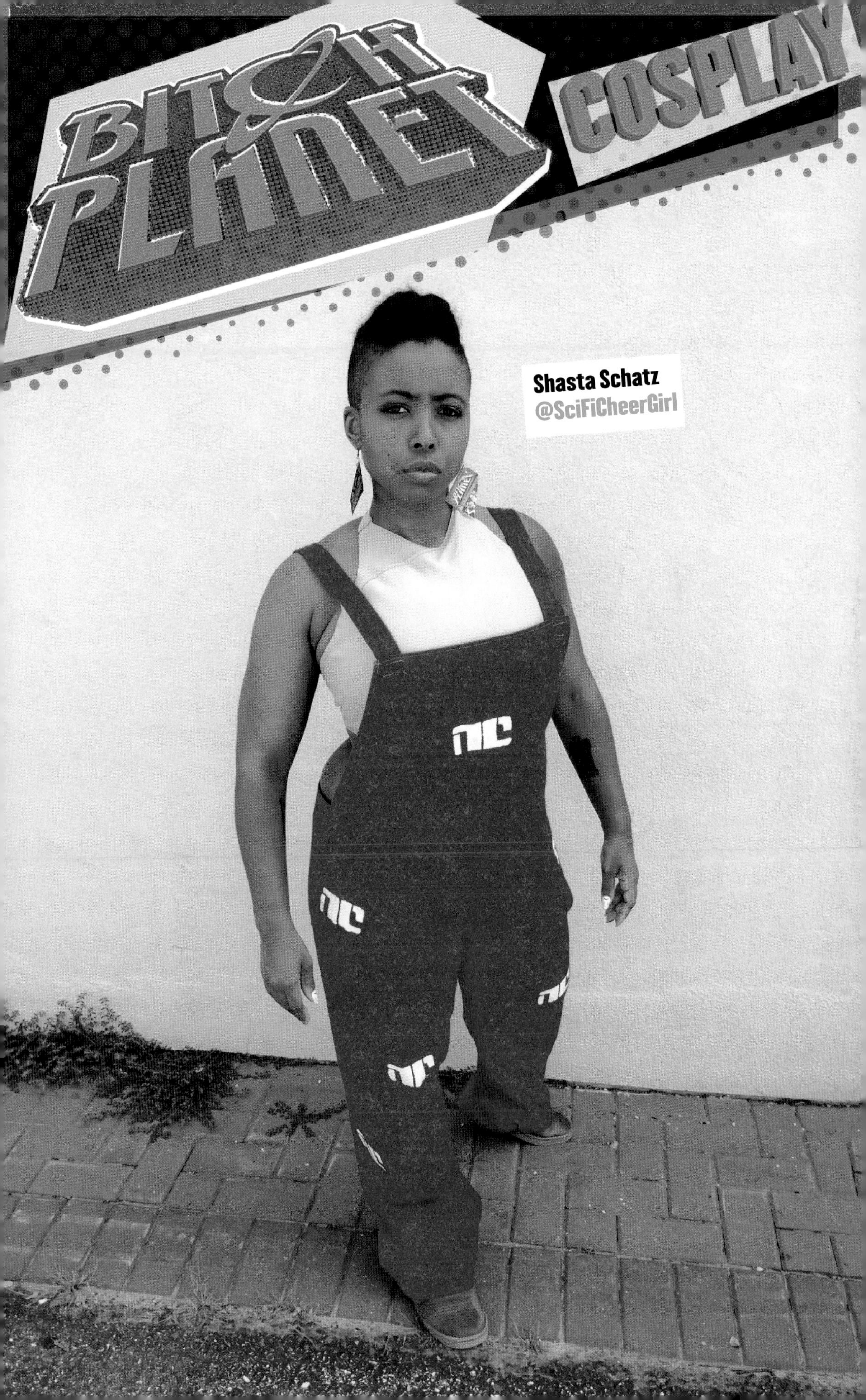
BITCH PLANET
COSPLAY

Shasta Schatz
@SciFiCheerGirl

*Triple Feature #3: Layout*

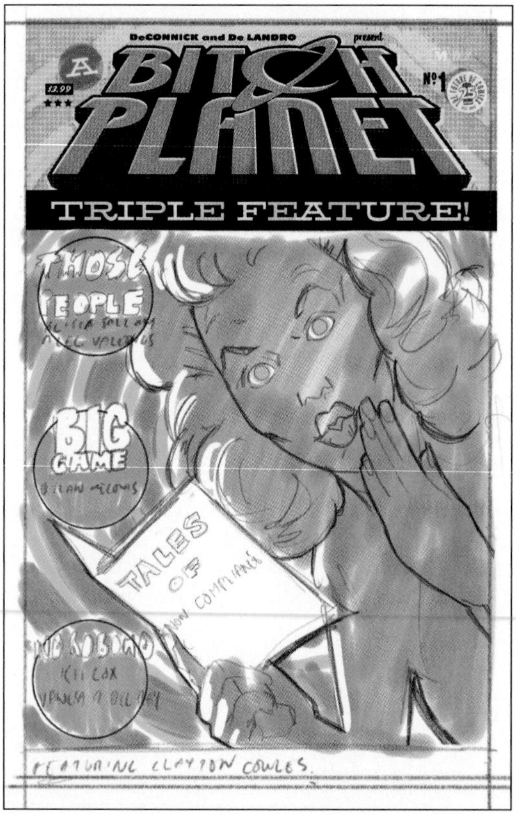
DeCONNICK and De LANDRO present
A
$3.99
BITCH PLANET
No 1
TRIPLE FEATURE!
TALES OF

*Triple Feature #3: Watercolor*

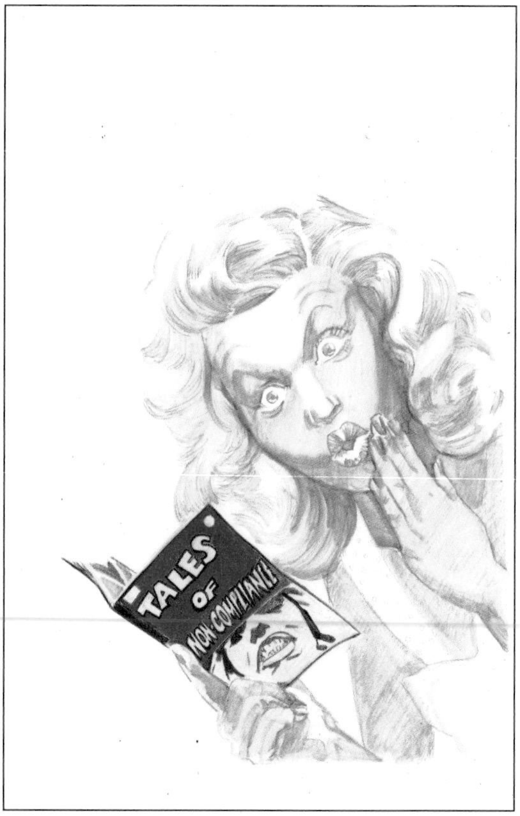
TALES OF NON-COMPLIANCE

# **BITCH PLANET** SKETCHBOOK

## Cover Process with Valentine and Rian

**1**

**Valentine:** The TRIPLE FEATURE covers were a particular challenge in comparison to the main series, which explored exploitation movie posters and political ads. For this anthology, the theme/style I aimed for was in the vein of the drive-in poster. For the first two issues, I had the benefit of seeing some of the short stories ahead of time and my concepts were inspired by the existing artwork. But, because comics solicitations have to be pulled together so far in advance (~3-4 months), by the time the third cover rolled around, we were still working out the details of the upcoming shorts. I realized I'd need to make a cover that was a bit more generic — for lack of a better descriptive.

The Model has been a very reliable character to build a theme around. She has a wide acting range that lets us use her in different scenarios from ultra creepy to silly and that has been very handy to lean on. There was also talk about basing a series of covers for a future arc on old pulp novels and comics. So that style was running through my brain, too.

**2**

**Valentine:** I only did one draft on this composition. I don't know if it was because I was confident in my initial idea or time (Narrator's Voice: it's usually time). This wasn't going to change much, other than The Model's expression or hand placement. There isn't a lot of variation when it comes to a composition like this. And making sure that there's clear room and direction for Rian to work his copy design has to be considered at this stage. The color palette is based off of The Model's distinctive pink and blue in BITCH PLANET proper. This step was so easy, kids.

*Triple Feature #3: Layered file*

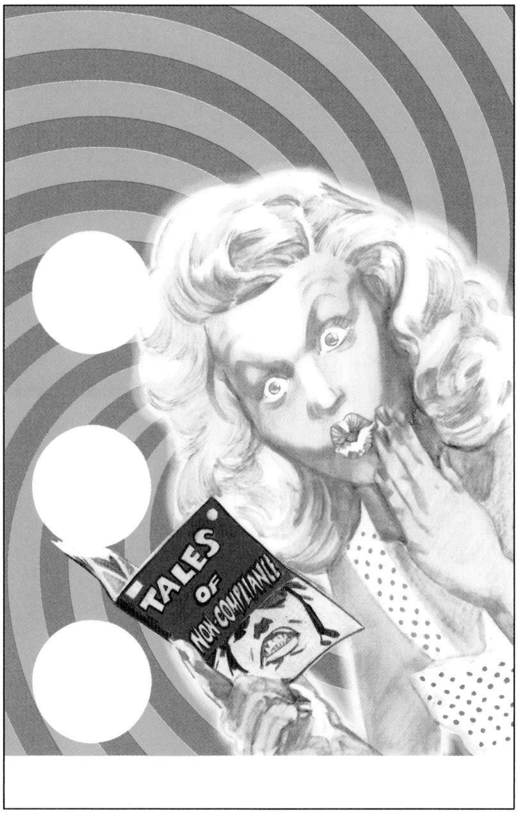
TALES
OF
NON-COMPLIANCE

*Triple Feature #3: Final mock-up*

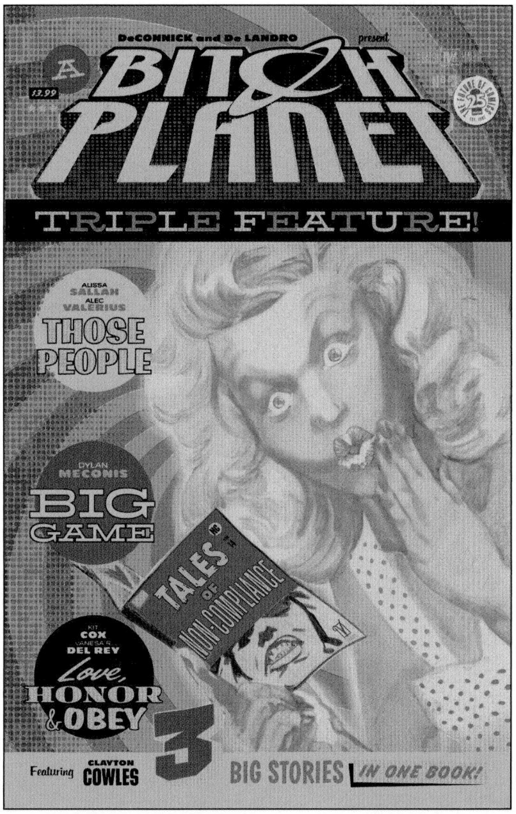
DeCONNICK and De LANDRO present
A
BITCH PLANET
TRIPLE FEATURE!
SALLAH
VALERIUS
THOSE PEOPLE
DYLAN
MECONIS
BIG GAME
COX
DEL REY
Love, HONOR & OBEY
TALES OF NON-COMPLIANCE
3
Featuring CLAYTON COWLES
BIG STORIES IN ONE BOOK!

**3**

**Valentine:** I did watercolors for the final... but I admit to smoothing out some of the brushwork digitally. Breaking in a new waterbrush is always cool, but flow control takes some time for me. I was hoping that hand painting would help sell the pulp look in the end.

**4**

**Valentine:** Once the digital was done, off to Rian it goes, where he continues to bring the magic and pull everything together for the final, fully mocked-up piece.

**Rian:** I place the Bitch Planet logo in Adobe Illustrator, add more dot screen textures and customized type using digitized period fonts from the Filmotype range, then import the whole into Photoshop where the colors can be knocked out of register to mimic cheap vintage printing techniques. A scan of yellowed paper is overlaid to age the colors and add some texture. The logo, here in yellow, is given a lighter overlay so that the color pops out, almost as if it's printed in a flouro ink.

*Issue #1 - Craig Yeung*

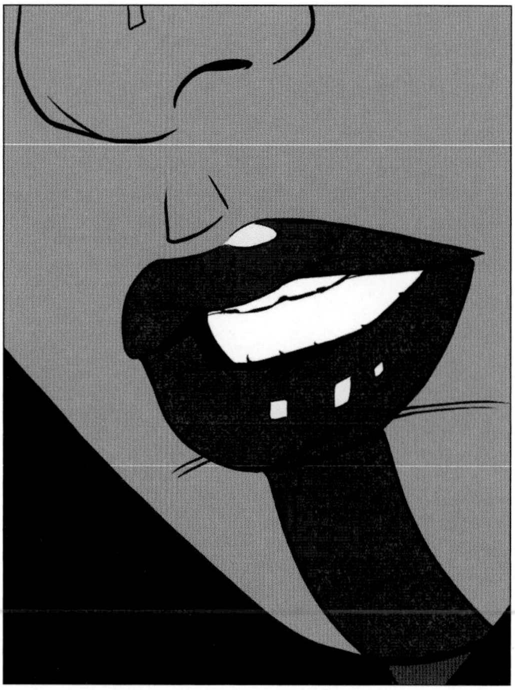

*Issue #1 - Joanna Estep*

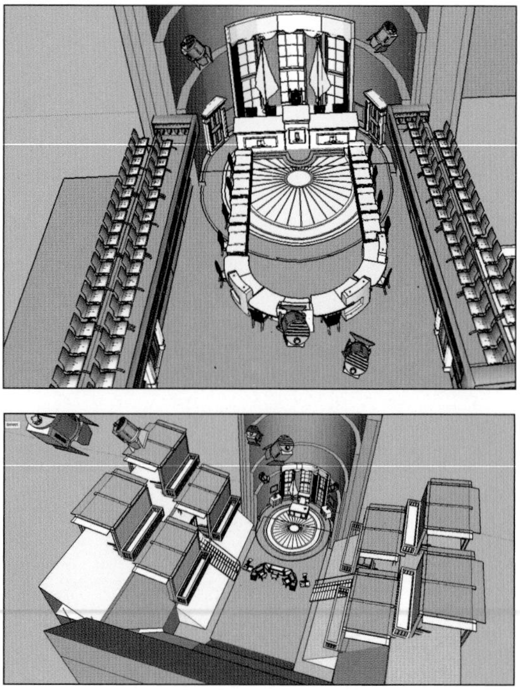

# BITCH PLANET SKETCHBOOK
## Designs and layouts

*Issue #1 - Joanna Estep*

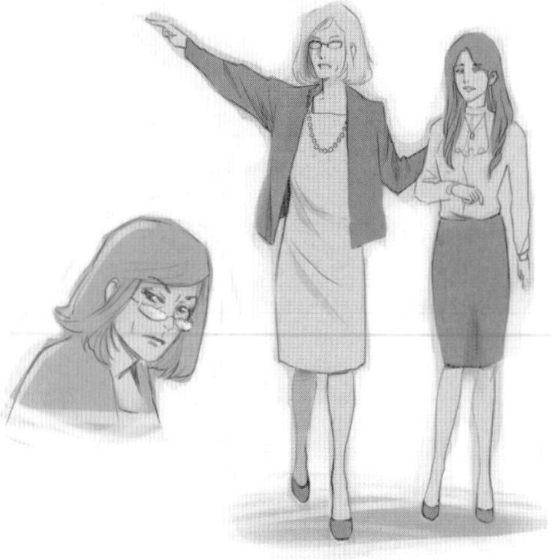

*Issue #2 - Sharon Lee De La Cruz*

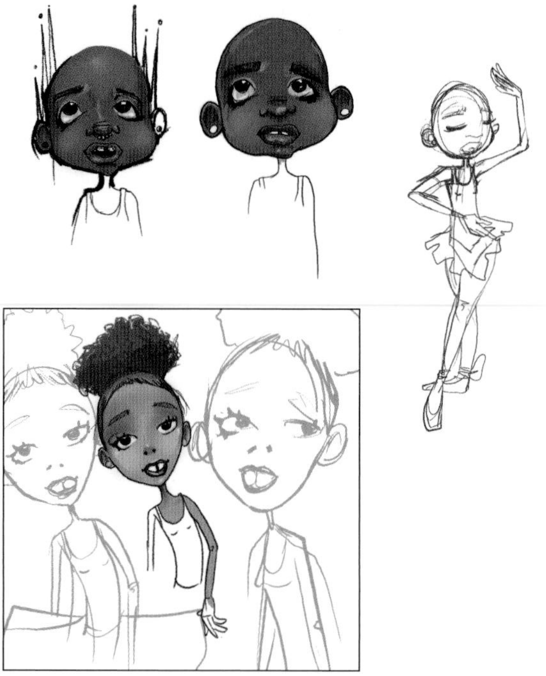

*Issue #2 - Ro Stein & Ted Brandt*

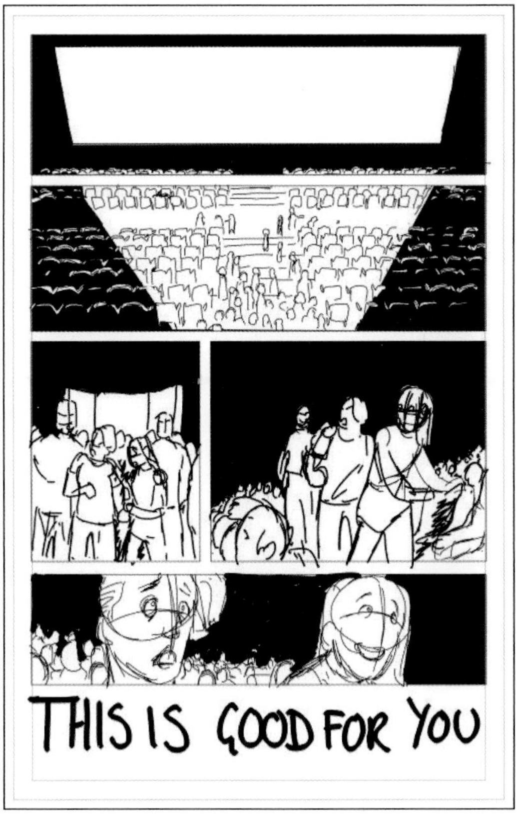
THIS IS GOOD FOR YOU

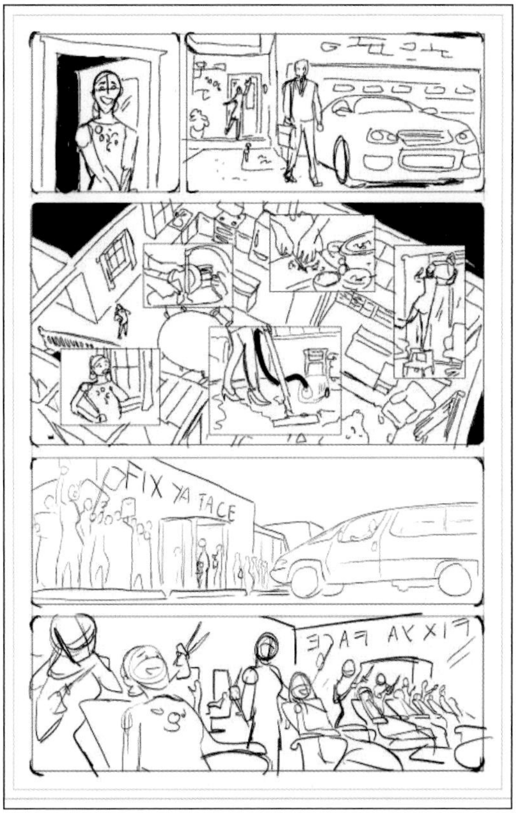

*Issue #2 - Naomi Franquiz*

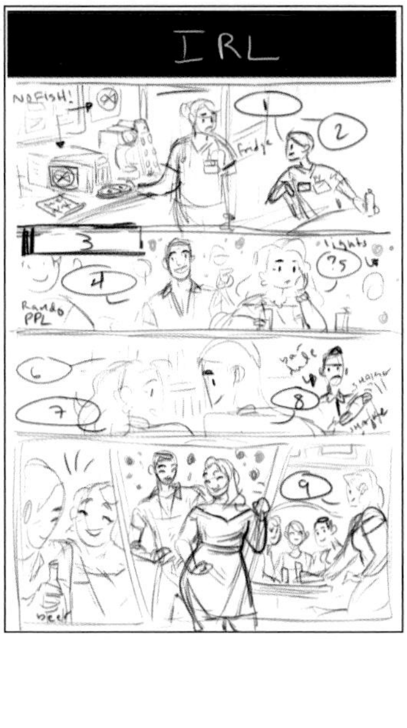
IRL
NO FISH!
Rando PPL

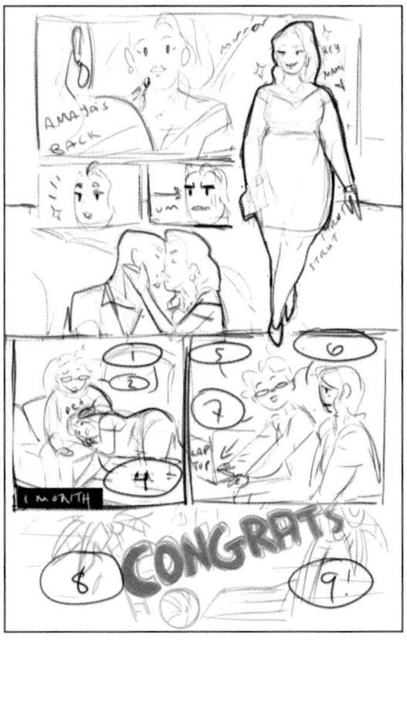
AMAYA's BACK
1 MONTH
CONGRATS

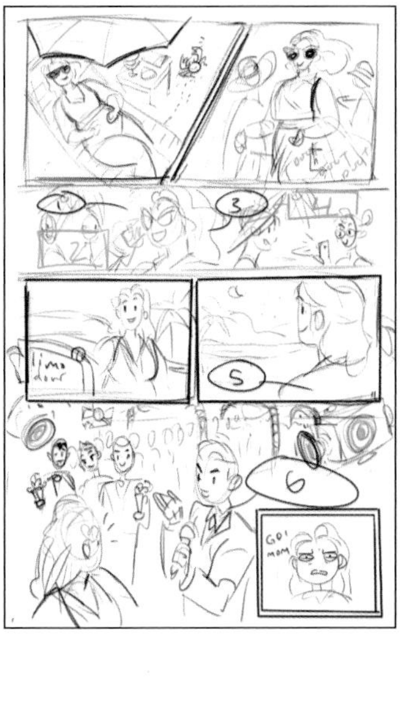

*Issue #3 - Alec Valerius*

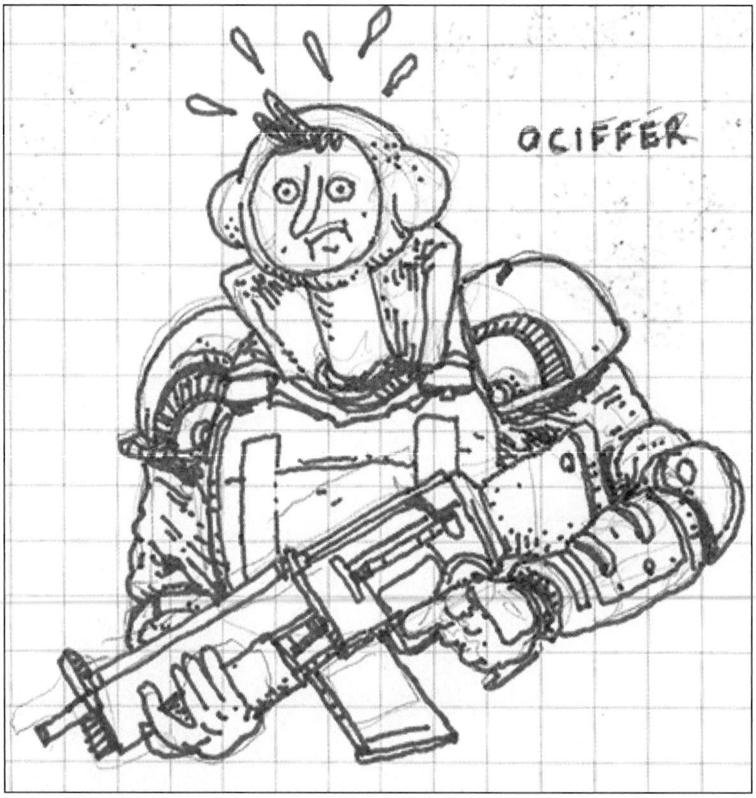
OCIFFER

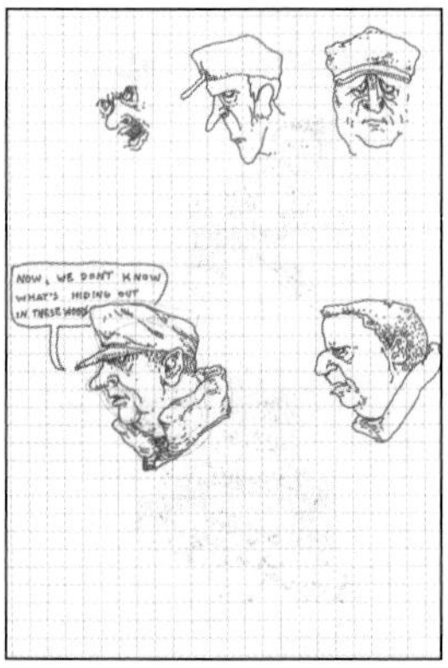
NOW, WE DONT KNOW
WHAT'S HIDING OUT
IN THESE

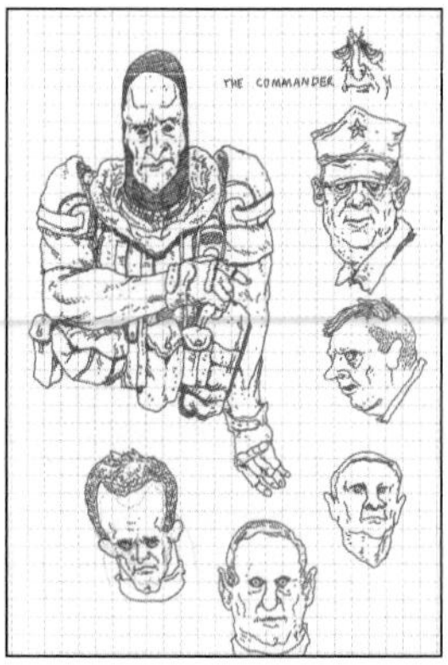
THE COMMANDER

## BITCH PLANET SKETCHBOOK

### Designs and layouts

*Issue #3 - Vanesa R. Del Rey*

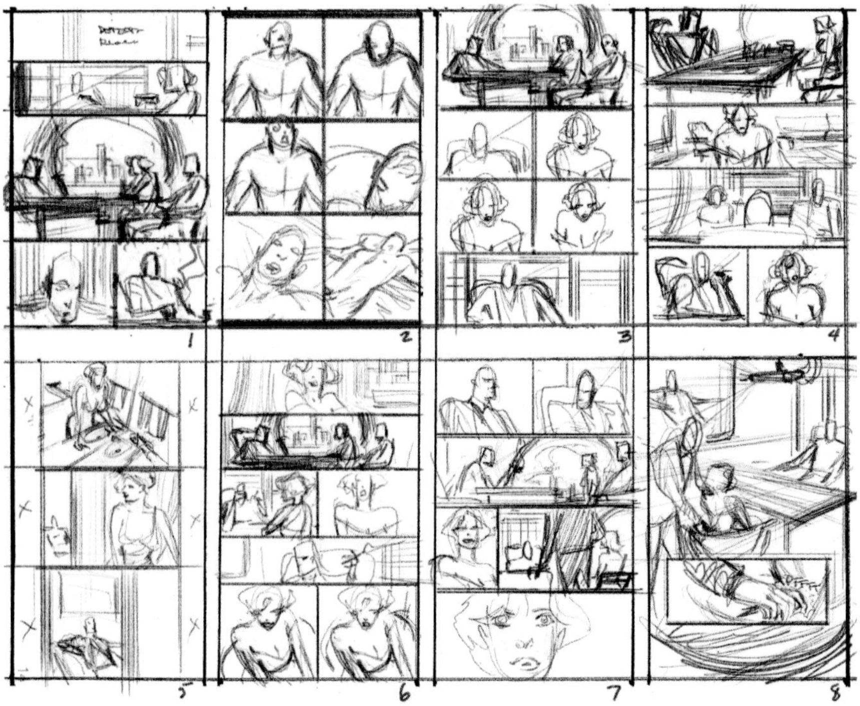
1
2
3
4
5
6
7
8

*Issue #3 - Dylan Meconis*

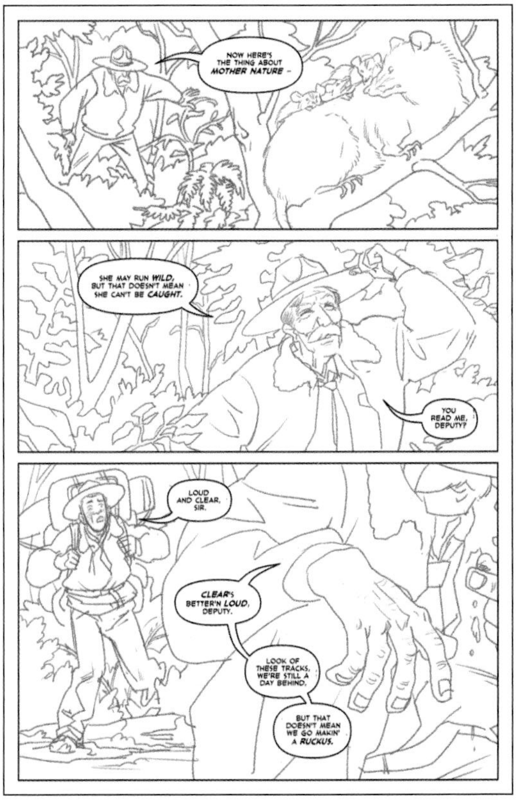
NOW HERE'S THE THING ABOUT ***MOTHER NATURE*** –
SHE MAY RUN ***WILD***, BUT THAT DOESN'T MEAN SHE CAN'T BE ***CAUGHT***.
YOU READ ME, DEPUTY?
LOUD AND CLEAR, SIR.
***CLEAR***'S BETTER'N ***LOUD***, DEPUTY.
LOOK OF THESE TRACKS, WE'RE STILL A DAY BEHIND.
BUT THAT DOESN'T MEAN WE GO MAKIN' A ***RUCKUS***.

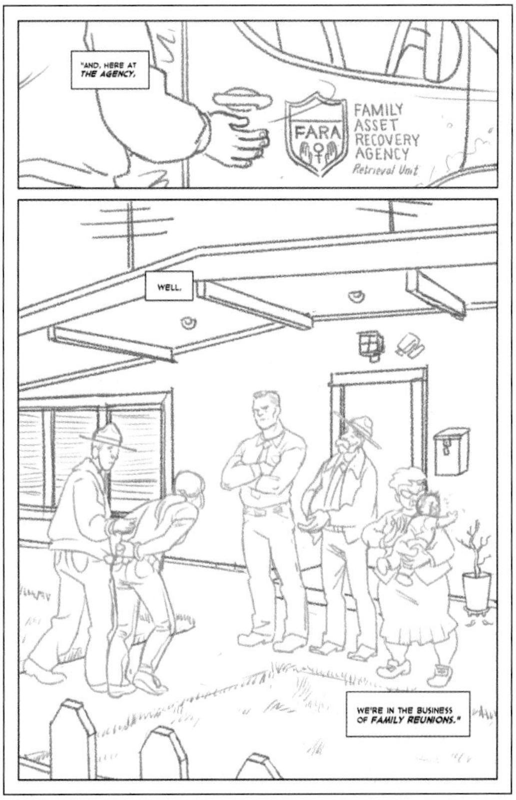
"AND, HERE AT ***THE AGENCY***,
FARA
FAMILY ASSET RECOVERY AGENCY
Retrieval Unit
WELL,
WE'RE IN THE BUSINESS OF ***FAMILY REUNIONS***."

*Issue #4 - Mindy Lee*

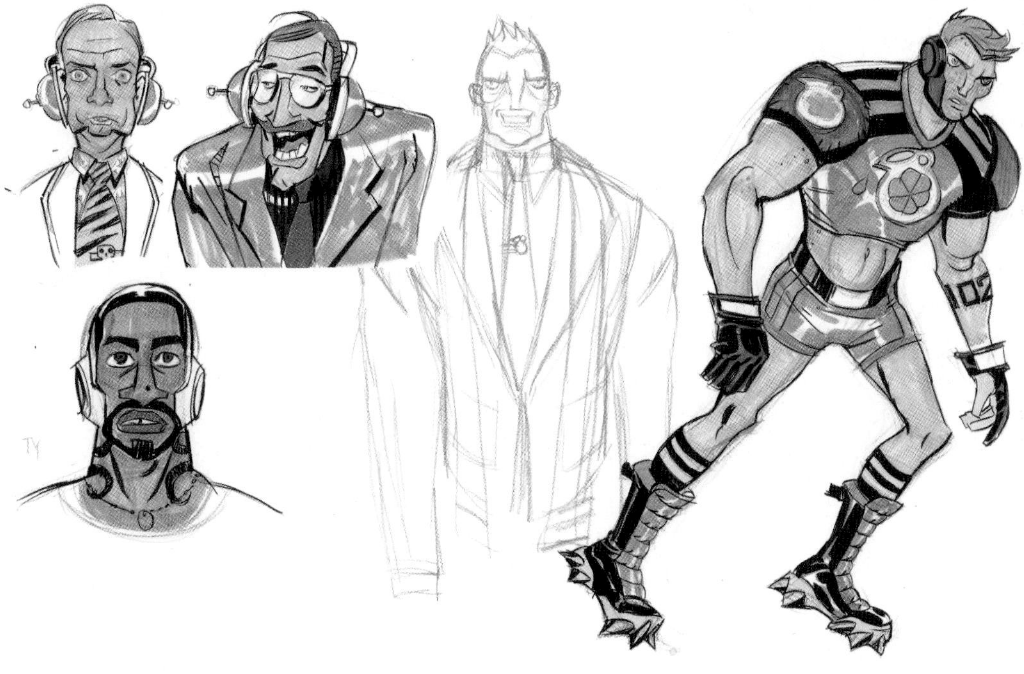

*Issue #4 - Rossi Gifford*

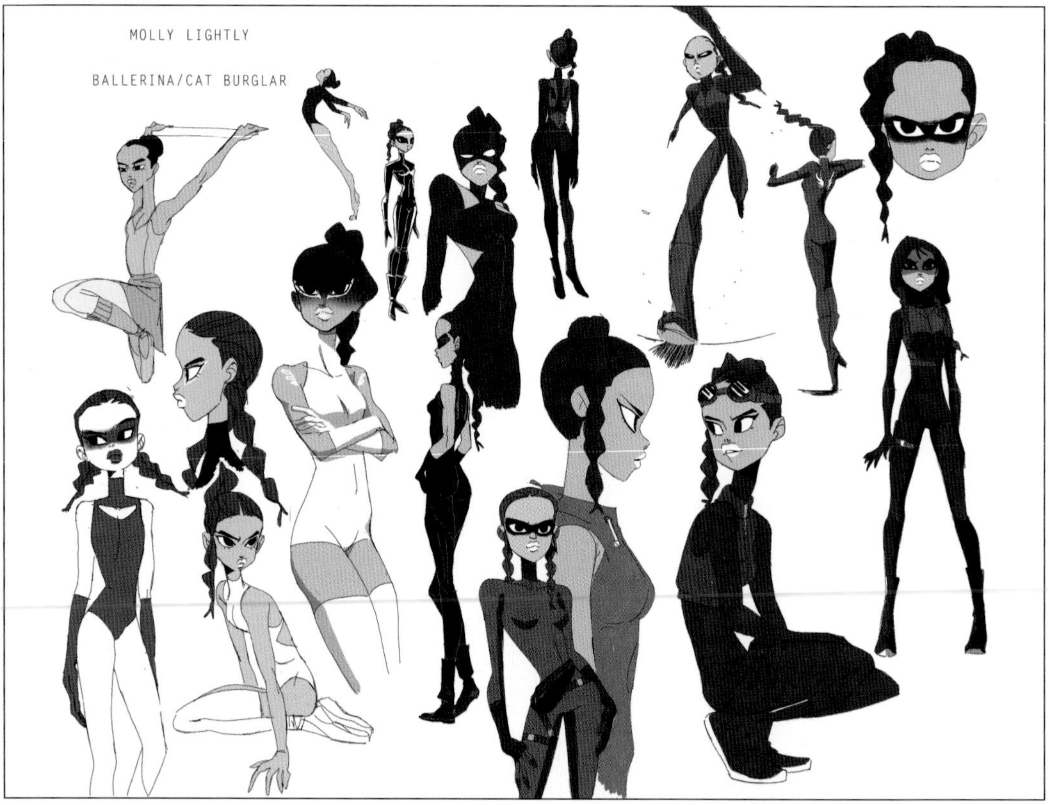
MOLLY LIGHTLY
BALLERINA/CAT BURGLAR



*Issue #5 - Saskia Gutekunst*

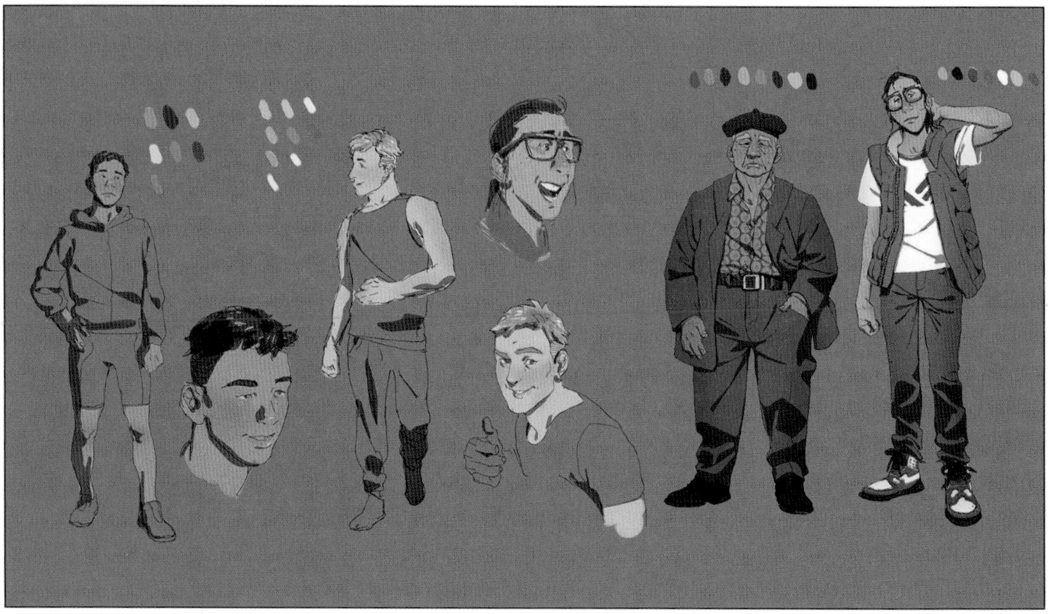

*Issue #5 - Chris Visions*

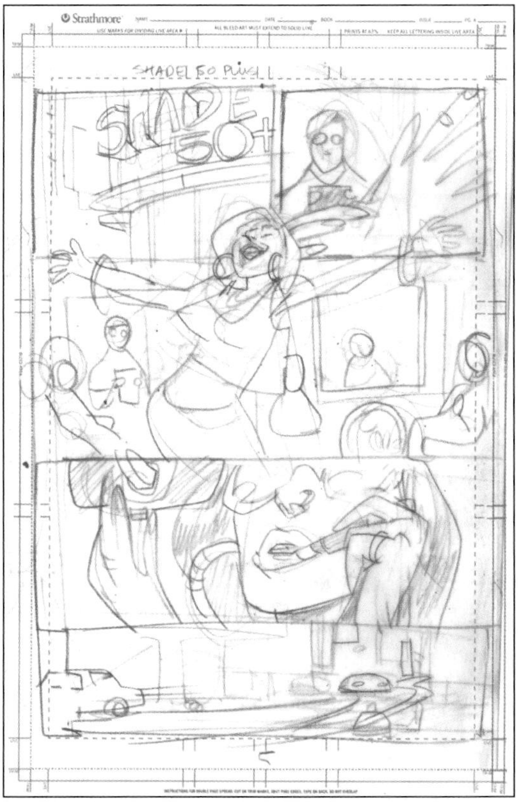
Strathmore
SHADE 50+

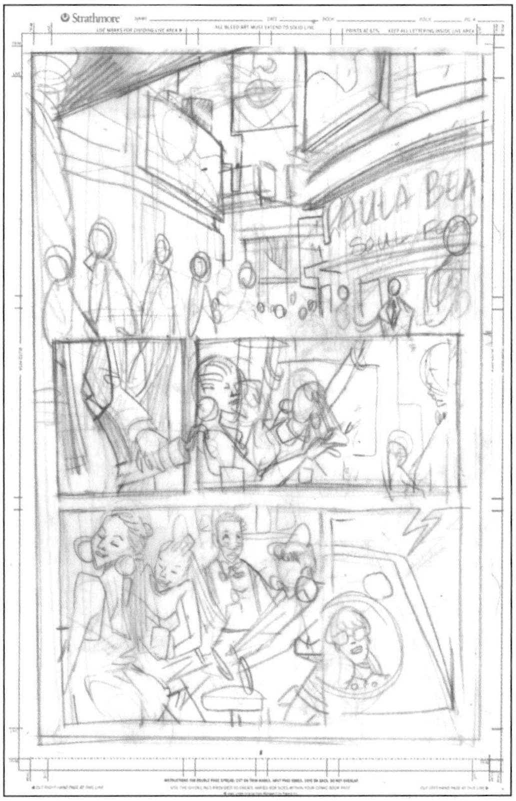
Strathmore
PAULA BEA

*Issue #5 - Elsa Charretier*

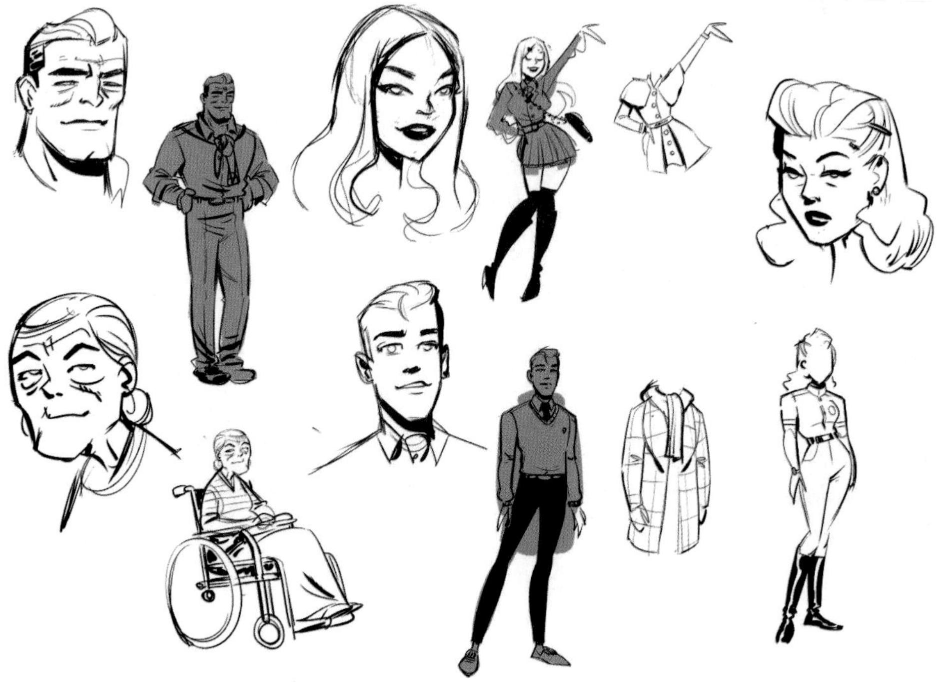

# **BITCH PLANET** CONTRIBUTORS

## Writer, artist and colorist biographies

**CHERYL LYNN EATON** is a writer, editor, and popular culture commentator focused on the intersection of race, class, the comic book medium, and the science fiction genre. She is also the founder of the Ormes Society, an organization dedicated to promoting the work of black women in the fields of animation and sequential art.

**MARIA FRÖHLICH** is a Swedish artist and writer, best known for her science fiction series MIRACLECITY published in the THE PHANTOM magazine in Sweden and Norway 2013-2014. She made her US debut in 2014 on IDW's SHADOW SHOW. She's currently working on NU LEKER VI! the latest book in a critically acclaimed children's book series co-created with bestselling author Sara Bergmark Elfgren for Rabén & Sjögren.

**ANDREW AYDIN** is a #1 New York Times best-selling and National Book Award-winning author and currently serving as Digital Director & Policy Advisor to Rep. John Lewis in Washington, D.C. Aydin is the coauthor of the graphic novel trilogy MARCH and has written for comics such as the X-FILES (IDW) as well as media outlets Creative Loafing and Teaching Tolerance.

**JOANNA ESTEP** is the critically acclaimed illustrator of such titles as THE FANTASTIC FOUR (Marvel Comics), DEATH HEAD (Dark Horse), and THE THRILLING ADVENTURE HOUR (Boom!/Archaia). Her work has earned her accolades such as the S.P.A.C.E. Prize, and nominations for Eisner and Harvey awards.

**CONLEY LYONS** is a speculative fiction writer who hails from western North Carolina. Her writing has appeared in BITCH PLANET: TRIPLE FEATURE (June 2017) and the speculative fiction anthology ATHENA'S DAUGHTERS, Vol. I (2014). She is currently working on a semi-autobiographical novel about her Native grandfather, set in the heart of 1890s Indian Country.

**CRAIG YEUNG** is an illustrator from Toronto, Ontario. He has worked on various titles that include RUNAWAYS, X-MEN and ARROW. Always looking to collaborate with unique voices and awesome people to create great comics, he can be found on Twitter @ csyeung and Instagram @craigyeung.

**MARCO D'ALFONSO** is a Canadian illustrator / designer who finds inspiration in animation, comics, contemporary art and pop culture. His work includes toy and video game designs, editorial illustrations, and comic book cover art and has been featured in various galleries such as Los Angeles' IAm8Bit and New York's Bottleneck Gallery. Marco is currently hiding out in Toronto.

**DANIELLE HENDERSON** is a TV writer (MANIAC, DIVORCE, DIFFICULT PEOPLE), freelance writer, and a former editor and staff writer for ROOKIE. A book based on her popular website, FEMINIST RYAN GOSLING, was released by Running Press in August 2012; you can still buy it, and you probably should. Her memoir, THE UGLY CRY, will be published in 2018.

**RO STEIN & TED BRANDT** are a single cartoonist implausibly split into two people. They live in the middle of nowhere in the U.K., but work mostly in the USA, which is a rotten commute they wouldn't wish on anyone. They've been working professionally in comics for 3 years, and in that time have drawn for Action Lab, Marvel Comics and Image.

**CHE GRAYSON** is a Brooklyn-based filmmaker and comic book creator. She is an MFA candidate at New York University's graduate film program, and is the creator and writer of the comic book series, RIGAMO. Che is a former TED Resident, and is currently an Associate Video Producer at Teen Vogue while developing her feature film debut, RED BONES.

**SHARON LEE DE LA CRUZ** is an artist and activist from New York City. She earned a BFA from The Cooper Union, is a Fulbright scholar, and obtained her Masters at NYU's ITP program. Sharon's work is in the intersection of tech, art, and social justice. She currently lives in New Jersey and is the Assistant Director of The StudioLab, a creative tech lab, at Princeton University.

**JORDAN CLARK** is a writer based out of Baltimore, Maryland. But enough about me...how are you? Good day so far? No? Well, go get some cake, that's what I would do. Anyway, I write about a bunch of different stuff from sentient zombies to the effects of the internet on identity. Tweet me @Jrsosa18, my website is Jclarkcomics.squarespace.com.

**NAOMI FRANQUIZ** is a freelance illustrator and comic book artist working out of delightfully dank Florida. Her original work has been published in the POWER & MAGIC PRESS anthology and self-published online. She is currently working on MISFIT CITY from BOOM!Box. You can find her online sleep-tweeting or aggressively enjoying video compilations of rude cats.

The midwestern masterpiece **ALISSA SALLAH** is the comics equivalent to LeBron James. She has worked in various anthologies such as the SPITBALL Comic Anthology, the BONFIRE Yearly Charity Anthology (SHONEN TRUMP, BLACK WATER) and now BITCH PLANET: TRIPLE FEATURE. She is currently editing & coloring the upcoming Image comic series SLEEPLESS and working on her first OGN.

**ALEC VALERIUS** is a cartoonist based in Columbus, Ohio. His work derives inspiration from underground comix and French illustration. His past work has been included in the Columbus College of Art and Design's SPITBALL anthology, where he collaborated with Evan Dorkin and Sarah Dyer. For more of his work, visit his website at alecvalerius.com

**DYLAN MECONIS** is a cartoonist whose work includes the graphic novels OUTFOXED, BITE ME!, and FAMILY MAN. She's a member of Helioscope, the largest studio of comics professionals in North America. She shares a home in Portland, Oregon with her wife (the attorney and speaker Katie Lane), an assortment of smaller mammals, and a cardboard standup of Captain Picard.

**KIT COX** is a writer and beautiful cat haver living in Portland, OR. She's a frequent BITCH PLANET backmatter contributor and co-wrote a comic short with Kelly Sue for the PRINCELESS Charity Anthology. You may know her from her not-so-secret double life as Kelly Sue & Matt Fraction's assistant.

Cuban artist **VANESA R. DEL REY** began her career doing concept art for animation. Her work in comics has been described as dark, gritty and mysterious with great dominance of figure work. She has illustrated SCARLET WITCH, DAREDEVIL ANNUAL (2016) for Marvel Comics and is a co-creator of REDLANDS, a new ongoing series at Image Comics. She currently lives and works by the beach in Miami, Florida.

**SARA WOOLLEY GÓMEZ** is an award-winning illustrator and graphic novelist based in Brooklyn, NY. Her work has been recognized by the Society of Illustrators in NYC and LA. Her creator-owned project, LOS PIRINEOS: THE MOSTLY TRUE MEMOIRS OF ESPERANCITA GÓMEZ, was singled out for award by the National Association of Latino Arts and Culture. She is illustration faculty at the New York City College of Technology, CUNY. sarawoolley.com

**MARC DESCHAMPS** is a Buffalo-based writer. He has had a number of stories published by Grayhaven Comics, and is currently working on an assortment of other comic projects. His Journalism degree is mostly reserved for ranting about gaming, sports and music through various publications, including Nintendojo where he serves as an editor. His favorite co-creation, however, is his daughter.

**MINDY LEE** has worked primarily as a concept designer on game projects such as DARKWATCH, LORD OF THE RINGS: CONQUEST, WILDSTAR and BREAKAWAY in addition to TV animation for COCONUT FRED'S SALAD ISLAND. She has enjoyed a fresh start in comics as of late, drawing for SPERA: ASCENSION OF THE STARLESS Vol. 1 & 3, and co-creating and drawing for BOUNTY.

**LEONARDO OLEA** has worked as a colorist for comics such as FAIRY QUEST, REVELATIONS, RUNLOVEKILL, and BOUNTY as well as various titles from Marvel, DC, Soleil, Aspen, Dark Horse and Image. As a graphic designer he has worked with Warner Bros, Disney and Nike. With his brand Mafufo, Leonardo has created products with J. Scott Campbell, Humberto Ramos, Francisco Herrera, Robert Valley, Sergio Aragones and Alex Ross. He hopes someday he can sleep.

**VITA AYALA** is a writer out of New York City who has done work for DC Comics (REBIRTH: WONDER WOMAN ANNUAL #1, SUICIDE SQUAD MOST WANTED: AMANDA WALLER & EL DIABLO), as well as creator-owned work with Black Mask Studios (OUR WORK FILLS THE PEWS). When not writing, they moonlight as a security guard, protecting art at one of NYC's oldest museums.

**ROSSI GIFFORD** is the creator of the critically acclaimed fantasy series SPIRIT LEAVES from Chapterhouse Comics, as well as being an in-demand illustrator and character designer. Recently arriving in Canada from Scotland, where she graduated from Duncan of Jordanstone of Art and Design, Rossi continues to produce artwork for clients overseas as well as in North America.

**MATT FRACTION** writes comic books out in the woods and lives with his wife, the writer Kelly Sue DeConnick, his two children, two dogs, a cat, a bearded dragon, and a yard full of coyotes and stags. Surely there is a metaphor there.

**ELSA CHARRETIER** is a French illustrator and comic book artist. After debuting on COWL at Image, Elsa co-created THE INFINITE LOOP with writer Pierrick Colinet at IDW. She has worked at DC (STARFIRE, BOMBSHELLS, HARLEY QUINN) and launched THE UNSTOPPABLE WASP at Marvel. Elsa is currently drawing WINDHAVEN (Random House), written by George R.R. Martin, and is co-writing THE INFINITE LOOP v2 and a forthcoming YA miniseries.

**NICK FILARDI** grew up going to Sarge's Comics in New London, CT. Studying comics at Savannah College of Art & Design, Nick now resides in Florida with his fiancée Shannon and 3-legged dog Deniro. You can find his work in CAVE CARSON HAS A CYBERNETIC EYE, POWERS, HEARTTHROB, and the odd DEADPOOL issue. His color work and terrible jokes are on Twitter (@nickfil) and Instagram (@nick_filardi).

**JON TSUEI** is best known for writing and co-creating the comic book RUNLOVEKILL. He has also contributed to the anthologies COMIC BOOK TATTOO and SECRET IDENTITIES: THE ASIAN AMERICAN SUPERHERO ANTHOLOGY. Jon currently resides in Long Beach, CA writing stories, fighting evil by moonlight and winning love by daylight.

Born in 1985, **SASKIA GUTEKUNST** is a German freelance artist for games and animation who happens to draw comics every now and then. When she isn't crunching on deadlines, she enjoys her free time away from computers.

**ALOBI** has over 10 years of experience crafting and advocating for federal nutrition and food assistance policy, spanning time on Capitol Hill, the non-profit sector, and most recently, the federal government. Alobi earned a BS in Political Science from the University of Oklahoma.

**BASSEY NYAMBI** has been jet-setting and pursuing her passion for human rights, working with a global women's reproductive health and rights nonprofit. She has also lead the youth wing of a Nigerian cultural organization based in the US and continues to work with young ambassadors of sexual and reproductive health through her current work. Bassey earned a BA in International Affairs from Lafayette College and an MS in International and European Politics from the University of Edinburgh.

**NYAMBI NYAMBI**, best known for six seasons as Samuel on the comedy MIKE & MOLLY, is also on the critically acclaimed CBS drama THE GOOD FIGHT as Jay Dipersia. He recurred on PBS' MERCY STREET and ABC Digital's AMERICAN KOKO. He continues to work in film and on stage while on the board for Almasi Collaborative Arts, developing emerging African artists. He also contributed to the Eisner award-winning anthology LOVE IS LOVE. Nyambi earned a BS in Business from Bucknell University and an MFA in Acting from New York University.

**CHRIS VISIONS** is a creator residing in Virginia, working in the fields of illustration and comics. He's drawn for books such as DEAD LETTERS (BOOM!), SPIDER-GWEN (Marvel), and CONSTANTINE (DC). Independently, "Chr!s" conjures projects from his sketchbook, a daily log of experiences and ideas drawn from his life, and hosts an online, live-drawing channel on Twitch, Instagram and Facebook.

**VALENTINE DE LANDRO** is a Canadian comic book artist, illustrator, and designer. His credits include titles from Marvel, DC Comics, IDW, Valiant, and Dark Horse. He's known for MARVEL KNIGHTS: 4 and X-FACTOR. He is the co-creator of BITCH PLANET with Kelly Sue DeConnick. De Landro lives east of Toronto, Ontario with his wife Maya and their two children.

**KELLY SUE DECONNICK** got her start in the comic industry adapting Japanese and Korean comics into English. Five years and more than ten thousand pages of adaptation later, she transitioned to American comics with 30 DAYS OF NIGHT: EBEN AND STELLA, for Steve Niles and IDW. Work for Image, Boom, Oni, Humanoids, Dark Horse, DC, Vertigo and Marvel soon followed. Today, DeConnick is best known for surprise hits like Carol Danvers' rebranding as Captain Marvel and the Eisner-nominated mythological western, PRETTY DEADLY; the latter was co-created with artist Emma Ríos. DeConnick's most recent venture, the Eisner-nominated sci-fi kidney-punch called BITCH PLANET, co-created with Valentine De Landro, launched to rave reviews in December 2014 and has received multiple awards. DeConnick lives in Portland, Oregon with her husband, Matt Fraction, and their two children. Under their company Milkfed Criminal Masterminds, Inc., DeConnick and Fraction are currently developing television for NBC/Universal.

Special thanks to Kelly Fitzpatrick.

BITCH PLANET created by Kelly Sue DeConnick & Valentine De Landro.

Kelly Sue DeConnick - @kellysue
Valentine De Landro - @val_delandro
Kelly Fitzpatrick - @wastedwings
Clayton Cowles - @ClaytonCowles
Rian Hughes - @rianhughes
Laurenn McCubbin - @laurennmcc
Lauren Sankovitch - @PancakeLady

#BITCHPLANET
Bitch Planet Tumblr: WWW.BITCHPLA.NET

IMAGECOMICS.COM

**BITCH PLANET: TRIPLE FEATURE, VOL. 1.**
First printing. December 2017. Published by Image Comics, Inc. Office of publication: 2701 NW Vaughn St., Suite 780, Portland, OR 97210. Copyright © 2017 Milkfed Criminal Masterminds, Inc. All rights reserved. Contains material originally published in single magazine form as BITCH PLANET: TRIPLE FEATURE #1-5. "Bitch Planet: Triple Feature," its logos, and the likenesses of all characters herein are trademarks of Milkfed Criminal Masterminds, Inc., unless otherwise noted. "Image" and the Image Comics logos are registered trademarks of Image Comics, Inc. No part of this publication may be reproduced or transmitted, in any form or by any means (except for short excerpts for journalistic or review purposes), without the express written permission of Milkfed Criminal Masterminds, Inc., or Image Comics, Inc. All names, characters, events, and locales in this publication are entirely fictional. Any resemblance to actual persons (living or dead), events, or places, without satiric intent, is coincidental. Printed in the USA. For information regarding the CPSIA on this printed material call: 203-595-3636 and provide reference #RICH-769882. For international rights, contact: foreignlicensing@imagecomics.com. ISBN: 978-1-5343-0529-8.